ASSEMBLING WORK

Assembling Work

Remaking Factory Regimes in Japanese Multinationals in Britain

TONY ELGER AND CHRIS SMITH

OXFORD
UNIVERSITY PRESS

Great Clarendon Street, Oxford OX2 6DP

Oxford University Press is a department of the University of Oxford.
It furthers the University's objective of excellence in research, scholarship,
and education by publishing worldwide in

Oxford New York

Auckland Cape Town Dar es Salaam Hong Kong Karachi Kuala Lumpur
Madrid Melbourne Mexico City Nairobi New Delhi Shanghai Taipei Toronto

With offices in

Argentina Austria Brazil Chile Czech Republic France Greece
Guatemala Hungary Italy Japan South Korea Poland Portugal
Singapore Switzerland Thailand Turkey Ukraine Vietnam

Published in the United States
by Oxford University Press Inc., New York

First published 2005

British Library Cataloguing in Publication Data

Data available

Library of Congress Cataloging in Publication Data

Elger, Tony 1946–
Assembling work: remaking factory regime in Japanese multinationals in Britain/
Tony Elger and Chris Smith
p. cm.
Includes bibliographical references and index.
ISBN 0–19–924151–1 (alk.paper)
1. Corporations, Japanese–Great Britain. 2. Foreign subsidiaries–Great Britain.
3. Manufacturing industries–Great Britain–Foreign ownership. 4. Industrial relations–
Great Britain. 5. Industrial management–Japan. 6. International business enterprises.
7. Globalization. I. Smith, Chris, 1953–II. Title.
HD2845.E44 2005
338.8′8952041–dc22 2004027667

ISBN 0–19–924151–1

1 3 5 7 9 10 8 6 4 2

Typeset by Kolam Information Services Pvt. Ltd, Pondicherry, India

Printed in Great Britain
on acid-free paper by
Biddles Ltd., King's Lynn, Norfolk

CONTENTS

ACKNOWLEDGEMENTS

The author order reflects the fact that Tony Elger did most of the detailed qualitative analysis and writing for this book. The research on which this book is based was a joint project, both in conception and implementation, and we have discussed the material and written about it together over a long period in joint conference papers and articles. More specifically the book draws upon some material that has been published elsewhere, especially a joint article in *Economy and Society* (1998, 27(4): 578–608) and a chapter by Chris Smith in Stephen Ackroyd, Rosemary Batt, Paul Thompson, and Pamela Tolbert (eds.) *The Oxford Handbook of Work and Organizations* (OUP 2004).

We would like to acknowledge comments received from colleagues at conferences where we have jointly reported preliminary research that has found its way into this book, especially: International Labour Process Conferences, *1996–2004*; 'The Globalization of Production and the Regulation of Labour', *Warwick, 1996*; Employment Research Conference, 'Manufacturing Matters', *Cardiff, 1996*; ESF-EMOT Workshop 'Globalisation and Industrial Transformation in Europe: National, Regional and Local Dynamics and Consequences', *Malaga, 1997*; International Symposium on Globalization and Industrial Relations, *Mexico City, 1997*; ISA World Congress, *Montreal, 1998*; WES Conference, *Cambridge 1998*; 15th EGOS Colloquium, *Warwick, 1999*; 4th European Conference of Sociology, *Amsterdam, 1999*; 18th EGOS Colloquium 'Reclaiming Hope: Organizational Politics and the Politics of Organizations', *Barcelona, 2002*; 'Multinationals and the International Diffusion of Organizational Forms and Practices', *Barcelona, 2004*; WES Conference, *Manchester, 2004*; IRRU Seminar, *Warwick, 2004*.

We owe a particular debt to all those who talked to us about their experiences and so made our research possible. We wish to thank the firms that allowed us to study them, and particularly the many managers and workers whom we interviewed. We are also grateful for the help and advice of people from the Telford Development Agency and Wrekin Council, especially Rob Rossen and Clare Bilsby, and other informants, especially Robert Hartley, Elwyn Jones, and Justin Bartlett, from the localities of the workplaces we studied. We also wish to thank Mandy Eaton who did an excellent job of transcribing many of the interviews.

The majority of the research was funded by a Leverhulme Trust Grant (F/250/J, 'Innovative Work Organisation in Japanese Transplants: A Regional Study') to Tony Elger and Chris Smith, held at Aston University, with additional funding from Warwick University Research and Teaching

Innovation Fund. We also benefited from the research of several Ph.D., M.B.A. and M.Sc. students who over the years have worked on topics related to the project. These include Simon Clark, Maria Daskalaki, Makiko Igarashi, Catrin Jones, Sampson Mann, Hoshang Noraiee, and Gerry Palmer; and we are grateful for their permission to reference their work. Minori Kusumoto and Hon Lam provided some help with tables. We would also like to thank participants (especially Andy Danford, Rick Delbridge, David Grant, the late Jim Lowe, Hoshang Noraiee, Gerry Palmer, Diana Sharpe) in the 'Japanese Transplants Research Seminar' that we organized in the late 1990s for debating many of the themes discussed in this book. We should also thank the many academic colleagues who have provided support and advice over recent years, especially Stephen Ackroyd, Ed Clarke, Simon Clarke, Maria Daskalaki, Rick Delbridge, Colin Haslam, Gerry Palmer, Ian Procter, Paul Thompson, and Karel Williams. Finally, special thanks to Ann and Yvonne for their support and patience.

LIST OF TABLES AND FIGURES

ABBREVIATIONS

ASEAN	Association of South-east Asian Nations
DFM	Design for Manufacturing
EDU	Economic Development Unit [Wrekin Council]
EU	European Union
EZ	Enterprise Zone
FDI	Foreign Direct Investment
FIEs	Foreign Invested Enterprises
GERPISA	Groupe d'Etude et du Recherche Permanent sur l'Industrie et les Salariés de l'Automobile [Permanent Group for the Study of the Automobile Industry and its Employees]
HQ	Headquarters
HRM	Human Resource Management
IAA	Intermediate Assisted Area
IMF	International Monetary Fund
ICT	Information Communication Technology
JETRO	Japanese External Trade Organization
JIT	Just in Time
MD	Managing Director
MITI	Ministry of International Trade and Industry [Japan]
NAFTA	North American Free Trade Agreement
NVQs	National Vocational Qualifications
PCBs	Printed Circuit Boards
QA	Quality Assurance
QC	Quality Control
QCC	Quality Control Circle or Quality Circle, depending on the terminology of the organization
R&D	Research and Development
SMT	Surface Mount Technology
SPC	Statistical Process Control
SSD	System, Society, and Dominance
TDA	Telford Development Agency
TDC	Telford Development Corporation
TPM	Total Preventative Maintenance
TQM	Total Quality Management
TUPE	Transfer of Undertakings (Protection of Employment) [Regulations]
WTO	World Trade Organization
YTS	Youth Training Scheme

I

THEORETICAL ISSUES

CHAPTER

1

Transplants, Transfer, and Work Transformation

INTRODUCTION

The study of the Japanese firm falls into different research and disciplinary camps. For those who invested time in learning Japanese and studying Japanese firms in Japan (Abegglen 1958; Cole 1971; Dore 1973; Fruin 1992), the debate sparked in the 1980s about the transplantation or transfer of Japanese practices to the West was rather a management fad and hence a somewhat superficial endeavour. For these writers, the Japanese firm is embedded within Japanese society, tied through social networks, national institutions, cultural practices and state policies to the territory of the country. It is not really possible to discuss the Japanese firm without studying Japanese language and culture, without *area* knowledge. As we discuss in Chapter 4, this approach is close to a 'societal effects' model, in which work organizations are always tied to national histories and logics, and hence management and worker practices and ideas are also societally bounded.

At the other end of the spectrum were those who sought to 'learn from' Japan, and take ideas, techniques and practices into other, non-Japanese spaces, especially firms (Ouchi 1981; Pascale and Athos 1982). Initially, these writers saw Japan as an *alternative model* to American practices, the latter frequently conceptualized as Taylorist or Fordist mass production methods of work, combined with antagonistic employment relations, governance structures, and supplier relations. Japan represented an alternative way of putting the firm together, based on principles of cooperation and high trust relations between workers and managers, suppliers and buyers, large firms and small. These writers express both an alternative, 'system' approach, and a 'dominance' view of the Japanese firm, as something different from, but also superior to, American forms of enterprise and work organization.

From the mid-1980s the Japanese firm abruptly began to move systematically from trading relations with Western countries and firms to joint ventures and independent subsidiary formation. From this period of massive acceleration in the spread of subsidiary formation, there was an explosion of writing on the *Japanese firm as transplant* (Elger and Smith 1994; Smith 1996). The transplant represented a mechanism for spreading Japanese ways of doing things to the rest of the world, and researching it shifted the terms of debate from Japan to learning and borrowing from Japanese practices. Overwhelmingly, writers in this field of 'transplant studies' were non-Japanese speakers, interested in different aspects of the firm *abroad* rather than any area-based perspective on the Japanese firm at home. These writers were therefore more dependent on secondary analysis of the character of the Japanese firm, lacking as they did linguistic and field research access to the firm at home. They were more driven by practical concerns of learning, borrowing and transfer, and less interested in examining the institutional linkages between Japanese firms and the Japanese economy and society. They were not linguists or area specialists, but rather practitioners or policy-orientated managers, management academics, social scientists, trade unionists, politicians or state officials. They had different motivations, but most were concerned with the implications of Japanese Foreign Direct Investment (FDI) for jobs. They were interested in the impact the new entrants would have on local firms, industrial relations, and the quality of jobs. More generally they were concerned with the possibilities of 'transfer' of more 'modern' manufacturing practices into local settings, and the leverage this afforded for changes in indigenous management policies, work practices, and industrial relations. This shift in focus had several effects that shaped the intellectual debate on the character of the new entrants.

First, the Japanese firm became disconnected from the Japanese economy, and abstracted as a stereotype, a model, decomposed into codified characteristics. All Japanese firms purportedly possessed common or stylized qualities that operated in a similar way in different times and places. This meant that considerations of difference (between firms and sectors), evolution and strategic choice were suppressed in favour of an image of a persistent repertoire of techniques. The stable reproduction of a constant set of qualities (lifetime employment, seniority wages, single unions, team working, total quality management (TQM), quality circles (QCCs), just in time (JIT), kaizen (continuous improvement)) was emphasized by this disconnection of the firm from historical developments.

Second, research and public attention focused on the issue of the *transfer* of all or a selective menu of these set qualities. Consequently, researchers devised tools for measuring the spread of decomposed and reified techniques, the ubiquitous presence of which offered proof positive that 'Japanese' practices were no longer tied to Japan. Rather they could be transmitted spatially within the Japanese firm and also become available to *all* firms as modernizing techniques.

Third, the attention to transfer meant local contexts were initially discounted, as the closed-system of Japanese firms or Western emulators could reproduce these techniques and therefore the *essence* of Japanese-style production success. In this closed-system view of the firm, environmental conditions were discounted against *internal* management practice and firm autonomy. Later, where externalities entered the debate, they often appeared, as in Oliver and Wilkinson (1988), in the form of 'functional supports' for the system dependencies required for the reproduction of Japanese-style production, human resource management (HRM), and supplier relations. Supportive environments, such as new towns, or rural or greenfield investment sites, represented areas fresh to international manufacture or with a surplus labour force, young, green, and keen for employment under new style (Japanese) management.

Fourth, for industrial sociologists and other scholars of work, studies of employment relations and the phenomenology of work in Japanese firms risked becoming mystified, as the colour filter of 'Japanese' practices mediated the investigation and perception of social relations in the workplace. The *experience* of assembly lines, team work or QCCs could not be revealed, except through polarized stereotypes—positive, unitary views (Womack et al. 1990; Kenney and Florida 1993), or negative, labour intensification models of Japanese production (Parker and Slaughter 1988). Both approaches strained workers' actual experiences into idealized supportive or negative judgements of 'Japanese practice'. As Milkman (1997: 15) has pointed out, both supporters and detractors of 'lean production' and 'Japanese-style' work organization spoke 'on behalf' of workers (and managers), often without adequately researching their experiences and responses to these 'innovative' work systems. This inhibited the empirical study of factory life in its own terms and discouraged the theoretical analysis of the specific corporate, sectoral, and local contexts in which Japanese subsidiaries operated. It also overemphasized the themes of novelty and change at the expense of attention to continuities in work routines and employment relations that might characterize firms in particular sectors, or capitalist firms more generally. In general, therefore, *transplant* research elevated national ownership—the *Japaneseness* of the Japanese transplant—above standard economic, sociological or organizational insights into the nature of work and social relations within the overseas subsidiary. Ownership was writ large, and hence established theoretical discourses on the work situation, from industrial relations, labour process theory and industrial sociology, were marginalized.

EARLIER WORK

Our initial intervention as non-Japanese speaking industrial sociologists was as reviewers of this field (Elger and Smith 1994). In the early 1990s we sought to introduce established middle-range analyses of corporate structures, employment relations, and institutional contexts into the agenda of *transplant* research. This prompted a critical appraisal of existing studies and generated an agenda for future research. This emphasized that the contextualization of Japanese transplants needed foregrounding, as the influence of well-established external contingencies, such as sector, country, and locality, would be likely to produce rather different policy repertoires and social relations within such firms (Elger and Smith 1994). Our objective in this intervention was to address the problems arising from reified modelling and the abstraction of the Japanese firm from history, and to counteract the tendency to reduce the firm to a repertoire of stable techniques removed from the dynamic of capitalist employment relations.

The research reported in this book pursues the critical programme outlined above. It explores management and worker experiences in a set of Japanese subsidiaries and seeks to analyse them through these middle levels of contextualization. We have studied a range of Japanese firms within one nation and region, with particular attention to one local cluster. Both the subsidiaries and the parent companies differed by size, sector, and their experience of internationalization. We interviewed workers, team leaders, engineers and managers within these firms, and also key figures in the attraction and reception of these firms to particular localities. We are therefore able to make an assessment of the work and employment experience of people within the subsidiaries of a range of Japanese companies, and compare their views with our understanding of the now considerable literature on work in the overseas Japanese firm.

Our commentary in 1994 was primarily a plea for the contextualization of the operations of internationalizing Japanese firms and their overseas 'transplants' at a series of different levels. First, we wished to re-emphasize that such firms and workplaces remained sites of capital–labour conflict and accommodation. Second, we wished to recognize that these enterprises had distinctive features that were rooted in corporate and sectoral as well as national institutional dynamics. Finally, we recognized the potential for such internationalizing enterprises to break down national barriers and local practices, with the intention of developing what Sklair (2001) has called 'world best practice', but also the uncertainties associated with this process. However, these features remain in tension and push firms, and the managers and workers within them, in contradictory directions. We hope that this book will reveal something of the contradictory character of the Japanese 'transplant', and provide an analysis of work in modern manufacturing which is also applicable to other international production platforms.

OUR APPROACH

This book draws particularly on labour process analyses of the indeterminacy of labour power and the active and contested construction of work regimes, and contemporary institutionalist analyses of the local and global contexts within which transnational firms operate (Smith and Thompson 1998; Elger 2002; Thompson 2002). Both these traditions of work seek to understand the active and strategic character of contemporary management and also the tensions and constraints which management confronts. Work organization is always *context-dependent*. Management policies and organizational or technological repertoires cannot determine the social relations of work independently of the wider contextual features that surround the enterprise and workplace. We are especially interested in the implications of context at factory level. On the one hand we are concerned to understand the relationship between the work and employment regimes within these subsidiaries and wider corporate structures and policies. On the other we wish to analyse the interrelationship between internal work regimes and local labour markets, local state policies, and national institutional arrangements. At the same time we continue to emphasize that contexts do not simply determine the character of workplace relations. While some elements of the context are more intractable than others, their significance is always mediated through the powers and agency of key actors.

Following labour process theory, we argue that management must be concerned with the control of labour within the workplace and can deploy substantial resources to support the achievement of such control, but also that the exercise of such powers confronts significant constraints and contradictions. In particular we are interested in the resources which transnational firms possess, such as their capacity to allocate investments to specific sites or their capabilities in what are regarded as leading-edge management systems. It is crucial to investigate the ways in which these resources are mobilized with or against local actors, such as British managers, local state agencies or organized labour, and to draw out the implications for workplace practices. As this implies, context and power are animated by *agency*—by people constituted as collective and individual actors. Within the subsidiary as a 'transferred workplace' the main agents are managers (both local and international) and workers who, within the employment relationship and the labour process, enact the day-to-day organization of work. These social agents, while positioned within firm hierarchies, capitalist social relations and the institutional rules of specific contexts, are reflexive, and able to resist, re-interpret and mediate actions in distinctive ways. Furthermore, the social structures they inhabit involve contradictory pressures and pose unresolved dilemmas, which necessitate active and creative responses. In this sense social actors are inevitably engaged in coping with structural constraints and deploying power in directions which remain uncertain, and thus they *remake* work relations in fresh and sometimes unpredictable ways over time.

The theoretical analysis that we develop on this basis is applied to the experience of Japanese manufacturing subsidiaries in the United Kingdom. To understand the nature of work organization within such transnational workplaces, we use a theoretical approach to comparative organizational analysis developed by Smith and Meiksins (1995). This locates three sources of structural constraint within the transnational workplace. The first comes through political economy as 'system' imperatives. The second comes through local, institutional forces derived from within a specific society and economy, so-called 'societal effects'. The third comes into the firm as 'best practices' derived from 'dominant' solutions to work organization problems within such workplaces, so-called 'dominance effects'. As we outline in Chapter 4, this approach helps explain the international interest in Japanese practices as global standards, but also deconstructs the different claims to dominance and efficiency that are associated with such practices through their potential transfer within the international firm. Through this approach we reject standard accounts of Japanese firms that treat novel employment or production practices as unproblematical points of departure. Thus this book explores the operations of Japanese manufacturing enterprises as examples of substantially and increasingly embedded workplaces, in which work and employment relations are actively developed and reworked through the interplay of context, agency, and power.

This analysis is applied to fieldwork in Britain, which represents a key location for the operation of international capital, and the major site for Japanese direct investment in Europe. This fieldwork focuses on the analysis of five case studies, involving eight workplaces, representative of different sectors and sizes of enterprise and different forms of Japanese manufacturing investment. On this basis the book develops an account of the importance of company, sector, size, and locality, as structural influences on the power of management to shape work organization at factory level. However, such shaping is not one-way. Local workers and local managers deploy resources such as claims to expertise or labour market leverage, which mediate and challenge the design intentions of international management. In greenfield sites, which supposedly represent a blank sheet for managerial prerogatives and plans, we find many low-key forms of worker resistance and non-compliance that mediate and reshape management plans. We explore these dynamics through four of our case studies located in one new town setting with a high concentration of Japanese manufacturing firms and other transnational companies, while the fifth case study, of a brownfield takeover, provides a distinctive comparison and counterpoint.

THE STRUCTURE OF THE BOOK

The book is organized in three parts:

- The first part interrogates existing debates and elaborates our analytical approach. In particular it focuses on the nature of the 'Japanese model' of employment relations and work organization and the internationalization of Japanese firms, as these inform the subsequent debate on diffusion and emulation of Japanese 'best practices'. It introduces our theoretical approach and justifies our use of multiple case-study methodology in workplace research.
- The second part focuses on similarities and differences between the operations of our case-study plants, and assesses the ways in which their work and employment practices have developed over time. It seeks to explain these features in terms of the distinctive corporate, sector, and local contexts in which the different workplaces operate, but also in terms of the active responses of management and workers to these distinctive circumstances.
- The final part of the book seeks to draw out the broader implications of the research by reassessing the scope and limits of the powers and agency of both managers and workers. This provides the basis for an overall assessment of the role of the overseas subsidiaries of international companies in remaking production regimes and working lives.

Chapter 2 outlines differing accounts of the nature of work and employment relations inside the Japanese firm, and the way these have been 'modelled' in the post-war period. We outline the core characteristics of the Japanese work and employment system and contrasting readings of the Japanese firm in terms of the production paradigms of neo-Fordism, post-Fordism, and Toyotaism. This provides the basis for identifying four interpretations of the rise of a distinctive Japanese model of work and employment relations: cultural, institutional, class relations, and political economy approaches. We examine the implications of each of these perspectives for the transfer debate, and find major problems with cultural and institutional approaches because they gloss over contradictions within the Japanese model. We conclude that an historical understanding of the Japanese model, which emphasizes the role of class relations, the state and wider geopolitical contexts, is important for understanding the rise of the Japanese economy in the post-war period and also the internationalization of economic activity from the 1980s.

The objective of Chapter 3 is to discuss the literature on the reasons for the internationalization of Japanese firms from the 1980s. We present data on Japanese FDI and its geographical spread. We then examine different interpretations of the rapid growth of FDI from the mid-1980s, and debates about the internationalization strategies and distinctive characteristics of Japanese multinationals. We explore the goals of such firms in establishing overseas subsidiaries, and argue that many earlier analyses were too optimistic in their expectations of upgrading, especially in the light of the ebb, flow, and international repositioning of investment.

Chapter 4 elaborates the theoretical basis of our perspective on the character of transfer and innovation in the modern overseas subsidiary, outlined earlier. Our theoretical framework builds on both an institutional approach, with its emphasis on the role of the social context in structuring relations within the modern factory, and a labour process perspective on the workplace as a site of social action and social control. More specifically it draws on the *system, society,* and *dominance* (SSD) effects model as a way of locating the sources of diversity within manufacturing subsidiaries (Smith and Meiksins 1995; Smith and Elger 2000). The operations of these factories do not simply reflect production concepts transferred from Japan, but are conditioned by such specific contextual features as corporate structures, sector dynamics, the local setting, and wider national institutions and traditions. In turn these features are themselves mediated and manipulated in power struggles between collective and individual agents at workplace level. Thus changes in forms of work and employment cannot be read off from existing organizational templates or external constraints, but involve tensions and struggles between managers and workers and, as important, between different groupings within management.

Chapter 5 outlines the methods we use in the book, which are directly related to our theoretical approach to workplace research. We review the limitations of survey and single case research, and argue that multiple case studies can make a distinctive contribution to the analysis of the phenomenon under investigation. It is widely recognized that case studies provide particular leverage on two features of social phenomena, namely their active *processual* character and the importance of social *context*. On this basis, case studies can contribute to the development of broader theorizing, by engaging with and reformulating theoretical claims about the social processes that animate Japanese subsidiaries and the ways in which social contexts impinge on these processes. This is especially pertinent to research on overseas subsidiaries, where there are strong claims for diffusion, transfer, and learning. Analyses of the nature of work organization within such subsidiaries are best developed through case studies, involving wide interviewing and extended fieldwork at the manufacturing sites themselves. Thus this chapter outlines the way in which this approach was pursued in conducting our own case-study research.

The four chapters in Part II develop an extended analysis of the development and dynamics of work and employment relations in our case-study firms. Together they demonstrate important contrasts between Japanese subsidiaries, which are intended to play different roles within their parent firms and occupy different positions in wider production and commodity chains. Here, contrasts between major assembly firms and smaller sub-contractors and between different sectors are particularly important. We also analyse the significance of the specific ownership patterns, management traditions, and experiences of internationalization that characterize each of our case-study plants. Our analysis shows that the protagonists in the evolution of these workplaces include not only corporate and on-site managers and their workforces, but also a wider array of actors such as the managers of sister plants and other firms in the locality. It also demonstrates that the contemporary operations of each of these factories have to be understood as the outcomes of change over time, involving problems, revisions, and learning. Finally, then, we argue that in none of these workplaces can we depict the existing patterns of work and employment relations in terms of the achievement of a settled production paradigm. Instead these relations remain unsettled and evolving, partly because of persistent tensions in the employment relationship and especially the wage-effort contract, and partly because of uncertainties arising from the product market and inter-site competition for investment.

Chapter 6 examines the issue of *space* within subsidiary research, especially the effects of the clustering of transnational corporations (TNCs) within distinctive localities, and the role of such concentrations in influencing factory regimes. This chapter sets the local context for the case studies discussed in Chapters 7 and 8 by examining the development of a particular local economy, at Telford in the English Midlands, which has the highest concentration of Japanese firms in the United Kingdom. In this context we argue that work regimes and employment rules within firms are strongly influenced by locality norms, constraints, and opportunities. For Japanese firms, in particular, close and cooperative relationships have helped to set 'the rules of the game' for many aspects of worker–management relations, and this makes locality a key influence on their *internal* factory regimes.

Chapter 7 compares two large assembly factories. It notes that these workplaces have implemented important elements of the repertoire of management techniques associated with the Japanese production model, and have done so in ways which underpin a continuing commitment of new products and/or new investment by their parent companies. They are substantial manufacturing workplaces, which appear well established and in important respects can claim to exemplify best practice in their sectors. At the same time, day-to-day work within these workplaces differs markedly from idealized accounts of Japanese production methods, especially in regard to forms of worker involvement, while the evolution of employment relations reveals persistent sources of tension and uncertainty. This prompts a reappraisal of the scope and limits of imitation and innovation in the design of production and employment practices at such subsidiaries, and a discussion of what might constitute 'good enough production' as enterprise and sector norms of performance coexist with problematical features of the employment relationship.

Chapter 8 examines small Japanese subcontractors within the same labour market as these larger firms. Here, we locate these subsidiaries in relation to interfirm relations of power, and especially the supply chain links between large assemblers and small subcontractors. Our case studies of these subcontractors suggest that such firms are more tightly constrained within their enterprise hierarchies and production chains, and possess fewer managerial resources to support the implementation of novel production and employment relations. Where smaller subsidiaries operate in the same locality as larger inward investors, often as a result of following the customers they supply, they also face similar problems in the recruitment and control of labour. Such circumstances prompt a selective and opportunistic adoption and adaptation of parent company management techniques, which may be characterized by the substantial autonomy of local management but can readily become a more fractious process involving conflicts among managers. In these firms Japanese-inspired employment practices are less evident than a resort to the familiar tactics of labour regulation in the domestic small enterprise sector, mixing elements of paternalism, informal mutuality, insecurity, and bullying.

In most of our assembly case-study plants there was little scope for research and development activity, as the main features of both products and processes were established elsewhere and innovations remained the preserve of the parent company. Technical workers were employed to facilitate the adaptation of processes and products to meet local conditions and standards, but there were few resources to go beyond this role. Thus the design and development activities of these firms remained highly circumscribed, firstly by their role in the wider company, which translated into limited resources, and secondly by skill shortages in the regional economy. However, in Chapter 9 we examine a case study where there was a more systematic commitment to local design and development. Here, a Japanese firm had bought a local company with innovative products and technical expertise, and managers were attempting to engineer new synergies between the professional competencies of Japanese and British technical staff. The new company and local management were granted considerable operational autonomy in the pursuit of this objective, but ultimately this subsidiary failed because of intense international competition and a programme of parent company rationalization. We use this case to explore the scope, vicissitudes, and limits of developing the local research, design, and development capabilities of Japanese-owned firms. On this basis we seek to contribute to the wider debate about the conditions under which inward investors upgrade their research and development capabilities or concentrate their resources on manufacturing activities.

Finally, the chapters in Part III reconsider the remaking of management and the remaking of working lives within these subsidiaries. In Chapter 10 we look across our case studies to reveal the ways in which Japanese managers attempted to build a cadre of local supporters within their subsidiaries, and how local managers worked within and against the new models of work organization and employment relations offered by the Japanese. We examine the stereotypical structural and cultural differences in the experiences and outlooks that Japanese and British managers brought into the transnational workplace. But we also explore variations in the ways these managers drew upon the two business systems and conformed to or challenged received conceptions, in ways that were influenced by their distinctive organizational and occupational histories. Our account highlights processes of argument, debate, problem-solving, mutual learning, and negotiation in management, both between British and Japanese managers and between various management specialisms. The chapter also outlines and seeks to explain the rather different ways in which such management micropolitics developed in the different firms.

The transferred workplace aspires to create new forms of employee relations in the context of a much wider reconstruction of forms of employment in Britain, involving the historical decline of workers' collective organization based on robust, male dominated trade unions. Rhetorically, the new relations are founded on worker commitment, participation and a unitarist conception of the firm. This is ostensibly based on a new social consensus, with a strongly individual character, reinforced by a more inclusive and egalitarian corporate culture. In Chapter 11 we examine the extent to which such new relations between workers and managers have emerged in the two large Japanese workplaces discussed in Chapter 7, and the extent to which older patterns of conflict based on structural inequalities persist. In particular we examine the persistence of instrumental bases of worker involvement, the mixture of accommodation and resistance which characterizes work relations, and the scope for individual and collective manifestations of conflict within a more constrained industrial relations environment. The chapter rejects idealized accounts of a strategic shift in worker–manager relations, and seeks to document contemporary patterns of acceptance and resistance, of survival tactics and opposition, in the two workplaces. Particular attention is given to informal understandings and bargains over effort and advancement, and to labour turnover and absenteeism as expressions of dissatisfaction which appear closely tied to these modern forms of work and employment.

Chapter 12 concludes the book by drawing out the wider implications of our research on Japanese subsidiaries and the analysis developed in the book, both for discussions of the local operations of transnational firms more generally and for debates about the transfer and hybridization of production models. Our analysis treats the transfer of management techniques and values within and between enterprises, and the evolution of work and employment relations within specific workplaces, as more multilayered and complex phenomena than is conventionally recognized. The actors in these subsidiaries seek to mediate and negotiate global, national, and local pressures by mobilizing individual and collective resources. Whereas Japanese companies have typically been treated as paradigmatic of new production or supply relations, we see them as one important contemporary setting for a more widespread dynamic of organizational evolution and innovation, characterized by substantial uncertainties and unresolved tensions.

CHAPTER

2

The Japanese Model and its Implications for International Transfer and Work Transformation

INTRODUCTION

Japan has recently fallen out of favour as an economic model, after a period of widespread but rather uncritical adulation, prompting a parallel re-appraisal of Japanese firms. Meanwhile, the American economy and companies have returned to favour as paradigms of success. In our view, however, it is important to develop more measured assessments of the strengths and weaknesses of each of these variants of capitalism, together with the distinctive international firms they have nurtured. We need to avoid the simplicities of adulation and condemnation that have been read off from specific periods of boom and stagnation in each case. Thus our approach to the analysis of the operations of Japanese factories in Britain is informed by a view of the Japanese 'political economy' which recognizes its post-war growth dynamic and its distinctiveness in terms of workplace and production regimes. But it also identifies important sources of tension in the model, including the costs involved for many groups of employees.

There are many accounts of the distinctive features that underpinned Japan's post-war economic recovery and emergence as a major actor in the global economy. These range from the specifics of work organization in leading firms, through the distinctive employment relations that have characterized large organizations, to the organized horizontal and vertical linkages among enterprises and, beyond these, aspects of state policy and the wider 'political economy'. This chapter examines such competing accounts of the Japanese model and their implications for debates about transferring or emulating Japanese work and employment relations internationally. We start with alternative accounts of work organization in Japan, which embody different conceptions of the production regimes that Japanese companies might offer for transfer or emulation. We then look at contrasting conceptions of the wider Japanese employment and business system, and consider the implications of these analyses for arguments about the transfer of Japanese work and employment practices to other countries.

ALTERNATIVE ANALYSES OF WORK ORGANIZATION IN JAPAN

Post-Fordism versus neo-Fordism

Discussions of the social organization of work in Japanese manufacturing have often become polarized between optimistic accounts that highlight the mutual benefits enjoyed by workers and managers and pessimistic accounts that highlight the oppressive character of these work relations for employees. The optimistic accounts (Kenney and Florida 1993; Womack et al. 1990) often draw sharp contrasts with work organization in Europe but more especially in the United States. The pivotal contrast is between highly specialized, fragmented and deskilled work tasks in the west and multiskilled, flexible teamwork in Japan. The typical Japanese worker gains cumulative experience on a range of tasks which are grounded in a continuing process of 'on-the-job' training. This expertise can be deployed to address day-to-day issues of production flow and quality, and also to develop better ways of working through team commitment to 'continuous improvement'. In turn, such flexible and creative teamworking provides the basis for reducing the stock of materials in process (through JIT systems) and increasing the speed, quality, and diversity of production. A crucial image involves the capacity of an assembly line worker to stop the line to rectify quality problems. The worker *controls* the line in contrast to the classical Fordist line which dominates the worker. This movement away from production standardization to 'continuous improvement' through worker engagement is sometime referred to as 'post-Fordism'. Furthermore, such networks of cooperation and innovation are not confined to the immediate production process within specific workplaces, but spread to incorporate design and development and to link the production activities of supplier networks.

The contrasting view of Japanese work processes retains the emphasis on team-working and flexibility, but stresses that the varied tasks undertaken by workers are generally specified in great detail, while the pace of work, closely tied to the virtually bufferless flow of the production line, remains relentless throughout a prolonged working day. In this account (Dohse et al. 1985; Durand and Durand-Sebag 1996) workers are incorporated as subordinate agents in quality assurance and 'continuous improvement', in ways that are tightly circumscribed by management imperatives and the powers of supervisors. Tight manning levels and production flows exert continuous pressures on workers to achieve production and quality targets. Supervisors conduct individual assessments of the conduct and commitment of workers, with substantial implications for their pay and prospects, thus reinforcing tight discipline within the work process (Endo 1994, 1997). Industrial engineers, always central to classical Taylorism and Fordism, are not banished from production, but remain key agents in designing work processes in ways which limit worker discretion. When workers do provide suggestions for improvements in work processes, this production intelligence is systematically integrated into new procedures and work rates, which represent renewed constraints on the workforce. This diagnosis is exemplified by management's use of 'andon' lights on the assembly line, not to grant control to the worker but to trim manning levels to the point where there is minimal slack and employees are stretched to the maximum. In this account, management hierarchy and management prerogative pervade workplace relations, and this also ramifies down the supply chain through the persistent requirement for suppliers to deliver reduced costs. Whereas the optimistic account in the previous paragraph is often labelled post-Fordist to contrast with an historical pattern of Fordist production in the west, this pessimistic analysis can be termed neo-Fordist, or even ultra-Fordist (Dohse et al. 1985; Naruse 1991; Tolliday 1998; Okayama 1986).

National models and sector and company differences

Many discussions of the social organization of production in Japan operate with clear-cut characterizations of the key features of the 'Japanese production model', both as the basis of post-war growth and as a model for transfer and dissemination. Sometimes this is justified by the claim that the model captures emergent 'best practice' among the most successful enterprises, but this begs the question of the relationship between such stylized models and real patterns of organization and activity. In particular, do such idealized models succeed in capturing the essentials, or do they abstract from important features of the phenomenon they purport to represent? As might be expected from research in other countries, more substantive studies have documented important differences in the organization of work processes in different sectors of manufacturing in Japan. For example, the extent of job rotation and the involvement of assembly workers in continuous improvement, both appear lower in consumer electrical and electronic goods than in the final assembly of automobiles

(Abo 1994*a*; Kenney and Florida 1988, 1993; Oliver et al. 1994). In turn such differences can be linked to distinctive features of the product and patterns of consumption, and to varied (and gendered) patterns of recruitment and organizational division of labour, echoing contingency theory critiques of 'one best way' management recipes. This suggests that accounts that focus on a uniform *national* model of work organization must at least recognize the differential salience of different aspects of the model for different *sectors*. But it may be necessary to go beyond this, to recognize that distinctive sector recipes may have greater relevance than stylized national models.

Furthermore, such sectoral contrasts are only part of the story. There are also significant differences of approach among major firms within specific sectors. For example, within the much discussed auto sector it makes sense to distinguish the different production trajectories of Toyota, Honda, and Nissan over long periods during the post-war era (Cusumano 1985; Hanada 1998; Mair 1994, 1998; Tolliday 1998; Tolliday and Zeitlin 1986). Such differences suggest that, even when managers are drawing upon a shared repertoire of sector practices, their innovations are marked by the specific contexts and external pressures facing their own enterprise, and that their responses continue to build upon distinctive enterprise traditions and competencies. Thus, when managers in one of these firms seek to borrow from another, their borrowing is influenced by an awareness of such features as their distinctive places in a shared product market, or differently configured local supplier networks or labour markets. Furthermore, established enterprise recipes and patterns of management expertise will also influence the formulation of management policies.

There have, of course, been wider movements supporting innovations in work organization in Japan over a long period. These have involved state agencies, employers' organizations, and such professional bodies as the Japanese Union of Scientists and Engineers, all of which have encouraged the discussion and dissemination of 'best practice' across different firms and sectors (Cole 1989; Tsutsui 1998). This has provided shared reference points and common elements to management repertoires across the economy, but the resultant 'family resemblances' (Liker et al. 1999) should not be overstated. Indeed, there are two particular reasons why specific *enterprise* recipes and competencies may be of special importance among Japanese firms. One reason is that the management cadres of large enterprises have generally built their careers within the firm that recruited them from college, so their expertise is primarily drawn from that firm (Storey et al. 1997). Strong internally structured careers reinforce a strong company consciousness. Thus managers often have wide experience of the operations of their own firms, but very limited experience of the practices and procedures of competitor firms. The other reason is that important features of Japanese production expertise remain relatively uncodified, available primarily as *tacit* knowledge displayed in the day-to-day practices of work organization (Abo 1994*a*: 12; Fruin 1997; Liker et al. 1995, 1999). This implies that an appreciation of the implications of such practices will depend upon the contact and involvement that are available to insiders, but will be difficult to communicate via decontextualized recipes that become readily available to outsiders. These organizational characteristics are shared across many leading Japanese manufacturing firms but, paradoxically, they reinforce the argument that stylized models of Japanese production management are likely to gloss over the central importance of enterprise-specific forms of work organization and innovation. This insight is important for assessing models of work organization in Japan, but becomes even more significant when these models are 'exported' through the Japanese international company. While such companies may be identified by their hosts as quintessentially Japanese, this obscures the distinctiveness of sectoral and company recipes and approaches.

Finally, several commentators have also suggested that generalized models of Japanese production systems ignore marked differences in the forms of work organization that characterize different *tiers* in the extended subcontractor hierarchies which are a widespread feature of Japanese manufacturing (Benson 1998; Chalmers 1989). One response to this is that it is only the dominant final assemblers and leading first-tier subcontractors that embody model characteristics or best practice, while the remaining firms deviate from best practice. They are thus less salient for understanding the strengths of Japanese manufacturing and the features that might be emulated in Japanese factories overseas (as well as by foreign competitor firms). However, this understates the importance of these supply chains in the overall pattern of operations of the Japanese final producers, because these operations often involve very highly differentiated activities in which a substantial part of the production process is carried out within the supply chain or by subordinate parallel producers. For example, in Toyota 85 per cent of the average car content was bought in through the supply chain, 50 per cent of assembly was subcontracted, and a network of eight subcontractors produced 45 per cent Toyota output (JETRO 2003: 25).

Once the centrality of these supplier networks is recognized, this adds a further dimension to debates about the internationalization of Japanese manufacturers. Some commentators emphasize the primacy of geographical proximity in such networks, allowing close coordination between the partners and tightly managed JIT logistics. This suggests that the effective internationalization of Japanese manufacturing requires the export of whole production complexes, to reproduce these features of the supply chain as integral features of overseas production (JETRO 2003; Ruigrok and van Tulder 1995). Other commentators place greater emphasis on the effective subordination of lower-tier suppliers to the cost, quality, and delivery imperatives of the dominant firms, with much less emphasis on the need for geographical proximity. This suggests that internationalization may involve the placement of different stages of the production chain in widely dispersed locations, so long as the prevailing circumstances allow the implementation of rigorous but low cost production regimes (Dedoussis 1994, 1995). Whatever the interpretation, and there may be important sector differences here, the message is that transfer and 'transplantation' involve more than stand-alone, isolated enterprises. Thus, our understanding of these processes has to embrace broader units of analysis such as production chains or supplier networks.

It is now appropriate to return to the contrasting stylized post-Fordist and neo-Fordist accounts of Japanese production regimes outlined earlier, to reconsider these accounts in the light of our discussion of sources of variation in enterprise and factory practices. One implication is that adjudication between these competing analyses is perilous if it is based on generalized claims about the organization of production across all firms, sectors, and contractor hierarchies. Instead, it is plausible to suggest that leading firms in capital goods sectors may be closer to the first, post-Fordist, model, but medium-sized producers of mass consumer goods will be closer to the second, neo-Fordist model. Meanwhile, many smaller enterprises towards the bottom of the supply chains are likely to diverge from both, in the direction of highly pressured and labour-intensive work routines which are more akin to Taylorism than Fordism.

Toyota, Fordism, and limitations of the enterprise paradigm

With this contextual and tiered approach to the Japanese production model in mind, it becomes appropriate to turn to an examination of the work regimes prevailing in specific leading firms, to assess them as *enterprise models* rather than extrapolating directly to a national norm (Wood 1992, 1993; Tolliday 1998). Analyses of the most obvious example to consider here, Toyota's production system, suggest that in this leading auto sector case, aspects of both models can be seen. However, the potentially post-Fordist dynamic of devolved operator responsibility and creative problem-solving is effectively subordinated to the supervisory prerogatives and tight routines emphasized by the neo-Fordist diagnosis (Cusumano 1985; Dohse et al. 1985; Ishida 1989; Okayama 1986; Shimizu 1998). The neo-Fordist approach may underestimate the ways in which the flexibility and tacit knowledge of line workers is mobilized to cope with production exigencies. However, supervisors clearly play the dominant role in kaizen within cost-down targets set by senior management, so the concept of neo-Fordism is much better at capturing the stringency and pressure involved within the Toyota production process.

At the same time it is apparent from detailed research on Toyota that summary accounts of the 'Toyota Production System' often fail to recognize important tensions and shifts involved in the development and institutionalization of this model (Gronning 1995; Sey 2000; Tolliday 1998). Its roots are primarily to be found in Ohno's programme for the rationalization of production developed in the late 1940s and accelerated after 1950. This followed upon the defeat of the Toyota Union's efforts to pursue an independent agenda, resulting in substantial redundancies and the entrenchment of management prerogatives (Cusumano 1985; Gronning 1995; Okayama 1986; Tolliday 1998). This rationalization programme, designed to cope with shortages of capital and materials, involved the specification of standard tasks and times, deskilling, multimachine manning and experiments in JIT assembly. It also involved a growing role for individualized merit assessments in determining pay and promotion. In the 1960s, a period of rapid expansion and considerable labour turnover, all these initiatives were pushed further and combined with a belated preoccupation with systematic QC. This resulted in a supervisor-orchestrated pattern of intense flexible labour, and a dynamic of productivity gains driven through the management hierarchy to work group level by payments for continuing above-norm improvements (Cusumano 1985; Gronning 1995; Ishida 1989; Nonaka, 1995; Okayama 1986).

By the early 1970s these features had been formalized into what became known as the Toyota Production System. This was still very much management dominated, but with a more subtle integration of workers through the institutionalization of merit pay and the extension of QC activities, as the proportion of temporary and seasonal workers among final assemblers fell rapidly (Gronning 1997; Ishida 1989; Shimizu 1998; Tolliday 1998; Udagawa 1995). However, the extent and form of implementation of this 'system' still varied between different areas of assembly and, more so, down the extensive supplier network (Williams et al. 1994*a*). There were further refinements in the 1980s, designed to cope with a more complex product mix and higher value models. These involved use of more flexible machines and line layouts, combined with a greater emphasis on preventative maintenance, but assembly work remained 'monotonous, repetitive and fast' (Shimizu 1998: 80). Finally, in the late 1980s and early 1990s problems with the recruitment and retention of labour, coupled with continuing competitive pressures, prompted some relaxations in the stringency of the production regime. This involved the modification of standard times, a reduced linkage of pay to productivity gains, the redesign of work stations, and experiments with shorter, buffered production lines (Gronning 1995; Nohara 1999; Shimizu 1995, 1998).

This résumé of the Toyota trajectory emphasizes two key points. First, stylized models of production regimes necessarily abstract from an evolving, uneven, and often problematical set of management policies and practices, and tend to attribute greater coherence and stability to those practices than are merited, even when they represent the codification of experience within a leading firm. Second, wider sets of conditions and contingencies are central to the strengths and limitations of such evolving policies, not simply through the 'anonymous' effects of changes in product and labour markets but through the organized efforts of governments, competitor firms, trade unions, and other institutional actors. Thus discussions of the potential transfer or translation of specific models of Japanese work organization from Japan to other parts of the globe must also consider the wider social, institutional, and economic contexts within which they have been developed in Japan. It is important to recognize that all 'production regimes' have a history and must be set in context, they are not 'closed systems'. Similarly, internationalization processes must also be viewed historically, and the operations of subsidiaries must be situated in their own evolving contexts.

THE PRODUCTION REGIME WITHIN A WIDER CONTEXT

There are many different analyses of the wider context of Japanese production regimes, but for our purposes we will identify four broad variants, namely *cultural*, *institutional*, *class relations*, and *political economy* approaches. The first focuses on the role of shared values in generating and sustaining a specifically Japanese social order. The second discusses the consolidation of a distinctive complex of institutional arrangements that constitute the Japanese business and employment 'systems'. The third analyses the class relations that underpin national institutional arrangements, highlighting evolving patterns of class conflict and accommodation. Finally, the fourth addresses the interplay between the political, economic, and social dimensions of class relations, including the ways in which national formations articulate with wider international developments. The first two approaches tend to emphasize the importance of relatively settled and self-contained national employment systems and their 'societal effects' (Maurice et al. 1986). However, the last two approaches emphasize that national social orders are characterized by internal tensions, conflicts, and change, and are also conditioned by their location in a 'changing global order' (Stubbs and Underhill 2000).

This section outlines key features of each of these approaches and considers the implications for our understanding of the embeddedness and relative autonomy of Japanese firms, both as national and international actors. As such it prefigures the framework for analysing the operations of international firms that is elaborated in Chapter 4, which emphasizes the interplay between 'system', 'societal', and 'dominance' effects in defining the terrain on which such firms operate (Smith and Meiksins 1995). First, these firms are capitalist enterprises, characterized by rivalry between competing firms and conflicts and accommodations between capital and labour. Second, they operate within and between competing capitalist societies characterized by different institutional legacies and class settlements. Finally, they are influenced by dominant modernization and innovation recipes that circulate across the global economy, cross-cutting and unsettling established national models.

The cultural approach

This approach emphasizes that specific cultural values and ways of being—especially loyalty to household, family, and nation; respect for hierarchy; and a situational sense of self—underpin all aspects of Japanese society (Abe and Fitzgerald 1995; Haitani 1976; Kondo 1990). In particular, this cultural framework provides the basis for reciprocal commitment and trust within the enterprise as a community. It furnishes the values that are embodied in the institutions of 'lifetime employment', seniority wages, and enterprise unionism and the meanings which inform team working and continuous improvement. It defines managers as organizational members, while shareholders are excluded from control and community membership (Inagami and Whittaker 2005). It also sustains the patterns of long-term trust and reciprocity that are held to characterize relations between specific enterprises and their network partners, whether funders, suppliers or customers. Strong versions of this approach (e.g. Hazama 1987) generally emphasize the distinctiveness of this cultural inheritance and thus argue that the transfer of Japanese production, employment or keiretsu practices to societies with very different cultural repertoires will be bereft of the appropriate cultural glue, and thus meaningless or impossible.

There are, however, major problems with such culturalist accounts, whether applied to Japan or elsewhere, which relate to the problem of explaining specific and varied institutional developments directly in terms of a shared and enduring cultural inheritance. First such analyses provide no way of addressing the discontinuities and non-correspondences between the various institutional features that are supposed to embody these values. For example, they fail to recognize the development of an industrial labour market in Japan characterized by widespread insecurity, labour mobility, coercion, and conflict in the 1910s and 1920s. Further, they fail to recognize that enterprise unions only became part of the institutional matrix after 1946, and then underwent further marked changes after significant conflicts during the 1950s (Sugayama 1995; Weiss 1993), while alternative approaches to enterprise union ideology and organization have continued to evolve and compete since then. In other words, culture is historically constituted, yet notions of shared 'inheritance' or 'traditional ways of being' imply immutable structures and values that seem to stand outside history.

Second, in offering a generalized explanation of shared features of Japanese society, cultural accounts offer little leverage for understanding how very different patterns of work and employment relations coexist, such as those in the large enterprises of the core compared with the small family enterprises of the periphery. In these respects culturalist accounts seek to explain too much but succeed in explaining too little. This is not to say that distinctive cultural discourses are irrelevant to an understanding of Japanese social institutions. However, the forms of these institutions cannot be derived from such discourses, because their meanings and implications are ambiguous, negotiated and changing, a point which is recognized in the more cautious and sophisticated analyses of Dore (1973) and Kondo (1990). As a result, we cannot conclude that this distinctive cultural matrix precludes the transfer of Japanese management practices to different social contexts.

The institutionalist approach

This approach is in part a response to culturalist arguments, and seeks to understand dominant features of Japanese industry and society in terms of an active and strategic process of institution building, rather than enduring cultural values. There are two influential but overlapping variants of this institutionalist approach, one arising out of historical discussions of Japan's 'late development' and the other addressing the institutional logic of Japanese capitalism in the post-war period. The *late development thesis*, associated especially with Dore (1973), argues that elites in Japan faced specific problems because they confronted the established economic and political power of rival imperialist states such as Britain and the United States, but at the same time late development offered distinctive opportunities to address these challenges. In particular it allowed state and business elites to learn from the positive and negative experiences of other countries in seeking to develop more effective industrialization strategies and institutions (Abe and Fitzgerald 1995; Dore 1973; Weiss 1993). This meant developing a form of 'organized capitalism', involving an active 'developmental state' and leading industrial sectors characterized by extensive organizational linkages and loyalties, as the basis for protecting Japan's political independence and securing its economic power.

Writers in this late development tradition have emphasized that key employment institutions, for example, were constructed by the interrelated initiatives of employers and state officials, as they sought to solve organizational problems, develop private industry, and forge a stronger state. Thus early experiments with internal labour markets and employment security for an elite of workers occurred in the 1910s and 1920s, when key employers in heavy industry were faced with problems of the retention and regulation of labour and incipient labour conflict (Gordon 1985; Littler 1982). Later, in the context of the mobilization of production for the war economy, state bureaucrats were the key agents in imposing wage controls accompanied by standardized patterns of seniority wages, extensive enterprise-based welfare measures and a rhetorical semblance of harmonistic worker involvement (Sugayama 1995; Weiss 1993).

Finally, the practices and expectations arising from these earlier developments were systematically institutionalized through the 'white-collarization' of the employment relations of manual workers in the core enterprises. This consolidated the 'three pillars' of the employment system (lifetime employment, seniority wages, and enterprise unionism) and supported the long-term development of worker expertise within the framework of the enterprise community (Koike 1988; Sugayama 1995). Such historical accounts of the construction and reconstruction of employment relations are paralleled by discussions of the organization and reorganization of corporate groupings, which resulted in distinctive patterns of long-term financing and integrated supply chains (Abe and Fitzgerald 1995). They are also accompanied by analyses of the development of JIT production arrangements to cope with shortages of capital and materials and limited consumer markets during the years of economic recovery after the war (Sayer 1986; Udagawa 1995).

Building upon such historical accounts, the new institutionalist economists then offer a more formal analysis of the logic of what they regard as the resultant organizational matrix. This is characterized in terms of high-trust, mutual-benefit relations between committed enterprise managers, shop-floor employees, members of supplier chains and providers of funding, reinforced by supportive state policies (Aoki 1994; Teague 1997). Their basic argument is that each of these relationships provides crucial advantages of flexibility and innovative capacity, whilst minimizing the costs which could arise from the sectional exploitation of the leverage which comes with expertise and barriers to substitutability. In particular, core employees are bound into the enterprise through employment security, the scope for continuing development and advancement, and payment based on individual development and merit. This is materially underpinned by the engagement of enterprise unions in joint-benefit productivity coalitions with management and also by the poor prospects of those excluded from the core.

Implications of institutionalist analyses for debates about transfer

This sort of institutionalist analysis has rather complex and ambiguous implications for debates about transfer (see Aoki 1994: 33–6). First, the emphasis on active institution building and the resultant scope for generating shared benefits suggests that key elements of the overall model are transferable, rather than being irrevocably tied to a distinctive cultural inheritance. Thus Koike (1988), in particular, is keen to emphasize the universality of the institutional logic involved, by stressing that what is distinctive about Japan is the 'white-collarization' of blue-collar work, through the extension of work and employment relations common among white-collar workers across capitalist societies to a wider working class constituency in Japan. Second, however, there are important path-dependent features of this analysis, highlighted by the particular contingencies which have influenced the uneven development and consolidation of this whole matrix of institutions in Japan. As a result Dore (1973), for example, argues that there is scope for others to learn from the Japanese experience through a process of 'reverse convergence', but this will depend upon institutional modifications and innovations which offer some approximation to Japanese models, both within the enterprise and, more problematically, beyond.

A major deficiency of most of these institutionalist analyses, however, is that they gloss over the inequalities of power which characterize these processes of institution building, inequalities which sharply qualify the claims of joint benefits they embrace. This is the key argument of the class relations approach, which emphasizes the subordinate role of labour in much of this process and the effort devoted to resubordinating workers at those moments when organized labour did gain real leverage over the terms of institutional innovation.

The class relations approach

An important starting point for class relations analyses is the disorganized and conflictual character of employment relations in many developing industrial sectors in the late nineteenth and early twentieth centuries. This led both to the repression of the nascent labour movement and to efforts by some of the large heavy engineering employers to stabilize their skilled workforces through the incorporation of subcontract relations within the enterprise and promises of job security (Gordon 1985; Littler 1982). This contradicts accounts of any smooth development from traditional to modern employment forms. Furthermore, this period also saw the active construction of an *ideology* of industrial harmony and enterprise community, through the appropriation and reconfiguration of an existing cultural repertoire. This then furnished an important basis of attempts by both employers and state officials to legitimate the subordination of wage workers, both to managerial prerogatives and to the demands of a strong, militarist state (Gordon 1985; Kinzley 1991). Thus these commentators emphasize the ways in which such institutions and ideologies sought to secure the effective subordination and exploitation of workers, rather than constructing a genuinely egalitarian 'enterprise community'.

A pivotal historical moment for analysts of class relations was the immediate post-war period. It represented a brief phase of radicalization and rapid growth in union organization, which in turn prompted a change of policy by the occupying powers and an employers' offensive that aimed to defeat such radicalism and reassert the prerogatives of capital within the workplace. It is evident that the form taken by this phase of class conflict was strongly influenced by earlier developments. This included the internalization of skilled labour by leading enterprises in heavy industry and, especially, the corporatist forms of employment regulation that had been imposed by the state during the war. However, the outcomes have been interpreted rather differently even within the tradition of class analysis.

Thus Kenney and Florida (1988) see the class compromise that issued from this period of crisis as one that embodied just those joint gains celebrated by the institutionalists, entrenching a relatively egalitarian and participatory class settlement at the origin and heart of the post-war economic miracle. Most other commentators, though, have emphasized a continuing conflict between the workers' version of the post-war settlement and the management revision of this settlement (Gordon 1985, 1993, 1996; Kumazawa 1996; Price 1997). In these accounts particular attention is given to the success of employers, aided by the state, in defeating the more radical trade union groupings and changing the terms of the accommodation between capital and labour even in the large enterprises. These changes entrenched management prerogatives in the production process, limited the scope and effectiveness of the remaining or replacement trade unions, and introduced discretionary elements into payment systems (Price 1997). Though major disputes in the early 1950s were pivotal to these developments and management's 'revision' appeared to be consolidated by the end of the 1960s, this reconstruction remained a persistently somewhat contested and incomplete process. From this vantage point, worker opposition to Ohno's reorganization of work at Toyota (Cusumano 1985); major episodes of industrial conflict such as those in the coal industry (Allen 1994; Price 1997); the caution with which craft workers guarded their tacit knowledge from management in medium sized enterprises (Cole 1971); and the occupation of small enterprises by workers threatened with redundancy (Turner 1995), all represent important aspects of the class struggle and accommodation that have marked the post-war economic trajectory of Japan. Alongside moments of organized conflict there were also more informal processes of resistance, signalled for example by difficulties of recruitment in periods of labour shortage. In other words, Japan is a capitalist society, in which structural conflicts between the major social classes remain central.

These analyses do not depend upon a simplistic class reductionism. For example, they recognize the tensions between state strategies and employer policies, as the state buttressed the war economy by extolling 'equality of sacrifice' or the post-war administration initially encouraged union organization to facilitate democratization. However, they suggest that, over time, state and employer policies have meshed to consolidate the subordination of labour. They also recognize the importance of divisions among workers, especially those between permanent male workers in the large enterprises and a range of temporary, insecure, and rarely unionized 'peripheral' workers. Indeed, a key argument of those writers who have emphasized class relations and class struggle is that the defeat of the more radical union currents and the consolidation of modern enterprise unionism served to institutionalize these divisions. This served to underline the value of job security for a compliant core workforce, thus making it difficult for other workers to organize (though not impossible, as Turner's (1995) ethnography of mobilization and factory occupation in small firms testifies).

This discussion of core and peripheral workforces also underlines the ways in which the post-war Japanese class compromise was also a gender settlement, involving the entrenchment of gender inequalities in both the domestic sphere and the labour market (Carney and O'Kelly 1990; Gottfried and Hayashi-Kato 1998). Women's position in Japanese society was powerfully defined in terms of obligations to both family and nation, but for working-class women this often involved low-paid wage labour. The industrialization of Japan was built upon the development of a textile industry that used predominantly female labour, subordinated by family indebtedness, the dormitory system, and authoritarian management, though not without rebellion and attempts at escape (Tsurumi 1990). In the post-war period women remained an important part of the growing industrial workforce, their position characterized by insecure employment and low pay, as temporary workers in the large enterprises or with interrupted work careers and often part-time employment in the small and medium sectors (Brinton 1993; Kumazawa 1996; Lam 1992). Again this pattern did not go unchallenged (Liddle and Nakajima 2000), and recently more women have made modest advances in internal labour markets (Inagami and Whittaker 2005), though the numbers in insecure employment have also grown.

Finally, the class relations approach illuminates contemporary debates about recent crises of the 'Japanese employment system' (Berggren and Nomura 1997; Gronning 1998; Inagami and Whittaker 2005; Kyotani 1999; Lincoln and Nakata 1997). First, it suggests that contemporary restructuring should be seen in the context of a persistent contestation and remaking of key features of that 'system' over the post-war period (Price 1997). Against this background, contemporary changes have often been quite incremental despite a rhetoric of transformation, but have nevertheless brought growing job insecurity across much of the economy. Second, it emphasizes the role of employers, and especially the Japanese Employer's Federation, as central actors in seeking to restructure employment relations in ways which enhance their autonomy in a period of recession and intensified competition. This has involved a stronger emphasis on 'ability' pay, the growth of 'intermediate labour markets' and insecure employment, and the shedding of jobs. Third, it emphasizes that in the face of such initiatives, coupled with the export of manufacturing jobs and growth of the service sector, Japanese trade unions have been losing members and are on the defensive. There have been some attempts to rethink union strategies and appeals, but the dominant response has remained cautious enterprise corporatism (Fujimura 1997; Suzuki 1998).

Implications of the class relations approach for debates about transfer

The class relations approach has four main implications for debates about internationalization and the transfer of Japanese models. First, the importance of class conflict highlights the contrasting agendas and criteria by which such models may be evaluated by employers and employees, and indeed by different groupings of workers, both within Japan and elsewhere. This suggests that there may be important parallels between the uncertainties and conflicts that have arisen over the terms of the implementation of Japanese management strategies at home and those that may characterize the operation of Japanese firms in overseas locations. Second, the distinctions between core and peripheral workers (and the gendering of these divisions) highlight important contrasts in the models of work organization and employment relations that may be drawn on by Japanese overseas subsidiaries. In turn, this raises questions about the relationship between choices among such models and existing forms of labour market segmentation and class accommodation in the host countries of such firms.

Thirdly, this approach directs attention to the ways in which the relative power of organized labour in host countries might influence the selection and adaptation of Japanese corporate repertoires in different subsidiaries. In this regard some optimistic commentators argue that stronger worker organization and higher worker expectations in some western contexts have prompted a selective implementation of the less negative elements of the Toyota model (Adler and Cole 1995). Meanwhile, more pessimistic commentators have highlighted the consequences of the absence or relative weakness of collective organization in many 'transplants', and have argued that these features are not incidental because they reflect some of the locational decisions made by Japanese companies moving production overseas (Milkman 1991). Finally, these analyses of class relations and class segmentation also illuminate the terrain upon which Japanese union federations have themselves responded to the internationalization of Japanese firms, and especially the limited role of any dialogue between Japanese federations and unions in host countries in influencing that process of internationalization (Williamson 1994).

The political economy approach

The final approach to the analysis of Japan's post-war economic success—and also its contemporary economic malaise—is that of political economy. By this we mean those analyses that seek to identify the totality of socio-economic relations within which Japanese manufacturing enterprises have operated, addressing both the interlocking features of these relations and the tensions or contradictions which characterize them and help to drive their evolution over time. There are many variants of such analyses, but our concern is to draw on a limited number to identify and comment on certain recurrent themes, rather than to intervene more fully in these debates (Burkitt and Hart-Landsberg 1996; Lapavitsas 1997; Leyshon 1994; Murphy 2000). In particular we wish to consider how these commentaries on the Japanese political economy may qualify and complicate the accounts provided by the institutionalists and the theorists of class relations discussed earlier. For this purpose the following paragraphs provide a selective outline of some important circuits of interdependencies identified by analyses of the political economy of post-war Japan, highlighting their unsettled and evolving features.[1]

The first is the important but also problematical role of state agencies in concerting and regulating the competitive strategies of the dominant Japanese firms and enterprise groupings. They have influenced both the rationalization policies applied to declining activities and the research and development (R&D) policies intended to underpin growth sectors. However, they have not been able to fully regulate the contrasting strategies of different firms or guarantee continuing strategic advantages in international competition (Berggren and Nomura 1997; Fransman 1995).

[1] One basis for developing a fuller analysis is provided by the regulationist approach. Thus the Japanese political economy has been conceptualized in these terms as a coherent and distinctive regime of accumulation (named variously Toyotism or Fujitsuism or Ohnoism), or as a progression of several such regimes (moving from pre-Fordist to post-Fordist forms). However, such analyses have all proved highly problematical. Peck and Miyamachi (1995) seek to defend the regulationist approach by emphasizing the disjunctions and conflicts that characterize any regulatory regime, but they also acknowledge a series of important difficulties with existing regulationist analyses. These are that (i) there are major unresolved differences among regulationist theorists in their characterization of basic features of these regimes; (ii) they differ in their periodizations of phases of consolidation and transition; (iii) the relationships between Japanese developments and wider global processes remain ambiguous; and (iv) there is a strong but inappropriate tendency to read off the broader configuration of social relations from a stylized account of production relations. In our view it remains unclear how regulationist approaches will overcome these problems, so we have not sought to deploy their conceptual framework here.

The second is the central importance of administrative guidance in the post-war reconstruction and continued operation of Japan's financial system. The state has drawn on the high levels of personal savings engaged in by ordinary Japanese, seeking to protect their economic welfare in the context of modest welfare state and pension provisions, and has circulated such individual savings in the form of long-term credit for major manufacturers (Burkitt and Hart-Landsbury 1996; Lapavitsas 1997). For a long period this provided 'patient capital' at the expense of low rates of return for ordinary savers, but it has been increasingly difficult to sustain as the economy has matured and economic growth has slowed.

The third feature has been the long-term hegemony (but more recent crises) of the Liberal Democratic Party, built upon economic supports for key interests in the countryside and in construction, sectors which have remained relatively fragmented and traditional compared with manufacturing.

The fourth, closely related to the previous two, has been the increasing importance of investments in land, both in the form of loans to farmer's cooperatives and in the form of speculative investment in urban commercial property. This served to underpin the financial system but also became a pivotal source of its contemporary destabilization (Lapavitsas 1997; Leyshon 1994).

Finally, all of these features of the domestic economy have been powerfully conditioned by the relationship between Japan and the United States, initially in terms of the democratization programme, which meant partial dismantling of pre-war and war time zaibatsu, but soon after, in terms of Japan's economic participation in the cold war alliance. Two key aspects of the resulting relationship were the early stimulus to the Japanese economy provided by its growing role in the provisioning of American military hegemony in the region and the later centrality of the American market for the Japanese strategy of export-led growth (Halliday and McCormack 1973). However, while Japan's recovery and miracle-era growth were conditioned by American hegemony in these ways, the resulting patterns of trade, competition, and financial flows also became increasing sources of economic and political friction between the two countries. This resulted in conflicts over trade barriers and exchange rates that have had profound implications for the more recent reshaping of the Japanese economy (Murphy 2000).

Implications of the political economy approach for debates about transfer

The first implication of these arguments is to reinforce the point that there have been substantial differences of corporate organization and performance in Japan, not only across firms and sectors but also over time

(Berggren 1995). Such differences are likely to influence efforts to 'transfer' Japanese management practices overseas, but also efforts to learn from international competitors or collaborators and even engage in 'reverse transfer' (Edwards 2004).

Second, such variations in competitiveness have to be understood not only in terms of the performance of specific work regimes or employment relations, but also in terms of prevailing wage levels, living standards, consumption patterns, and exchange rate regimes. These have in different ways supported and constrained management policies and practices in Japan (Williams et al. 1994*b*). This suggests that processes of internationalization cannot simply be seen in terms of processes of transfer or non-transfer, but also have to be understood in terms of efforts to manage or cope with such external contingencies, as they are experienced in different ways at home and abroad.

Third, they therefore emphasize that internationalization itself has been driven by wider pressures of economic and political rivalry within the global economy. As such internationalization in turn feeds back into challenges for the domestic political economy, signalled by debates about the 'hollowing out' and servicization of the Japanese economy and its implications for domestic social and class settlements. Indeed, even within the confines of specific enterprises, internationalization has this reciprocal character, as the operations of subsidiaries influence the range of activities of the home plants in a variety of ways.

CONCLUSION

Three important implications flow from our evaluation of these different approaches to analysing the context in which firms have operated in Japan. The first is that institutionalist characterizations of the positive dynamic of a socially regulated high-trust economy are inadequate, not only because they gloss over class inequalities but because they fail to address important limitations and contradictions that characterize the Japanese political economy (Coates 2000). The present long recession of the Japanese economy has helped to expose these features, and we do not need to embrace a caricature account of 'crony capitalism' based upon an uncritical celebration of neo-liberal market capitalisms to recognize their significance.

The second implication is that analyses of class relations cannot simply focus on the organization of work and employment relations. They must consider other aspects of class and gender relations, involving the social organization and regulation of consumption, savings and political representation. They also have to address the ways in which such relations within Japan are conditioned by the country's position in the global political economy.

The third and final point is that many firm-focused approaches to the transfer debate neglect some of the important but problematical conditions surrounding the successful operation of major Japanese firms. In particular the class relations and political economy approaches emphasize the importance of the specific historical conjunctures represented by post-war reconstruction and economic growth, and the pivotal role of American hegemony over this period. From this perspective, the positive dynamic effects of MITI-orchestrated strategic restructuring and the administered supply of low-cost capital were vulnerable to erosion, as Japan's mass-production based growth reached maturity, international competition intensified and overcapacity grew.

Such developments have clearly altered the terrain upon which Japanese manufacturing firms and their managements operate, in ways which are a far cry from the usual debates about the scope and limits of the transferability of the Japanese model. In particular these arguments have emphasized some of the *structural* challenges that confront contemporary Japanese enterprises even in their efforts to sustain their existing modes of operation in Japan. A mundane but important example concerns the shift from growing mass markets which facilitated the operation of factories at near full capacity, to more nearly saturated markets which readily translate into fluctuating demand and costly overcapacity. As Williams et al. (1994*b*) show, the post-war competition between auto manufacturers in the United States, Japan, and Europe was both a competition between producers embedded in different social or class settlements and a competition between producers facing distinctive national market conditions. While American motor manufacturers had to sell their products and operate their factories in increasingly mature markets characterized by fluctuating cycles of replacement demand. Meanwhile Japanese manufacturers grew in conditions of continuing domestic market growth, which allowed some of them to run their operations at near full capacity, strongly reinforcing their competitive advantages. However, market saturation has made it much more difficult to reap these advantages on the basis of the home market. Furthermore, such processes of maturation, increased competition and incipient overcapacity have been played out on an international and not just national level, in this and other sectors. In particular, the growing Japanese penetration of and reliance upon the American market prompted the American administration to impose trade restrictions and to pursue major revisions to the exchange rate regime, leading to the Plaza Accord in 1985. While the former provided a direct incentive to move some manufacturing activities to such major markets as the United States, the latter involved a massive revaluation of the Yen and radically altered the international competitiveness of manufacturing for export in Japan.

Two decades of substantial FDI and one decade of recession have stimulated considerable internal debate in Japan on the durability and efficiency of the 'Japanese model' at home. Meanwhile, the global reach of Japanese investments has created a new generation of Japanese managers and engineers with genuine international exposure and experience, against which to evaluate indigenous practices. There has also been some, though still modest, foreign investment penetration into the Japanese economy, and this, too, has placed strains on the stability of existing Japanese practices. However, the conclusion from Inagami and Whittaker's (2005) survey and case-study data is that there has still been more continuity than transformation in Japan's 'corporate communities'. From our perspective in exploring the nature of work in Japanese subsidiaries abroad, this may suggest that Japanese managers will still remain confident about transplanting their home-grown employment relations and production regimes to overseas factories. Nevertheless, Japanese manufacturers have had to confront the pressures and uncertainties of an unstable, even volatile, national and international political economy in recent decades, across a period that can be characterized as a long, complex domestic recession (Berggren 1995: 60). As we show in Chapter 3, this has influenced the patterns of Japanese FDI, and challenged many assumptions about the 'Japanization' and revitalization of western economies popular at the end of the twentieth century.

CHAPTER

3

The Internationalization of Japanese Manufacturing

INTRODUCTION

This chapter develops a critique of linear evolutionary approaches to the analysis of Japanese FDI that suggest a progressive movement up the value chain with associated upgrading of physical and human capital. We argue that such approaches gloss over the persistence of mundane assembly operations and also the continued geographical repositioning of subsidiaries through competitive pressures across the international division of labour. We outline the trends in Japanese FDI and manufacturing capital formation from the 1970s, and the associated debates on the character of subsidiary formation. We suggest that debates in the 1980s were far too optimistic and unidirectional, in the light of the recent ebb and flow of investment and the emergence of China as a key site of global assembly lines. However, we do not suggest that Japanese subsidiaries are simply cost-cutters. Rather, some are likely to remain routine manufacturing plants, some may move up the value chain and others may face contraction or closure, and these different trajectories will help to shape the production regimes and employment relations of specific subsidiaries. Thus recognition of these different possibilities prepares the ground for our substantive discussion of our case-study plants in later chapters.

TRENDS IN JAPANESE FOREIGN DIRECT INVESTMENT

There was an established, though modest, pattern of Japanese service sector investment overseas before the 1970s but Japanese investment in manufacturing operations in North America and Europe was negligible, and the bulk of productive investment was in Asia, primarily directed at the extraction of raw materials but with growing involvement in low skill, labour-intensive manufacturing (Dicken 1991: 22, 33). In this period Japanese manufacturers relied almost totally on the export of goods from Japan to North American and European markets, while Japanese commercial, finance, and service investments in these regions supported this trade in goods produced in Japan.

In the 1970s the volume of Japanese FDI remained quite low, but there was modest growth as it became easier because of deregulation. This period saw significant Japanese manufacturing FDI in North America and Europe for the first time, but the shift should not be overstated. First, overseas investment in services continued to outweigh investment in manufacturing, though Dicken (1991: 26) suggests that one distinctive feature of the flow of manufacturing investment was that the large trading companies helped to support the internationalization of relatively small and medium sized Japanese manufacturing firms, resulting in a greater involvement of such firms compared with the manufacturing FDI of other countries. Second, Japanese exports still massively outweighed overseas production. Dunning (1993: 134, 140) suggests that even by 1990, overseas operations still accounted for less than 10 per cent of the production of large Japanese manufacturing companies. Third, there was a much lower level of internationalization of production by Japan than among comparable US or European firms.

The 1980s witnessed a qualitative shift in the pace of overall Japanese FDI, peaking in 1989. During this period both the location and composition of this FDI also changed, moving from a focus on developing economies to growth in developed economies, and from an overwhelming emphasis on service, commerce, property, and raw material supply, to growth in manufacturing and final assembly, and to a limited extent design and development (although this activity remained, and remains, primarily a Japanese affair). In Asia, Japanese firms developed manufacturing and export bases to reduce the costs of home production and counter the effects of the appreciation of the Yen. Japanese manufacturing operations, especially final assembly, were moved to the United States to counter the threat to Japanese exports as the balance of trade between the two countries worsened. Similarly, in Europe, FDI was principally targeted to avoid trade friction and tariffs, and to capitalize on business opportunities presented by the creation of a Single European Market. The Plaza Accord of 1985, a response to trade friction between the United States and Japan, propelled the appreciation of the Yen against the Dollar, making Japanese exports more costly and American assets much cheaper, and this stimulated a huge increase in Japanese FDI. Japanese manufacturing investment grew rapidly through the 1980s and the first half of the 1990s, with Europe following behind the trend set in the United States, and this investment was particularly concentrated, and had a disproportionate effect, in a few key sectors, especially electronics and car manufacture.

During the late 1980s Japan experienced the 'bubble economy', when unrealistic expectations of continued growth fuelled huge property speculation and inflation, which was corrected at the end of the decade when the Japanese economy entered and remained in a long recession. In the 1990s FDI growth was no longer on an upward trajectory, as it had been in the 1980s, and it wasn't until the end of the 1990s that volumes started to reach the levels of the peak year of 1989. The 1990s saw the consolidation of regional economies, in the North American Free Trade Agreement (NAFTA), the European Union (EU), and Association of South-east Asian Nations (ASEAN), and the consolidation of Japanese manufacturing investments within these regions. This involved some closures and intra-regional relocations. For Japanese firms in the United States, this meant moves to Mexico as a low-cost NAFTA platform for the US market. In Europe, as we shall elaborate, there was more FDI in Eastern Europe as opposed to Western Europe, especially from the middle of the 1990s. In Asia, China has increasingly been the country of choice for low-cost production.

However, this re-division of investment was not only a regional phenomenon, and some low-value production has moved to China from Europe and North America, while some high-end R&D has moved back to Japan. Such changes suggest that some Japanese firms are taking an increasingly integrated global view of their international operations, and Kusumoto (2003) reports global corporate organizational change rather than internal regional problems as the primary reason for (small numbers of) Japanese firms withdrawing from Europe. Finally, there was a dramatic slowdown in overall Japanese FDI from 2000 to 2002 following global recession, which meant that in 2002 there was only half the FDI (by value) recorded in the peak year of 1989, underlining a recent pattern of volatility.

Turning to a closer examination of patterns of Japanese manufacturing investment in one region, Europe (broadly defined to include Turkey in this investment space), we can develop a more detailed picture of the division of manufacturing investments between countries over the period 1984–2002 within this region (see Table 3.1). This highlights some of the shifts between countries over time that have become central to the analyses reviewed later in this chapter, and also helps to frame our own case-study research on British manufacturing subsidiaries discussed in later chapters.

From 1984 to 2002 the United Kingdom led in terms of share of Japanese manufacturing affiliates, having over double the number of subsidiaries at the end of the period compared with nearest rivals France and Germany, which alternated between second and third places. Between 1984 and 1990, 100 new manufacturing affiliates were added in the United Kingdom, and between 1991 and 2001 another 100. The United Kingdom has seen the most

Table 3.1. *Japanese manufacturing affiliates in Europe and Turkey by country (as at the end of 2002)*

End of the year	1984	1985	1986	1987	1988	1989	1990	1991	1992	1993	1994	1995	1996	1997	1998	1999	2000	2001	2002
United Kingdom	45	50	60	75	92	120	145	162	173	181	188	203	215	226	237	250	258	262	266
France	28	34	41	49	55	67	78	84	87	90	98	106	117	120	128	130	137	139	140
Germany	41	43	49	54	58	74	86	93	102	105	107	115	121	121	124	127	128	129	129
Netherlands	14	17	18	19	22	27	27	34	37	38	40	42	46	49	52	55	56	57	57
Belgium	16	17	19	20	22	28	34	36	39	40	40	42	42	44	44	46	46	46	46
Luxembourg						1	2	3	3	3	3	3	3	3	3	3	3	3	3
Ireland	7	7	9	9	10	13	15	17	18	19	19	22	22	23	24	24	24	24	25
Spain	20	20	23	26	29	35	40	45	47	50	53	53	55	57	60	61	64	65	67
Italy	21	22	23	24	28	33	42	45	45	47	50	54	57	59	62	64	65	66	66
Finland									1	1	2	2	3	4	4	4	4	5	5
Norway														1	1	1	1	1	1
Sweden	5	5	6	7	7	7	7	8	10	12	12	12	15	15	16	17	18	18	18
Denmark	2	2	2	2	2	2	3	3	3	3	3	3	3	4	4	4	4	6	6
Austria	3	3	5	5	5	5	5	5	8	8	8	8	8	9	9	9	10	10	10
Portugal	4	4	5	5	6	7	9	9	10	11	11	13	14	14	16	16	16	16	16
Switzerland	2	2	2	2	2	2	2	2	3	3	3	3	3	3	3	4	4	4	4
Greece	3	3	3	3	3	3	3	3	3	3	3	3	3	3	3	3	3	3	3
Total in Western Europe	211	229	265	300	341	424	498	549	589	614	640	684	727	755	790	818	841	854	862

Poland										1	1	4	5	7	10	13	13	15	18
Czech Republic								1	4	5	5	6	8	11	11	13	17	30	42
Slovakia											1	1	3	4	4	4	6	8	8
Hungary				1	1	1	2	5	5	6	8	10	11	15	18	22	30	33	35
Romania															1	1	3	5	7
Lithuania																		1	1
Total in Central and Eastern Europe				1	1	1	2	6	9	12	15	21	27	37	44	53	69	92	111
Turkey	1	1	1	3	4	4	5	6	8	8	8	10	10	11	11	11	11	13	13
Total	212	230	266	304	346	429	505	561	606	634	663	715	764	803	845	882	921	959	986
Number of affiliates established	21	18	36	38	42	83	76	56	45	28	29	52	49	39	42	37	39	38	27
Increase over previous year (%)	11.0	8.5	15.7	14.3	13.8	24.0	17.7	11.1	8.0	4.6	4.6	7.8	6.9	5.1	5.2	4.4	4.4	4.1	2.8

Notes: This table shows the trend in the number of affiliates at the end of each year for 986 Japanese companies arranged by the year established. These figures are for manufacturing affiliates only; they do not include independent R&D/Design Centers.

Source: *Japan External Trade Organization* (JETRO) 2003

consistent growth in such FDI and remains the most popular location. In terms of affiliates, the British share of Japanese manufacturing operations in Western Europe was 21 per cent in 1984; 29 per cent in 1990; 30 per cent in 1995, and 31 per cent in 2002, while France showed a similar trend at a lower level (13 per cent, 16 per cent, 15 per cent, and 16 per cent). However, Germany's share dropped slightly (19 per cent, 17 per cent, 17 per cent, and 15 per cent), and in the latter part of this period. This involved a very modest arrival of new affiliates, eight between 1996 and 2002, compared with forty-one in the United Kingdom during the same period, perhaps reflecting the low growth of the German economy during this period. Obviously, these figures do not indicate the value of the affiliate investment, but if we take one year, 2002, France took 12.4 per cent of all European Japanese investment by value, double that of the United Kingdom, due very largely to Nissan's investment in Renault (JETRO 2003).

Within Europe, however, the main story in terms of new Japanese capital formation has been the expansion eastwards as former state socialist countries were economically integrated with Western Europe, and FDI flowed to benefit from intra-regional cost reduction and also local market access. In 1990 Japanese affiliates in Eastern European countries accounted for just 0.4 per cent of the total European (including Turkish) affiliates, in 1995 the figure was 3 per cent, but by 2002 it was 11 per cent. This represented a really striking increase in the rate of new affiliate formation. New Japanese establishments in Eastern Europe accounted for about 1.3 per cent of all new establishments in Europe in 1990, 11.5 per cent in 1995, 24 per cent in 1999, and 70 per cent in 2002, when the overall pace of new establishment formation fell. Japanese enterprises followed American and major European (especially Germany) firms in this movement, reflecting shared strategies from firms across the triad, rather than any specifically Japanese approach, but for all, the race eastwards was significantly accelerated in this period. The longer term implications of this move for Japanese companies in Western Europe is not yet clear but, as we later speculate, it is likely to redefine the regional division of labour, and lead to closures and rationalizations, especially in Japanese subsidiaries on the continent.

Finally, if we look at industry and country together, we can see that Japanese manufacturing FDI has partly followed a pattern of capitalizing on host country competitive advantages, hence more investments in food industries in France and the chemical industries in Germany, both of which are strong sectors within these respective economies. However, the pattern of internationalization also reflects home rather than host country strengths, hence the weight of investments in electrical and electronic parts and transportation machinery parts across a range of European countries, reflecting the strengths of these two sectors among Japanese firms and in the Japanese economy. As many of these sectors featured strongly in FDI growth in Eastern Europe and in Britain, it is likely that we will see some challenges to British–Japanese affiliates on costs grounds from new rival subsisiaries in Eastern and Central Europe (see Table 3.2).

INTERPRETING NEW JAPANESE MANUFACTURING FDI

The evolution of Japanese manufacturing investment in North America and Europe since the late 1970s can be charted through a succession of interpretations. These started with accounts of Japanese manufacturing firms as 'reluctant multinationals' (Trevor 1983). They preferred home manufacturing and the export of goods to overseas markets, but when they engaged in overseas production this was seen to involve overseas assembly 'warehouses' (Williams et al. 1991) designed to overcome barriers to market entry, with little value adding activity. Other writers then traced the development of such minimal foreign assembly operations into more substantial manufacturing branch plants (Munday et al. 1995). However, there were differing assessments of the extent to which such factories had implemented the more routine or the more sophisticated aspects of the operations of the parent factories in Japan, usefully signalled by the distinction between 'reproduction' and 'learning' factories (Kenney et al. 1998). Finally, later phases of Japanese manufacturing FDI were interpreted in terms of the growth of complementary activities around established plants. This involved both clusters of subcontractors and new research and development capabilities, which were sometimes seen as emergent 'integrated production networks' (Ruigrok and van Tulder 1995).

The development of Japanese manufacturing FDI can, then, be read as an evolutionary sequence, representing a process of consolidation of Japanese foreign investment and perhaps leading to the establishment of a series of regional design, development, and production clusters across the globe. This was the trajectory that was projected by some of the most influential analyses of the rapid growth of such investment in the developed world in the 1980s and early 1990s (Dunning 1993; Kenney and Florida 1993; Morris et al. 1993). More recently, however, discussions of the spatial distribution of such activities across the international division of labour have suggested that factories devoted to different phases of this sequence may continue to coexist at different sites, and that the redistribution of such activities over time can involve downgrading as well as upgrading (Dicken 1998; Kenney et al. 1998; Wilkinson et al. 2001; Morgan et al. 2002). This suggests that a linear progression through this evolutionary sequence is much more problematical than earlier accounts implied.

One influential interpreter of Japanese manufacturing FDI was Dunning, who sought to trace and project the pattern of this investment on the basis of his 'eclectic paradigm' for the analysis of the interacting roles of

Table 3.2. *Japanese manufacturing affiliates in Europe and Turkey by country and industry (as at the end of 2002)*

	Total	Total in Western Europe	United Kingdom	France	Germany	Netherlands	Belgium	Luxembourg	Ireland	Spain	Italy	Finland	Norway	Sweden	Denmark	Austria	Portugal	Switzerland	Greece	Total in Central and Eastern Europe	Poland	Czech Republic	Slovakia	Hungary	Romania	Lithuania	Turkey
Food products, agricultural, and fisheries product processing	43	38	8	20	2	5	1			1								1		2				1	1		3
Textiles (yarn, fabric)	9	8	2		1					1	3						1			1		1					
Clothing, textile products	19	18	8	5	1						3					1				1				1			
Timber, wood products (excluding furniture, interior products)	6	6			0							3		2		1				0							
Furniture, interior products	1	1		1	0															0							
Paper, pulp	9	9			6	1				1		1								0							
Printing, publishing	3	3			2	1														0							
Chemical and petroleum products	153	149	35	25	18	17	15	1	2	13	11		1	2	1	2	4	1	1	4		2		2			
Pharmaceuticals	34	34	3	7	5	1	5		6	2	4	1								0							
Rubber products	26	21	4	4	4	2	1		2	2	1						1			3	3						2

Ceramics, soil, and stone	14	13	3	1	2		4			2	1									1		1					
Steel	4	4			1	1				1									1	0							
Nonferrous metals	10	8	3	2	1			1	1											2				2			
Metal products	30	27	10	2	1	1				7	1					1	3	1		3		1		1		1	
General machinery	104	97	32	7	29	7	3		2	2	9			5		1				7	4	2		1			
Electric machinery	59	53	24	6	9	1	2		1	5	4						1			6		3	2	1			
Electric and electronic parts	111	92	32	12	17	3	4	1	8	4	5			3	1	1	1			19	1	5	3	9	1		
Transportation machinery	25	20	3	4	1	3				5	2			1			1			2		1		1			3
Transportation machinery parts	171	116	50	18	5	4	5			12	15			4			3			51	8	25	3	12	3		4
Precision machinery	70	67	25	15	16	5	1		2					1		1		1		3		1		2			
Other manufacturing industries	85	78	24	11	8	5	5		1	9	7				4	2	1		1	6	2			2	2		1
Total by industry and countries	986	862	266	140	129	57	46	3	25	67	66	5	1	18	6	10	16	4	3	111	18	42	8	35	7	1	13

Note: These figures are for manufacturing affiliates only; they do not include independent R&D/Design Centers.
Source: *Japan External Trade Organization* (JETRO 2003)

ownership, coordination, and locational effects. He suggested that the *ownership* advantages of Japanese companies grew in the 1970s and 1980s, but played an equivocal role in overseas investment. On the one hand it remained uncertain how far the ownership specific knowledge of key Japanese firms could be abstracted from their home bases and transferred overseas, because such knowledge was often embedded within disaggregated but closely coordinated networks and hierarchies of suppliers. On the other hand Japanese companies were still weaker in some areas of technological innovation. This may have influenced attempts to gain technical know-how through FDI, though Dunning suggests that Japanese firms showed a distinct preference for acquiring technological expertise through such routes as licensing or reverse engineering, rather than direct investment.

Thus *locational* factors appear to have played a more central role in stimulating FDI in the 1970s and early 1980s. First, there were often growing push factors, such as rising real wages in Japan and especially the appreciation of the Yen, which made home manufacturing more expensive. Second, there were important pull factors, associated with growing trade frictions and the imposition or threat of export quotas (Dicken 1991: 31). A graphic demonstration of the role of threatened trade sanctions is provided by Dunning's data on the correspondence between the initiation of European Commission (EC) surveys to monitor the import of specific products and the establishment of Japanese manufacturing facilities in Europe (Dunning 1993: 143, Fig. 6.1). For example, the first video cassette recorder factories date from 1982, the same year as an EC investigation, while two sites for manufacturing photocopiers predate the EC study of that sector, but eight more were established in the following five years (ibid.; also Dunning 1997: 332).

These developments led Dunning to identify two broad corporate strategies in play in the period of rapid growth of manufacturing FDI in the US and then Europe, in the early 1980s. The first and dominant strategy was that of 'defensive market-seeking investment', primarily in response to actual or potential trade barriers. This was undertaken by firms with strong organizational advantages that discouraged them from taking over existing firms or pursuing joint ventures, but also strong locational advantages to retaining core production activities in Japan. This typically involved greenfield plants 'which performed relatively low levels of value added activity... at worst these operations were "screwdriver" factories; at best they were branch plants which replicated the output of the parent company' (Dunning 1993: 141). Alongside this pattern, Dunning suggested that there was also some 'offensive, supply oriented investment', intended to facilitate learning from foreign competitors, both to upgrade Japanese home operations and enhance international competitiveness. However, he acknowledged that such efforts to acquire new organizational capabilities did not alter the pattern whereby strategic and high value activities remained in Japan. Furthermore, it was the first strategy that dominated the logic of overseas investment until the late 1980s.

Dunning argued that this logic of *market access* explained both the earlier and higher rate of Japanese manufacturing investment in the United States and the later and lower but parallel trend of such investment in Europe. Not only was the United States the larger market for key products, but it had 'lax inward investment and tight trade protection policies' compared with Europe (Dunning 1993: 144). Nevertheless:

> The underlying motives for Japanese investment in the two locations were fundamentally the same, viz. primarily market seeking, export substituting FDI, with little or no rationalised (efficiency seeking and/or cost reducing) investment, the latter being concentrated in low cost Asian countries (Dunning 1993: 145).

Morris (1988; 1991*b*) explored the specific implications of these processes for the patterning of Japanese investment in Europe, and especially in the United Kingdom. His critical commentary drew both on Dunning's (1986) pioneering work on Japanese investment in the United Kingdom and his own survey research, and again highlighted dual effects of the appreciating Yen and European protectionism in stimulating the move to European production operations. Against this background, Morris then argued that several features had combined to make Britain the most attractive location for Japanese manufacturing investment. These included the welcoming stance of the government and the associated regional incentives for inward investors, the weak position of consumer goods manufacturing in Britain which facilitated penetration of the domestic market, and low wages, especially compared with Germany. Thus, while *market access* was pivotal, *cost considerations* also played a role in guiding the location of specific investments within Europe, with a disproportionate flow of routine assembly investment to the declining industrial regions of Britain. However, while such British plants were often oriented towards production for the wider European market, sister plants were also being established in other European countries to serve these markets, underlining the continuing importance of the politics of market access.

An important feature of the analyses of both Dunning (1993) and Morris (1991*a*, 1991*b*) was their emphasis on the evolving character of Japanese manufacturing investment through and beyond this period. Thus Dunning suggested that towards the end of the 1980s there was an important shift in the international strategies of Japanese firms, from this defensive trade-replacement approach towards a more offensive pursuit of 'global competitive strength'. In his account, this shift had two components, firstly the consolidation of extensive production operations as 'insiders' in these key markets, and secondly the acquisition of leading edge expertise where this was possessed by competitors. While the differences and relationships between these two priorities were not fully explored by Dunning, they were both seen to support the upgrading of overseas production activities, giving priority to overseas production rather than export from Japan.

Three causes of this shift of strategy were identified. The first was the revaluation of the Yen following the Plaza Accord, which eroded the cost advantages of exports from Japan. The second was the continuing competitiveness of American firms in key sectors such as computers. The third was the emergence of the single European market. Dunning argued that all three features pushed Japanese firms to more offensive but also more technology and knowledge-intensive internationalization strategies. In his account a fairly uniform erosion of the organizational advantages of Japanese firms meant that 'the risks of building greenfield facilities sharply increased', and all these firms had to pursue new organizational advantages, either through increasing value-added at existing sites or through acquisitions, joint ventures or strategic alliances.

However, it is necessary to disaggregate these influences as they affect different regions, sectors, and firms more clearly than Dunning does. He did note that Japanese electronics companies in Europe were more likely to acquire the assets of local firms than those in the United States, and that Japanese motor firms in Europe had not developed such integrated production complexes as in the United States. However, the latter was treated as an historical lag rather than a product of the different structure of the European supply industry highlighted later by Fujimoto et al. (1994). Dunning also registered some differences between sectors, for example in the local content levels of transport equipment versus electricals. Overall, however, he argued that Japanese manufacturing FDI was becoming more strategic, which meant more design, development, and research investment, more reliance on local management and increasing management autonomy. His judgement of likely developments in the later 1990s was that, 'in short Japanese multinational enterprises are strategically positioning themselves to acquire or create new organisational advantages which will complement their existing competitive strengths and power their future growth' (Dunning 1993: 164).

Morris (1991*a*, 1991*b*) offers a parallel account of the evolution of Japanese investment in Europe and the United Kingdom. He portrayed an important shift from Head Quarters (HQ) controlled branch assembly factories, driven by protectionism and the high Yen, to *global localization*. This involved the integration of component supply, a full range of production activities, and growing R&D, driven by the need to respond flexibly to market demands to gain local market share. Sony and later Nissan were seen as exemplars of this pattern in the United Kingdom, just as Kenney and Florida (1993) regarded Honda as a pioneer in the United States. Morris argued that Japanese overseas investment in more capital-intensive production could only be understood in such terms. He suggested that this involved the emergence of flexible transnationals, oriented towards more rapid innovation cycles to meet local market needs. Like Dunning he also highlighted the role of strategic alliances with non-Japanese firms in building such flexibility.

However, Morris (1991*a*) introduced a slightly different emphasis by arguing that this development had not marginalized the role of cost considerations, of the sort emphasized by analyses of the 'new international division of labour' (Frobel et al. 1980). Rather, he recognized that 'there are clear signs that different spatial divisions of labour have emerged, both at an intra-regional and a national scale', and in the context of Europe this had involved 'Spain and the UK emerging as low cost centres for production' (Morris 1991*a*: 10).

JAPANESE INVESTMENT AND REGIONAL LOCALIZATION IN THE UK

Thus for Morris (1991*a*, 1991*b*) the extent to which global localization was generating a substantial upgrading of branch plant operations or coexisted with a complex international re-division of labour remained open. This prompted more extensive research on Japanese investment in South Wales, on the basis of which Morris et al. (1993; Munday et al. 1995) provided a broadly positive assessment of the evolving logic of investment in the United Kingdom over this period. They were critical of both the 'warehouse thesis' of Williams et al. (1991) and Morris's (1988) own earlier reservations. Against the warehousing argument they emphasized that 'relatively little employment is provided by assembly-only plants utilising a high number of imported kits' (Munday et al. 1995: 7), while more positively they suggested that the organization and activity of Japanese manufacturing firms in Wales had developed in several significant ways.

First, while the early firms were all final assemblers, later investment (from 1985–92) was dominated by a wave of parts and components suppliers. These acted as subcontractors for the first wave firms, largely as a response to continuing pressure to increase local content and the problems of sourcing from domestic firms (Munday 1995). Second, though most factories continued to produce a single product range, most of the larger electronics firms were diversifying across product ranges, while even those with a single product could embrace 'very broad ranges of single products plus substantial component manufacture' (Morris et al. 1993: 19). Third, the percentage of Japanese managers in these enterprises was lower for larger and older plants. This suggested that, as the plants matured, Japanese managers were gradually replaced by local managers, though these establishments also encountered quite widespread difficulties in recruiting local engineering staff. Finally, a few high profile firms had several large factories and also R&D capabilities. The most advanced factory complex was that of Sony, sometimes regarded as the most vertically integrated television plant in the world, with both in-house manufacture of complex equipment and R&D activities.

Against this background, their survey data on the composition of the workforce suggested that 'the nature of some of these plants is changing... developing away from the assembly-only stereotype and employing, in some cases, large numbers of managers and engineers' (Morris et al. 1993: 24–5). This suggested that 'certain of these investments have matured and "deepened" from assembly operations to manufacturing concerns and even added development work in some cases' (ibid.: 28). However, what was less clear was the *extent* of this shift, as the implication that developments across these firms would follow a similar trajectory remained much more problematical. First, the second wave subcontractor firms, though more recent arrivals, were less likely to follow this trajectory because their role in the supply chain remained distinctive. Thus, with few exceptions, the second wave subcontractors were involved in labour-intensive final assembly and testing, where 'the technology used was often fairly advanced but the human skills required were basic for assembly and ancillary operations' (Munday 1995: 14). Second, the integrated R&D and manufacturing complex developed by Sony was clearly exceptional even among the established manufacturing plants. Indeed, 44 per cent of the firms surveyed by Morris et al. (1993) still characterized themselves as primarily assembly operations, while only 24 per cent were involved in any form of development work, the remainder being manufacturing operations (with or without assembly) or process plants.

In addition, the evolution of these factories apparently continued to involve quite tight control from headquarters, consistent with the production of standardized mature products, as these factories had 'a limited amount of autonomy with respect to minor decision-making, but little freedom with respect to capital investment and strategy' (Munday et al. 1995: 9). Finally, this evolving mix of operations at best had rather ambiguous consequences for the pattern of worker skills and competencies. Thus the authors note:

> the skills required in Japanese plants vary greatly. The majority of jobs are semi-skilled, with opportunities to learn other skills and rotate jobs. Multi-skilling, or more accurately multi-tasking, is encouraged and a favourable factor within personal appraisals and promotions. Established Japanese transplants had a strong emphasis on training. However, a caveat is needed here: typically training was on-the-job and was low-skill based. (Munday et al. 1995: 8).

Overall, then, the evidence from research in the early 1990s was of an increasing *differentiation* of the roles of various Japanese manufacturing subsidiaries, rather than of a broadly based upgrading process.

THE GLOBAL CHOICES OF JAPANESE MANUFACTURING

Both Dunning and Morris acknowledged that the internationalization of Japanese manufacturing operations involved substantial investments in Asia, but other commentators have placed the analysis of developments in Europe and North America more firmly within the framework of the international configuration and reconfiguration of disaggregated production operations. In particular, Dicken (1991) and Steven (1991) emphasized that Japanese manufacturing investments in East and South-east Asia shifted over time, in ways which also had ramifications for the pattern of imports and investment in the West. Japanese manufacturing investment in Asia moved from an initial market-oriented pattern to the relocation of labour-intensive production from Japan as part of an increasingly elaborate regional division of labour (Morris-Suzuki, 1992). This generated an evolving hierarchy of production, with some upgrading of operations in the leading newly industrialized countries but also the entrenchment of predominantly low value production operations in other countries (Wilkinson et al. 2001; Elger and Smith 2001). These Asian production operations have increasingly become platforms for export to the West, as well as the offshoring of Japanese manufacturing (Itagak: 1997; Tejima 1998).

A crucial consequence of this evolving international division of labour across both East and West is that it has created the basis for the production strategies of some Japanese firms to take on a global character, and this has allowed some production activities to return East from the West, for example to take advantage of the costs of production in China, while China is rapidly becoming an important market as well (Taylor 2001; Gamble 2003). Thus the pattern of Japanese FDI became more varied in the 1990s, as recession at home prompted both increased production in East Asia and also regional relocation in the mature markets of North America and Europe. Globally China appeared to be the country of preference for cost-based FDI from all countries, but within the triad regions there was also cost-competition, from Mexico within NAFTA, and from Eastern and Central Europe (and increasingly Turkey) in Europe. Given such regional and global movements, analyses of upgrading or downgrading on a national stage look increasingly naive.

These features suggest that an understanding of contemporary developments in the overseas investments and operations of Japanese companies must attend to the strategic options opened up by both the changing *global* terrain of potential operating sites and the active coordinating role of regional centres. This is a theme that has been taken up by Morgan et al. (2002), in their review of patterns of Japanese manufacturing investment in the United Kingdom at the start of the new century. Their discussion highlights the growing importance of both East Asia and Eastern Europe as locations for cheap labour-intensive mass production operations. They also note the increased pressure that Japanese companies are under to generate revenues, both from stronger competition from global competitors and because of the losses they have suffered following the collapse of the bubble economy at home. One of the features of stronger international competition, especially from American firms, has been a new vulnerability of some Japanese firms in sectors where they had earlier been dominant, reinforced by the exposure of significant weaknesses in such new product areas as telecommunications and biotechnology (Berggren 1995; Fransman 1995; Morgan et al. 2002).

One consequence of these changes has been a decline in the number of new foreign operations being established by Japanese firms and an increase in withdrawals from such activities. Thus Morgan et al. (2002: 1029) emphasize that we cannot assume 'that Japanese subsidiaries [have] a sure and stable place within the plans of Japanese companies... [because] as new areas of economic activity are opened up the strategic purpose of UK subsidiaries might change'. Having diagnosed the dominant pattern of past investment in the United Kingdom as one of relatively standardized mass production, they suggest that such production sites will now be under increasing pressure from alternative locations of cheap production, in East Asia and also in Eastern Europe. Thus 'standardised mass production will only survive in the UK as long as costs can be pushed further down and productivity increased, both of which are difficult conditions to meet given possibilities elsewhere in the world for cheap mass production' (Morgan et al. 2002: 1023).

FUTURE TRENDS IN THE OPERATIONS OF JAPANESE MANUFACTURING FIRMS IN EUROPE

This leads Morgan et al. into a necessarily somewhat speculative assessment of likely future trends in the operations of Japanese manufacturing firms in the United Kingdom, trends that may involve divestment, relocation and/or strategic alliances, as well as the hitherto predominant stand-alone investments. In this regard Morgan et al. identify two major trajectories, with each operating at both global and regional levels. The first is the relocation of standardized mass production to cheaper locations, and the second is the pursuit of a science-based upgrading of design, development, and production capabilities. Each can operate on a global scale, with China as an ultimate location for cost reducing operations because of 'the huge possibilities that lie there for reducing wage costs' (Morgan et al. 2002: 1031) and Japan and the United States as key destinations for R&D-intensive investment. However, these same tendencies operate at a regional level, through the development of what Steven

(1996: 71) characterizes as 'zone strategies'. Morgan et al. emphasize that, as Europe has become more of a common economic space, Japanese firms have looked beyond the United Kingdom and widened their horizons in terms of investment locations designed to serve the European market.

In particular, Morgan et al. suggest that Eastern Europe (we would add Turkey) has become an increasingly attractive location for labour-intensive manufacture, while Germany represents the preferred European destination for high technology investments. On this basis they suggest that Japanese subsidiaries in Britain (and elsewhere in Western Europe) may be squeezed from both ends. Many will become vulnerable to competition from standardized manufacturing plants located in areas of cheaper labour, while competition will intensify between the United States, Germany, Britain, and others for growing investment in R&D and high technology activities. Morgan et al. suggest that one consequence of this squeeze will be greater pressure to increase productivity and reduce costs in standardized production transplants and their subcontractors in the United Kingdom. This will mean efforts to control wage levels and incremental seniority gains and to increase labour discipline and the intensity of work, with layoffs and the ultimate possibility of closure of UK sites that cannot compete with those located in cheaper settings. They conclude that Japanese plants will increasingly look like any other manufacturing plant in Britain, having lost any ownership distinctiveness in terms of work participation or employment conditions (Morgan et al. 2002).

Another more positive consequence might be the development of substantial R&D facilities, whether free-standing, linked to production facilities, or involving strategic alliances. These could involve less centralized control from HQ and more active cooperation between Japanese and British managers and scientists. However, not only will the United Kingdom be competing with Japan, the United States, and other parts of Europe for such investments, but these authors also raise questions about the extent to which Japanese management practices will prove compatible with such open collaborative learning organizations. This bleak hypothesis has the value of emphasizing the ways in which specific overseas operations are influenced by the *temporal* and *spatial* evolution of wider corporate investment and competitive strategies. At the same time it raises several questions that remain unresolved.

First, the development of R&D activities in the United Kingdom has been more positive than they allow. While we should be cautious in interpreting the significance of the number of R&D centres because they cover different levels and forms of activity, the data on trends in manufacturing affiliates with R&D/Design Centres does not support the case for a characterization of Britain as the low road and Germany as the high road for such activities. At the high point of Japanese overseas manufacturing capital formation in 1989, the United Kingdom had 31 per cent of Japanese European R&D/Design Centres and Germany had only 20 per cent, while in 2002 the

United Kingdom had exactly the same share and Germany had declined to 17.5 per cent (JETRO, 2003: 6). There has been a marked slowing in the overall rate of formation of such centres in Europe, with the peak of 24.7 per cent in 1989, an average of 10 per cent per year between 1990 and 1995 and just 2.8 per cent between 1996 and 2001, but the United Kingdom has more than held its own in this context (JETRO 2003).

Second, though, this latter trend raises broader questions about positive views of the increasing salience of R&D-focused operations. Japanese firms have traditionally retained the bulk of their R&D activities at home (Lam 2003; Odagiri and Yusada 1996, 1999), and much of their existing overseas R&D has in fact been design and development work 'associated with supporting local manufacturing and sales by adapting products to local conditions' (Morgan et al. 2002: 1035). It remains unclear how far Japanese multinationals are breaking with this pattern and internationalizing basic or core R&D activities, and if so which firms and sectors are most affected. Certainly it could be argued that the imperatives of R&D internationalization are likely to be greater for some sectors (pharmaceuticals, software) than for others, though there are also important contrasts between offensive and defensive moves towards international alliances and R&D operations among firms within such sectors (Fransman 1999). As Morgan et al. recognize, there are some sectors, such as car styling, games software and pharmaceutical development, where Britain hosts leading R&D sectors, but for other sectors other locations are likely to be more attractive.

The final problem area in the diagnosis offered by Morgan et al. concerns the relative significance of *regional reconfigurations* of manufacturing investment ('zone strategies' for Europe and North America) and any other thoroughgoing *global relocation* (concentration of labour-intensive operations for world production in East Asia and more specifically China). It remains unclear which sectors or phases of the production chain are likely to be implicated in one or the other of these processes. It might be expected, for example, that final assembly of heavier and higher value products is more likely to stay in Europe or North America, while global mass production of component or sub-assembly manufacture is more likely to be relocated to China. Different stages in the product cycle may also be important, with Western branch plants having to compete for investment but the more successful such plants more likely to capture business in higher value, more customized product lines. Furthermore, Morgan et al. (2002: 1029) themselves recognize that the existing sunk costs of branch plant operations, which we can couple with more recent limits on investment capital, represent important constraints on the pursuit of relocation, though it remains unclear how far this may moderate the trends they project. Our evidence from an important cluster of Japanese firms in the United Kingdom, reviewed in Chapter 6, suggests that exits remain limited, but marked fluctuations in employment levels within subsidiaries are more evident consequences of intense global competition for production mandates within these firms.

Nevertheless, the main contribution of Morgan et al. is to draw out the current implications of the *spatial analysis* of investment strategies developed by such writers as Dicken and Steven. This powerfully qualifies the positive evolutionary progression mapped by Dunning and others, and thus identifies central themes of a research agenda to address the varied and evolving character of contemporary Japanese transplant operations, in Britain and elsewhere. In this regard they place major emphasis on the changing matrix of pressures and opportunities that structure the strategic choices of Japanese managements, but they also address the question of the social organization of management, and the way in which this might influence responses to these strategic choices. For example, they note that the development of more autonomous and collaborative R&D units might face difficulties because they would challenge the relatively tight control that Japanese corporate HQs have tended to exercise over their overseas subsidiaries. Lam (2003: 678) reinforces this point by identifying difficulties for Japanese firms in breaking away from an 'inward learning pattern' for R&D, compared with the more decentralized US firms which rely more on 'financial performance based' management controls. Such considerations introduce the final theme of this discussion of the internationalization of Japanese manufacturing capital, namely the distinctive *forms* of Japanese strategic management of such international operations, and the ways in which these have been analysed over recent decades.

THE DISTINCTIVE FORMS OF JAPANESE INTERNATIONAL STRATEGIC MANAGEMENT

Westney (1999) provides a valuable overview of this topic, grounded in an appreciation of the extent to which early theorizing about multinational companies was designed specifically to address the experiences of American manufacturing multinationals. This tended to regard divergences from the American trajectory (from multidomestic production to increasingly strongly coordinated global product divisions) as curious aberrations from an American-centric norm. Against this yardstick, key features of the initial phase of post-war Japanese internationalization, such as the emphasis on sales and servicing to support heavy reliance on exports, and the role of trading companies as joint venture partners, appeared anomalous, though compatible with a view of Japanese manufacturers as *reluctant multinationals.* However, once Japanese firms began manufacturing operations overseas other distinctive features emerged, in particular the more extensive use of expatriate management cadres and the relative exclusion of local management from corporate decision-making processes. This contrasted with the use of robust impersonal rules and structures by American firms, administered by local management integrated through wider corporate norms, rather than directly by expatriate managers (Edwards et al. 2003; Edwards and Ferner 2004).

Westney (1999) notes that such features prompted debate about the relative importance of temporal and country effects in explaining the distinctiveness of Japanese management. Was it primarily a temporary feature, characteristic of an initial phase of multinational operations, or did it reflect a more enduring distinctiveness in the cultural and institutional form of Japanese management, with a particular bias towards broadly defined roles, consultative decision-making and tacit knowledge? The growing number and apparent viability of Japanese factories overseas, coupled with the continuing importance of Japanese expatriate managers, suggested that it was more a country than a temporal effect. At the same time, however, it became increasingly difficult to treat these firms as anomalous divergences from a multinational norm defined by the operations of American firms, and they came to be seen as exemplars of an alternative strategy for managing internationalization. This came to be termed the '*global multinational*', and was characterized by the continuing importance of exports from the home base, an emphasis on overseas production being close to the market place, and global coordination oriented towards the full range of corporate activities rather than primarily production operations.

This reappraisal viewed features that had hitherto been seen as weaknesses of Japanese firms as strengths, by emphasizing the way in which dense communications between HQs and branch plants, facilitated by a substantial expatriate management cadre, could achieve a close coordination of local and central policies. However, as Westney notes, any such celebration of the distinctive form of Japanese internationalization was rapidly overtaken by the emergence of a new prescriptive model of the *transnational multifocal* firm, characterized by heterarchy rather than hierarchy and a capacity for distributed organizational learning (note the echoes of Morgan's discussion of competing logics in R&D management). Against this benchmark the self-confident export of domestic Japanese management strategies was once more judged wanting compared with the encouragement of devolved capacities for organizational learning, especially if this was viewed as primarily a country rather than temporal feature.

However, Westney queries whether international firms from any country have actually conformed to this prescriptive model, and suggests that less prescriptive and more analytical attention should now be paid to the 'distinctive evolutionary trajectories' of international firms based in different countries. Furthermore, she suggests that an understanding of such trajectories must escape from contrasts between simple models, to develop a more fine-grained analysis of the dynamics of management processes and the evolution of corporate capabilities. This should give more attention to 'differences across industries, across firms and across locations' (Westney 1999: 25), and qualify the contemporary overemphasis on country effects.

CONCLUSION

This chapter has outlined the shifting geographical distribution of Japanese FDI, and reviewed the reasons why firms internationalize their operations. We noted several key trends, including the slowdown in Japanese capital formation in Western Europe during the last decade and the movement eastwards as the economies of Central and Eastern Europe were opened and integrated into the EU. Globally, Asia (especially China) and the United States continue to take a disproportionate share of global Japanese FDI. Japanese international investments involved strategic calculations about market access, production costs, and sometimes design and development opportunities that guided an increasingly complex pattern of investments across the international division of labour. However, the implications of such strategies were not as clear-cut as Morgan et al. (2002) suggest, and the United Kingdom continued to attract a substantial share of R&D investments in Europe. This reflected the weight of Japanese investment in the country, and the openness of British institutions to international investment, including universities (Lam 2003). What is clear from the pattern of Japanese FDI in Britain is that, while the main period of capital investment was during the 1980s, new investment has continued to flow in, something that did not happen in smaller economies.

Against this background, we have emphasized a significant heterogeneity of modes of managing internationalization among Japanese firms, which fits comfortably with our earlier critique of evolutionary projections of a progressive upgrading trajectory among Japanese overseas manufacturing operations. Different firms may have different corporate strategies and assign different roles to their subsidiaries. Some may retain or extend routine assembly operations, others may seek to augment such activities in ways which allow the more complete production of higher value product lines, and yet others will try to develop a new level of R&D capability. This highlights the need to locate Japanese practices inside corporate and sector strategies and to see both in temporal and spatial terms. While Chapter 2 identified the historical context of the development of Japanese firms and their evolving employment and production models, this chapter has tracked the shifting pattern of internationalization of such Japanese firms and their distinctive strategies of subsidiary formation and operation in different territories. We have stepped back from earlier writing which viewed such formation largely as a sequential development of more complex production operations within most subsidiaries based in western countries. Instead we have stressed a more complex and differentiated pattern of formation and evolution of the overseas subsidiary operations of Japanese manufacturers. This arises from the responses of Japanese companies to changing economic conditions at home, intra-regional competition within and regional rivalry between the still-dominant centres of FDI flow (North America, Asia and Europe), and rising global centres of low-cost production (especially China).

To address the implications of these trends we need a framework for analysing transfer, diffusion, hybridization, and adaptation processes within subsidiaries. This should take seriously the distinctiveness of Japanese models and policy repertoires, but also their dynamic spatial and temporal evolution and interaction in new contexts through the process of internationalization. This is the purpose of Chapter 4.

CHAPTER

4

A Framework for Analysing Work Organization and Employment Relations in the International Company

INTRODUCTION

In the debate on the transfer of Japanese practices around the globe there are a number of competing claims about the processes of internationalization, convergence, and divergence which require careful interrogation. As we have noted in Chapter 1, the movement of Japanese firms out of Japan and into mature markets in the 1980s created a strong interest in the idea that such firms were successful in manufacturing because they had evolved *production practices* superior in efficiency terms to other national standards. Thus these innovations would become 'best practices' through emulation and transfer—*systemic* requirements for all manufacturing companies. Hence, we had universal or systemic claims for Japanese practices, which detached such practices from historical development and political economy, and hence from the cycles of boom and bust within capitalism, and projected a process of convergence on this basis.

An alternative reading of these practices tied them to Japanese society as cultural and institutional artefacts, hence neither accessible nor transferable to non-Japanese firms. These were *societal* claims for the limited utility of Japanese practices and for the persistence of divergencies in the operation of competing capitalisms. A final strand in these arguments suggested that some variants of capitalism were more resilient than others, so that by locating in declining or developing economies, Japanese firms could *dominate* through their economic power, and force the transfer and adoption of their practices through subsidiary 'transplantation'. The recession in Japan throughout the 1990s made this claim more problematical and reminded commentators of sources of crises within Japanese capitalism, while also underlining the contemporary vitality of other, more market-based, variants of capitalism.

In all of these arguments what we have witnessed in the last twenty years has been a rerun of the debates on the Americanization of Europe, when Taylorist and Fordist production and business practices were carried by American companies that interacted with indigenous ways of working but also appeared as dominant efficiency standards (Tolliday and Zeitlin 1986; Kogut and Parkinson 1993). It therefore seems that there is a tendency for capitalist competition to become institutionalized in national and company-based terminology, and for this language to have symbolic as well as real effects. The aim of this chapter is to present a framework to explain this tendency, and more specifically, to analyse its implications for understanding the characterization of the Japanese firm and subsidiary formation.

As a critique of the dichotomous contrast between convergence and divergence within comparative organizational analysis, we can say that the operations of international firms and workplaces are better seen in terms of a three-way interaction of contextual and interest group effects from different structural sources. This triple influence involves political economy or mode of production ('system effects'); different national institutions, cultures, and histories ('societal effects'); and the diffusion of best practices or modernization strategies by the 'society-in-dominance' in specific periods of global competition, such as the United States or Japan in recent years ('dominance effects'). This framework of *system, society, and dominance effects* (SSD), which is summarized below, grew out of comparative research on the engineering profession (Smith 1990; Smith and Meiksins 1995), and was extended through our research on Japanese transplants in Britain (Smith and Elger 1997, 2000). It seeks to provide a dynamic, synthetic, and integrated approach to cross-national organizational analysis, building upon and responding to the work of Child (1981) and Lane (1989). There are three aspects to the construction of this framework. First it involves the characterization and critique of three influential discourses on developments in work organization and employment relations in the capitalist enterprise, each of which offers only a partial account. Second, it involves the critical deconstruction of these discourses to provide a more adequate understanding of the processes involved. Finally, it brings together the three sets of processes as a basis for understanding the active construction and reconstruction of work and employment regimes within specific firms and workplaces.

Thus the SSD framework argues that the international firm will be a site for the social interaction of these three sets of processes, and not simply a universal set of economically 'efficient' organizational practices or a local set of institutional rules, customs, laws, and relations. On this basis the

SSD framework also highlights the agency of the enterprise and its subsidiaries in managing the constraints, opportunities, and tensions that arise from the confluence of the SSD effects that bear upon the firm. Our approach supports the work of others (Clark and Mueller 1996) who have tried to interrogate the action of the large firm within the context of societal constraints, developing an analysis of what Mayer and Whittington (1999: 936) call a 'reflexive recombination of local and international practices'. Therefore, our approach to Japanese subsidiaries in Britain emphasizes the agency of the firm in responding to and *reshaping*, rather than simply carrying its host country and corporate heritage or reflecting home country institutional and locational effects. We will say more about the strategies of international firms and the internal politics of corporate strategizing following our presentation of the SSD framework. The final section of the chapter then draws these elements of our analysis together through a discussion of competing conceptualizations of the role of international subsidiaries as transplants, hybrids or branch plants.

THE SYSTEM, SOCIETY AND DOMINANCE EFFECTS FRAMEWORK

Figure 4.1 represents a way of examining work organization within the international firm that aims to capture the complexity of influences on the firm in terms of SSD effects.

System effects—shared underlying properties

By *system* effects we mean those effects which arise from dominant social relations and priorities within a political economy—for example, the desire to work for private gain, rather than enhanced community status or common bonds of group or collective interest. System is the underlying dynamic of a 'political economy'—such as capitalism or state socialism—which produces common interests and similar problems, regardless of the country context within which those social relations are located. For example, state socialism had generic features, typically an accentuated role for the state in economic affairs, in planning and management of the firm, control of labour allocation, and constraints on managers' freedom to hire and fire workers.

System is therefore both 'political' and 'economic'. *Systemic* features of capitalism begin with property rights, owners and non-owners, and the capitalist employment relationship. Paid work in a capitalist society requires waged labour which is always dependent on employers for work and is structured by the drive for capital accumulation and profitable

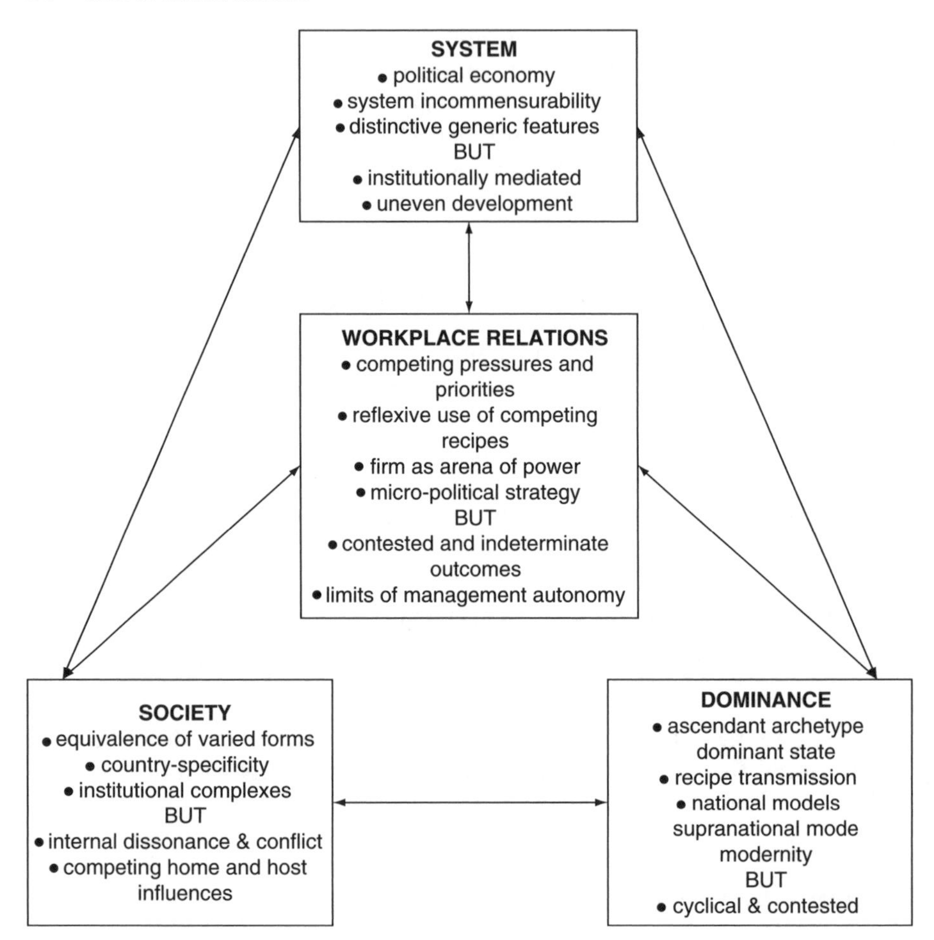

Fig. 4.1. System, society, and dominance effects framework

production. These relationships mean that the firm is constituted by managers and workers who are drawn into definite social relations for the purpose of profitable production. Workers are motivated (compelled and facilitated) to sell their labour power to survive. Managers have to take this human 'raw material' and combine it with the technical means and objects of production as a social force of production and profitability. In the relations between waged workers and employers (or their 'representatives') there is an exchange, an employment relationship, in which wages are exchanged for labour services. However, the precise amount of work and effort to be expended for this economic return remains open-ended, as do the precise tasks to be performed, the standards of work, the performance criteria, and the quality of the authority and human relations between those who employ and those who are employed.

This does not ignore the importance of particular variants of a capitalist political economy, for example Anglo-Saxon or Germanic Capitalism (Albert 1993; Hall and Soskice 2001; Hyman 2004). Such differences involve both different paths of capitalist development and distinctive institutional arrangements, but there are also generic features which are embodied in capitalism as a global system (Crouch and Streeck 1997; Elger and Edwards 1999; Coates 2000; Sklair 2002). In this sense capitalism is a global system at one level of abstraction, but a particular set of institutional practices at another. Nevertheless, system effects become embodied in those forces of production, such as prevailing forms of technology and ways of working, that are diffused as common standards across capitalist economies. Capitalist competition, technological dynamism, and capital–labour conflict underpin and exert common pressures on all specific manifestations of capitalist social relations, within enterprises, sectors or national economies. It is these underlying dynamics, with their associated conflicts and uncertainties that can be regarded as *system imperatives*.

These underlying dynamics are necessarily mediated through more specific institutional complexes that take distinctive forms in different national variants of capitalism, while capitalist firms that originate within particular national contexts also share distinctive features. Nevertheless, some manifestations of the dynamic of capitalism can be seen as more directly systemic than others. Capital flows facilitated by contemporary technologies, technical innovations involving combinations of hardware and knowledge, and even innovative forms of social organization may be seen as highly mobile and readily transferable across the global economy. As the debates about the new international division of labour remind us, the forms of international corporate coordination which may be fostered by such developments interact with a strongly differentiated international economy in ways which are likely to reproduce such differentiation, albeit in changing ways. In this sense uneven development rather than convergence is also a systemic feature of capitalism. Thus, we need to characterize labour processes and business organizations more generally as subject to competing and emergent globalizing and localizing pressures, rather than direct expressions of either systemic tendencies or path dependent distinctiveness.

Purely universal or 'systemic' theorizing assumes a standardized or standardizing workplace in which technology, science, and managerial discourse aim at creating common methodologies regardless of the sector or country in which the firm is operating. Such system thinking tends to operate deductively from claims about system properties without giving attention to the competing social processes in play and the ways in which system properties are mediated in specific contexts. This contrasts with critical realist analyses that seek to identify both the underlying system dynamics and the varied mediations and manifestations of these underlying social processes (Ackroyd and Fleetwood 2000). Thus major problems exist in discussing the action of firms, and the social relations of workers and managers within them, only through the concepts of political economy—firms as capital; managers and workers as representatives of capital and labour. Human beings are conceived as carriers of predetermined structures and social roles (e.g. capitalist firm, worker, boss) without reflexivity, or interpretative and strategic capabilities. It is therefore important to see the systemic features of capitalism and of management–worker relations in the capitalist firm as critical starting points for our analyses of the operations of international firms, but we must also recognize that these systemic features are in key respects open-ended and contradictory. It is in this context that established societal cultures and institutional arrangements constitute more specific resources and constraints that influence the actions of corporate managers and employees, but this context also implies that such societal formations do not resolve underlying contradictions or foreclose innovations that contest institutionalized path dependencies.

Societal effects—diversity, coherence, and equivalence

In the late twentieth century, claims of convergence across capitalist societies, whether premised upon economic or technological imperatives, came under sustained criticism from a range of institutionalist approaches. These critics of the convergence thesis emphasized that the operations of capitalist markets and enterprises were historically embedded within and strongly conditioned by distinctive institutional arrangements and cultural dispositions that sustained a variety of different national or regional forms of capitalism.

One of the most influential proponents of this position has been the 'societal effects' school, which emerged within organizational sociology in the 1970s and has been influential in industrial relations as well as industrial and economic sociology. It emphasizes that the operations of business enterprises and the organization of work differed between societies in ways that are strongly influenced by the specific configurations of institutional arrangements that surround the workplace. In particular it builds upon comparative cross-national studies to emphasize the reciprocal interdependencies that sustain the distinctive character of such features as the social organization of education, training, industrial relations, and the workplace division of labour in specific societies. The strength and distinctiveness of these interdependencies mean that the implications of innovations in business and employment practices are filtered through processes of selection and translation to gain a specific character within each society, which is broadly consistent with the existing institutional configurations.

In an extreme form, this approach discounts the idea of the *capitalist labour process*. All that exist are national variants of 'ways of working', menus of social relations generated by national histories rather than any dominant organizational forms or overarching economic processes of an underlying capitalist system. Thus there is no 'best way' of managing work and employment relations, but rather a variety of 'functionally equivalent' ways of organizing social and economic institutions such as the capitalist firm. The 'rules of the game' under which managers and workers interact are formed by nationally specific cultural and institutional codes. As these codes or rules emerge through historical processes within each country, they are unique. In this way the 'societal effects' school suggests an *irreducible* diversity of forms of work organization, regardless of common factor inputs or modes of systemic rationalization (Maurice and Sorge 2000*a*, 2000*b*).

Related arguments have been taken up in a wide range of comparative national institutionalist approaches that have analysed the distinctiveness of national employment systems, patterns of industrial relations, or more inclusively 'business systems' or 'industrial orders' (Ferner and Hyman 1992; Whitley 1992*a*, 1992*b*; Crouch 1993; Lane 1995). These analyses have sought not only to understand the specificity of a range of more 'organized' European and East Asian variants of capitalism, but also to identify the specific institutional characteristics of British and American liberal capitalisms. Such institutionalist approaches are by no means homogeneous in their theoretical underpinnings. Nevertheless, they often share an emphasis on the role of specific national institutional complexes in the construction of the interests and obligations of individual and collective actors, so that change is strongly conditioned by these existing institutions and bears the mark of a powerful 'path dependency' (e.g. Hollingsworth et al. 1994: 278–9).

These arguments are important because they recognize the real differences between specific variants of capitalism and important continuities in these differences over substantial time periods. It is sensible to concede that the national, the state, and institutional arrangements within states, create practices that are *relatively* stable. These authors have also identified the significance of both socialization processes *and* institutionally structured choices and trade-offs in reproducing national distinctiveness, so that nationally specific forms of conflict and accommodation are also recognized in some of these accounts.

However, this broad family of 'societal effects' approaches also risks overstating the coherence and persistence of specific national institutional configurations (Smith and Elger 1997; Amoore 2002). First, such approaches often give little recognition to the heterogeneity of institutional arrangements or the tensions between different institutional forms within specific societies. They may also neglect those conflicts of interest between key actors, such as capital and organized labour, that persist beneath existing national institutional compromises. Such features dilute the force of path dependency and open more scope for internal contention and change. They also mean that external agencies, such as international firms, may have more leverage and gain important allies in diverging from aspects of established host country practices.

Second, these approaches focus heavily upon the delineation of societies through the bounding of nation-states, and tend to assume that organizations and processes that cross-cut such boundaries are assimilated into established national patterns. In this respect, it is instructive to compare the societal effects approach with the neoinstitutionalist approach developed in the United States, which highlights a set of social processes (normative, cognitive, and coercive) that generate institutional homogeneity in specific 'organizational fields' (DiMaggio and Powell 1983). On the one hand, the analysis of such 'institutional isomorphism' has strong parallels with the 'societal effects' literature when state regulatory policies and other nationally bounded influences predominate. On the other hand, however, 'organizational fields' may be constituted across national boundaries, for example, by industrial sectors or corporate networks (Katz and Darbishire 2000). Whereas a strict 'societal effects' analysis would suggest that the foreign operations of international firms would generally be assimilated into the institutional pattern of the host country (German firms in Britain become British, Japanese firms in Germany become German), the implications of institutional isomorphism are more open-ended. Thus, from this perspective Ferner and Quintanilla (1998) identify not only conformity with host country practices, but also the potential influence of the firm's own distinctive corporate repertoire or approaches drawn from the home country or global corporate networks, to which we could add internationalized sector and supra-state regional influences among others.

Of course, international firms will be influenced by the societies in which they operate. However, the home countries of such firms may remain particularly influential in terms of providing a legal framework, a model of organization, key managerial personnel, a major market, and a base for such strategic functions as head office and R&D. In this sense, it remains appropriate to characterize them as national firms with international operations. However, such firms are not simply constrained by the national contexts, either home or host, in which they operate. Capital can be highly mobile, providing opportunities to develop management practices in many different societies and leverage for change at each site of operation, while key employees can also be moved across national borders. Thus leading international firms are dynamic forces that challenge settled national institutions, by changing ownership and integrating activities cross-nationally, operating with a global reach that few states (or national institutions) can possess as they are tied to *territory* in a way that capital, and to a lesser extent labour, are not.

Indeed, in recent years, many institutionalist commentators have recognized that the assumption of national boundedness overvalues national institutional contexts. In particular it understates the power of major international firms to manipulate national territory to suit their needs, and to create internal institutional communities which can at least challenge and reinterpret national rules, if not overturn them. It therefore becomes an open research question whether host or home practices, or those drawn from other sources, or a hybrid or combination of these, shape work organization and employment relations in these firms. The *range* of practices brought into action means the international firm is able to draw upon divergent policies, and individuals with differing orientations to work, beyond those present within the host or home society.

A third criticism of institutionalist analyses is that, when they have addressed the economic viability of different 'national business systems' or variants of capitalism, they have often assumed that each has its own economic advantages, so that each will continue to occupy its own distinctive niche in the international division of labour. This extends the concepts of functional equivalence and path dependency to the level of the international economy, but in so doing neglects the unsettled character of both international competition and the international division of labour. States do not compete in the same way as firms, because states do not easily go bankrupt or get taken over (Krugman 1994). However, their policies and institutions do come under pressure, both as a consequence of the rivalry and innovation of competing firms that cross-cut national borders and as a result of the policy initiatives of supra-national institutions, such as the World Trade Organization (WTO) or the International Monetory Fund (IMF), themselves arising from the strategies of dominant coalitions of states.

Thus, international firms may create global, regional, and trans-state forms of interdependence and integration, often based on cost-driven and market-driven business strategies, or the construction of different 'global commodity chains' (Gereffi and Korzeniewicz 1994). Such strategies do not suppress institutional and value differences between societies, and they may indeed reinforce such differences. However, they do encourage similar policy initiatives among states desperate to attract FDI, including tax breaks and incentives and special labour codes, as found in 'special' development regions and enterprise zones (Dicken 1998; Sklair 2002). The 'competition state' (Cerny 1990; Elger and Burnham 2001) and globalization reinforce each other, so that national policies do not simply reproduce diversity, but also encourage convergence to standards that fit the process of the internationalization of capital. This forms the context in which firms, consultants, and national policy makers persistently seek to borrow and transfer organizational practices from firms and countries that come to be regarded as models of 'best practice'; a process that is inexplicable within a pure 'societal effects' perspective, in which countries compete with each other through divergent but functionally equivalent organizational means.

Overall, then, the assumptions of institutional coherence, national boundedness, and economic equivalence mean that societal effects approaches struggle to account for the impact of external challenges and the pressures for convergence that represent recurrent features of capitalist development. The theorists of societal effects have begun to develop valuable accounts of the sources of diversity in national trajectories of capitalist development and class relations. However, these accounts have concentrated upon the internal logics of institutional development which are held to explain persistent distinctiveness, while giving little attention to the ways in which evolving relations between states and firms, and among states, alter the terrain upon which national 'systems' operate.

Dominance effects—ascendancy and diffusion

As suggested above, the third element in the SSD framework concerns the uneven nature of economic development and economic power, and the tendency for one society to take the lead in evolving work organization and business practices considered more efficient than those operating within other countries. These lead societies create 'dominance effects', that circulate as 'best practices' or global standards that are emulated by other societies. In this way, societies do not face each other as equals, but with uneven capabilities, which encourages the processes of diffusion and dominance by some and learning and borrowing by others. In this context, international companies play a key role, though they are not the only agencies of such processes, with state and supra-state agencies, management consultancies, academics, and NGOs, all potentially involved. However, as the internationalization of capital means that international companies operate across several regions and societies, this opens the possibility that they will act as key agencies in carrying ostensibly superior practices from home to host countries. Moreover, this may also mean that home practices are only retained if they are judged to yield competitive advantages to the firm, opening up the possibility of 'reverse diffusion' if host country practices experienced by subsidiaries are deemed to be superior to those of the parent firm in its home country (Edwards 1998, 2004).

Within the contemporary debate on competing capitalisms, there are those who emphasize a plurality of equally effective national solutions to common economic problems, and those who search for a 'best' solution, and hence an arrangement of social institutions that delivers superior economic performance. But as Crouch (2001: 132) has noted, the identification of each new 'best' model—Sweden, Germany or Japan in recent years—has had only short-term currency, as the economies of these countries face challenges and crises. What Crouch does not explain, however, is why the 'search for excellence' or the 'best model' of capitalism continues. This appears to be driven not only by systemic competition between states and capitals, but also by the recognition of patterns of uneven development which imply a succession of dominant economies and societies.

In debates on the Japanese model there was a clear relationship between the economic success of Japan and an intense interest by firms and governments in wishing to 'learn' from and 'borrow' Japanese ideas. But in order to make such borrowing more acceptable or to neutralize its societal origins, generic rather than societal technical terms, such as 'lean production' or 'TQM' or 'continuous improvement', were invented by academics, consultants, and other ideas traders. While originating in Japan, the circulation of such repertoires created a different discourse, and association with the Japanese context could be broken. This was especially important as the 'dominance' of the Japanese economy faded in the 1990s. Dominance effects signal the idea that such practices may originate in one society, but then be disseminated as new standards, as a distillation of the ideas into 'societal' and 'systemic' elements occurs through the process of diffusion. This is clear in the debate about Japanese production innovations, but it was also evident in earlier debates on Taylorism:

> Taylorism . . . was initially bounded by the constraints of American capitalism; but its diffusion transformed it into a 'best practice' which was seen as a system requirement in some economies. . . . The identification of Taylorism with American economic success made it difficult to resist. Disentangling the three influences of society, system and dominance has always been part of the critique of Taylorism as it became a dominant ideology and began to diffuse to Europe and Japan; but we could say that it was only with the emergence of other dominant capitalist states, in Europe and Japan, that such a critique has been able to separate these levels, and identify what in Taylorism is specific to America, what is part of capitalism, and what held sway only through American economic hegemony and not intrinsic qualities of Taylorism itself. (Smith and Meiksins 1995: 263–4)

Thus symbolic claims to dominance are usually tied to cyclical patterns of economic success of one nation or region, or at least of leading firms in such a location, as 'efficiency' is understood in terms of a dominant national business system rather than simply abstracted concepts of growth, output, and productivity. Institutionalist theory suggests that the urge to emulate such dominant economies is stimulated by conformity, fashion, and efforts to overcome the uncertainties of capitalist competition (DiMaggio and Powell 1983). But when the cycle moves, stars of yesterday become dogs of today, and the 'learning from' literatures move on to new talents. In this way, 'dominance' has a strongly symbolic element, as well as representing real, although always historically conditioned, efficiency differences between societies. Model making tends always to dehistoricize debate, and hence there is a cyclical musical chairs, as societal models rise and fall without ever challenging the rules of this particular game.

The SSD framework recognizes that the organization and rationalization of capitalist production has 'national' traits, though these are often exemplified by particular, leading enterprises, such as Ford in the United States or Toyota in Japan. However, it also suggests that the diffusion of new production and employment ideas through international firms, consultancy channels, and internationalized management education (such as the global commodity of an MBA) serves to de-link the sources of ideas from national contexts through the process of diffusion (Kogut and Parkinson 1993; Smith and Meiksins 1995). Delinking stresses the universal efficiency gains that all organizations will receive from the adoption of new 'best practices'. Nevertheless, the application and adaptation of novel practices, especially within the subsidiaries of international companies, will raise themes of national 'ownership', until techniques become 'global best practices' (Sklair 2001), denationalized but also diluted or altered through the diffusion process.

In summary, the SSD model aims to capture the complexity of innovations in work organization and employment relations and their 'transfer' within the modern, internationalized enterprise. By identifying 'societal effects' it recognizes the origins of particular innovations in specific societal settings and the extent to which those settings (whether in home or host societies) continue to influence the conduct of managers and workers within the firm. At the same time the partial character of such effects is emphasized by underlining the extent to which national production regimes may be characterized by differentiation, conflict, and reconstruction. Moreover, by identifying 'dominance effects' it recognizes that practices that have been developed in leading national economies, or industrial sectors or indeed specific firms, have the potential to exert a distinctive influence on key actors in and around a wide range of business enterprises situated in different societies, by virtue of their apparent efficacy. Finally, the identification of 'system effects' recognizes that certain practices gain influence by virtue of their claims to general, systemic relevance, but it also cautions against an easy attribution of such systemic status. Instead, it uses the concept of 'system effects' to identify fundamental social relations and processes that underpin and condition the specific institutional patterns and organizational practices that characterize the evolution of competing capitalisms and competing firms. From this vantage point, particular management repertoires and techniques never attain more than a provisional systemic status because they remain beset by the contradictory features of the capital–labour relationship and the unsettling rivalry between competing capitalist enterprises.

FIRM AND WORKPLACE RELATIONS—MEDIATING AND REFLEXIVE

As Child (1972) and others have emphasized, the policies and practices of business enterprises are rarely a direct result of structural forces and contingencies, as organizational actors and hence the organizations themselves are reflexive and they strategize in response to such conditions. Moreover, our discussion of SSD effects has underlined the contradictory and shifting pressures and priorities faced by capitalist firms, and the varied repertoires of practices that managers may draw upon in response to such pressures. As we have seen, managers within such firms may be influenced by and draw upon home or host country models, internal corporate or wider sectoral or network recipes or exemplars drawn from dominant countries or leading firms.

Thus, we have suggested that work organization practices and HRM techniques coalesce within firms and workplaces through the deployment of a combination of systemic, societal, and dominant ways of working, especially in internationalized segments of capital. This means that we need to be sensitive to the ways in which these elements are brought together within specific firms and workplaces, as managers and employees address and meditate the effects of globalizing capitalist forces, national institutional rules and 'world best practice' work and employment standards within distinctive local contexts. It is only through micropolitical processes of argument, interpretation, conflict, and compromise that groups and individuals negotiate how these different (and perhaps competing) ways of working, standards of quality, authority relations, and methods of employment will actually shape particular work situations.

At the same time, of course, the interests and powers of different actors within the capitalist enterprise differ and conflict (Amoore 2002). The dominant coalition of owners and top managers will be differently structured and may have different priorities in different national variants of capitalism, but in any case will possess some strategic capacity to shape the ways in which the firm organizes itself at home and abroad. The various widely referenced typologies of the strategies and structures of international firms, such as multidomestic, international, global, and transnational corporations, may capture some of the strategic options open to top management, though they are often presented in terms of an idealized prescriptive progression rather than as coexisting but problematical alternatives. Nevertheless, they underline the importance of different ways of organizing relationships between the centre and other operating units and imply different pressures for centralization or devolution of policymaking. At another level, Bélanger and Edwards (2004) have highlighted the leverage that top managers may possess to shape state policies, either through direct representations or through organized business lobbying, though they also note the tensions and limitations that may beset such leverage.

Senior head office managers clearly possess considerable resources to control the activities of subordinate managers, both at home and in overseas subsidiaries, through the promulgation of rules and targets, the monitoring of performance, and financial and career inducements and penalties. Almost by definition, it is they who define the objectives and priorities of newly established subsidiaries, though in circumstances (such as national regulatory frameworks or the moves of rivals) that may constrain their options. However, the managers of such subsidiaries are also likely to possess some scope to negotiate and modify their position vis-à-vis head office, for example, by arguing the case for increased autonomy in detailed policy formulation or by developing organizational capabilities which justify agreed changes in the objectives of the plant (Birkinshaw and Hood 1998; Edwards et al. 2004). Such initiatives and negotiations can be pivotal to the consolidation and growth of specific subsidiaries though, as Birkinshaw and Hood also emphasize, the initiatives of subsidiary managers may not be reciprocated and subsidiaries may evolve in a more precarious rather than more secure direction. Furthermore, the importance of local management policy initiatives and lobbying activities in the evolution of subsidiaries does not preclude top management decisions to expand, contract or close such operations because of changes in wider corporate priorities over which local managements have no influence.

Finally, employees other than managers and some key technical or professional workers are generally excluded from the hierarchical and micropolitical processes through which both corporate and subsidiary policies are formulated (though in some national contexts highly institutionalized forms of representation and consultation such as works councils may allow organized labour a limited formal voice in such processes). Nevertheless workers, more generally, remain an active presence in relation to such processes, even when they are weakly organized or unrepresented by unions. This is partly because formal and informal bargaining around the consequences of management policy decisions is likely to influence outcomes and, in turn, future management policy stances, and it is partly because even unbargained worker responses (such as changing patterns of effort, absenteeism or turnover) will also impinge on management calculations, especially at the level of the workplace. Of course, such observations themselves underline the limits of worker leverage even in propitious conditions such as tight labour markets or advances in collective organization, while in less favourable circumstances such inequalities of power will be all the more marked. Our point, however, is that managers can rarely take employees and their labour power entirely for granted, and in this sense they remain an active presence in the workplace, albeit with limited and variable leverage.

In this context both the national provenance and the local relevance of alternative policy repertoires remain contested within international subsidiaries. Nationality of ownership differentiates the local from the international enterprise, but we need empirical research to uncover how and how far different groups invoke nationality in seeking to legitimate or undermine activities that reconstruct work and employment relations within the workplace.

For example, recent research on HRM practices within American multinationals in different European societies was noted that 'diversity management' was diffused to subsidiaries by American corporate management, but was resisted as a strictly *American* recipe, appropriate for the parent firm but not the subsidiaries (Edwards 2004). This was especially the case where these subsidiaries were located in ethnically homogeneous societies, such as Ireland (Almond et al. 2003; Gunnigle et al. 2004). In this context, local management resistance drew upon indigenous societal norms to resist dominant practices, the nationality of which (Americanness) was highlighted to emphasize their specificity and inappropriateness. Milkman's (1991) research on Japanese firms in the United States provides another example, where Japanese managers sometimes used work sharing, reduced hours, flexible allocation of labour, and other practices to retain labour through downturns in trade, when the first reaction of the American managers was to lay-off workers. In turn, American managers argued that such labour security was inefficient when hire-and-fire could weed out unproductive workers. In this contest, Japanese managers applied home-influenced company practices which conflicted with local management approaches, but American workers could ally with Japanese managers in seeking to maintain employment security through a downturn. Thus nationality was contested, and normal class divisions between workers and managers complicated by the addition of *competing* management practices and worker preferences.

A key objective of our own research is to explore the different ways in which nationally designated repertoires of work organization and HRM practices are debated and deployed within Japanese manufacturing subsidiaries in Britain, and to analyse the implications of this for our understanding of the interplay of SSD effects in the operations of such subsidiaries. The final section of this chapter therefore outlines three influential but contrasting accounts of the operations of such Japanese subsidiaries that are to be found in the existing literature.

THE SSD FRAMEWORK AND JAPANESE SUBSIDIARIES: TRANSPLANTS, HYBRIDS OR BRANCH PLANTS?

In broad terms, analyses of the operations of Japanese manufacturing subsidiaries outside Japan have developed three different types of argument, which treat these subsidiaries as *transplants, hybrids* or *branch plants,* with most of the contributions concentrating on the first two variants. As will be seen, these three variants do not exhaust the terms of debate because they each contain different strands and they can also be combined in the work of specific authors, especially as their work develops over time, but they nevertheless represent distinctive and contrasting approaches (see Table 4.1).

The transplant—from dominance to system effects

The terminology of transplantation, which appears to have been developed specifically to address the experience of Japanese rather than other international subsidiaries, implies a quite simple transfer of management practices to overseas operations. It is directly underpinned by the claim or

Table 4.1. ***Contrasting perspectives on the operations of subsidiaries: transplants, hybrids, and branch plants***

	Transplant	Hybrid	Branch plant
Logic of management techniques	Universal best practice	Practices adapted to location	Practices adapted to role of plant
Character of class relations	Direct joint benefits	Negotiated accommodations	Subordination and conflicts
Model of globalization	Hegemonic model moves from national to universal	Societal effects mediate and moderate hegemonic models	Persistently uneven and contested redevelopment, through interplay of system, societal and dominance effects
Development over time	Linear development to maturity	Blocked progression or perhaps emergent new model	Conditional development and decline
Criticisms	Reifies best practice and glosses over conflicts of interest	Ambiguity of claims: emergent models, functional equivalents, or second best survivors?	How to theorize roles and trajectories of different subsidiaries?

assumption that these practices provide the basis for the competitive strength of the parent firm, both at home and in its overseas subsidiaries. This makes it necessary for transplantation to take place, but also facilitates this process, because it becomes attractive to all participants by offering mutual benefits from competitive success. Hence the transplant should be characterized by a convergence of interests between workers and managers which is likely to overcome mutual suspicions grounded in earlier class relations or cultural traditions. At its most benign, this may be construed in terms of shared interests arising from an egalitarian and participative production regime (as in the analysis of 'innovation mediated production' by Florida and Kenney 1991*a*, 1991*b*, and Kenney and Florida 1993, 1995). At its most stringent it may be seen in terms of shared subordination to the disciplines of 'waste elimination' in pursuit of enhanced job security (as in the advocacy of lean production by Womack et al. 1990).

Within this transplantation approach to the analysis of Japanese overseas operations, the trajectory of subsidiary development tends to be seen as linear and progressive, as the overseas site takes on a widening range of activities and comes to mirror the capabilities of the parent production clusters. Overall, particular corporate practices of the Japanese parent company are identified as elements of a hegemonic national repertoire, and are thus translated directly into 'system effects' across international operations that readily override and subsume local 'societal effects'. Thus this approach tends to work with a reified conception of a model of 'best practice', formed within but emancipated from specific national and corporate contexts. It also glosses over conflicts of interest within the employment relationship, either by conceptualizing the model as a basis for the reconciliation of such conflicts or by subsuming remaining tensions within an overriding shared imperative to adopt the model to allow competitive survival. In this sense the 'dominant' model is translated directly into a transformation of 'system' characteristics.

The hybrid—home and host societal effects with contradictory implications for dominance

It is evident that an unqualified model of transplantation makes very strong claims about the universal pertinence of parent company practices and about their unhindered transfer overseas. Thus almost any qualification to these assumptions moves the discussion towards branch-plant, or more often hybrid, theorizing. However, hybridization arguments may challenge and qualify the claims for transplantation in relatively weak or rather stronger terms. Perhaps the weakest version of a hybridization argument, and one which remains close to the universalism of the transplant approach, is that which identifies distinctive 'functional equivalents' for some components of the parent firm's management repertoire. In this approach some elements of that repertoire (such as specific production arrangements) are identified as core best practices which must be pursued by the subsidiary, but others (such as payment systems) are seen as supportive but secondary. The latter are then seen as open to replacement by alternative arrangements, which are similarly supportive but tailored to the circumstances of the local subsidiary. Many of those who use the language of transplantation nevertheless allow for such secondary hybridization, or even see it as central to the process. In particular, this is an important part of the influential analyses of Japanese auto transplants in the United States (Kenney and Florida 1993) and of Japanese transplants in the United Kingdom (Oliver and Wilkinson 1988, 1992; Morris and Wilkinson 1995). In these approaches 'societal effects' are recognized but are seen to have little effect on the dominant and increasingly systemic model because of the availability of functional equivalents.

However, other analysts of hybridization depart more clearly from any conception of unproblematical transplantation. The most common move of this sort is exemplified in the work of Abo (1990, 1994*a*, 1994*b*, 1996, 1998*a*, 1998*b*) and his colleagues, who chart the ways in which subsidiary practices often deviate from model versions of Japanese work organization, personnel practices, and industrial relations by moving some way towards (model versions of) local, domestic patterns in these respects. Abo and his colleagues map the resulting profiles and see them as charting adaptations to local conditions and expectations. In turn, such adaptations are interpreted as dilutions of the Japanese model and are thus seen as serving to weaken the effectiveness of the subsidiaries involved. Thus this diagnosis is underpinned by an emphasis on the strength and coherence of an ideal-type Japanese model, which is seen as compromised and diluted by pressures and constraints arising from the host society. Here, then, 'societal effects' clash with 'dominance effects' and may limit their translation into systemic features. There is considerable latitude within this broad approach to highlight rather different sources of pressure and constraint, involving different institutional complexes (such as the training system or supplier networks) and social agents (such as unionized workers or local managers) (e.g. Broad 1994). In general, however, this view of hybrids construes them as sub-optimal operations, which are thus potentially vulnerable and only survive as second best.

The final important variant in analyses of hybridization challenges this last assumption, to suggest that institutional constraints and compromises may actually impel enterprises to develop new configurations of work and employment relations with their own distinctive strengths. A relatively weak version of this argument has been developed by commentators (such as Fruin 1997, 1999, and more generally Liker et al. 1999) who emphasize that any transfer of existing socially-embedded workplace practices necessarily involves an active process of interpretation for, and translation within, new settings. In some cases this process may be channelled (both constrained and enabled) in directions which limit the effectiveness of the arrangements constructed at the overseas site. But in others, it may be channelled in ways which enhance that effectiveness. A particularly interesting version of this approach is found in the work of Adler (1993, 1999*a*, 1999*b*) and Adler et al. (1995, 1998), who discuss organizational innovations in unionized brownfield and non-union greenfield Toyota factories in the United States. They argue that strategic management responses to local conditions, including distinctive power relations with unions and regulatory bodies, involved subtle modifications to the Toyota production system and more marked departures from Japanese employment practices. Furthermore, in some respects these innovations facilitated the productivity and viability of the plants, though they did not create an unproblematical pattern of joint benefits for management and employees. Thus Adler et al. highlight the capacity of management for active organizational learning and institution building at these sites of inward investment. However, they also address the significance of the varied leverage of unions and state agencies and the continuing sources of tension surrounding any emergent hybrid repertoire. In this view, then, societal effects may challenge and modify a seemingly dominant model, underlining the provisional character of such dominance. In turn, possible new model variants may emerge but any translation of these models into systemic features will also involve their provisional character and the unresolved tensions and conflicts that surround them.

Fruin and Adler each provide quite cautious interpretations of innovation as hybridization. However, the strongest and most systematic version of such a positive hybridization analysis has been developed by theorists working within the French 'regulationist' tradition, whose arguments highlight the possibility of what, following the biological metaphor, may be called 'hybrid vigour'. This regulationist analysis seeks to systematize the findings of a wide-ranging collaborative research programme on the evolving patterns of corporate strategy and production organization among the world's large auto firms (Boyer et al. 1998*a*, 1998*b*; Freyssenet 1998; Freyssenet et al. 1998; Durand et al. 1999), and thus addresses developments in both the parent plants and overseas subsidiaries of American, European, and Asian producers. The arguments are therefore generic, at least within the auto sector, but a particular focus of the research on overseas subsidiaries is on Japanese companies and their affiliates (Boyer 1998*a*).

Two key arguments serve as points of departure for the discussion of hybridity in this context, and each constitutes an important advance on approaches that extol the transplantation of 'model' production regimes. The first is that active processes of remaking and innovation undermine the utility of static models of best practice, a point comparable to the emphasis on creative translation noted earlier. The second is that the social organization of production models confronts a range of substantial dilemmas that can be addressed in several distinctive ways. Thus a range of relatively coherent configurations of corporate strategy and work organization are likely to coexist, none of which will resolve all of the problems but several of which will be viable at some of the available locations. Thus the interaction of home and host societal effects underpins a variety of contested but potentially dominant models, and a feature of the 'system' is continuous competition between such evolving and contending models, rather than a clear resolution of the claims to dominance by any one model.

On the basis of the above propositions Boyer (1998: 27) argues that 'the notion of hybridization becomes significant, not just as a more short-term adaptation to environmental resistance, but as a principle of transformation, indeed of genesis, of industrial models themselves, through their interaction with social and economic systems which are different from those in which they first developed.' However, this transformative development represents only one among a range of possible outcomes. Thus Boyer identifies a spectrum of possible trajectories for the successful operation of subsidiaries, ranging from effective imitation (transplantation), through hybridization as the more or less successful utilization of functional equivalents, to hybridization as relatively successful adaptation to local conditions and only finally hybridization as innovation of a new model with broader potential. Alongside these possibilities are others, characterized by greater dissonance between context and strategy and/or greater tensions and incoherences between elements of management policy, which would represent failed imitation, sub-optimal forms of hybrid compromise, or opportunistic but incoherent, and thus unviable, mixes of policy. According to Boyer, the prevalence of these various outcomes is likely to depend on the dynamic interplay between the evolving strategies of the parent companies and the institutional configurations of constraints and opportunities characteristic of the sites of their overseas subsidiaries.

As this implies, the analytical principles emphasized by Boyer et al. (1988*a*, 1988*b*), when combined with the substantive findings of the Permanent Group for the Study of the Automobile Industry and its Employees (GERPISA) researchers, have generated a rich map of possible trajectories of hybridization. This map subsumes the earlier discussions of 'functional alternatives' and compromised forms of adaptation whilst highlighting the scope for the emergence of innovative repertoires. It also converges with other research which emphasizes significant differences among Japanese companies in their orientations towards their subsidiaries, especially in regard to their commitment to the generalizability of their parental model and their willingness to adapt that model to local circumstances (see especially Beechler et al. 1998; Beechler and Bird 1999; Bird et al. 1999). However, there are also some problems in utilizing this analytical framework, which arise primarily from the high level of abstraction at which it is formulated.

First, Boyer provides a valuable discussion of the difficulties (for both analysts and top managers) of adjudicating between those subsidiaries displaying optimal and sub-optimal levels of performance, and he emphasizes both the inappropriateness of narrow and abstracted benchmarking exercises and the pertinence of satisficing rather than maximizing strategies. Nevertheless, it remains unclear how this informs his discussion of different trajectories of hybridization. Second, only brief attention is given to the substantive character of the production and employment relations involved in concrete examples of these various forms of hybridization, and this leaves the forms of subordination and insubordination of labour that may be involved rather opaque. As with other regulationist analyses, there is a tendency to divide cases into those characterized by the integration of labour and those characterized by a crisis of employment relations, rather than exploring the scope and limits of the subsumption of labour in each case. Finally, the whole approach neglects the possibility that the parent company may pursue a policy of selective transplantation and hybridization, conditioned by the specific role that is envisaged for the subsidiary within its overall internationalization strategy. Boyer's model gives particular attention to the strength or weakness of a parent firm's commitment to export its production model, but gives little attention to any principles of selectivity which might apply to that process.

The branch plant—system, societal and dominance effects

The final set of analyses identified here, namely those that focus on the branch-plant role of overseas subsidiaries, directly address this last limitation of the hybridization approach, while remaining compatible with the positive insights provided by such authors as Boyer, Adler, and Fruin. There is a long tradition of analysis of foreign direct manufacturing investment sites as branch plants (e.g. Foster and Woolfson 1989; Hudson 1989), and these analyses tend to stress two key features which are glossed over in the discussions of transplantation and hybridization. First, the analysis does not start from the assumption that the parent company is concerned to produce a *replica* of its home operations at the subsidiary. Instead, the subsidiary is seen as a specific site within a wider international division of operations, and is thus expected to play a specific, selective role in that wider context. Second, the notion of a branch plant emphasizes the conditional character of the investment and thus the leverage which is afforded to the parent company both by its decision to invest and its continuing capability to switch investment elsewhere. Together, these themes are exemplified by the image of the small branch plant that adopts a low wage, labour-intensive production regime, to perform limited assembly operations as part of an integrated international commodity chain, and the related image of the powerful corporate centre that uses its capacity to grant or withdraw investment, or even to close the factory, to maintain the conditions which make such an operation viable.

Such a pattern of operations would be compatible with the selective transfer of low-end production arrangements and employment relations from elsewhere in the parent company, either from more routinized operations at the parent plant or from other subsidiaries at home or abroad. This is the scenario highlighted by Dedoussis (1994, 1995; Dedoussis and Littler 1994) through his argument that Japanese firms may have selectively transplanted the work and employment relations of Japan's subordinate subcontracting networks and peripheral labour market to their overseas operations. It is also compatible with forms of adaptation that draw heavily on the indigenous management practices of the host country, especially when they involve harsh conditions and union exclusion. This is the pattern identified by Milkman (1991, 1992) in her analysis of the operations of many Japanese factories in California, where they draw heavily on a low wage immigrant workforce and appear to have self-consciously copied American union-avoidance strategies. Thus there is a significant fit between the branch plant argument and several substantively based challenges to the transplantation model.

It could nevertheless be argued that a substantial weakness of the branch plant approach arises precisely from its direct equation of branch plants with routine assembly operations, when there is evidence of important variations in the character of subsidiary operations (see Henderson 1989), and this includes both upgrading and divergence from the basic assembly factory. Our response to this criticism is that the branch plant approach should be able to accommodate such developments, because it focuses on the varied roles of these branch factories in complex international production chains (Dicken 1998; Gereffi 1996; Gereffi and Korzeniewicz 1994; Henderson 1989, 1994, 1999). However, from this vantage point we would continue to see such higher value-added operations in the context of the overall global strategies of the parent companies, thus contingent on the development and modification of such strategies rather than part of an automatic process of transplantation and upgrading. Furthermore, the issue of the leverage afforded to employers through their international, multisite, operations, remains pertinent, even though the extent of sunk costs and ease of relocation will vary according to the specific role being played by each subsidiary. In these respects the branch plant perspective adds a new, more critical dimension to debates which have usually been conducted in the language of transplantation or hybridization. In particular, it attends to the class relations involved, both through attention to the strategies and leverage of international manufacturers and through consideration of the leverage and vulnerabilities of workers based in the settings where these firms establish their subsidiaries.

This conception of the role of the branch plant also reconnects the discussion of the operations of Japanese overseas subsidiaries with a wider literature on the operations of international manufacturing companies. These focus on the ways in which power relations in subsidiary operations are affected by the range and character of a firm's international operations (Dicken 1998; Edwards et al. 1996; Mueller 1996). This wider literature explicitly addresses the ways in which HQ-led comparisons across production operations may be used, often in quite subtle and incremental ways, to modify the priorities of subsidiary managers and the specific ways in which they conduct their operations. Among the features of this process that have been highlighted in recent years are the extent to which corporate policy debates and guidelines may involve both the forcing and fostering of evolutionary modifications in branch plant policy and the scope for senior managers to use the allocation of investment streams to reward and punish subsidiaries over time.

At the same time, contributors to this literature have also recognized that international companies vary in both their propensity and their capacity to demand compliance with centrally formulated operating principles. In particular, vertically integrated production companies are much more concerned to develop common design principles and production standards than are conglomerates or multidomestic firms, while international firms also differ in the size and experience of the international management cadre they have available to manage their foreign subsidiaries. Thus the branch plant approach places a valuable emphasis on the location of specific subsidiaries within their wider corporate strategies and structures, whether as low-end assembly operations (the traditional image of the branch plant) or in some other role. This reminds us that any engagement between dominant production models and local societal effects, and indeed any processes of hybridization, are mediated through distinctive corporate management structures, strategies, and power relations.

CONCLUSION

International companies are globalizing, not globalized, as Sklair (2001) suggests, and therefore their organizations will be marked by their origins in specific national economies and by the strength of the local practices embedded within any particular subsidiary, as well as the prevailing forces within the world market and production system. States or national business systems are always penetrated by the international division of labour, the world market, and competition between rival capitalist societies, and are never 'islands' of self-sustaining diversity. However, the idea that globalization, best practices or the latest, 'one best way' modernization recipe will sweep away diversity is misleading. Our argument in this book is that the interplay of different processes, often pulling in contradictory directions, is a more feasible scenario. As such the new international division of labour within global capitalism may confirm some countries within already dependent, peripheral or subordinate positions within the order of global capitalism. But new entrants may also create different ways of organizing the firm, employment relations, work organization, and supplier relations and redefine themselves and influence others in the system. Japan played this role from the 1980s, with a profound influence on work organization outside of Japan. Finally, whatever value there is in particularizing the nature of organization, work, and employment relations by reference to country or production metaphor (e.g. Fordism or Toyotaism), the universal or systemic social relations of capitalism will always underpin these diverse representations or appearances. In other words, capital–labour contestation is structurally endemic to capitalism, but is expressed in manifold ways, and mediated through a great variety of institutional forms.

The international subsidiary condenses the effects of the underlying social relations of capitalism, national institutional legacies of home and host societies, and 'best practice' work and employment standards in specific localities and workplaces. But it is only through social interaction that groups and individuals negotiate which of these different (and perhaps competing) ways of working, standards of quality, authority relations, and methods of employment will actually shape particular work situations. It is therefore important to retain a research focus on the workplace, as it is here that the working out of workplace rules and practices emerges. The *unpredictability* of workplace relations arises both from underlying systemic contradictions and from more particular tensions and dilemmas. These may arise from the specific location of the workplace in relation to wider corporate hierarchies and networks, market relations with suppliers, customers and competitors, national and local forms of state regulation, and the social organization and supply of labour. Our commitment to case-study research arises from a concern to investigate and analyse the ways in which managers (both Japanese and local) and workers experience, respond to, and cope with these tensions and dilemmas, and thus mediate the interplay of SSD effects.

CHAPTER

5

Researching Japanese Subsidiaries: The Strategy of Multiple Case-study Research

INTRODUCTION

Our research was conducted through a set of case studies of Japanese-owned workplaces. Each case study involved initial discussions with workplace 'gatekeepers', opportunities to observe and discuss the work process, semi-structured interviews with a wide range of staff, the collection of documentary material both within and outside the workplace and discussions with key informants inside the factory and in the locality. The most intensive phase of each case study involved two researchers over three to six weeks, but contacts were maintained with some of the research sites or workplaces over a much longer time period, allowing revisits and further discussions with key informants. This chapter sets out the rationale for adopting this approach to the research, discusses the way in which the case studies were conducted in more detail, and comments on the strengths and weaknesses of such a research strategy.

RESEARCH STRATEGIES: SURVEY OR CASE-STUDY RESEARCH

Our commitment to a case-study approach to research is underpinned by a long established tradition of such studies in industrial sociology and organizational analysis, but it also gained strength from a critical engagement with survey research on Japanese firms. In particular, a key theme in the critical discussion of much of the earlier literature on Japanization and hybridization was that the use of survey research methods has failed to illuminate the day-to-day realities of management, work, and employment relations within the workplace (Elger and Smith 1994).

Surveys of enterprise policies were central to four of the landmark studies on Japanese inward investors in Britain and North America, conducted by Oliver and Wilkinson (1988), Kenney and Florida (1993), Morris et al. (1993) and Abo (1994*a*). The best of these survey-based studies have made a valuable contribution to discussions of Japanese subsidiaries, especially by mapping their geographical and sectoral distribution and charting the views of senior managers regarding key features of their operations. What they all share, however, is a heavy (sometimes total) dependence on management informants and considerable emphasis on charting the presence or absence of key attributes of a stylized Japanese model of work organization and employment relations. These are not the only sorts of surveys that have been used in research on Japanese manufacturing workplaces. Several researchers have conducted employee attitude surveys as part of their case studies of specific factories (Adler 1993, 1999*a*; Rinehart et al. 1997; Babson 1998 in North America, and White and Trevor 1983; Grant 1994 in Britain). However, it was the multi-enterprise surveys that played the primary role in defining the research agenda of the mid-1990s, when we commenced our research.

While these studies had set the agenda, they provided limited leverage on the critical questions their research had raised. The reliance on senior management informants made it difficult to know how management policies are actually enacted in the workplace, especially when responses were confined to statements about the presence or absence of particular practices. Furthermore, these approaches to research generally lacked robust evidence of how employees respond to management policies, and this applied to such key shop-floor agents of management as supervisors or team leaders as well as regular workers. Finally, even elaborate mapping of checklists of policies gave little insight into the dynamics of policy formation and revision over time. To address these sorts of questions requires more in-depth case-study research, involving gathering information from a wider range of participants in the workplace and examining the evolution of specific policies and practices over time.

The major alternative to multi-enterprise surveys reliant on key management informants is case-study research, but such case studies vary considerably in their design. The fieldwork involved may vary in depth from short visits and discussions with a small number of key informants (in which case they have important similarities with the enterprise surveys, but without their systematic comparative character) to prolonged and extensive engagement with participants in the research setting. Studies that are closer to the latter pattern may also differ among themselves, according to the mix of research methods used. There are now several valuable examples of intensive ethnographic case studies based primarily upon participant observation (Graham 1995; Sharpe 1997, 1998, 2001; Delbridge 1998; Palmer 2000) but other detailed case studies have used a varied mixture of observation, discussions with key informants and (as noted above) attitude surveys.

As these variations imply, one important dilemma facing case-study researchers is that between depth and breadth of focus. While participant observation provides unparalleled access to the experience of a particular work group and work process, its intensity limits the range of such settings that can be examined. It often limits the vantage point of the researcher and it also demands considerable commitment from the organization being studied. Alternative case-study methods may be less demanding and constraining for the field researcher (and for the 'gatekeepers' of the workplaces under study), and may also allow a wider angle of vision, either within a given workplace or across a number of case-study sites. However, they will also offer less intensive and nuanced insights into day-to-day conduct than participant observation. Of course, responses to the resulting set of choices of research strategy depend upon both the analytical priorities of the researchers and the resources they have available.

Our analytical priorities were to investigate the enacted character of management practices and worker responses in a variety of different Japanese manufacturing subsidiaries, and thus to be in a position to analyse and compare the key features of the social relations of management, work, and employment across these workplaces. This suggested that we should adopt a less intensive and narrowly focused approach than participant observation, but one which would nevertheless use a mix of observational, interview, and documentary methods to develop a detailed and rounded account of developments in each of several case-study workplaces.

A particular view of the ways in which case-study research can contribute to a cumulative understanding and analysis of the phenomenon under investigation also informed our approach to the case studies. It is widely recognized that case studies provide particular leverage on two key features of social phenomena, namely their active *processual* character and the importance of social *context*, but there remain sharp differences of view regarding the contribution that case studies can make to the development of broader theorizing. One view, often developed by the proponents of survey research, is that case studies have only the subordinate role of testing hypotheses about 'process' derived from a sophisticated statistical analysis of survey data (Goldthorpe 2000: 84–9). A contrasting view, associated with the symbolic interactionist tradition, seeks to derive generalizations entirely inductively through a systematic interrogation of qualitative data sets (Glaser and Strauss 1967).

However, we believe that neither of these approaches captures the dominant logic of case-study work, which is based on engaging with and reformulating theoretical claims about social processes and social contexts during a theoretically informed engagement with case-study evidence (for defences of this approach see Burawoy 1991, 1998; Halford et al. 1997; Stoecker 1991; Vaughan 1992). Burawoy (1998), in particular, has drawn out the role of the 'extended case method' in the analysis of active social processes within the research setting, but also in the identification of the (necessarily reified) wider social forces which impinge upon that setting. We have sought to develop this approach throughout our substantive discussion of our case studies, and it also informed our decisions regarding choice of cases and our organization of the research process. The next section outlines the process of selection of the case-study sites, after which the process of case-study research itself is discussed.

SELECTING CASES FOR COMPARISON

Multiple case studies have often been used in organizational research to allow comparisons between cases and shed light on the sources of similarities and differences between them (a classic example is the work of Burns and Stalker 1961). Our basic research design involved the study of firms from one country, Japan, operating in one regional setting, the English Midlands, rather than comparisons of cases across different 'home' or 'host' countries. Instead, we were interested in other sources of variation in management policies and workers' experiences within the 'one home/one host' format. In particular, our analytical approach highlighted the potential importance of company and sector differences, as has emerged from earlier chapters. Against this background, the debates about Japanese 'transplants' provided suggestions about a whole range of pertinent differences among such firms, including sector contrasts, different forms of ownership (especially joint ventures versus wholly-owned subsidiaries), size variations and unionized versus non-unionized workplaces. In turn, these bald differences gained potential analytical significance in relation to particular social processes. For example, joint ventures might be important because they involved influences from different parent companies, while size might be an indicator of distinctive locations in supply chains. One of our research objectives was to select a range of cases that would allow us to consider the relevance and role of such differences for understanding the day-to-day character of work and employment relations within Japanese subsidiaries.

We did not have the resources to conduct substantial fieldwork in sufficient cases to be able to subject our findings to statistical analysis, by correlating such variables as size or ownership structure with workplace practices. In any case we were sceptical about the extent to which such statistical exercises would allow us to explore the social processes, of management micropolitics, effort bargaining and the negotiation of workplace order, that we regard as crucial mediators between structural variables and the lived experience of work and employment. Thus our concern was to explore the relevance of the social processes signalled by these structural features, both by considering the direct accounts of their influence according to our informants and by using our broader findings to reassess how these factors impinged on the social relations of the workplace.

The time and resources which could be devoted to the research as a whole, coupled with our assessment of the work required to produce rich cases, governed the number of cases we could consider. Thus we worked backwards from the presumption that we would spend six to twelve 'person-weeks' on each site and that we would work together on a substantial proportion of our interviews. This was important since these were our main research tools and this would allow us to review and discuss our research material and interpretations as we went along. Joint interviews were less efficient quantitatively speaking, but richer and more effective in fashioning shared understandings and collaborative analysis as the fieldwork progressed. On this basis we decided that we would conduct research at six production sites, each owned by a different company. In the event, this book reports on five firms, as the sixth did not commence significant production until after the period of research, but actually covers eight sites. Since one of the features we were interested in was the size of the firm (at least as size itself indicated rather different forms of insertion into wider production networks and forms of social relations in the workplace) these sites differed considerably in terms of numbers of employees. This obviously influenced the time we actually spent at each location around the average duration for the case-study work.

We were able to identify an appropriate population of companies to consider for our research by using an almost complete English language listing of firms engaged in 'Japanese Overseas Investment' (Too Keizai 1992). This was supplemented by a similar listing in the regular 'Survey of the European Operations of Japanese Companies in the Manufacturing Sector' compiled by the JETRO (various dates), and other published listings provided by local state agencies. These databases provided information on ownership (including joint venture partners), location, date of establishment, acquisition or first operation, areas of activity, number of employees, and often number of Japanese 'dispatched' employees on site. We identified all of the relevant enterprises operating in the Midlands area of England, a constraint we imposed both for practical reasons of relative proximity and because there had been few published studies of Japanese firms operating in this distinctive regional context, representing the heartland of British engineering. We worked through appropriate cases in several tranches (influenced by the progress of existing studies) while seeking examples with different ownership patterns, from different sectors and different sizes, until we had accumulated sufficient cases.

We experienced several rejections in this process, raising questions about how this may have skewed our selection. Several rationales were given for non-involvement in the project. One was that other researchers had already studied the firm. However, sometimes the research mentioned by those that rejected our approach was quite limited and superficial, while several of the firms we did study had also been the subject of earlier research, so our feeling was that this was rarely the pivotal reason for refusal. The other reasons given related to current circumstances within the firm, sometimes related to changes in management and sometimes related to the sensitivity of industrial relations. If we take these reasons at face value they each suggest that our cases may be characterized by greater stability and less conflict than the firms that refused us entry. Management was more in control, or felt they were. In particular, we had more refusals at 'brownfield' sites, where older management traditions and established patterns of trade union representation and industrial relations may have been in contention.

Certainly, our original plan had been to include some workplaces with these features, but while the final selection of cases included 'brownfield' sites, none of these was unionized (usefully underlining the ambiguity of the brownfield/greenfield distinction). The absence of unions is clearly an important and distinctive feature of our case-study panel, which deserves further comment. First, it can be seen as an opportunity to research precisely that subset of cases where management has had the strongest hand in constructing employment relations in their preferred form. Second, however, our analysis will show that the workplaces we studied were not devoid of tensions in employment relations. Furthermore, over time they have faced a variety of pressures and changes which mean that they cannot be said to represent a particular unproblematic subset of cases for management, either in commercial or labour market terms. Thirdly, almost all of the greenfield Japanese factories in the Midlands region have avoided union recognition (Toyota in Derbyshire is an important exception). In this respect our case studies can be regarded as typical of a distinctive regional pattern, especially when compared with the almost universal pattern of union recognition in South Wales (see Wilkinson et al. 1993; Danford 1999).

We set out to look at Japanese firms in a variety of locations across the English Midlands, but the geographical concentration of such firms meant that four of our five case studies came to be conducted in the locality which has the greatest concentration of Japanese inward investment in the region, Telford in Shropshire. These firms not only shared a common labour market and local economic development agencies, but also regarded themselves as participants in a *cluster* or *community* of Japanese enterprises, so this added a further dimension to our research. On the one hand they represent four enterprise case studies (discussed in Chapters 7, 8, and 11), but on the other hand they also represent a single case study of this locality and cluster (discussed in Chapter 6). For this locality we also drew on the findings of several other researchers on aspects of employment relations in the town (Forde 1997, 2001; Mann 1991; Palmer 1996; Sharp 1997, 1998; Waye 1983) together with the work of several research students and research assistants in parallel projects on employment agencies, labour turnover, and induction (Clark 1996; Jones 1996; Igarashi 2000; Daskalaki 2001).

The identification of each enterprise with a single-site case study was also qualified in another way, through attention to multiple sites when this appeared appropriate to gain a coherent view of the manufacturing operations and social relations of the relevant firm. As noted earlier, this meant we actually visited eight sites owned by the five companies, though several of these sites were quite small. Furthermore, one of these sites was a manufacturing operation in Scotland, but this was included alongside the firm's R&D operation and HQ which *were* sited, like all our other workplaces, in the Midlands. Where we studied only one site this was always the main site, and usually the sole manufacturing location in the United Kingdom. Thus in each case we sought to gain a rounded view of the production operations of the firm in Britain.

Time and resource constraints, however, did not allow us to visit the Japanese HQs of these companies. This is an important limitation of our research. Our understanding of relations between the British operations and the parent company in Japan had to be developed almost entirely from information and documentation gathered at the British sites. This also applies to relations between the British factories and other factories elsewhere, whether 'mother factories' in Japan or 'sister factories' in other countries. Nevertheless, we were able to address these relationships through our discussions and interviews with both Japanese and British informants who were involved in communications and travel between different parts of the company (see Table 5.1).

CONDUCTING THE CASE STUDIES

We gained access to each case study on the understanding that we wished to study the way work and employment relations were organized in a variety of Japanese-owned firms. Interviews with a wide range of employees constituted the primary research method, but these were coupled with opportunities to observe and discuss the production process and the collection of appropriate documents and statistics. This meant that granting access was more onerous for the participants than it might have been if the request was for just one or two interviews, but less demanding than a request to engage in lengthy participant observation. Nevertheless, negotiating the scope of access remained a continuing process in each

Table 5.1. ***Features of the case-study workplaces***

Pseudonym	Copy-Co	Part-Co	PCB-Co	Assembly-Co	Computer-Co
Ownership	Japanese	Japanese/European joint venture	Japanese	Japanese/US joint venture	Japanese take-over of UK firm
Product	Office equipment and consumables	Complex car components	Printed circuit boards	Plastic parts and assemblies	Computers and servers
Role of site	Manufacturer supplying to marketing division	First tier supplier to several final assemblers	Supplier of PCBs to several final assemblers	Supplier of parts to several final assemblers	Product division reponsible for design, development amd manufacture
Established	1983	1990	Opened 1987 Closed 1999	1989	Purchased 1990 Closed 1999
Employees at time of main fieldwork	550	720	92	180	475
Sites	One	One	One	Two	Three
Total interviewed (as percentage of all employees)	43 8%	50 7%	16 17%	17 9%	41 9%
Japanese expatriates	9	8	2	1	4
UK managers/ engineers/technicians	15	12	4	6	19
UK supervisors/ team-leaders	4	8		2	5
UK maintenance/ production workers	15	22	11	8	13

enterprise. The period of intensive research varied between three and six weeks on site, depending upon the size of the workplace, but the fieldwork usually involved additional revisits to fill gaps and update our accounts.

We undertook to protect the anonymity of our informants and, though we did not promise to disguise the identities of the firms, we have chosen to use pseudonyms to help fulfil our commitment to individuals. We also undertook to provide a brief and general résumé of our preliminary findings. One further feature of our access follows from the fact that none of these workplaces was unionized. This meant that the details of our negotiation of access were entirely mediated through management and we did not have the opportunity to define our independence from management concerns through any process of parallel access. This made it particularly important for us to spell out our distinctive research agenda and independence from management in our interaction with employees, both at the start of the interviews (which were usually the moments of initial face-to-face contact with employees) and during other encounters, but we felt that we were generally successful in this regard. Managers often had their own agendas in granting access and providing particular individuals for interview. For example, at one plant we were cast in a counselling role by management, and in others particular groupings of managers hoped that our findings would help their cause. However, we soon became aware of these ascribed roles from informants and were able to negotiate our way around them, while they also provided interesting insights into the dynamics of management.

We sought to interview a representative range of employees on a quota sample basis. Thus, though we were dependent on management and supervisory permission to interview specific people, our emphasis on a spread of informants by occupation, section, employment status, tenure, age, gender, and ethnicity constrained management selection and allowed us to hear voices from all sections of the workforce. Combined with our assurances about confidentiality, this was successful in creating the conditions for reflective and informative interviews, with few of our interviewees displaying any reservations about responding to our questions. As Table 5.1 shows, we interviewed around 8 per cent of the workforce at each of our larger case-study employers, and substantially higher percentages in the small firms.

We aimed to avoid the tendency in the literature on Japanese transplants to work with a top-down checklist of 'Japaneseness'. We deliberately decided to talk to informants about their work history, current work relations, and general attitudes towards working in the particular factory, and not lead with questions about Japanese ownership or working for the Japanese. Our interviews were semi-structured and followed a common range of topics, tailored slightly to be appropriate to managers, engineers, supervisors, and shop-floor workers respectively. The shared agenda in all of our formal interviews covered:

- work history
- recruitment and selection into the firm
- job history in the firm
- current role
- significant events and policy developments
- patterns of influence over the work process and employee relations
- opinions on the overall character of the firm

The interviews were tape-recorded and lasted from one to two hours. This allowed our informants to deviate from our agenda and elaborate where appropriate, while we could listen and draw out further responses.

In common with other case-study researchers, we found that such interviews allowed a 'dialogue between researchers and respondents, to provide much more detail on context and process' (Halford et al. 1997: 59) than would have been produced using questionnaires or highly structured interviews. However, Halford et al. (1997: 61) also expressed concern that such interviews also invite informants to 'let off steam' by articulating criticisms and confidences that would not necessarily be expressed explicitly in day-to-day work. While we recognized that some of our informants used their interviews in this way, we were less concerned with the ambiguous status of such comments. This was because it seemed to us that the positions being rehearsed were rarely ones that had not been articulated to other confidants within the organization, such as trusted colleagues or workmates, while other interview, conversational, and observational material allowed us to place these comments in their appropriate contexts.

The first objective of the interviews was to listen to the range of experiences and opinions in each workplace. However, we did not see each interview as an entirely discrete event, but also treated the sequence of interviews as a cumulative and iterative process. We suspect that this is an important feature of case-study interviewing in many settings, and perhaps especially in formal organizations, though it is one that has hardly been discussed in the literature. We were, after all, interviewing a series of informants who shared a common employer and usually a common workplace. They participated in shared working arrangements and common institutions and many interacted directly with one another more or less frequently. In our interviews we sought not only to elicit attitudes or opinions but also to gather accounts of events and processes which were part of this shared experience. In so doing we gained impressions, insights, and uncertainties in our early interviews in each workplace which informed our probes or queries in later interviews.

Accordingly we sought to capitalize on these iterative features of our research process in an explicit fashion. First, we sought to concretize the process of cumulative and iterative analysis through brief but systematic résumés of themes and issues arising from each interview and through our own discussion and interim commentaries during the fieldwork. Second, this helped to structure the sequencing of interviews and requests for further information. For example, it proved valuable to be able to interview senior managers in each firm relatively late in the sequence, if necessary by arranging a second interview. This allowed us to ask more informed questions and to probe in a meaningful way beneath the well-rehearsed scripts that are inevitably a stock-in-trade of those who present the public face of these organizations.

As this suggests, our semi-structured interviews with diverse participants provided the main resources for developing our understanding of workplace social relations, but we also used observations, documentary sources, and informal conversations to test, modify and develop our analysis. For example, an examination of the minutes of consultation meetings at one of the factories complemented our interview material on these meetings. This enriched our understanding of the scope and limits of employee 'voice' in the workplace, while observations of, and informal conversations about, work processes enabled us to clarify key features of the organization and experience of production.

Our iterative approach to interviewing, combined with these other aspects of fieldwork, often allowed us to draw out accounts of shared experiences from several vantage points and thus deepen our understanding of the events in question and the ways in which they were variously interpreted. In one workplace, for example, we gathered contrasting accounts from managers and workers about the reorganization of supervision in one area of the factory. Managers talked about overcoming problems of 'horseplay' and indiscipline, while workers talked about the ending of informal understandings and 'give-and-take'. Thus, there were contrasting characterizations of developments but the informants were recognizably talking about the same events and processes. Just occasionally we found that the accounts we were being given by different participants were radically at odds, apparently referring to experiences and events which had little in common. In such instances, however, further investigation tended to reveal that the contrasts arose from entrenched divisions between these participants, in one case, for example, between administrative and production management, with attendant divergences of interpretation and recollection.

In general, however, our experience was of various interviewees and other informants talking about a recognizably shared configuration of social arrangements and social processes, though from a range of different standpoints and coloured by different judgements. In turn such standpoints evidently arose from the specific circumstances of different sets of informants. In part they matched particular positions in the workplace hierarchy or division of labour, but they were also related to distinctive labour market and biographical experiences, differentiated in terms of gender, age, and ethnicity. Thus our interviewees, like those of Halford et al. (1997: 62, 190), gave us access to alternative narratives about workplace social relations that were interwoven with wider biographical narratives. For example, several of the senior British managers in the Telford workplaces had experienced the crises and sharp decline of British manufacturing in the Midlands in the 1970s and early 1980s, including having to make workers redundant and experiencing their own redundancy. As we will show, this informed their receptivity to Japanese management policies in distinctive ways.

It is worth emphasizing here that these narrative threads were themselves often explicitly part of a shared social matrix of experiences and understandings in the workplace, not merely private or individual accounts. Most obviously this was evident from the recurrence of common themes in the accounts of different informants, and in the shared vocabulary informants used to characterize the range of outlooks and opinions among their fellow employees. Finally, on some occasions interviewees self-consciously sought to articulate what they believed to be shared experiences and sentiments among co-workers, either because they were repeating views they had expressed as explicit spokespersons in their work settings or because there had been discussions among workmates about the points the interviewee should make on their behalf. These later features once more underlined some of the ways in which the sub-texts of our interactions with informants were embedded within, and provided a basis for a fuller understanding of, wider social processes in the workplace.

CONCLUSION

Our research strategy was designed to allow us to engage with and reformulate existing theoretical approaches to the overseas operations of Japanese manufacturing firms. We did not simply seek to test and refute theoretical propositions in a deductive fashion because this would have failed to explore the social processes that were generating such outcomes. Neither did we commit ourselves to a strictly inductive process of grounded theory generation because we wished to engage with and build upon existing middle-range analytical approaches. In these respects, then, our approach to case-study research was theoretically driven but open, designed to engage critically with existing theoretical approaches and thus to develop more adequate analyses, in ways consistent with recent defences of theoretically informed case-study research.

This approach informed our selection of a range of cases for study, and our conceptualization and reconceptualization of the features that differentiated or represented commonalities among these cases. First, we wanted to locate our case-study firms and workplaces within their wider contexts, in terms of such features as ownership structures, enterprise networks, production chains, product markets, national and local industrial relations patterns and regulative frameworks, and local employment structures and labour markets. Second, however, we did not wish to treat this array of contextual conditions as an unproblematical set of determinants of social relations within the enterprise or workplace. Instead we sought to use our understanding of internal social processes and comparisons between cases to tease out the salience and influence of these and other features of the broader social context.

Similarly, the iterative processes of investigation and analysis, which characterized both the sequence of interviews and the combination of different research materials, involved the deployment and revision of existing analytical ideas about the social processes of management and the dynamics of employment relations within these firms and workplaces. This analytical agenda was then carried over into the detailed re-examination of our data after the completion of our case-studies, which involved a systematic review of the topics and themes covered in the interview transcripts and other materials for each workplace. This allowed us to explore the scope and limits of different phases in the formation and implementation of management policies, and to analyse the forms of worker accommodation, compliance, and contestation associated with such policies in the different workplaces.

II

MANUFACTURING SUBSIDIARIES: CLUSTER AND COMPANIES

CHAPTER

6

Inward Investment and the Construction of New Production Spaces: The Case of Telford

INTRODUCTION: SPACE AND LOCALITY EFFECTS

Capital is globalizing but production always takes place *somewhere* (Dicken 1998: 11). Specific territories and spaces may be by-passed through the movement of capital, and owners and managers may seek a 'spatial fix' (Harvey 1982: 415) as they work to resolve problems of accumulation through the use of relocation as a power resource. The international reach of capital clearly creates opportunities for the use of space to suit corporate needs, as in the movement of production from high- to low-cost regions or the concentration of R&D in specific centres. But despite such mobility, workplaces must be set within a specific locality to ensure that surpluses are appropriated within a given time-frame, whatever the acceleration in the mobility of capital (Harvey 1982; Massey 1984). Thus there are always local conditions that influence the operation of the firm, when employers, managers and workers come together in a specific locality for the purpose of production. The capacity of enterprises to move and choose between production sites provides them with powerful levers in bargaining with state agencies and constructing workforces that conform to their requirements. However, sunk-costs and local linkages also represent important constraints on the mobility of capital, generating a complex and contradictory field of power relations and corporate strategies (Harvey 1982: 373–412).

Meanwhile it is generally acknowledged that labour is more local and less mobile than capital (Castells 2000: 504), and Campbell (1994: 186–7) suggests that 'the real *problematique* of globalisation is, arguably, the growing disparity between the mobility of labour and capital'. However, this emphasis on the immobility of labour also risks overstatement if it fails to recognize that, at a variety of scales, labour mobility also remains fundamental to capitalism. Not only may workers move between workplaces or local labour markets in search of work or improved pay and conditions, but wider patterns of regional and international labour migration remain pivotal features of contemporary capitalism (Castles 2000: 124–32; Cohen 1997: 155–76; Smith 2003). As Harvey (1982: 382–5) argues, a critical issue then becomes the extent, bases, and limitations of any resulting mitigation of the dependency of labour upon capital. On the one hand labour mobility may provide some leverage for workers, especially where there are shortages of labour. But on the other hand the institutional framework within which such mobility takes place (involving legal and welfare rights or exclusions) is critical, while mobility may itself disrupt locally embedded forms of mutual support among workers.

In this context, national and local state agencies continue to play important roles, both in competing for mobile investment through the provision of infrastructures and incentives and in coordinating the development of new production spaces, such as new towns or investment zones. In these respects states address the needs of labour (for jobs and social infrastructures) primarily through efforts to meet the requirements of capital (for suitable production sites and labour forces). However, the resultant state policies are also likely to be fraught with tensions and limitations, for the 'requirements' of capital are often contradictory while their reconciliation with the needs of labour remains difficult (Tickell and Peck 1995; Peck 1996). In this context inward-investing firms not only seek to influence state policies but also develop their own strategies for managing local labour markets and communities. Thus we see the social organization of new production spaces evolving out of the intersection of pre-existing institutional frameworks, national and local state initiatives, the strategies of individual enterprises, and the responses of employees and wider communities. The objective of this chapter is to provide an analysis of the development of one such new production space, Telford 'New Town', which has attracted a disproportionate volume of Japanese inward investors during the last two decades. This provides the spatial context for four of our detailed case studies of Japanese manufacturing subsidiaries, presented in Chapters 7, 8, and 11.

Japanese firms investing in Britain have sought out particular forms of 'spatial fix', involving distinctive labour market features. Some have located in established manufacturing centres, perhaps attracted by the density of industrial, commercial, and R&D networks that can support their operations. More often, however, they have focused on areas of high unemployment, especially within traditional but declining industrial regions (such as Wales and the North-east of England), or on new towns, characterized by a growing supply of youthful labour and often weak union organization (such as Telford or Milton Keynes in England or Glenrothes in Scotland). While government grants played a role in attracting firms to some of these locations, commentators have emphasized that declining regions and new towns were attractive because they allowed inward investors to construct a workforce and production operations of their choosing. This is exemplified by the availability of 'greenfield' sites, which are contrasted with older, established 'brownfield' sites because they are thought to offer greater opportunities to deviate from existing institutional patterns of work and employment (Smith and Elger 2000).

In these terms our discussion of Telford represents a case study of the development of one of the characteristic British 'greenfield' locations for foreign, and especially Japanese, manufacturing subsidiaries since the surge of Japanese inward investment in the early 1980s. However, the notion of a 'greenfield site' embraces an amalgam of features (new firms in new factories, in new settings, recruiting a new workforce) that may come together in a variety of ways with different effects, and it also has an ambiguous temporality as novelty is qualified by the passage of time (Hallier and Leopold 2000; Leopold and Hallier 1997). Thus our discussion of Telford has to problematize these features to consider how far and in what ways the development of this new town may have encouraged firms to diverge from traditional workplace and employment practices, and to consider how firm practices and labour market dynamics evolved over time.

TELFORD

Telford is a new town located North-west of Birmingham in the county of Shropshire, on the edge of the English Midlands. It has grown considerably since the 1960s, has enjoyed significant success in attracting FDI and boasts a large number of foreign invested enterprises (FIEs). Most of these firms are manufacturers, with concentrations in electrical assembly, office machinery, computers, plastics, and auto parts assembly, and Telford still has a relatively high proportion of jobs in manufacturing compared with the West Midlands and national averages. The labour force is comparatively young and also relatively unskilled, although the proportion of managerial and professional employees has grown in recent years. Wage rates are low in comparison with the rest of the West Midlands. The town is weakly unionized and the vast majority of foreign firms are non-union. It had high unemployment when many of these firms arrived, but now has low unemployment, drawing workers from a wide area, including rural Shropshire, the Black Country and the wider Midlands. Telford represents, therefore, a low wage, non-union, FDI dominated locality, close to a major centre of manufacturing industry, the West Midlands, but distinctive in terms of employment and industrial relations traditions. In these terms it has offered an attractive 'spatial fix' to inward investors through the establishment of non-unionized assembly factories (and more recently mass service industries like call centres) employing mainly low paid, semi or unskilled workers. In turn, these features have been reinforced by the very concentration of such workplaces, as this has encouraged liaison between firms in the development of their employment policies, though this has not guaranteed a fully compliant or committed workforce.

Following our earlier discussion of the construction of new production spaces, our account of the evolution of Telford as a centre of new manufacturing investment focuses on the interaction between three key agencies—the state, new capital, and labour. In this context we give particular attention to the unresolved tensions and unforeseen consequences characterizing this interaction over time, rather than simply privileging the capacity of employers, aided by state development agencies, to regulate the labour market and construct the workforces of their choice.

THE EVOLUTION OF AN FDI-BASED NEW TOWN DEVELOPMENT STRATEGY

The Telford Development Corporation (TDC) was the government body responsible for planning and developing Telford New Town. It was formed in 1963 and wound up in 1991, when the local Wrekin Council assumed many of its functions. Telford was designed to draw an 'overspill' population from the Birmingham conurbation, but this also involved the regeneration of a cluster of long established industrial and mining settlements dating back to the first industrial revolution, as these were subsumed within the boundaries of the new town. As the local planning and management agency, the TDC purchased land, built and managed housing, organized infrastructural facilities, and provided major services to inward investors. Eventually this involved the construction of a series of modern 'greenfield' industrial estates, in part through the rehabilitation of older industrial and mining sites (De Soissons 1991).

As part of the prosperous West Midlands, a key feature of Telford's development in the 1960s and 1970s was that it had no access to regional development grants, but was seen primarily as a means of relieving housing and labour market pressures in the Birmingham conurbation (Aldridge 1979; De Soissons 1991). Thus the availability of low rent housing was the initial motor for the growth of Telford, and it generally had to rely on firms relocating from Birmingham and the Black Country to create new employment. Through the 1970s and into the 1980s the generation and retention of local inward investment proved increasingly difficult, existing manufacturing and extractive industries inherited from the old industrial settlements continued to decline, and the mismatch between housing development and employment provision in Telford worsened. Unemployment rose above the regional average from the late 1960s, and was the highest in the West Midlands by the mid-1970s.

It was in this context that TDC policy evolved towards the attraction of overseas investors. Efforts to gain Assisted Area status, which would have provided grants to attract new investment, were unsuccessful in the early 1970s and again in 1980. As a result 'the Development Corporation began to look at the possibility of going overseas in order to by-pass the Industrial Development Certificate controls. Tentative feelers were put out in the USA and Germany' and by 1978 it 'had redoubled its efforts at overseas recruitment of industry and began the "wooing" of Japanese business' (De Soissons 1991: 107, 110). In 1982 the TDC finally gained an Enterprize Zone (EZ), which covered one of the town's industrial estates for ten years, giving incoming firms exemption from rates, development land taxes and some planning constraints, and in 1984 Telford was designated as an Intermediate Assisted Area (IAA), along with the rest of the West Midlands.

It is generally agreed that the pursuit of FDI was already having some success before the positive financial inducements of EZ and IAA status became available. Nineteen foreign-owned companies, including the first Japanese firm, were operating in Telford before 1983, and one interviewee claimed that 'the tide had turned in our favour by that stage'. Other TDC informants stressed that financial aid was usually a subordinate consideration in the location decisions of later arrivals, outweighed by the position and communications links of Telford and the availability of a substantial and relatively cheap workforce. This is consistent with Hill and Munday's (1994) finding that new FDI jobs were much more sensitive to relative labour costs than they were to grants, and that of Collis and Roberts (1992: 119) that 'in contrast to many of the traditional Assisted Areas, financial assistance has not in general been a significant factor in attracting [FDI] to the West Midlands'. Nevertheless, the latter authors also found that more foreign-owned firms gained financial assistance after 1984, while the availability of such assistance sometimes influenced their further investment in the region (Collis and Roberts 1992: 119).

The recruitment of such firms must also be placed in a wider national and international context. By the early 1980s mass unemployment had become an instrument of British state policy, coupled with the first phases of deregulation and the enactment of restrictive anti-trade union laws, and against this background the Conservative government also viewed the encouragement of inward investment as a lever in changing established patterns of work and industrial relations. At the same time Japanese companies were extending their overseas investments to protect market access, and in so doing were capitalizing upon the financial inducements and labour market conditions available in the United Kingdom, especially in the older industrial regions. However, the character and implications of such national conditions were also mediated in important ways by locality. As noted earlier, national constraints on industrial recruitment strategies in the 1970s had pushed Telford to seek FDI, capitalizing upon the advantages of their location in the West Midlands and their capacity to provide greenfield sites. Meanwhile, the very difficulties which the TDC had faced in encouraging national relocation, coupled with the accelerated decline of traditional industries, had created favourable labour conditions for winning foreign investment. In this regard the continuing expansion of the New Town population as well as high unemployment underpinned the availability of an attractive workforce. By the mid-1980s a slack labour market then came to be accompanied by more favourable financial assistance, and the TDC built on this combination in its search for inward investment.

THE PATTERN OF FDI AND THE ROLE OF JAPANESE INWARD INVESTORS

During the recession of the early 1980s, state policy tolerated a massive decline in British manufacturing employment, from 8 million in the late 1970s to just over 4 million in the mid-1980s. This fuelled the highest levels of unemployment in OECD countries, but the economy was sustained by revenues from North Sea oil, avoiding recourse to an *active* industrial policy and reinforcing the neo-liberal politics of Thatcherism. In turn, Thatcherite policies eroded union autonomy and strengthened management prerogatives, while reinforcing such features of Britain's existing institutional inheritance as decentralized bargaining and an absence of collective employment rights (Edwards et al. 1992; Visser and Ruysseveldt 1996). In this context fierce competition to attract inward investment, both among local English development agencies and between Scottish and Welsh development agencies, fitted the neoliberal agenda and reinforced the long-standing role of foreign investment in Britain. Furthermore, foreign firms were encouraged to introduce new industrial relations policies and working practices, but these innovations were guided by corporate decisions and management preferences, without any steer from the national level. Thus the switch to foreign capital as a basis for rejuvenating British manufacturing should not be seen as a strategic industrial policy (Kim 1999: 117). From the early 1980s the government began to see attractions in an FDI route to recovery, but the reshaping of the industrial relations environment was largely about settling internal scores, not an effort to *prepare* for foreign investment as in some 'developmental states'. Nevertheless, in some older industrial districts and several new towns such as Telford, *new capital* became almost synonymous with *foreign capital* as inward investors accounted for a high proportion of manufacturing employment.

Table 6.1. ***Inward investors in Telford: establishments and employees by country, 1994–2002***

		United States	Germany	Japan	France	Others	Total
1994	Firms	41	28	22	15	37	143
	Employees	2,309	1,187	3,972	1,494	2,559	11,521
1996	Firms	40	29	21	16	41	147
	Employees	2,501	1,740	6,316	1,795	2,855	15,207
1998	Firms	40	30	16	18	48	152
	Employees	3,163	1,852	6,521	2,605	2,662	16,801
2000	Firms	42	36	15	17	39	149
	Employees	5,926	1,785	4,565	2,151	2,557	16,983
2002	Firms	42	32	18	21	41	154
	Employees	5,176	1,844	5,356	1,665	2,067	16,108

The TDC established liaison offices in the United States, West Germany, Japan, and France; all countries which became major sources of FDI in Telford (Table 6.1). While nineteen foreign investors had arrived in Telford before 1983, another ninety-seven came between 1983 and 1990, a period of rapidly growing inward investment. In the early 1990s firms continued to arrive, but at a slower rate, and 1995 marked the peak year with 163 FIEs in the town. Fifty-five of these were American, twenty-seven German, nineteen Japanese, seventeen French, and forty-five from elsewhere. Most were the result of new manufacturing investment, establishing new 'greenfield' facilities in the town. By 1995 these companies represented 5.4 per cent of the workplaces in Telford, but employed 12,719 employees, accounting for 20 per cent of total employment. Since 1995 the number of such firms has fluctuated at around about 150, as arrivals and departures have more or less balanced. However, the numbers employed in these firms continued to grow, to a peak of 16,983, accounting for around 23 per cent of local employment, in 2000. This suggests that after 1995 overall job growth came more from the internal expansion of existing firms than through new arrivals. The last available figures, for 2002, show 154 foreign companies in Telford, employing a total of 16,108 people, a slight drop since 2000 but still around 20 per cent of employment in the area.

While American and German companies have consistently outnumbered Japanese firms, many of the largest inward investors have been Japanese. In 1994 the average number of workers in the Japanese companies was 181, while the figures for American, German, and French firms were 56, 42, and 100 respectively. Of course, trends for average employees per firm by national ownership (Table 6.2) show the overall outcome of several processes, including growth and decline of existing firms, and

Table 6.2. ***Average employees per foreign firm in Telford by major countries, 1994–2002***

	Japan	United States	France	Germany
1994	181	56	100	42
1996	301	63	112	60
1998	408	79	145	62
2000	304	141	127	50
2002	298	123	79	58

entrances and exits of firms with different workforce numbers. Nevertheless they show that the average size of Japanese firms has remained substantially larger than those from the other main investing countries, though the Japanese average declined slightly from the late 1990s. The patterns for the other countries varied, with German workforces consistently small, the French average fluctuating, and American plants showing modest but uneven growth. The Japanese firms generated the largest aggregate employment among foreign-owned firms almost continuously throughout the period, only being overtaken by the smaller but more numerous American factories in 2000 before returning to pre-eminence in 2002, when they accounted for nearly 7 per cent of local jobs.

While the TDC always sought inward investment from the United States and Europe, they paid particular attention to Japan, being the only UK Development Corporation to establish a permanent office in Tokyo. They used the first major arrival, Maxell, as an 'ambassador' with other Japanese firms, and later published promotional literature in Japanese, focused on the experience of the initial cohort of arrivals. In 1990 this featured the nature of the labour force, reporting that inward investors had chosen Telford 'because it has a flexible, adaptable and enthusiastic workforce', while the 'young workforce in the newly built factories' had not inherited the 'harmful labour habits' of the past (quoted in Mann 1991: 27). These activities succeeded in gaining Telford the highest concentration of Japanese firms in a single town in the United Kingdom, and Japanese investment in the West Midlands became particularly concentrated there (Collis and Roberts 1992: 122). Table 6.3 lists the twenty-two Japanese firms that have operated in Telford over the past two decades, highlighting the largest workplaces in bold and indicating product lines, establishment dates, and whether they were still operating in 2002, our last census date.

These firms arrived in what the local Economic Development Unit (EDU) has since identified as several different 'waves'. The first wave, between 1981 and 1987, consisted mainly of large manufacturers, often with existing overseas subsidiaries but seeking a European production base prior to the formation of the Single European market in 1992. Firms

Table 6.3. ***Japanese firms in Telford***

Company	Product Line	Operating 2002	Established
Epson Telford	Printers & computers	Yes	1987
General Imaging Technology (UK)	Office consumables	Yes	1990
Hoshizaki	Ice-making machinery	Yes	1994
ICL	Computer consultancy	No	1990
IK Precision Co	Plastic injection moulding	Yes	1989
Inabata Europe SA	Chemical & plastic products consultants	Yes	1990
JRI Technologies	Interior trim for automotives	Yes	1989
Kiyokuni Europe	Precision pressings	Yes	1987
Makita Manufacturing Europe	Power tools manufacture	Yes	1989
Marusawa (Telford)	Metal shafts manufacturer	Yes	1989
Maxell (UK)	Video & audio tapes, floppy discs	Yes	1981
Mitutoyo (UK)	Measuring tools	Yes	1979
Denso Manufacturing	Automotive components	Yes	1990
NEC Technologies	Monitors, facsimile, mobile phones	Yes	1981
Nippon Express (UK)	Freight forwarding	No	1990
Ogihara Europe	Car body pressings	Yes	1995
Omron Telford	Control panels and PCB assemblers	No	1987
Ricoh (UK) Products	Photocopies and copier consumables	Yes	1983
Toyota Tsusho UK	Logistics & engineering support	Yes	1995
TP Mouldings	Plastic injection mouldings	Yes	2000
Yokohama HPT	Tyres	No	1990

(*Source*: Telford Development Corporation)

such as Maxell (1981), NEC (1981), Ricoh (1983), and Epson (1987), all large final assemblers who soon employed in excess of 500 staff, were part of this first wave. The second wave, between 1987 and 1990, consisted of smaller manufacturing firms, often supplying critical components to Japanese companies in Telford. They were suppliers to some of the large firms in Japan, and came as affiliate companies in the wake of such firms. This group included Kiyokuni (1987), Omron (1987), TP Consumables (1989), Marusawa (1989), IK Precision (1989), and JRI Technologies (1989). A third wave of firms, arriving in 1989 and 1990, were major manufacturing companies with existing overseas subsidiaries but needing a European base to supply growing markets. They included Makita (1989) and Denso (1990). One of the features of these later arrivals was that they entered an established Japanese manufacturing cluster, with established links and common conventions, so they were potentially able to 'learn from' existing players. These first three waves mirrored the wider pattern of growth of Japanese FDI in the United Kingdom and internationally (Elger and Smith 1994; Munday 1995), and our research includes firms from each of these phases of investment. A fourth wave of arrivals, from 1991 onwards, consisted of smaller, privately owned or specialist suppliers, including Mitutoyi (1991), Hoshizaki (1994), Toyota Tsusho (1995), and Ogihara (1995), each with small workforces.

Since the late 1990s some Japanese firms in Telford have experienced downsizing or closure, while others have continued to expand. In 1999, Omron, the first to leave Telford, closed its factory after eleven years (and established a new plant with a different product in nearby Dudley, transferring only a few staff). In 2002, Marusawa, a precision engineering company in Telford for thirteen years, closed with the loss of over fifty jobs, and in 2003, Mitutoyo, a precision instrument manufacturer, closed with similar job losses. The latter firms, as small high-end companies, had reportedly faced problems with shortages of skilled labour. IKP and TP Consumables (later TP Mouldings), both significant subcontractors to Epson, downsized operations in the late 1990s because of cost pressures and a decline in production at Epson. Others among the early arrivals, such as Maxell, Ricoh, and NEC, saw falls in employment as products reached the end of their life cycle and overseas competition intensified. Several companies downsized because of the strength of the pound, which altered parent company calculations about manufacturing in cheaper locations, such as Thailand, China, or Eastern Europe. However, some new Japanese investment also flowed into Telford. Denso, Makita, and Toyota Tsusho, all expanded operations through extensions to their existing sites, while others brought outsourced work in-house. Epson opened a call centre on site, creating 100 new jobs and retraining existing staff, while Orix, a financial services company, arrived in 2002. Overall, however, the pattern has been an uneven one, with growth, contraction, and further growth (see Tables 6.1 and 6.2).

So far, then, we have shown that during the 1980s the TDC pursued a strategy of economic development based largely on the recruitment of FDI, that it had appreciable success in this policy, and that Japanese firms played a major role, especially in terms of employment numbers. Before turning to a discussion of the management policies pursued by these firms, both individually and as a 'cluster', we now need to establish the broader parameters of the Telford labour market, which forms the evolving context in which these firms have operated but also reflects their impact.

EMPLOYMENT GROWTH AND THE OCCUPATIONAL STRUCTURE IN TELFORD

Employment growth in Telford has been dramatic: the number of employees more than doubled between 1968 and 2001, from 37,000 to 80,318 (Telford and Wrekin EDU 2004). However, population growth and employment growth did not always move together, so Telford also experienced very high unemployment during the 1980s, with a smaller peak in the early 1990s. Throughout the 1980s, at the time of the early waves of Japanese inward investment, unemployment in Telford was markedly higher than in the West Midlands or the country as a whole, peaking at 21.6 per cent in 1985, when the figure for the West Midlands was 16 per cent (Table 6.4). After a net loss of jobs in the early 1980s, more new jobs were created than

Table 6.4. ***Unemployment rates: Telford, West Midlands, and Great Britain, 1980–2002***

	Telford (%)	West Midlands (%)	Great Britain (%)	
1980	13.7	9.5	8.3	Narrow base
1981	20.9	15.1	12.2	
1982	20.9	15.8	12.7	
1983	20.9	16.0	13.1	
1984	21.4	15.9	13.4	
1985	21.6	16.0	13.6	
1986	20.5	14.4	12.1	
1987	15.4	11.5	10.1	
1988	11.3	8.9	7.6	Change to workforce based rate
1989	6.5	5.9	5.6	
1990	6.0	6.1	5.6	
1991	9.2	9.3	8.5	
1992	10.8	11.0	9.9	
1993	10.4	11.1	10.3	
1994	7.8	9.4	9.0	
1995	6.3	8.3	8.1	
1996	5.2	7.6	7.4	
1997	3.5	5.4	5.3	
1998	3.3	4.8	4.6	
1999	3.2	4.7	4.2	
2000	2.5	4.8	4.1	
2001	2.6	4.4	3.7	
2002	2.9	4.2	3.7	

were lost through the rest of the decade (Elger and Smith 1998*b*: 586), but a growing supply of labour meant this had little impact on the unemployment rate until 1987. As one TDC interviewee reported:

> by the middle 1980s we had started to recruit companies who were employing large numbers of people, yet the unemployment rate didn't seem to be shifting and didn't shift until 1985.... We began to despair around about the middle 1980s because we were getting these new jobs in, but the unemployment rate was still over 20%.... But eventually we started to build up firmer ground, and once the unemployment rate dipped below 20% in, I think, the latter part of 1985, it did then drop like a stone to bottom out at about 5% in 1990.

Thus the new firms arrived and began to recruit in the context of large scale unemployment and a plentiful supply of local labour, but their arrival itself contributed to an eventual decline in unemployment.

In the early 1990s the unemployment figures for Telford then converged with, and later fell below, the regional and national averages (Table 6.4). Even when unemployment peaked again at 10.8 per cent (calculated on a revised basis) in 1992 this was similar to levels elsewhere, and from 1994, Telford's figures remained below the wider averages while participating in a broader decline. By 1998, unemployment in Telford was 3.3 per cent, compared with 4.8 per cent across the West Midlands. In summary, continuing job creation had a delayed impact but Telford moved from an unemployment 'blackspot' in the 1980s to become a 'tight' labour market during the consolidation of Japanese inward investment in the late 1990s. This shift represents a critical context for our research, as we can explore the implications of high unemployment at the time of the arrival and initial operation of the first two waves of Japanese investors but also the ramifications of the move to a tighter labour market during our research.

Alongside these changes Telford also moved from being a net exporter of labour during the 1980s to become a net importer during the 1990s. Thus a Telford Development Agency (TDA) informant noted that 'in the early 1980s people streamed out of this town to work in Wolverhampton and the Black Country. [But in the mid-1990s], it rather pulls people in from the surrounding market towns within rural Shropshire, and from the wider West Midland conurbation'. The TDC and its successors always advertised the availability of wider pools of labour beyond the district (in 2002 they indicated that an economically active population of 325,883 lived within thirty minutes commute from Telford), and by the mid-1990s almost 30 per cent of the working population in the town were in-commuters, a percentage that remains similar today. Such commuters included not only managers and skilled workers but also operators, who were often bussed-in by firms to relieve recruitment difficulties within the town. It remains important, however, to look at the character of the jobs which have been created through the success of the TDC policy of recruiting FIEs, and also at the evolving dynamics of this increasingly buoyant labour market.

Table 6.5. ***Manufacturing as a percentage of employment: Telford, West Midlands, and Great Britain, 1980–2002***

	Telford (%)	West Midlands (%)	Great Britain (%)
1994	45.8	28.3	20.2
1996	43.0	26.1	18.1
1998	40.0	30.0	20.0
2000	32.1	22.9	16.1
2002	28.1	19.4	13.9

The vast majority of the FIEs in Telford have been manufacturers and this has helped to sustain a distinctive feature of the local economy, namely the persistent importance of manufacturing employment. As elsewhere in Britain, there has been a substantial long-term decline in the percentage employed in manufacturing, with matching growth in the proportion of service sector employment. But in 1994, Telford was quite disproportionately dependent on manufacturing, with 46 per cent of jobs, compared with 28 per cent across the West Midlands and 20 per cent across Great Britain. As Table 6.5 shows, the proportion of jobs in manufacturing in Telford fell a little more rapidly than the regional and national figures in the mid-1990s, then paralleled the regional and national decline more recently, marking a substantial shift to service employment. However, in 2002, Telford still had 28 per cent of jobs in manufacturing, double the national average. Meanwhile, the gender composition of manufacturing employment has remained predominantly male (66.8 per cent in 1994, increasing to 71 per cent in 2002), though men also increased their involvement in the growing service sector (from 41.6 per cent to 46 per cent), against a background of relative stability in the overall ratio of men and women employed in the town.

The continuing relative importance of manufacturing has been attributed to 'the steady inflow and expansion of modern companies in the automotive components, electronic and polymer sectors' (Telford and Wrekin EDU 2004: 11). In turn, this reflected a clear TDC policy of targeting manufacturing, and particularly labour-intensive manufacturing. The intention was to capitalize upon the existing pool of relatively unskilled and cheap labour and to secure a substantial and sustained jobs yield. As one of our TDC informants in the late 1990s argued, the policy could be judged a success in these terms:

> That was a decision that we made when we had 20 or 25 per cent unemployment, that we should go for manufacturing companies . . . we were looking for jobs that were going to stay—discarding the warehousing element—and it actually worked. Because this time when we had the recession in the early

> '90s we did not suffer as a town anything like the region as a whole.... What happened was that a lot of the companies stayed here, they just reduced their workforce, they didn't up and go.

As this suggests, the success of the TDC in attracting manufacturers, and especially foreign manufacturers, made a substantial contribution to employment in the town through the 1990s and beyond. Nevertheless the decline of manufacturing from the mid-1990s was absolute as well as relative, with a loss of 6,446 jobs between 1994 and 2002, while service employment grew by 23,020.

Telford, then, was a locality that grew rapidly in both population and employment; that moved from disproportionately high unemployment in the 1980s to comparatively low unemployment from the mid-1990s; and in which FDI played a central role in sustaining an important place for manufacturing, despite a substantial shift towards service sector jobs. It remains important, however, to look in more detail at the character of employment in Telford, in terms of skills, occupations, and wages.

LOW SKILL, LOW WAGE EMPLOYMENT

In 1995, 36 per cent of employees in Telford, 25,500 people, worked in operative and unskilled jobs, when the figure for Britain as a whole was 18 per cent, prompting the TDC to acknowledge that a disproportionate number of jobs were 'concentrated in the sales, operatives, and unskilled occupation categories' (TDA 1997: 14). In 2002, it remained the case that 'a high proportion of jobs are concentrated in the operatives and unskilled occupational categories', 34.5 per cent in Telford compared with 20 per cent for Britain (Telford and Wrekin EDU 2004: 12). By the late 1990s, TDA officials were pointing to a modest growth in professional employment associated with the recent relocation of service sector firms, and the latest workforce survey notes that 'the percentage of managerial and professional [jobs] continues to move towards the national average' (Telford and Wrekin EDU 2004: 12). Nevertheless, a substantial concentration of semi-skilled and unskilled jobs remains a characteristic feature of the Telford labour market.

This was already an established feature of the locality before the investment and growth of the 1980s and 1990s (Waye 1983: 23–5), while the persistence of this pattern during the expansion of service employment suggests it is not simply a feature of manufacturing. However, the pursuit of routine, labour-intensive manufacturing investment appears to have reinforced this pattern. As a council document candidly commented, 'the nature of much modern manufacturing work is that to a large extent jobs have been deskilled. A consequence of this is that fewer employees have sufficient work-related qualifications to be classed as a craftsperson or even as a technician' (Wrekin Council 1996: 10). TDA officials also recognized that many of the larger manufacturing FIEs 'basically employ a large proportion of assembly type workers'. Indeed, among Japanese companies 70 per cent of employees were classified as operatives or unskilled at the time of our research, covering 59 per cent of men and 82 per cent of women (unpublished survey data provided in interview). Officials hoped that 'some of the earlier Japanese companies are starting to introduce more skills now they have got their basic assembly lines up and running', but our own research suggested this was quite limited during the 1990s.

Another established feature of the local labour market which was reinforced by the dynamic of inward investment was low wages. Telford had a long-standing reputation for low wages compared with the West Midlands conurbation, and several of our informants talked of the area as retaining some of the features of a semi-rural economy in this regard, though some of the older major employers, such as GKN, had the reputation of paying much closer to the Midlands rate. Documenting this pattern in the early 1980s, Waye (1983: 34) reported that TDC officials regarded their role as 'to attract industry to the area irrespective of rates of pay', while 'many of the employers in the town who are tenants on the industrial estates are continuing to pay low wage rates'.

While the press reported bluntly that 'wage rates are among the lowest in the country' (Seton 1994), our informants with experience of recruiting inward investors highlighted their emphasis on an abundant and flexible supply of labour rather than low wages. One commented that the relatively low wages in the area 'could have been sensitive, and was not something which we majored on, but I guess that companies would have done their own research and I guess that is what they would have found'. Another reiterated the dilemmas perceived by such officials:

> We do not promote this town, in the sense of 'come here and you can pay your staff less and make more profit', because we don't want to attract low-wage, unskilled jobs . . . [and] I'd be surprised if they led on low wages [in the early 1980s]. Remember the days when we had 23 per cent unemployment. If you're given a choice between a hundred low paid, low skilled jobs or nothing, you're going to take the jobs . . . There's a macroeconomic argument, the more jobs you can pull into the town, the more demand for labour goes up, the higher the wage rate goes.

Despite an undoubtedly tighter labour market, however, Telford in the later 1990s was still characterized by comparatively low pay. Data for 1996, during our fieldwork, suggested wages averaged 17 per cent lower for manual workers and 21 per cent lower for non-manual workers, compared with south-east England. Starter wages for assembly workers in manufacturing were between £3.30 and £4.10 per hour, averaging £3.70. Among the larger employers, especially, wages could rise with length of service, attendance allowances, seniority pay or upgrading within internal labour markets, but such rises were generally modest and still left basic pay very low. For indirect manual workers, such as security guards, wages could be below £3.00 per hour. For supervisory and junior managerial grades, wage rates were at least a third less than those paid for equivalent work in older areas of the West Midlands.

Furthermore, inward investors were not just passive recipients of this pattern, but actively contributed to its maintenance. In particular, wage rates and related costs were key concerns in meetings of managing directors (MDs) from the larger Japanese firms, and they acted in concert to monitor and limit departures from established patterns. While this policy came under pressure from some of the firms towards the end of the 1990s, it remained true that the inward investors both occupied and helped to consolidate a labour market dominated by routine, low wage manufacturing jobs.

Such features of the Japanese inward investors (and the wider Telford labour market) were paralleled, though perhaps in a less clear-cut fashion, among several clusters of Japanese firms in old industrial regions of Britain. For example, Morris et al. (1993: 24, 44) avoid any overall characterization of skill trends among Japanese firms in South Wales, but note that 'the majority of the jobs could be described as being of a semi-skilled nature'. However, the Japanese workplaces in Telford stand apart from those in such areas in terms of industrial relations arrangements. Whereas all but one of the Japanese companies in South Wales eventually recognized a trade union, none of the companies in Telford does so. In this respect, Telford is similar to some New Towns (like Milton Keynes and Livingstone), but Japanese firms in others (like Newton Aycliffe and Washington) have recognized unions, so it is not simply a New Town effect. Indeed, trade unions apparently played a significant though subordinate role in the initial recruitment of FIEs to Telford, before being excluded from the new factories, so the evolving role of organized labour in the locality requires further discussion.

THE ROLE OF THE UNIONS AND THE EXCLUSION OF ORGANIZED LABOUR

Organized trade unionism and formal industrial relations in Telford were largely phenomena of the twentieth century, despite the long industrial history of the area (Trinder 1973). Unions appear to have gained ground on the coat-tails of developments in Birmingham and the Black Country, but they remained relatively weak into the post-war years. By the 1960s, workplace trade unionism and shop-steward organization were established features at the larger employers (Waye 1983: 11, 44–52), and union membership expanded during much of the 1970s, but in retrospect TDC officials regarded the area as non-militant (Waye 1983: 69). Nevertheless, the inflated fears which many overseas managers harboured about British trade unionism led the TDC to make considerable efforts to reassure potential inward investors. They publicized the low number of working days lost through industrial disputes in the district and arranged face-to-face meetings between inward investors and union officials to communicate their commitment and 'responsibility'. One union official of the time felt the agenda of the TDC was to show that 'everything in the garden was friendly', while a TDC official reflected that:

> here locally the unions have always been absolutely superb, very supportive. We used to, in those early days, introduce prospective overseas companies to representatives of the local union . . . And they were fine, very realistic people, sensible, looking forward.

However, this helpful stance was not translated into union recognition, even of the constrained sort associated with the 'Single Union Deals' and 'beauty contests' characteristic of recognition by Japanese companies elsewhere (Wilkinson et al. 1993).

Machin's (2000) wider findings on the predominance of union exclusion in new plants established across Britain from the mid-1980s suggest this was not simply a product of the New Town setting, but reflected the changed economic and political environment. Thus Waye (1983: 38, 48–50, 59–60) notes that in the early 1980s, in the context of high unemployment and government hostility towards trade unions, employers in Telford became increasingly resistant to union organization, as evidenced by an increase in recognition disputes, tactics designed to undermine organizing campaigns and withdrawal of recognition in some smaller firms. Meanwhile many centres of union strength suffered large-scale redundancies, sometimes falling disproportionately on union activists. This was the climate in which the first Japanese company was courted by the TDA and, despite several rounds of discussions with union officials, decided that 'we basically desired to operate our factory without labour unions, if possible, in the future as well' (Nagai 1985: 8).

In turn, this set the pattern for later Japanese arrivals. A TDC survey of fifty-one British and thirty-five FIEs captured the emergent pattern in 1985, showing both a declining likelihood of unionization and a lower union presence among later inward investors. While 37 per cent of British companies recognized unions, only 20 per cent of FIEs did so, and the disparity was most marked among companies employing more than 100 people (with 66 per cent of British firms unionized but only 29 per cent of FIEs). Furthermore, union recognition was substantial among both British and foreign firms in the traditional engineering sector, but it was entirely absent among companies from the modern sectors of polymers and plastics, electronics and electrical assembly. Finally, among FIEs, German subsidiaries were most likely to recognize unions, American companies were much less likely to, and neither of the Japanese arrivals had done so. Thus a new pattern of industrial relations was developing in Telford, and this has been sustained through into the new century.

There are competing accounts of the circumstances surrounding the capacity of so many inward investing companies to avoid union recognition. TDC officials suggested that employees were disinclined to join unions when given the opportunity, because of earlier negative experiences with unions or because of the effectiveness of the alternative consultative processes in place. In our four case-study companies, however, the small minority of employees who expressed antipathy towards unions was more than offset by another minority who were union-minded, though many workers remained agnostic and younger workers often had no direct experience of unions. Furthermore, employees in these firms voiced a varied range of shop-floor grievances (not least regarding low wages) and there was widespread dissatisfaction with the failings of consultative procedures, though this sometimes coexisted with appreciation of paternalistic management concern for individual employee welfare. Finally, it was widely believed that Japanese companies would not tolerate trade unions, and at one factory (which had been leafleted by outside union activists after encouragement from a section of the workforce) management had gently threatened that the price of union recognition would be the ending of a tacit commitment to job security (see Chapter 11).

This suggests that, in an economic and political context where, as one union official remarked, 'boat-rockers were in short supply', managements actively played upon uncertainties, fears, and divisions among employees to maintain union exclusion. At the same time, however, there was little evidence of a concerted union challenge to this pattern, and unlike in Wales, no political or institutional pressures at a state level to ensure trade unions maintained a presence in the new factories. After the initial failure of efforts to 'organize from above', unions found themselves increasingly pressed for resources (several local union offices closed in the 1990s), beset by challenges in their existing centres of organization and confronted by companies and workplaces which differed significantly from those where trade unionism had traditionally operated. In these circumstances the unions appear to have made few efforts to actively 'organize from below'.

Thus, unlike in South Wales, organized labour was not an active political agent in the remaking of employment relations in Telford. Unions were tentatively involved in TDC overtures to early Japanese investors but then rapidly marginalized, and appeared unable to respond when incoming firms rebuffed their requests for opportunities to recruit and represent employees. Meanwhile, management continued to exercise its powerful role within the workplace and upon employment relations—in structuring tasks, instituting flexibility, and sustaining low wages. As we have seen, the flow of inward investment into Telford has created relatively secure jobs, but in workplaces characterized by low paid, low skilled, non-union labour with little collective voice. These are all features which appear to be associated with unrelieved management hegemony. However, the situation has been more problematical and contradictory for employers than this suggests.

GREENFIELD WORKPLACES AND THE LIMITS OF MANAGEMENT HEGEMONY

Having chosen a location with a plentiful labour supply and excluded trade unions, the first Japanese arrival (Maxell) sought to transfer many aspects of their Japanese operations to the new site. An early study reported that

> Maxell has given a great deal of effort to developing a replica of its Japanese parent factory in Telford. This includes the technology in manufacturing, much of the social organisation of production, training policy as well as management–labour practices. Most machinery was duplicated from the parent plant at Kyoto. The key local staff were sent to the parent factory in Japan for training. (Mann 1991: 31)

In many respects the firm embodied stereotypical features of the Japanese greenfield 'transplant'. They called employees 'members', used the language of 'family' to characterize social relations in the workplace, established company uniforms for all, a single-status canteen, a works council, and an open-plan office. They instituted morning exercises and appraisal pay, used few job classifications, and emphasized the flexible deployment of labour. They pursued a preference for recruiting young workers for shop-floor jobs, whilst offering the prospect of advancement within an internal labour market. Finally they offered employment security but also sought to screen potential employees systematically.

As new Japanese investors arrived in the town in the second half of the 1980s Maxell represented an influential model, particularly for the larger firms. Not only was its approach to wages and non-unionism accepted, but its emphasis on single status, flexibility, and the recruitment of a youthful workforce encouraged the new arrivals to adopt similar policies. The development of an informal network and a formal MD's forum, attended by the larger Japanese firms, further consolidated a common approach to personnel matters, not only by monitoring wage costs but also by implementing an understanding that employees would not be allowed to move directly between these companies (Elger and Smith 1998*b*).

However, important aspects of this model, especially the recruitment of a youthful workforce but also aspects of labour discipline, quite rapidly came under pressure, even in the conditions of high unemployment which still prevailed in the mid-1980s. In this sense the policy of implementing a Japanese model of work and employment relations faced important limitations. Furthermore, the very success of the TDC policy placed some aspects of such employment relations under particular strain by the late 1980s, as unemployment declined, employees grew bored with poorly paid routine assembly work, and labour turnover became a major method of expressing discontent. Finally, in the 1990s, the substantial expansion of several of these Japanese firms placed further pressure on a tightening labour market. Thus the complex interaction between the employment regimes *within* particular Japanese companies and external labour market conditions moved through several phases, but we can reconstruct some of the key features from the vantage point of our case-study plants, information from local agencies and the labour market histories of our workplace informants.

Initially, high unemployment provided the context for a multitude of job applicants and systematic recruitment and selection procedures by the early Japanese investors, intended to create a young, inexperienced, pliable, and responsive 'green' workforce. One attraction of the New Town was that the age structure of the population promised a large pool of young workers, a feature highlighted by the TDC. Such workers seemed to offer inward investors cheapness, dependability, and control—thus minimizing labour's organizing and voice capability and maximizing management's power in the employment relationship. At this stage these Japanese firms appeared to conform to the pattern documented elsewhere, in South Wales and in the United States: they utilized quite rigid selection criteria, limited recruitment to young workers, and aimed to reproduce home country institutional arrangements within their 'transplants'. However, even at an early stage these firms are reported to have experienced high levels of labour turnover and absenteeism among such workers.

Thus a primary focus upon building a young workforce came to be experienced as a problem of (a) recruitment (as young women workers in particular appeared to be in short supply), (b) 'indiscipline' (especially in relation to punctuality and 'application'), and (c) retention (as people moved on). On the one hand the jobs at the new factories of the 1980s appeared somewhat different (both more intense and lighter) compared with entry jobs in British companies. On the other hand, as we have seen, the work on offer across the 'greenfield' plants was generally quite similar—routine assembly jobs at low wages. Since jobs were equivalent and the costs of exit were low, even minor differences in wages or conflicts at work could encourage workers to leave. The high proportion of young workers with relatively few obligations, coupled with the limits of alternative channels of representation, appear to have amplified this response.

As more Japanese firms arrived, one of their shared responses was to cooperate in the unofficial but widely known non-poaching policy, intended to discourage workers from seeking to move from plant to plant and thus encourage labour stability, but while this constrained the labour market options of workers it did little to solve the turnover problem. One of our informants captured a widespread management perception of these difficulties:

> We talked to the Job Centre in [the] early days when we got here, to try and find out what was happening. All we could hear was everyone was suffering from the same sort of thing... the person I was talking to at the Job Centre said 'Oh, we class it as the herd of wildebeest syndrome at Telford', and they reckoned that there were about 5,000 wildebeest just sort of swaying around [from one plant to another].

From the comments of our respondents, all Japanese firms experienced similar problems, as their matrix of wages, conditions, and internal management regimes proved incapable of retaining and developing a large core of stable employees. Furthermore, both labour turnover and indiscipline on the line were experienced as especially disruptive in the context of the tight manning levels, tough quality targets, and stringent production schedules which often characterized these firms. Thus the attempts of Japanese managers to construct key aspects of the Japanese employment system proved extremely difficult to sustain, especially when external labour market conditions improved and made labour mobility easier. Far from being particularly loyal or committed, such workers maintained an instrumental orientation to work and a willingness to leave in response to grievances or just because they wanted a change. As one of the case studies in Chapter 7 demonstrates, in these conditions British managers were in a powerful position to offer arguments against Japanese approaches which were experienced as failing.

One response was a growing use of temporary workers, not as a strategy to stratify the workforce into core and periphery, but rather as a piecemeal response to recruitment difficulties or production uncertainties (Elger and Smith 1998*b*: 598–600). Some managers had reservations about the cost or flexibility of temps, but most made some use of Temporary Employment Agencies and there was a dramatic growth of such agencies in Telford, from one in 1979 to twenty-one by 1996. Furthermore, managers who had used these agencies often found them useful as filters in recruiting employees, so their role became institutionalized in many firms, reducing fringe benefits, keeping entry wages low, and significantly extending probationary periods. In the mid-1990s most agencies in Telford served the manufacturing sector while agency workers were predominantly unskilled young men performing routine assembly jobs (Clark 1996; Jones 1996). Given the non-poaching policy, temping could offer opportunities to sample work in different workplaces, but the predominant objective of temps was to escape unemployment, to gain an immediate salary and work experience (Forde 1997, 2001). By the late 1990s, however, a tighter labour market meant that fewer workers would accept temporary contracts, and the competing agencies were reported as 'struggling for business'.

Meanwhile, managers in these factories also sought to stabilize their permanent workforces in a variety of ways. Most elaborated their checks on attendance and absence, with associated bonuses and penalties; some developed more explicit training arrangements and promotion pathways; some offered extensive overtime to compensate for poor basic wages; and several sponsored sports and social clubs in a bid to retain employees. The main response, however, was to widen recruitment away from reliance upon young people, though the extent and the emphasis of this move differed between companies. The most common move was a shift in recruitment towards older workers, especially mature women (a development also noted in South Wales, by Morris et al. 1993: 80–1). This was largely a result of British management suggestions, *against* the preferences of Japanese managers who were sceptical that older workers would accept flexibility or cope with the pace of the line. One TDC informant in the mid-1990s suggested that, among the large firms, there was a clear correlation between the subordinate role of British personnel managers, a reluctance to move away from recruiting young workers and continuing problems of high labour turnover. Meanwhile our company informants generally believed that the presence of older workers had a 'calming' effect on labour turnover and work culture, and this approach became the norm among later investors who sought to learn from the experience of earlier arrivals. Some companies also searched for new pools of labour in areas of high unemployment, by bussing-in workers from outside Telford, or in one case through the creation of a satellite factory and the use of home workers on sub-assemblies (see Chapters 7 and 8).

There was thus a switch from seeking to 'build in' worker diligence and commitment, by recruiting young workers and moulding their attitudes and conduct, to trying to 'buy in' the required attitudes and behaviour (particularly a basic work ethic of attendance, obeying orders, and not quitting) by recruiting older, experienced workers. A more marked development of internal job ladders coincided with these moves, especially after the recession of the early 1990s, with efforts to place loyal and experienced workers in senior operator and supervisory positions. Such policies resulted in an increasing average job tenure and age of employees, as they settled into the benefits of being in one company or worried about the negative consequences of leaving and starting at the bottom again. However, while the increased recruitment of older workers helped to alleviate problems of attendance, discipline, and turnover, there were also costs for management. On the one hand the previous employment experience of such workers had generally habituated them to patterns of 'responsibility' and work discipline. They had often experienced the employment insecurities or redundancies associated with restructuring, evoking 'gratitude' at having regained employment. They also tended to have more to lose than younger workers, who could switch jobs more easily and sometimes had fewer family responsibilities. On the other hand, however, the employment histories which mature workers brought with them into the new workplace provided benchmarks of fairness and equity which were not always matched by management policies, and they were more likely than younger workers to articulate their dissatisfactions in these terms.

Since the different factories varied somewhat in terms of pay systems, supervisory practices and production pressures, the interplay between management policies and worker expectations in different workplaces generated an uneven profile of dissatisfactions. Nevertheless, they commonly embraced such themes as disparities between limited rewards and high levels of effort, unfairnesses in the operation of appraisals or promotion procedures, an inadequate responsiveness to shop-floor concerns, or inappropriate expectations of enthusiastic participation in activities like QCCs. Our evidence suggests that, though such grievances often remained private, older workers were more likely to voice them rather than deciding to quit, sometimes even acting as 'surrogate shop-stewards' in the absence of trade unions. Thus these workers were more likely both to 'buckle-down' to their work and to 'resist' those aspects they experienced as most irksome. In this regard they not only drew upon their wider experience to judge both the positive and negative features of their present employment, but could also appeal to the authority of age and experience to challenge younger supervisors or managers (see Chapter 11).

The expansion of several of the larger inward investors in the late 1990s, coupled with the broader economic upturn, worked against the stabilization of the workforce by creating more external job opportunities and encouraging significant job hopping. Thus labour turnover at many of the factories remained relatively high while recruitment became more difficult (Elger and Smith 1998*a*: 191). The persistence of a narrow band of wages for work at these companies, despite the fall in unemployment, suggests that employer liaison and mutual monitoring continued to deliver substantial employer control over wage pressures in the local economy. However, there was also evidence that the wage cartel was becoming more difficult to sustain, especially in periods when firms recruited substantial numbers of new workers. Such circumstances prompted debate in some firms about the scope for wage increases. Still, even managers in companies with scope to make such a move were very conscious of the risks of bidding up wages, and looked for ways of finessing the old norms and repositioning themselves in the local wage hierarchy whilst minimizing such risks. By the end of the 1990s managers talked of the non-poaching agreement as a thing of the past, eroded by labour market pressures, though many workers still believed that it operated.

Such pressures were, of course, concomitants of the very success of the prolonged phase of FDI-led growth in Telford, but serve as reminders of the uncertainties which still accompany such a growth trajectory. Finally, we would add that there is no need to embrace an uncritical 'globalization' thesis to appreciate the ways in which Telford's growth strategy, based so heavily on the labour-intensive branch-plant operations of international companies clustered in a small number of manufacturing sectors, also remains vulnerable to corporate rationalization and the reconfiguration of production operations across countries and localities. The risks are already evident in a small way in the oscillations in staffing levels in some of the large Japanese plants and the closure of several of the smaller factories.

CONCLUSION

This chapter has shown that during the 1980s, the TDA sought to constitute Telford New Town as a new production space attractive to foreign manufacturing firms. In key respects Telford was constructed as a 'greenfield site', as newly arriving firms occupied new factories in a new town with new workforces. However, we have also suggested that the character and implications of the construction of this new production space cannot be understood just in terms of these new settings, in which managers and workers engaged on new terms.

First, the scope for innovation in this setting was also conditioned by some long-standing features of the British 'production system' and employment relations, especially the relatively unregulated character of the labour market and the highly fragmented and decentralized character of industrial relations. Such features have long afforded inward investors and the managers of new production sites more latitude for autonomous policy making than has been the case in more strongly regulated or centrally bargained employment systems.

Second, however, the character of such relative autonomy was also strongly conditioned by major changes in the British political and economic terrain presided over by Thatcherism. The 1980s saw a profound shift in the balance of power in employment relations, with the reinforcement of managerial prerogatives and the erosion of union leverage and organization, though these changes did not simply reflect the Thatcherite political project, which itself embraced unresolved tensions (Edwards et al. 1992; Marsh 1992; Smith and Morton 1993). These developments enhanced the scope for new and varied management initiatives, while reinforcing the attractions of relatively low-skill, low-pay, labour-intensive routes to manufacturing competitiveness (Ackroyd and Procter 1998; Elger 1999; Almond and Rubery 2000). This, then, was the context in which Japanese investors arriving in Telford avoided union recognition, paralleling developments in many other newly established workplaces during this period elsewhere in the country (Machin 2000). It was also the context in which inward investors, responding to the efforts of the TDC, established production operations that generated many jobs but also fed off and reinforced an emphasis on lowly paid, semi-skilled, routine machining and assembly work in the district.

At the same time another key argument of this chapter has been that managers have still faced important constraints and challenges in 'greenfield' Telford, which have modified and reshaped the ways in which work and employment relations have been organized in these factories. In part this arose because an initial preference for the recruitment of young workers confronted the volatility of such workers when faced with the exigencies of tightly paced, routine and disciplined factory work. However, it also arose because the very success of the TDA policy of attracting inward investment, and the later expansion of some of these operations, contributed to a tightening of the local labour market. In these circumstances, and coupled with the absence of union recognition or other effective collective voice mechanisms, worker dissatisfactions were reflected in turnover, absenteeism or a lack of commitment to discretionary activities such as 'continuous improvement'.

In some respects these responses may themselves be regarded as echoing long-standing strands of instrumentalism, and scepticism about management policies, among British employees and, as elsewhere, they were also interwoven with more positive and cooperative responses. Again, however, we wish to suggest that the persistent importance of labour turnover, however amplified by the circumstances of new start-ups or fresh phases of expansion, also represented something of a distinctive response to wider features of the new 'greenfield' production space created in Telford. In particular, such turnover represents a predictable response to the availability of a range of rather similar, though subtly different, work opportunities within routine manufacturing operations (and now perhaps within routine service work), coupled with a lack of effective channels for the collective articulation of grievances, especially in a relatively tight labour market. Clearly, we cannot simply extrapolate from Telford to other new production spaces, because particular political, economic and social conditions (with both temporal and geographical specificities) have influenced the forms taken by factory regimes and the patterning of the wider labour market in the town. However, we would expect that similar patterns of labour turnover will arise where other new production spaces are constructed in similar ways and generate similar conditions, notwithstanding the costs and limitations of such responses for workers themselves.

A final important feature that emerges from our discussion concerns the relationships among the inward investors themselves. As we have noted, the managers of new Japanese arrivals were not only influenced by the experiences of existing firms, they also joined a group of enterprises that in important respects monitored one another and sought to coordinate their management of the local labour market, especially in such matters as wage rates, labour costs, and other personnel policies. Thus these firms became participants in a *cluster* of firms, united primarily by a shared labour market and common management problems, rather than the value-chain linkages characteristic of local production *complexes* (Ruigrok and van Tulder 1995). The firms differed in their influence over such concertation. In particular, the larger firms were most directly involved, while the smaller firms participated at one remove, as subordinate partners with limited influence. Furthermore, these firms also varied in some of their priorities. A major argument in later chapters is that even the larger subsidiaries operated in distinctive corporate and sectoral contexts, while management coalitions and policies evolved differently within each workplace. Nevertheless, the formal and informal linkages between these firms served as a basis for wielding significant influence as a cluster, evident especially in their capacity to sustain relatively low pay rates across the firms even in tightening labour market conditions.

Such influence represented an important constraint on the actions of managers in specific firms. While managers debated how to finesse agreed policies, and sometimes sought to justify and gain approval for departures from established practice, the consensus on key issues had considerable force. Furthermore, this was not based on the presence of one dominant firm, as is often the case in local production complexes, and it did not involve a differentiation between higher-paying 'sophisticated paternalists' and lower-paying 'standard moderns', as noted by Findlay's (1993) study of the Central Scotland electronic assembly industry. In this sense we should regard this coordinated cluster of firms as an important actor in the construction of this new production space, qualifying any emphasis on the autonomy of the managers of specific 'greenfield' factories.

However, there were also significant limits to the capacity of such concertation to control developments in this new space. In part, these arose from the limited reach of such coordination, as the wider dynamics of a buoyant labour market made it increasingly difficult to sustain such arrangements as the no-poaching policy. In part they arose from internal tensions among companies that had different priorities in coping with the intractable features of labour management in the area, as was particularly evident in continuing discussions in some firms about making a break from the wage norms set by the cluster. In all these respects, then, Telford offered real opportunities for innovation by new firms operating on new sites with new workforces, but neither the development strategy of the local state nor the concertation of policies among the cluster of Japanese companies delivered an unproblematical management hegemony as they sought to manage their 'greenfield' sites.

CHAPTER

7

Work and Employment Relations in Large Assembly Firms: 'Good Enough' Production Despite Problematical Employment Relations

INTRODUCTION

Two of our large firm case studies were taken from among the half dozen larger Japanese factories in Telford. Both were engaged in a range of manufacturing processes to produce electrical goods and both were dominant in their sector, but operated in different segments of this diverse market. Copy-Co was a relatively early arrival in Telford and, by the time of our research, had reached a relatively steady state in terms of both production and employment. Part-Co was a more recent arrival, but was expanding substantially and has continued to do so over the following years. Thus this chapter considers the organization of production and employment relations in two factories that could be expected to transplant production operations fairly directly from well-organized and successful home plants. They might also be expected to utilize a hybridized pattern of personnel policies to support these production operations, but one that was 'functionally equivalent' to personnel policies in Japan.

In line with our argument in Chapter 6, however, our research found that in both subsidiaries, management efforts to translate and adapt production processes and personnel policies faced signficant problems and complexities. Thus our research suggests that the permissive character of a greenfield location, some distance from large industrial conurbations and in a lightly regulated national labour market, did not automatically facilitate the transfer of policies from the home factories of these leading

Japanese companies, even in a period when Japanese manufacturing was internationally pre-eminent.

These companies shared important similarities. Many jobs in both firms involved routinized production work, while managers faced substantial challenges in recruiting workers and gaining the commitment of their workforces. Despite the rhetoric of unitarism and the absence of trade unions, most employees in these firms remained predominantly instrumental in their approach to work and sceptical about the meaningfulness of the forms of involvement on offer, and this translated particularly into significant labour turnover and qualified commitment on the shop-floor. These responses were underpinned by a widespread assessment that wages for the work at these firms were relatively low and certainly failed to set them apart from similar jobs elsewhere in the district, though job security was valued, especially by longer service workers.

These features influenced the ways in which managers at these firms implemented and adapted their production arrangements, encouraging extensive 'foolproofing' of job designs and circumspection in the involvement of operators in continuous improvement, though other commercial and production imperatives, especially the variety of products and limited automation, also had a bearing on these outcomes. Thus managers in these enterprises were engaged in debate and experimentation, in which British managers claimed particular expertise in the management of local labour while Japanese managers retained primacy in the implementation of technical innovations. The resulting policies did not resolve the problematical features of employment relations, but did succeed in sustaining production regimes that delivered acceptable levels of productivity and financial returns for the parent companies. In this sense both these firms were characterized by 'good enough' production, despite the difficulties they faced.

However, there were also significant differences between the two factories, in corporate strategies, employment relations, and patterns of work organization. This suggests that we should be cautious in generalizing about practices and experiences even across the larger companies in this cluster, let alone the smaller companies to be discussed in Chapter 8. First, the two firms differed in the balance of power and initiative between Japanese and British managers, with a more central role for British managers at Copy-Co than at Part-Co. The earlier establishment and longer history of Copy-Co may have influenced this, but the distinctive roles of the two subsidiaries within their parent firms also coloured these relationships within management. Second, the problems faced by managers in coping with worker instrumentalism and labour turnover were more acute at Part-Co than at Copy-Co. Again this was influenced by the rapid expansion of the more recent arrival, but it was also linked to the more stringent demands of its production process, again reflecting distinctive sector and firm dynamics. Finally, however, the continuing expansion of Part-Co had sustained more scope for the progress of key workers within the internal labour market, while the relative stability of Copy-Co, combined with management efforts to recast supervisory relations, had precipitated a crisis in such internal progression. These differences had particular salience for the distinctive outlooks of the team leaders as they performed their pivotal roles within each workplace.

Our analysis in this chapter seeks, therefore, to combine an understanding of the commonalities across these workplaces with an exploration and explanation of significant variations around such common themes. In so doing it tries to explain the specific processes through which work and employment relations in these factories were actively constructed by Japanese and British managers, in ways that move beyond the common metaphors of transplantation, dilution, or hybridization. First, we show that production and employment arrangements drawn from parent plants and sister subsidiaries were selected and modified in ways that were influenced not only by existing workforce characteristics and responses but also by the distinctive roles of the branch plants within their wider firms. Second, we suggest that managers in these factories continued to face quite significant difficulties in the management of labour. This prompted continuing efforts to recast work and employment relations, even as managers succeeded in delivering sufficient production and profitability to sustain the subsidiary. Finally, we argue that differences between the two case-study factories were not simply a reflection of differences in their age, but also indicate the importance of sector and firm effects that should be central to our understanding of the operations of Japanese (and indeed other) inward investors. In exploring these features we will begin by discussing developments at Copy-Co because it arrived earlier and thus provides a longer history of translation, implementation, and adaptation of management policies.

COPY-CO: TENSIONS AND DILEMMAS IN THE MAKING OF A DISTINCTIVE LOCALIZED PRODUCTION REGIME

Corporate internationalization, regionalized manufacturing, and 'localization'

Copy-Co is one of the dominant firms in its sector in Japan and a leading player internationally, very successful in developing its products for the home market and a sector pioneer of new quality regimes in production. It started overseas production in the early 1970s and steadily increased the number of its factories in East Asia, the United States, and Europe through the 1980s. The establishment of British production at Telford in the mid-1980s reflected both the push of an appreciating yen, which increased the costs of Japanese home production, and the need to respond to European moves to restrain Japanese imports through 'anti-dumping' rules. Copy-Co's internationalization, like that of other leading players in the sector, was characterized by regional production for regional markets, and this was reinforced by regulatory requirements for local content, especially in Europe (Industrial Bank of Japan 1994: 10). Parts suppliers associated with the sector were also encouraged to internationalize to provide locally produced components, and several (including one discussed in Chapter 8) set up operations in Telford to supply Copy-Co and its competitors across Europe.

However, the operations of Copy-Co were never simply multiregional but also involved elements of a more global division of labour, most conspicuously in the retention of much research and development and high-value production in Japan and in the transfer of mass production to factories established in China from the early 1990s (Industrial Bank of Japan 1994: 12–13). By the mid-1990s the British factory was part of a successfully internationalizing company whose European operations were best understood in terms of regional specialization in the context of elements of a global division of labour. By then about 20 per cent of production from Telford was for the British market while the remainder went elsewhere in Europe, so the factory was firmly regional in its role. However, a significant number of more complex components were still imported from Japan, while Telford competed with factories in other countries, including China, for the opportunity to manufacture new product lines of increasing complexity.

An important consequence of the regional role of the factory was the scale and mixture of its activities. First, the scale of production was much smaller than in the parent plants in Japan, though similar to that in other overseas subsidiaries. For example, one production area at Telford had a daily output of around 65 units, while a roughly equivalent production line in Japan was producing 400. Furthermore, the Japanese lines used more bought-in sub-assemblies and were more highly automated. As we will see, such differences meant the transfer of processes from Japan to the United Kingdom was never straightforward and involved considerable adaptation to these different conditions. Moreover, these differences created difficulties in comparing and benchmarking across these production operations.

Second, however, the Telford factory was involved in an extensive portfolio of production operations, because it produced not only complex office machinery but also key replacement components and consumables. The manufacture and sale of such consumables were crucial for profitability (Industrial Bank of Japan 1994), and in the mid-1990s just over one-third of the factory's turnover and a substantial investment in new production capacity were accounted for by these products. The Telford factory had also brought some parts production in-house from outside contractors, adding further to the mix of operations on the site. Thus the subsidiary, which employed about 550 permanent staff and around 100 temporary staff, was involved in a diverse range of production activities: line assembly of complex office equipment, process production of consumables, small batch machining and processing of high specification components, large batch manufacture of low value plastic components and routine packaging of consumables. Some of these activities were outsourced in Japan and others were performed not only at separate locations but also within separate divisions of the parent company, making the subsidiaries different from the parent factories in this regard.

The firm's customers lease products and purchase consumables from a separate marketing division, or less frequently from other suppliers part-owned by Copy-Co. Thus these marketing organizations are the immediate customers of the manufacturing plants, and changing market conditions are strongly mediated through their internal structures and policies. The role of the factory as a production centre supplying regional marketing organizations, coupled with the way in which the leasing of equipment helped to stimulate the market for consumables, created something of a buffer between the factory and the ultimate customers. However, this sometimes frustrated manufacturing managers, as production targets changed unpredictably or customers' equipment problems were not relayed to the factory.

Both the mediating role of the marketing organizations and the scale and mix of production activities had important implications for management priorities at the subsidiary. The factory was not expected to make a profit on every activity but rather to prioritize efforts to control costs and quality in relation to past performance. Thus one British manager drew a sharp contrast with his earlier experience at a British multinational:

> At [British firm] you had to make a profit on every job, but I've never noticed any pressure specifically to make a profit here. I think we're here to be Copy-Co's European manufacturing plant, and the company can take their profits anywhere they like, they take them out of sales companies, take them out of selling us parts.

As far as personnel policy was concerned this had two main implications. First, it meant that Copy-Co generally conformed to the wage norms set among the local cluster of Japanese manufacturers, but also had some latitude in managing their overall wage bill. British labour was markedly cheaper than at home in Japan, while the sunk costs of capital investment and the requirements of local content represented significant protections from losing work to cheaper production centres such as China.

Second, there was little evidence of the application of strong productivity comparisons to set production targets across different Copy-Co operations, especially as comparisons with the parent plant were complicated by the lower production volumes, smaller batch sizes and less capital-intensive production arrangements:

> One of the things that we don't do at the moment, production control, is actually measure productivity strictly, there's no productivity measure at the moment. So, OK you can see by the manpower against the number of machines historically, but it's not really an accurate and technical way of doing it I don't think.... Quality is the key factor really. So if you've got ten extra people and the quality's right then it doesn't matter. I wouldn't say it doesn't matter but that in the past history that is the priority.

Thus the emphasis was on quality measures and on improvement within the plant in its own terms.

Nevertheless, while corporate HQ did not expect the factory to generate an immediate profit stream for the parent company, it was expected to generate internal funds for investment on the site and to establish a financial record that would allow it to raise further investment funds externally, and it had been quite successful in meeting these objectives. In these respects, the factory operated in a slightly more sheltered commercial environment than our other case-study companies. However, it remained vulnerable to decisions about the allocation of new models between subsidiaries, and potentially to major shifts in corporate strategy which could redraw the international division of labour in the firm and the sector in a more global and less regionalized form.

By the mid-1990s Copy-Co had codified policies at corporate level to guide the development of its growing number of overseas subsidiaries. These envisaged the initial establishment of an 'assembly-only' factory and moved through localization of parts sourcing, engineering capabilities and contribution to exports, to finish with localization of management, and finally financial independence. Managers at the Telford plant reported major progress under each heading, while acknowledging important limits to localization. Thus they had levels of local sourcing that met local content requirements, an accomplishment that had required a major commitment of resources. A high proportion of output was exported to Europe. By the mid-1990s the senior management team contained equal numbers of Japanese and British managers, while junior managers were predominantly local and the Japanese staff usually became 'advisers'. Finally, the factory successfully financed its own recent investment programme.

However, important components continued to be sourced from Japan or elsewhere in East Asia, and the factory was largely reliant on R&D conducted in Japan. Japanese engineers continued to play a key role in the factory, not only as advisers but in some areas as production managers, while the financial viability of the plant rested on the costing regime of the parent company. Thus the extent of localization remained incomplete, and implicitly or explicitly a matter of negotiation, not only between managers in Telford and at the corporate HQ but also among managers within the factory, each group with their different priorities and powers.

The localization policy placed 'management' quite late in the sequence and failed to give explicit attention to personnel and employment policies, but the explicit corporate articulation and endorsement of localization opened the way for internal debate between British and Japanese managers regarding such policies. At Copy-Co the terms of this debate were heavily influenced by changes in senior management that were themselves part of the process of localization. First, a British manager was appointed to the senior management team for the first time in 1990, a man with considerable industrial and personnel management experience, though he had never worked for a Japanese firm. He became a powerful advocate of the view that local managers should take the initiative, not only in personnel matters but also in the wider social organization of the factory, and mounted a direct challenge to some policies developed by the Japanese staff. Second, soon after, the founding Japanese MD, who had overseen the establishment of factory and its initial personnel policies, returned home. A new MD, who was both personally committed and mandated by HQ to further localization, replaced him. This set the scene for an alliance between these two key figures to support major changes in personnel and employment policies. The British manager encapsulated this arrangement in *his* characterization of the Japanese MD's position:

> We have got to localize everything because at the end of the day that's where it's got to go, and I will be the link to Tokyo very much on the technical side and the product side, and you will advise day-to-day, and unless I heartily disagree with you, you have a free hand to do almost what you want.

These management successions led to substantial changes in personnel policies and also in the wider management of the plant. However, the changes were not always straightforward and sometimes remained contested, though not simply between British and Japanese managers.

An early casualty of the refashioning of personnel policies was the original British personnel manager, regarded as insufficiently experienced and assertive to make the required changes. Another dimension of the reorientation of policy was evident at this point because his replacement was female, the first woman to be appointed to such a post within local Japanese firms. We have already noted that the established expectations and policies of these firms, as represented through the social network of MDs and meetings among management specialists, exercised important influence on the policies of each firm in the Japanese manufacturing cluster. First, firms in the cluster raised questions about the apparent departure of other companies from established norms, as happened to Copy-Co regarding the funding of works buses. Second, Japanese managers within a company could also question existing policies on the basis of comparisons with other plants, as happened at Copy-Co regarding levels of absenteeism. In both cases British managers were able to demonstrate that differences were more apparent than real, though this still underlined the potential influence of the broader cluster. However, the appointment of a female personnel manager had to be defended in more proactive terms. This meant portraying the firm as a pioneer in developing an innovative policy, and the willingness of the Japanese MD to argue this case was further evidence of a convergence of views at senior management level.

The perspectives of British and Japanese managers

Our main research took place after the factory had operated for a decade, but sought to reconstruct the earlier history of the plant as well as understanding its contemporary operation. An influential British management gloss on the early years argued that the founding Japanese managers were preoccupied with the transfer of existing products and processes from Japanese factories and tended to assume that personnel policies informed by Japanese priorities and assumptions would work well alongside these technical transfers. Thus they began with an emphasis on recruiting young workers, providing internal promotion pathways, and enforcing stringent standards of quality and work discipline. The outcome was unexpected but perturbing for the Japanese, with limited worker commitment, significant absenteeism, and substantial labour turnover, especially when the company was recruiting heavily as it increased the scale of production. From a British management perspective such developments showed that their knowledge was essential to manage the local workforce in an appropriate and effective way.

Interviews with Japanese managers suggested they often shared a perception of weak worker commitment and 'poor morale' in the factory, though they sometimes suggested that this reflected the inadequate implementation of the intended policies and procedures by local managers. In this respect, the contrasting orientations of the Japanese and British managers at Copy-Co were similar to those Broad (1994) identified in his valuable study of the tortuous and limited implementation of 'high involvement' work practices at a Japanese-owned electronics factory in Wales in the late 1980s and early 1990s. In that case, Broad argued, Japanese senior management pursued such innovations over a substantial period, but a key reason why their ambitions were largely frustrated was that British managers defended a more traditional and directive approach (and their own role) on the grounds that this was appropriate to the management of the local workforce. Meanwhile, British workers were also critical of British managers, but British management scepticism was reinforced by their limited role in policymaking and the way they were monitored by Japanese managers.

At Copy-Co there were echoes of such views: some Japanese informants suggested that local managers had failed to implement Japanese practices properly, while some shop-floor workers contrasted British managers unfavourably with the Japanese staff. Furthermore, some British managers felt the Japanese failed to share important information and there was a sense that the two groupings participated in distinct but unequal policy-making processes:

> They're very easy to work with on a one-to-one basis [but] I think we tend to have two management structures here. We tend to have a Japanese management structure and a British management structure. And they'll go off and have meetings about things and they'll be discussing product development and things like that. You feel very left out.... But then again we do exactly the same. We'll have British meetings without the Japanese.

However, the overall dynamic of management policy formation and its repercussions at Copy-Co were different to those in Broad's case, for the shifts and inconsistencies in policies over time did not involve the sort of polarization that he suggests.

Instead an effective alliance was forged between senior Japanese and British managers committed to a process of localization and substantial changes in the social organization of management–worker relations in the factory. In turn, this nurtured a greater willingness on the part of key Japanese staff to regard both the production and employment exigencies characteristic of the Telford plant as justifications for a selective and negotiated implementation of Japanese domestic policies. Thus one remarked that

> The worst thing is to force the locals to follow the Japanese way, even if we feel that 'it was like this in Japan'. The local people are different from the Japanese...ideally it would be best if we can combine the good points of each country, since the objectives are the same as a company, that is how to increase the profit.

Furthermore, most British managers acknowledged the strengths of Japanese management approaches, especially in terms of technical expertise and a commitment to systematic procedures, while remaining sceptical about their skills in people management. A British characterization of one Japanese manager provided a sharply formulated version of this:

> He understood how to use, like the hard science of management, perhaps data analysis. God bless him, he knew the expertise about consumables. He could make that plant sing, he could make it that we had the best yields in the world. But the people where demoralized, oh, the problems they had.

These limitations were ascribed partly to Japanese experience of a more cooperative home labour force, which fostered a 'systems' orientation, and partly to the limited overseas experience and limited English of many Japanese staff. However, the consequences of this technical bias were not seen as uniform: in one instance it might cut across the sensibilities of local staff and thus create grievances, in another it might foster an 'indulgency pattern', either directly or by failing to regulate informal staff practices.

While this was a dominant motif of the British management view, there were nevertheless important differences in their experiences and attitudes to Japanese management. Many younger British managers had little experience elsewhere and often identified quite strongly with the guidance and development provided by their Japanese mentors, even feeling that good Japanese innovations had been compromised by later developments:

> Each department more or less had a Japanese protégé almost. They were brought up to spread the belief or the gospel as it was at the time [but] a lot of those people have either left or moved or gone to different jobs in the organization.

This young manager saw this as a consequence of localization and the growing influence of senior British managers, but he also recognized that immediate resource constraints were critical when he tried to apply the lessons he had learned to his current work:

> At the moment it's difficult because of the amount of workload and the expansion is just incredible at the minute. So basically we're trying to follow the same principles as we can without being as diligent as maybe we should be. So we are fighting a little bit in that. Balance all the plates that crash into one another [laugh].

Thus some younger managers adapted rather reluctantly to the shift in management style involved in localization, though others came to embrace this change in a more positive way, as will be evident in our discussion of quality management later in this chapter. Older British managers, with wider experience of British personnel policies, tended to voice more scepticism, especially about the capacity of the Japanese to manage British workers. Nevertheless, they had often experienced the failures of British manufacturing management, with growing insecurity or redundancy from British firms, and they too could be very receptive to Japanese management expertise.

Overall, then, the positions of Japanese and British managers at Copy-Co were less polarized than in Broad's study. Senior British managers certainly claimed particular expertise in managing British labour but usually recognized and sometimes learned from the organizational competencies of Japanese managers, while younger British managers were often particularly impressed by Japanese technical expertise but wrestled with the ways in which it could be adapted to local conditions. Meanwhile, Japanese managers also registered some of the complexities involved in using their expertise in the Telford factory. To trace the implications of these positions more fully it is necessary to explore debates about innovation and implementation in specific areas of policy, covering the broad areas of the making of production organization, and the remaking of personnel policies.

The construction of a local production regime

The Transfer of Products and the Reconstruction of Production Processes

Since the British factory manufactures products designed, developed, and usually produced in Japan, each new product involves a transfer of production capabilities from one country to the other, though sometimes other subsidiaries with relevant experience may also become involved. Such transfers involve not only methods of working but also performance comparisons between plants, covering such matters as labour productivity and quality standards. As one team leader remarked 'it's like an uphill battle between the three companies. We've got America's report [on quality levels] coming in and the Japanese report coming in, but they [the Japanese head office] set the actual standards.'

As we have already noted, however, the scale and conditions of production are quite different in Japan and Britain, so more than a straight transfer of production processes and performance measures is involved (as the complexities varied from process to process we have focused here on the main assembly line). Thus one British manager who favoured tighter productivity measures in the Telford factory lamented that:

> Unfortunately we tend to assemble them differently here to anywhere else. In Japan for example they have fewer people on their production lines, usually at the higher level.... Because their more routine jobs are done by subcontractors, they buy that level in.... In Japan their volume is a lot higher. It's three times as high, over three times as high... obviously they're not doing as much process, but they're doing higher volumes.

Nevertheless, an influential Japanese production manager indicated that in his view worker effort in the British plant, defined in terms of the standard times for specific operations rather than job cycles, was not too far from that in Japan, especially as labour was much cheaper in the United Kingdom:

> We are using 120 per cent Japanese standards—it's a little slower than Japan, we never achieve Japanese time [laughter].... Production volume is one of the big factors [behind] the difference in standard time here and in Japan... it is very difficult to achieve the same productivity with different volumes.... In Japan there are a lot of automatic systems but we [in the United Kingdom] are always calculating costs. If we have a big automation to our line it's not so

> effective on the cost side. In Japan, the operator's cost is almost 5 times more than here for one person. It's a big difference. Manpower is cheaper than automation.

Against this background, the process of transfer was addressed by project teams of engineers and supervisors sent from the United Kingdom to visit the relevant plant, usually in Japan but sometimes elsewhere. This involved looking at the existing 'process books', one-to-one training, and practice in stripping and rebuilding the new products. However, this then had to be translated into production procedures and work stations appropriate to lower volumes of output and more in-house sub-assembly operations.

> We come back and we tailor it to what we need, adapt it to what we need. And we go from there, from there we start to go our separate ways. Japanese operators may do things differently; they may be better at this than us, or we may be better at some other things than they are. I think we tend to be a little bit slower than Japanese operators [are]. Japanese operators tend to be quicker, but because they have only got one minute takt [cycle] times and we have got sort of twelve minutes takt times, it's vastly different.

Thus production volumes and labour intensity influenced the job cycle time at each work station, with a range between seven and seventeen minutes in complex assembly in the United Kingdom compared with much shorter cycles in Japan. This had quite profound implications for the character of the work:

> So the operator's job changes quite dramatically.... They have to remember in their heads seventeen minutes worth of work. Two minutes is fairly easy and in Japan they are producing something like 400 a day off their lines so they've got less than 60 seconds worth of work so maybe two brackets fitted, two screws done, finished, stand there waiting for the next one.... Our production set-up is vastly different to Japan.

Furthermore, the salience of these differences was reinforced by experience. Thus a team leader recounted how, during one model transfer from Japan, 'we undermanned the line to try to cut costs [but] it didn't work. We had to stop production, we had to recruit, we had to train people up and increase the line capacity.' Consequently, when experience at an American subsidiary was used as the benchmark for introducing another new model at Telford, the project group built in some leeway, even though the scale of production in the United States was much closer to that in the British plant. In turn, such caution underpinned reliance on internal historical experience in the specification of manning levels.

Two further points are relevant here. First, this account suggests that the adjustment of job times was influenced by local power relations and tacit bargaining on the shop-floor, in ways which echo long-standing analyses of effort bargaining (Roy 1955; Baldamus 1961; Burawoy 1979). In the course of his interview a senior operator captured various facets of this process:

> You'll find, as they've got used to a job and they've got spare time, they'll be going round talking to their friends, you know. They've got time to walk off and talk to someone, and you find that's when defects are happening, that they've rushed their job and they walk off. We all do it, I've done it, I'm not saying only the operators, we've all done it like. You get bored; it's nice to have a chat to take your mind off your job. You find eventually [management] turn the line up and you stop at your station then, you haven't got time to walk off.... Eventually I'll have to time all the operators, but time them without them knowing; you know what I mean. If they know that you're timing them they'll slow down a bit, they'll allow a bit of time for them to have a rest, see, but sometimes you do it without looking at them... but at the end of the day I can't upset my operator because I've got to work with him.

At Copy-Co, then, management efforts to control the pace of work sought to 'balance the line' and capture the gains accruing from worker familiarization with the work process by surreptitious timing and by nudging up line speeds. Meanwhile, workers tended to use time gains to relieve work pressures and tried to avoid tighter job times, and tacitly their conditional cooperation set some limits to the scope for speed-up.

Second, we should note an instructive anomaly in the commentaries of the British managers concerned with transferring products and organizing production processes in the British factory. One comparison of Japanese and British manning practices suggested that the model mix on lines in Japan was more varied, and linked this to the high level of expertise of the operators, while also acknowledging that the cycle times were short. However a more experienced manager suggested that the model mix in Britain had often been greater, and emphasized that the longer cycle times at Telford involved more complex and extended assembly routines even if the Japanese operators were quicker. These differences remind us that new models were associated with significant changes in production processes and manning arrangements in *both* countries, involving shifts in model mixes and cycle times, so we should not oversimplify the broad contrasts made by our informants.

However, we also suspect that gender inflects perceptions of different aspects of the internal division of labour in Japanese factories. The most experienced and skilled operators in Japan are invariably male workers who often concentrate on rectification, while most routine in-house assembly involves 'temporary' young women workers. As one Japanese manager remarked, 'in the case of manufacturing in Japan, there are a lot of young girls, because young girls are a cheaper cost, and they are leaving many times. If you employ a man, they want to stay and it costs too much.' Thus, by focusing on the male rectifiers, the Japanese workforce could be perceived as more skilled in coping with more complex production demands, while the 'temporary' women workers who performed the most standardized and fragmented tasks were sometimes lost sight of. By comparison, the gendered division of labour in the assembly areas of the British

Copy-Co plant was rather less rigid so there was less scope for such selective perception in characterizing the British workforce.

Negotiating the Relevance of Parent Factory Recipes: Quality and Foolproofing

Quality control (QC) has long been seen as a central strength of Japanese manufacturing companies like Copy-Co, and considerable attention was given to quality management at the Telford factory from its establishment. However, from the early 1990s the approach to these issues also changed substantially as a result of the consolidation of the new senior management coalition. A key participant, who had risen from working as a quality inspector under Japanese leadership to become a senior quality manager, provided a telling account of this process. He had learned much from his Japanese 'mentor' but was later forced to reconsider his approach. This was a painful process for people like him because he was a committed advocate of what he regarded as a superior Japanese approach, and change involved direct conflict with his erstwhile mentor as he realigned himself with the new senior management team. However, top management also provided a fresh language to guide and rationalize this change, as a shift from a highly technical enforcement role to a more collaborative problem-solving orientation:

> Things have changed a great deal in terms of the relationships between the Quality Assurance Department and Production.... In the past we were seen as a very, very strong police force. Highly critical, and I'm as guilty as my mentor was of being very highly critical at quality meetings, with very little support for production. We would tend to look at all the figures... and we would write a report that practically reduced the production manager to tears. And that we saw as our goal, as a stimulus for improvement, to shock managers into action.... But at the start of the 90s I was realizing that all of the development I had gone through, the teaching in terms of management style, management approach, were basically not appropriate. And I had to work very hard re-establishing different relationships with local management, becoming more cooperative, not banging their heads with a stick, but more looking to areas of support.... We are now seen as far more proactive, supportive, and we have worked hand-in-hand with production and it's been extremely successful.

These reflections suggest that this manager, operating in a key arena of Japanese management techniques, moved more decisively away from his original orientation than did some of the other protégés of Japanese management. In particular, he came to regard the *enforcement approach* advocated and encouraged by pioneering Japanese management cadres as inappropriate for the Telford subsidiary. This was not simply because British production managers would not accept this approach. It also reflected conditions and structures in Copy-Co in Japan, such as stable market dominance, massive scale, and the development of large specialist departments, which were quite different to those of the small and somewhat more vulnerable British subsidiary.

It was evident from other informants, however, that the character and effectiveness of quality control regimes on the shop-floor remained uneven and contested, especially in the more complex production areas. Thus another successful protégé of Japanese management remained less convinced by the newer senior management approach and emphasized the limitations of the contemporary quality regime:

> I think the quality is very poor at the moment. The quality has been the worst I've ever known it, and it's just very poor. Delivery delays have gone back to what it was when I first started here. Where we did get it down to a reasonable level, that actually went back up again.

Though he recognized this judgement was made at the time of a complex and demanding model change, he explicitly claimed that the problems were more systemic. Indeed, he suggested that Japanese managers were also raising questions that were prompting a further reappraisal of the quality regime.

In this context it is important to register the relationship between engineering innovations designed to secure quality and improve productivity in the production process and the initiatives of the shop-floor workers themselves. Despite sharing the rhetoric of employee involvement in quality improvements, Copy-Co continued to place most reliance on the activities of engineering management, and quality improvements remained primarily the property of process engineering. Worker involvement in quality initiatives remained rather limited and superficial and the more complex production lines used a kiting system that was designed to minimize worker discretion.

The firm had some experience of both suggestion schemes and Quality Circles (QCCs), and the Japanese MD had returned them to the agenda, following his participation in a meeting of overseas subsidiary managers in Japan. This sponsorship prompted British managers to visit various other companies in Britain to draw on their experiences and, according to a leading British manager, the first result was a 'very simple, quick fire suggestion scheme' which offered a financial reward to operators. However, it was widely recognized that the initial flow of small suggestions had 'dropped off' as the novelty wore off, and one shop-floor verdict was that 'it's a bit of an insult really because you implement a good idea and they'll give you a pound for it. . . . So you think, "no forget it'." QCCs had been tried before but had collapsed: 'two or three years ago we tried, we played at it, but it wasn't supported from above, . . . it really failed because we hadn't got the support'. Now they were trying again with some pilot QCCs on a voluntary basis, though managers recognized the substantial difficulties in bringing them to fruition. One problem was that only minorities of workers were interested, while another arose from the movement of people between production areas as a result of changing production exigencies and the reorganization of supervision:

> We have to come down in volume or go up in volume so moving people around, so we are continually smashing all the circles. I mean we have moved half the supervision... we are now splitting the workforce [between different lines]... so we are losing all the circles all the time. It's a real nightmare trying to hold it all together but the operators, some of the operators, see the value.

Nevertheless this manager regarded the initial efforts as very promising ('the first presentation we had, the enthusiasm and the energy that it generated, it was electric'), while emphasizing that he believed it was the process of involvement rather than substantive achievement that was important.

This view was not widely shared down the hierarchy, however. Supervisors tended to be much more sceptical and highlighted the different demands on QCCs by British and Japanese managers. One claimed that:

> They wanted to integrate it within the company, looking at it from an English point of view, changing some of the things to adapt to this company, but again they differ from what they were wanting from QCCs. I know what the Japanese want, they want to see these groups working on problems that are affecting quality, that are affecting efficiency, and solving them, so it's what these groups achieve, that's what they want.... Whereas the English management, they were more 'let's get these people working as a team, let's get them presenting this work', and not so much emphasis on what they've done.

Indeed, this reversed the management assessment by perceiving the rhetoric of involvement as a substitute for efforts to make real improvements. In part, this reflected sympathy with what he saw as the Japanese emphasis on technical virtuosity, but it also reflected a belief that real difficulties in constructing cohesive and committed work teams were being glossed over. In particular, he suggested it was fairly easy to mobilize a minority of volunteers who were already 'quality minded', but this ignored the non-involvement of a majority of more sceptical and instrumental workers.

A broader critique was provided by one of the most experienced and well-regarded team leaders in the factory:

> Well, they are playing at it really. They are playing little quality circle games, but there is no commitment to it. They've fallen apart, the QCCs have, but management haven't admitted to that.... What they did, they trained all the supervisors—quite an intense training course on QCCs.... The supervisors built up their QCC groups, and they disbanded the supervisors, promoted all these team leaders and put them in charge of the QCCs... so these new team leaders had to take over the team and the QCC, for which they had no training, and there was no training coming... and then they kept saying, 'Oh, don't forget your QCCs'... I mean, it's ridiculous. There is no commitment from above with the QCCs. They started sending operators out to presentations, thinking this would be such a wonderful incentive for them,

> but it isn't because they don't care. . . . QCCs are a good thing, you can get some brilliant work done, you can get the team going, but if the people on the shop-floor don't see the involvement from above they don't care either . . . they started cutting corners on our hour-a-fortnight, so during that hour we would have to do re-work rather than quality circles, and it's just failed.

From this perspective, production pressures and the reorganization of supervision raised major questions about management priorities, and in such circumstances worker (and indeed team leader) involvement was unlikely to be sustained.

Against this background, the views of workers who were enthusiastic *advocates* of quality underline difficulties facing any management efforts to mobilize worker involvement, as frustration and scepticism were often dominant themes in their testimony. For example, one such informant persistently contrasted the formal features of management concern with quality—management meetings, quality circles, graphs and diagrams—with the practical expertise of committed employees, and claimed that:

> They spout quality but I think they're more concerned with image, and I think a lot of the time the only people that do actually care, I mean properly care, not just say they care but they don't, are the actual people building a machine.

Furthermore, this judgement was dramatized by vivid stories that evidently rehearsed aspects of shop-floor debate on these issues. One such account emphasized the obstacles the operator had faced when she sought to alert supervisors and managers to a practical quality problem:

> I was on the line and one of my jobs was to put a [part] into a [sub-assembly] and as I was fitting this [part] the plastic was splitting and you could see it widen and it was stretching and stretching . . . and the problem got worse so I went to my relief and I said 'I'm not happy about this'. I went to another supervisor and this one day I went to him four times. But he was in the office and . . . nothing was getting done. So I went to my relief and said, 'get [name]', he was an investigator at the time. So he came out and he started a part investigation, and he asked me to monitor everything, so I did, and it got worse . . . So I went down to the final station and says to the girl that checks these, 'there's a problem [part], will you keep an eye out for it?, if you spot it put your light on and get some help'. So she got her [boss] to come over and she said 'well this should never be made', and I said . . . 'this has been going on for three days now, I've been to see [senior operator], I've been to see [the supervisor] and they're starting an investigation but I'm not happy'. I said, 'I'm just not happy going through the system' . . . They all stick together. Because it was all their problem. The problem had got through QC and at the end [the area manager] had to go through four days production. Now that could have been averted. It's no good telling the operators 'quality' if it stops with the operator, and it very often does.

As these comments suggest, this person saw herself as a committed employee who placed a high value on quality. She also expressed positive views about many aspects of employment relations in the factory, at one point declaring that 'the company is basically an extremely good company, and everything about the company is good'. At the same time, however, her frustrations and scepticism about management systems and management commitments fuelled a strong sense of a gulf between 'us' and 'them'. This prompted the claim that 'operators are treated as the lowest of the low... it's as if you've got no value, and that's a common feeling, the operator is just a number', so 'you find here that operators tend to look after operators'. We are not claiming these views were typical. However, they demonstrate how difficult it may be for managers to develop quality assurance and improvement policies that articulate effectively with the concerns of even quite well-disposed shop-floor workers at Copy-Co, because of the cross-cutting management priorities and highly standardized production routines.

In the context of such arguments about quality regimes and worker involvement, one aspect of the social organization of the production process at Copy-Co was particularly revealing about the ways in which techniques were borrowed and modified to address differences in both production parameters and the orientations of employees. This was the adaptation of a kiting system called 'haizen', used quite sparingly in Japan to enhance QC at specific work stations but developed and applied as a widespread form of 'foolproofing' on the British Copy-Co production line (see also Palmer 1996). The basic idea was that the various components for an assembly task were laid out systematically on a tray by parts supply, so that assemblers could use them in a routine and reliable fashion.

The origins of this innovation went back six years, to a period when Japanese production management were facing serious quality problems at Copy-Co UK. A team of Japanese engineers had tackled these problems by helping to install 'haizen' arrangements similar to those used in Japan, but these first efforts had only a temporary effect. This then prompted a lengthy period of experimentation, involving visits to plants in Japan and the United States and experiments to develop improvized wooden kit trays. This was partly a question of tailoring the method to the specific circumstances of British production, but the key Japanese manager emphasized that it was also intended as an 'educational' process:

> There is a lot of history to the introduction to this kind of system. I wanted to introduce the system, but it was difficult to do just like that... If the team leader and the operator do not want to follow the rule, then the system has no meaning. Therefore, I teach them what is the 'haizen' system, so they are doing the 'haizen' system themselves before we introduce it.... After that they understand what 'haizen' is, what the purpose is.

On the basis of this dual process, of technical experimentation and practical induction into the principles of foolproofing, a distinctly British version of 'haizen' was developed for the semi-automated flow lines.

Both Japanese and British managers argued that this process reflected differences in the attitudes of Japanese and British operators, though they recognized that distinctive production exigencies were also relevant. Thus the Japanese sponsor of these developments highlighted the extent to which Japanese workers monitored one another in the production process, but also acknowledged that many of the Japanese assembly tasks were simpler in the context of high automation and short cycles. Meanwhile the British manager most involved in the project highlighted the propensity of British workers to seek shortcuts, but also noted that the scope for mistakes was much greater on the Telford lines because of the long-cycle times and more varied models. As a result, the British variant of haizen differed from the Japanese version in several key respects. It was more tightly structured in terms of sections and labels, placing less reliance on decisions by the assembler:

> Ours tends to be more foolproof. The Japanese way is basically just a tray with segments in. Ours has actually got a tray with segments, with drawings, with part numbers, with numbers. So ours is sort of belt and braces where in Japan they teach the operator like 'you put this part in that segment', and they'll do it.

It also tended to involve more components on each tray to match the longer, more complex job cycles, and finally it was used more widely across the assembly process rather than just for particularly difficult operations. This illustrates how the details of the design of production operations were influenced by contrasting circumstances in the parent and subsidiary factories, but also underlines the extent to which a technical foolproofing solution was adopted in Britain to cope with the problems of QC that arose from this cluster of circumstances.

Overall, then, Japanese factories provided important models and resources regarding production procedures and standards, both for expatriate Japanese staff and for British managers. However, the contrasts in the scale and organization of production in Britain and Japan, coupled with the distinctive features of employment relations in the locality, also afforded managers in the Telford factory considerable operational autonomy in constructing the details of the social organization of the local production process. This was underlined by a senior British manager who argued that:

> We are very independent. Even though we [Japan and the United Kingdom] are producing the same models there is very little communication between the two plants.... We tend to stand alone and we tend to solve our own problems. If we have major problems, then we contact Japan 'have you had this problem'? And they might say 'yes', but they haven't told us.... It seems a little bit strange but it's to get us to stand on our two feet as well. If they are always telling us 'do this and do this', I mean we'll never stand on our own two feet and where is the cut-off? What do they tell us and what don't they tell us?

> We have problems *every* day. We make defects *every* day. So we can be telling Japan every day, or they can be telling us every day, we have this defect, do this. So where do you draw the line?

At Copy-Co the line appeared to be drawn in a way that emphasized the local construction of the production regime through a selective adoption and adaptation of production arrangements strongly influenced by both local labour market conditions and the distinctive mix and scale of production processes.

The Scope and Limits of Localization: Design and Development

While the products manufactured at Copy-Co were generally designed and developed in Japan, there was some limited localization of design and development work. There had certainly been significant local innovations in *process* engineering when, after initial overtures from British engineers and support from the Japanese MD, the parent company encouraged work on recycling a major component, resulting in a British award for environmental engineering. One of those involved emphasized the distinctive position that the British plant came to occupy in this regard:

> We have received more autonomy. We have got the environmental award which I was involved with. We have developed technology ourselves here.... All the other factories are taking turnkey operations from Japan.... Whereas we said 'no, we'll resource that... we can get it a third of the price you can get it from Japan', and it's developing our own technology and particularly in [this area of] manufacturing we have been allowed to do more than any other plants have been allowed to do.

Furthermore, this innovation had been adopted by factories elsewhere in the company, including Japan (where there was initially some resistance to a solution from abroad), so there had been some 'reverse transfer' (Edwards 1998) in this specialist area.

The involvement of the British subsidiary in *product* development was more fraught but also revealing about the relationship between the subsidiary and parent company. Management had failed to gain an expected new product to replace an established but ageing model range, as the new model went to China instead. The response of Telford managers (both British and Japanese, though with most urgency among the former) was to try to develop their own design and development competencies, by undertaking development work on a product that had been mothballed in Japan. The emphasis was primarily on demonstrating the development of local engineering capabilities but with the possibility that a new product line might result:

> This is the first time now we've had our chance to get our teeth into something, actual product design and development, and I find it very difficult but I really enjoy working on it. I'll go home about nine o'clock tonight and there'll

be engineers still there working on it. So although they're finding it difficult, and it's stressful for them, they're actually thoroughly enjoying working on this type of product.... Two years ago we knew that it's not going to be a profit-making product, but the main purpose of it was to develop our personnel, and they really have developed working on it for the last two years.

This underlined the significance of the project but also its limitations. There was little prospect of generating a mainstream product locally, and the loss of a replacement model emphasized the continuing dependency of the factory on research, design, and development activity conducted in Japan. The demonstration of local expertise apparently made a favourable impression at HQ and helped the factory to gain another new model a year or so later, but it was only one element in the negotiations. Managers at the factory also made a more direct pitch, emphasizing the availability of production capacity and a novel alliance with the European marketing division to delivering closer links with customers. Furthermore, the new line required the redeployment of most of the existing engineering staff, making further development work a fringe activity. As a result, this effort at innovation remained incomplete and made little direct impact on the overall standing of the Telford factory.

In all these respects, then, the implications of playing the role of a regional production centre, and especially the character and implications of localization, had to be worked out among Japanese and British managers at Telford in negotiations with the centre. In large part these confirmed the established role of the subsidiary, serving regional marketing organizations by producing product lines allocated from Japan. The parameters within which the plant operated were set by HQ and translated and negotiated by Japanese managers in the business-planning department in Telford, but this left much of the detail of the technical and social organization of production to be worked out by local British and expatriate Japanese staff within the branch factory itself.

At the same time this relative operational autonomy coexisted with exchanges of experience and expertise with other plants, including other overseas subsidiaries. One manager remarked that:

I've been to Japan three times; America once, France two or three times. Germany, Sweden.... We go to our French factory every other year and go and have a look and swap ideas. The Japanese think its important to go and look at other people and try and benchmark yourself and move along, and help each other.

As this suggests, the strongest 'lateral' link was with France, the other Copy-Co factory producing in and for the European market, though managers also commented on uneven and shifting relations between these two subsidiaries. More generally, Telford had pioneered the recycling processes discussed earlier and some of the work on the mothballed product line had also been fed back to Japan, while other minor product and process innovations had been disseminated to other subsidiaries. Meanwhile, the British factory had adopted some of the software developments and ideas about team-based QC from France, and had drawn on process engineering expertise from the United States. Apparently the American plant was seen as an easier source than the Japanese 'mother' plant because of language, a similar scale of production, and an absence of direct competition, which facilitated openness.

Thus there was certainly a degree of 'transverse diffusion' between subsidiaries and there was even some modest 'reverse diffusion' of specific technical solutions to Japan. But these are minor qualifications to the overall picture, of a substantial operational autonomy in the social organization of production within the centrally defined mandate of production of specific products for the European regional market.

The negotiated reorientation of personnel policies

Discipline, Recruitment, and Job Security

It was in the sphere of personnel policies that British managers were most critical of Japanese management and made their strongest claims to distinctive expertise. In particular, they argued that problems of discipline, absenteeism, and labour turnover had arisen as a result of an initial policy of recruiting young inexperienced workers and promoting from within. This reliance on aspects of Japanese employment practice was, they argued, inappropriate in the circumstances of the British, and especially Telford, labour market.

Some of the changes advocated by British managers were relatively minor but symbolic. For example, the relaxation of rules about wearing hats sought to avoid turning the demeanour of employees into a disciplinary issue:

> Well the uniform was OK, though perhaps we were not used to it in this country, but the mountain of effort that went into getting people to wear hats was absolutely ridiculous, and some would . . . wear them on back to front and that was the fashion (laughter) and then the Japanese would complain that it looked sloppy.

However, such moves were not simply designed to produce a more relaxed disciplinary regime in the factory. Rather, they were informed by a widespread British management view that Japanese staff, operating in a foreign country and language, understandably lacked finesse in their management of employment relations, sometimes making decisions that offended local sensibilities and provoked disgruntlement, sometimes tolerating or overlooking practices that needed more active management. For example, British managers argued against the imposition of a 'forced distribution' in awarding merit pay, because it invited shop-floor criticism and disillusionment, but they still advocated a tightly focused version of performance related pay, aimed particularly at good attendance:

> The [project] group decided that we wanted performance-related pay, and why shouldn't we pay the people who do perform, why should we pay the people who don't perform anything? And for the last three years we actually haven't paid shop-floor people who haven't performed.... On the shop-floor there is a checklist and there are two main criteria—one is quality and the other is attendance. They *have* to be here.... If you have less than seven days [absence] you are automatically accepted. That's good attendance. Seven to twelve days, the manager and the supervisor or team leader can make the decision whether we accept that person or not, so if they have had some illness and they've crept over. Anything over twelve days is a special case.... But it's the people who are having Mondays or Fridays. Obviously the team leaders are looking for that anyway and we've got maybe a few people in discipline, but very few.

Thus British managers regarded their policies as more appropriately designed and easier to legitimate, rather than softer than what went before.

However, while employees often regarded the Copy-Co factory as a fairly relaxed environment when compared with other workplaces they had experienced, long-standing employees often felt that in some ways British managers had actually promoted greater stringency on the shop-floor. One worker suggested that 'now, if you start going for your break a couple of minutes early they're standing around watching annd writing things down, that's what its like in a British factory... [whereas] the Japanese weren't really interested, as long as the job got done'. A team leader endorsed this view: 'It seemed a lot more relaxed, if I can use that word, when I first started.... It's got to be good quality and you've got to achieve your production quota, so they seem a lot firmer, a lot more stricter... so [it's] tightened up a little bit, especially on the attendance and that sort of thing.' However, the extent to which managers succeeded in enforcing labour discipline and also gaining legitimacy remained heavily dependent on the ways in which supervisors exercised their discretion. Many workers continued to resent penalties imposed for 'unavoidable absences' and some felt that too much emphasis was given to attendance compared with other aspects of performance (see Chapter 11).

The most obvious shift in personnel policy, though, concerned recruitment, where British managers had tried for some time to persuade Japanese staff to recruit more mature workers. By the time of our research, the earlier problems of managing a youthful workforce had become part of the litany of all long-serving British managers, though it was recognized that these problems had been exacerbated by the expansion of the workforce as production had grown. One manager who had pushed the case for recruiting more mature workers over a long period reflected that:

> We had such trouble when I arrived. First, when I arrived here there was lots of 16- and 17-year-olds. I think [this reflected] the Japanese attitude of get

> them young and train them, develop them, mould them into what we want. In this country that is quite naïve, it wouldn't work.... And I remember the fight I had, to bring other people in and some of the comments and the merriment actually produced with the Japanese managers when they saw older people coming in.... they couldn't understand the concept of bringing older people in who had worked in other industries, who had gone through redundancy and change, and even people we had previously used. They couldn't understand the concept of mixing people up at all.

Thus, patterns of recruitment were initially modified informally, in areas where lower management were willing to experiment, but later, following the successions in senior management, the new approach became formal company-wide policy.

This broadening of recruitment was widely believed to have helped reduce absenteeism and labour turnover, though it should be noted that conditions in the external labour market also changed in ways that helped to stabilize the workforce. An employee who reflected on experience in his section highlighted this:

> Just before the recession, there was quite a bit of work around. People were moving in and out. People get disillusioned, boring, boring jobs. If they're not very motivated within themselves they find it difficult to maintain the same sort of pace. They just get tired and move on.... Then I joined right at the beginning of the recession. Sort of six months later all of a sudden the recession was there. The job market started really getting difficult, and you saw the effect on people leaving. After the first three years I was in [that department] I think only two people left, and one of those transferred to a different department within the company. So it was a drastic sort of change in the structure.

Thus there was a significant policy shift, but its initial effects were underpinned by a period of growing unemployment.

During the same period, however, some aspects of personnel policy remained more distinctively 'Japanese', though both Japanese and British managers were involved in their implementation. In particular the firm adopted a policy of avoiding redundancies during a downturn in production, redeploying workers not only to other production areas but also to factory refurbishment and training activities. Several interviewees recalled that the Japanese MD of the time met the staff and told everyone that if they accepted these moves he guaranteed that there would be no redundancies. This clearly echoed domestic Japanese corporate policies of job security for core workers, though some British managers claimed that their own experiences in the early 1980s also predisposed them to pursue this approach. A senior personnel manager commented that:

> I think we have gone a long way to try and stabilize our workforce and get out of this moving around, 'yes, I'm about to be dismissed because of my timekeeping, I'll get a move on now'. So yes, I still think it exists, but I hope that we

> are able to retain our people more because of what we have just gone through. We obviously haven't had the work and one major difference I would say about a Japanese company to a British company, redundancy is the last on the list and not the first on the list and we have maintained our workforce.... I think the managers, most managers within the organization have gone through redundancy of some sort, so I think they would try and avoid this redundancy as much as they can. They have been on the sharp end of that.... So I think the willingness to try and look at other things was there with the managers. However, the ability to enable us to do this definitely came from the Japanese, to carry the cost. If they hadn't wanted to carry the cost then we would have had to implement a redundancy programme.

This policy generated quite positive responses among employees, but they were less convinced of the role of British managers. One reflected:

> Every time there was a rumour they'd stand up and say 'no'. By the end of it you knew they weren't going to make anybody redundant.... I was pretty impressed actually, because I thought they were under quite a bit of pressure. But like I said, when you talk to the Japanese they don't worry about one year or two years or three years, they worry about ten or fifteen, which British gaffers, they can't ever see that.

It also generated a sense of reciprocal obligation. The same worker commented that 'none of us like to admit it, but... they've done us a favour, so you tend to do them one good favour like', while a team leader argued that 'they're helping you, they're bending over backwards, they're losing money by keeping you employed, so you do what they want you to do'.

In turn, managers noted the costs incurred by the firm, and took the promise of job security as an opportunity to highlight where they thought any reciprocity should lead. One suggested:

> It was at a cost because you weren't getting the production that you would want, but we made as much use, and got as much value from that cost as we could. Also I think it gave us a value in, hopefully, the attitudes.... We have tried to sell that as well... every opportunity we got, if people complained about the flexibility, we took an opportunity, not to throw it at them, but to show why we are doing it and why we need them to be as flexible as we need them to.

The policy on job security was not only used as a lever to extend flexible deployment, but also to discourage employees from considering trade union organization. At one point when external union efforts were being made to recruit members, a senior British manager commented publicly that British industrial relations arrangements might have to be accompanied by British traditions of job insecurity.

Finally, the employment of temporary workers as a counterpart to the permanent workforce might also be regarded as following Japanese parallels, though it actually appears to have been driven primarily by pragmatic considerations. Initially the emphasis was on recruitment of permanent staff and it was only during recovery from the downturn that temporary workers began to be recruited, primarily because of uncertainties about whether the recovery would last. Once temporary workers had been used, however, Copy-Co managers found advantages in using Temping Agencies not only to cover peaks in demand but also as a channel of recruitment to permanent posts, though the costs involved meant this happened primarily during periods of major recruitment.

From Supervisors to Team leaders: a very British Reorganization

Such developments as the broadening of recruitment and the revamping of merit pay suggest that the emergent senior management alliance accomplished a relatively successful reconfiguration of personnel policies in line with British conceptions of the practicalities of managing a British, and more particularly a Telford, workforce. However, this did not mean a simple switch to older British personnel policies, but retained such distinctive features as relative job security and union avoidance.

In other respects, though, changes in policy were more protracted and problematical, and this was especially the case where personnel policies impinged more directly on the social organization of production. A pivotal area in this respect was the reorganization of workgroup supervision by the replacement of existing supervisors with team leaders and the removal of a layer of leading hands. The rhetoric of this reorganization again contrasted the technical sophistication of Japanese management with their limited skills in social relations and stressed the central role of local management expertise in 'people management', though how far the new policy could accomplish the results this rhetoric promised remained contentious.

There were several strands to the British management argument for change. First, they claimed that first-line supervisors often lacked appropriate 'people management' skills, resulting in grievances and disciplinary problems on the shop-floor. Fairly typical was the remark that:

> We had a lot of very young supervisors, inexperienced . . . we would have situations where supervisors would tell the operators to do things and in the manner they were told, they didn't like it, and they just walked out.

Second, and in line with the overall framing of the discussion of localization, these managers saw this as the legacy of an initial Japanese emphasis on in-house promotion that developed and rewarded detailed technical expertise but neglected personnel competencies. However, they also acknowledged that the sheer rapidity of early growth encouraged internal advancement. Thus a British production manager suggested that:

> We had started people at the young age and we promoted them very quickly, and all the supervisors that were in here then were promoted internally. They made good operators but good operators, as we found out later, didn't necessarily make good supervisors.

It was also claimed that the existing structure led to ambiguity in responsibilities for such issues as discipline, leading to confusion and inconsistency. The same manager continued:

> With these four tiers [supervisors, leading hands, senior reliefs, operators] the operators didn't always know who they reported to... and sometimes you would say to the supervisor 'have you done so and so?' 'No, the leading hand is doing it.' The leading hand would say 'no, I haven't done it, he's doing it'. There was no responsibility out there, people were ducking issues.

Such concerns prompted the formation of a project group composed of experienced British managers, who spent nearly two years developing what became a quite radical strategy to reorganize supervision across the factory.

Even members of the project group had to be persuaded of the need for change. In particular those directly responsible for line management had reservations:

> When we started I think we were all perhaps a little sceptical. It was somebody's idea to take a second layer out, and I think we were all sceptical on how the hell are we going to run the lines, and how are we going to manage.

In this sense the project group was a forum in which personnel specialists sought to convince their colleagues about the changes required:

> We had to change managers' views, and that's not an overnight thing, for them also to recognize the problem. They may have felt there was one, but by recognizing and admitting to it they had to deal with it as well. There was a reluctance to do that. So we went through a process of project group meetings and bringing five key production managers on board with the concepts.

The project group was, then, a forum for both persuasion and policy formation.

As with QCCs, this involved visits to other innovating firms alongside internal discussions:

> We went out and looked at companies like Rover and how they had managed to change from their old style of working with foremen.... Rover had actually gone a lot further than we were going... the team leaders weren't actually supervisors, they were just sort of the leader of the gang and were picked by the operators. We thought that was perhaps taking it a bit too far.

As this suggests, however, the agenda remained very much domestically defined. The result was a radical overhaul of existing arrangements. A new team leader role was to replace supervision, to combine technical and personnel responsibilities more effectively. The old leading hand was abolished, senior operators were redefined as technical experts without wider responsibilities, and the role of the managers immediately above team leaders was also addressed. Helped by an external consultant, this reconstruction of the job hierarchy also involved systematic assessment of all existing supervisors to decide whether they had the appropriate skills for the new role.

British managers also sought to persuade their Japanese colleagues of the legitimacy of this change from arrangements that had been developed under earlier Japanese tutelage. The alliance between the Japanese MD and the senior British manager was again crucial in this respect, though this did not mean that disquiet disappeared. Thus one local manager commented that:

> Officially they support it (chuckle). The MD... he totally supported it I believe. I think some of the Japanese further down the line support it because he does. They are very loyal people. But I honestly believe that my [immediate Japanese] boss doesn't think it's the right thing. He had his head in his hands once and told me privately... that he thinks, because of problems we are generating, quality problems we are generating now, he feels that it's not the way to go.

First, then, the capacity of the senior British managers at Copy-Co to formulate and implement this major change represented a telling form of localization. In particular, it underlined their ability to develop the argument about their necessary role in the management of British labour, in a way that gained the active support of top Japanese management within the plant. Second, however, this did not guarantee active support of the policy across the factory, and it was widely seen as very much the property of British management.

Implementing Team Leadership: Increasing Pressure, Declining Support?

The existing supervisors were most directly threatened by the proposed changes, as the diagnosis of past failings implied that some were not suitable to become team leaders and the assessment process was designed to determine who. Understandably this process generated considerable disquiet, as was acknowledged by one of the managers directly involved:

> They hated it, they were very, very resentful. They felt as though they were applying for their own jobs basically... so it was a very tense time, a lot of unsettled people.

In the event, the selection process included not only existing supervisors but also many 'leading hands' and several other employees nominated by management, so the pool of potential team leaders numbered over sixty people. However, expanding production and plans to cut the size of some big teams meant that more team leaders than supervisors were needed. From around twenty-five supervisors about three-quarters became team leaders, together with several other internal candidates, but at least eight new people were also recruited from outside directly into the new role.

The biggest impact of these changes was on those supervisors who were rejected. One commented:

> I was devastated. I was a good supervisor, ... I'd been a supervisor for six years and I'd never been sat down and told that I wasn't suitable for being a supervisor. On the contrary, I'd got one of the highest assessments. I still believe it wasn't the right thing to do to take me off that line.... They basically put people into this new team-leader role that were far less capable than myself. I mean that's not just my opinion that's everybody's opinion.

Our interviews suggest this was, indeed, a widespread opinion on the shop-floor, though the impact was mitigated by a commitment to re-deployment to provide job security to those affected, with relocation and sometimes retraining in ancillary technical or administrative jobs.

However, more telling were the criticisms by some of the supervisors who did become team leaders. Many of their points were well articulated by a woman who was recognized as an informal spokesperson. She was sympathetic to the *idea* of teamwork, but much less convinced by the rhetorical contrast between old autocratic supervisors and new participative team leaders:

> So they took away the leading hand and then called us team leaders, and said 'what we want you to do now is to be an integral part of the team, more hands-on, be involved with the people'. I've been doing that for the past five years, so they have basically just taken the name, taken out leading hands, changed the name. I can't see any difference.... Just a little bit more work now because we don't have the leading hands that could take care of quality things; certain aspects of investigations and what have you, for want of a better word, some of the donkey work, some of the leg work the leading hands were there to assist with. And also the leading hands were trained to become supervisors, so there was motivation there for them. These leading hands are now senior operators; they have lost a status. There is no motivation, and we are now busier—team leaders are now busier. But the job hasn't changed.

Abolishing leading hands simultaneously increased the work of team leaders and undermined hopes of promotion. Furthermore, managers now provided less day-to-day support, further increasing the pressure. Finally, she argued that all this was experienced most acutely by the newly recruited team leaders, who had little training or back-up:

> It's [some of] the new ones that is sinking, and I can see that they are going to go. They're not going to last very much longer because the pressure is showing. They are not coping; they are not getting any support. They are just thrown in. And all the normal problems that you get within production, they are not coping with. The absenteeism, the defects in machinery, the quality problems, which you can normally take in your stride and it's just all part of the way it is, and you can usually control it and overcome it, but you can see it, it's just piling up.

However, even those who were reappointed often had to cope with being moved to new areas, which disrupted established relationships and existing knowledge.

Senior British managers recognized the dilemmas involved in these changes. One remarked:

> Unless they understand processes and have got some technical skills it is very difficult to move along the quality improvement road. But primarily we were looking for people with better man-management skills who would take care of the team.... But they have to have the technical knowledge, you can't just have somebody in there with man-management skills and no technical knowledge, although to a certain extent you can get support from people beneath you. But one of my problems at the moment is team leaders that I have recruited from outside, is that they haven't any technical knowledge.

However, they tended to view lack of technical expertise as a necessary transitional cost rather than a more enduring problem, and hoped that the tensions arising from the restructuring of supervision would be overcome in time. Japanese middle managers, however, were more sceptical. As one Japanese production manager commented:

> From my understanding the team-leader system is a little bit stronger on the man-management side. That's the difference, it's too strong on that side. This is a little bit upside down. I said man-management was very important, but a more important matter is the quality awareness or technical skill of the team leader.... They can't manage or supervise without the technical skill, but sometimes [the company] brings team leaders from the outside. This is one of the big problems for me [to understand]. I agree they have good man-management skill, good capability, but they haven't any experience for the technical side.

Thus Japanese managers tended to reverse the terms of the British diagnosis by emphasizing the pivotal importance of technical competencies and also the costs of undermining an internal labour market that had nurtured such competencies.

Criticisms of the way the reforms had altered the internal labour market were also widely shared on the shop-floor. A senior operator emphasized the ramifications in terms of disappointed expectations:

> It was a bad move because you've got nowhere to go. I mean I don't know if I'm going to make it to team leader, whereas before I would probably have made it to leading hand. And it means now they've got a lot of people going nowhere and the younger lads behind me aren't going to get my job. So it's a bit of resentment now about that...I suppose it makes sense for them because it saves them money, but in the long run it'll probably cost them, four or five people will leave.

Meanwhile, a new team leader who *had* moved up the job ladder emphasized that this remained a major issue:

> I don't think it was handled very well. Obviously I don't know what the options were to them, but I'm very close to the shop-floor area and I know what the feeling is there and I can gauge that. The disappointment from the leading hands who didn't make it was tremendous.

Thus the downgrading of leading hands and the appointment of staff from outside undermined existing expectations among experienced employees about the scope for promotion within the firm, a theme highlighted not only by team leaders and senior operators but also by other shop-floor workers.

Finally, shop-floor criticisms of promotion and demotion decisions often involved allegations of favouritism. An operator gave us a vivid example:

> When I started there were more Japanese here than we've got now, and you used to be able to get promoted from within the factory straight up, but since English management took over the running of things, its like who you know [rather] than what you do, so people get preference to other people. There was one where the supervisor, his girlfriend—he started going out with this girl—she got made up to relief; then he dumped her, and they demoted her. And now he is married to another girl and she got made up to relief. People looking at these things are thinking, 'well we never actually got the job'.... Even if you had brilliant qualifications for the job, you aren't going to get it.

Such claims of favouritism were not ubiquitous but they were fairly common and embraced diverse aspects of working life. They extended upwards to include the selection process that had produced the new cohort of team leaders, but they also extended downwards to include the exercise of discretion over day-to-day matters of job allocation and discipline. We will return to the theme of favouritism in Chapter 11, but our argument here is that the restructuring of supervision had been quite corrosive of existing expectations and commitments among longer service workers and in this context charges of favouritism gained currency.

In summary, then, the British managers at Copy-Co had, over a two-year period, successfully developed and implemented both a substantial reorganization of the structure of supervision and major changes in the occupancy of supervisory roles. This had involved the consolidation of a shared view among senior British managers, in alliance with top Japanese management, and the resulting changes had entrenched the priority of 'people management' over both technical skills and the integrity of internal promotion pathways. However, the legacy of this transformation remained quite contested during the period of our research, as groups outside the policymaking process measured the new arrangements against what they continued to regard as the virtues of the old structures. In this regard *shop-floor* views did have parallels with those found in Broad's (1994) study, as it was often British managers who were seen as having disrupted more acceptable Japanese-inspired arrangements.

It will be evident from our discussion of shop-floor views in Chapter 11, that there were subtle but significant differences in the ways these changes were experienced in different parts of the factory. In some areas, characterized by quite small work teams clustered around specific pieces of equipment, both team leaders and shop-floor workers perceived a relatively benign pattern of continuity between the arrangements involving the old supervisors and the new team leaders. In the complex assembly areas which have been the focus of our discussion the changes were experienced as more contradictory, but the dominant view from below highlighted the disruption of established competencies, expectations and social relations, and increased pressures on the new team leaders. However, in still other areas, especially where there was process production, the experience was of an unequivocal increase in work pressure and a tightening of discipline, particularly in relation to the night shift. Thus in many parts of the factory the impact of the restructuring appeared to be quite substantial but it did not match the positive transformation envisaged by the management proponents of change and it remained a focus of uncertainties and tensions.

PART-CO: THE FORM AND LIMITS OF A STRINGENT PRODUCTION REGIME IN CONDITIONS OF EMPLOYMENT TURBULENCE

The strategic internationalization of Part-Co

Part-Co has often been seen as a pioneer and exemplar of sophisticated product design and lean production methods because of its role in the historical development of close collaborative relations in the upper reaches of the automobile sector supply chain in Japan. Indeed, its very integration into the disaggregated production complex of Japanese auto production probably helps to explain the relatively late internationalization of the firm's production operations, as the late 1970s and early 1980s were characterized by a massive expansion of production capacity in Japan. However, the first overseas factories were established in East Asia in the late 1970s, and investment in Asia has continued since. This was followed by the establishment of major production facilities in the United States in 1986 and 1990 and then investment in Australia, Brazil and the United Kingdom.

Thus the establishment of the Telford plant in the early 1990s represented the first Part-Co investment to manufacture its product line in Europe, but this was part of what was by then a well established strategy of the internationalization of production. One important consequence of this timing was that Part-Co had by then established an organized programme of training for Japanese managers destined for overseas duties, and had a significant cadre of managers with international experience to draw upon in the foundation and development of newer sites such as that at Telford, though some informants suggested that the pace of internationalization was still outstripping the availability of appropriate staff. In particular, the firm could call upon managers with experience of working in its American and Australian plants, and this appeared particularly pertinent both in terms of communicating in English and in terms of labour market institutions and employee attitudes. However, as will be seen, this did not resolve all of the problems facing Japanese managers in the British plant.

The pressures that stimulated the internationalization of production by Part-Co were similar to those that have been identified elsewhere. The most immediate pressures for investment beyond East Asia arose from the demands of the Japanese car manufacturers that were the firm's main customers. As they began to move their production to the United States and later Europe they expected suppliers to move with them. The broader context of these moves was the rivalry between Japanese, American, and European automobile producers and the threat of restrictions on imports to both the United States and Europe. This formed the background both to the strategy of internationalization and also, in the British case, the pursuit of a joint venture with a European firm, albeit with Part-Co as the dominant partner. The internationalization of production was further reinforced by two additional considerations. One was the experience of the high yen in the 1990s, which tilted the balance further away from production for export from Japan. The other was the concern of Part-Co to widen its customer base, to include European car makers alongside its established Japanese customers, premised on the assumption that European producers would increasingly develop new models requiring their product.

This last feature underlines the strategic and proactive character of the firm's overseas investment. The requirements of the Japanese final assemblers were pivotal in the timing and development of its overseas investments and these companies retained considerable leverage as dominant customers. However, Part-Co is itself a major international company with its own strategic capabilities, and by the late 1980s, the company could claim to have overtaken both of the major American producers of car components in its product market. Thus the expansion of its customer base to include serveral European manufacturers reflected its existing strengths in design and production and reinforced its bargaining position in relation to its major Japanese customers. Nevertheless, international competition between the major automobile producers and persistent tendencies towards global overcapacity (Williams et al. 1994*b*) exerted pressures on even the largest component manufacturers.

The production regime at Part-Co reflects these pressures, both through competition for orders and the quality and delivery demands exerted on production lines dedicated to production for particular models and customers. In these respects, then, this firm is a major and proactive player within the auto industry production chain but also subject to the broader competitive pressures that have stimulated the pursuit of so-called lean production methods across the sector (Harrison 1994: 161). Thus the role of the British subsidiary was to produce established product lines and implement established production processes, both to serve existing customers and gain new customers. To achieve this objective, the parent company was prepared to invest substantial sums; at the time of our research they were investing over £30 million—about a third of the value of the turnover of the factory at that time—in a key phase of their longer term expansion. The expectation was that this investment was to be recouped within four years, while it was reported that the factory had moved into profit in its established production facilities a year ahead of projections.

The primacy of Japanese management in implementing the production regime at Part-Co

Five years after the establishment of the Telford plant, Japanese managers remained predominant in the management team. Below the Japanese MD the senior management team consisted of seven Japanese and two British managers. In the first few years of the new factory the most senior British manager on site had been the representative of the European minority partner, and had played a particularly important public relations role. However, when he resigned he was not replaced, and one British informant characterized the European company as a 'sleeping partner'. Below the senior managers were fourteen other Japanese and twelve other British members of the management team. Twelve of the Japanese managers were designated 'coordinators', and formally they had a substantial guidance and liaison rather than direct line management role, while four of the locals were designated 'assistant managers'.

These titles implied a gradual process of transfer of responsibility from Japanese to British managers. According to both British and Japanese informants, the Japanese managers in the second wave (in terms of four- to five-year tours of duty) would hold less direct responsibility than the first wave, while the third wave would have the most difficult job, as they would have to negotiate policy with the local managers, some of whom would graduate from the role of assistant manager. At the time of our research, however, localization remained quite uneven. Japanese managers continued to play the leading role in all areas apart from personnel matters, while the coordinators were also concentrated in planning, engineering, and production activities. Meanwhile, the primary responsibility of the senior British manager was personnel and we were told that British managers had taken responsibility for 'man-management from day one'. One British manager summed up by saying that 'the engineering side, the purchasing side, the system side, they are very much done by Part-Co in Japan . . . so I would say we were the only function probably in the company that were given reasonable freedom to do things the British way, but influenced by Japan'.

The three successive Japanese MDs had extensive experience as production engineers or manufacturing managers, both in Japan and overseas, but their expertise was also tailored to different phases in the development of the factory. Thus the first MD had particular experience of starting up an American factory, while the most recent was characterized by a British manager as 'very much a production engineer, the right man at the right time', because his role was to 'rack up production'. Some of the more junior Japanese managers had also worked in the United States, though others had been despatched direct from Japan. These managers were in regular contact with their counterparts in Japan (and sometimes in the United States) by phone, fax, and e-mail: for example one technical manager reported that 'I spend all morning, talking on the phone every day, and I also have TV conferences a few times a month'.

Such managers saw themselves as implementing parent company approaches at the British subsidiary, with a focus on developing an intense work regime and increasing output as the factory expanded. Comparing Part-Co with other firms in the area, a Japanese manager reflected that 'the pressure on the shop-floor worker is larger than in other companies. The auto industry is particularly strict in quality and delivery. It tends to be strictly controlled and the line speed is faster as well than other companies'. At the same time Japanese managers registered several ways in which the British operation differed from those they were used to. First, it was producing smaller production volumes but for a wider range of customers, compared with Japan and even the American factories. This meant that the level of mechanization was lower than in Japan, while there was more variation in the expectations of customers. Second, labour turnover was a particular problem, exacerbated by the continuing recruitment associated with the process of expansion. As one Japanese manager remarked 'the turnover rate is high, so human resources and technical knowledge are not accumulated very well and quality control is not so easy'. This meant that more time had to be invested in basic training while it was more difficult to develop more extended training, and these features reinforced an emphasis on labour-intensive production using 'fool-proofed' job routines.

Alongside the features of production volume, customer diversity, and labour turnover, some Japanese managers also highlighted what they saw as contrasting patterns of commitment among British and Japanese workers. Thus one Japanese manager, interviewed by a Japanese research student when directly involved in production in the British factory in the late 1990s, argued that:

> Japanese [workers] try to do 120% of the target when they complete 100% just in case. British workers tend to be satisfied with 70%. When they achieve 100% of the target within the time they tend to be like 'Well done! Let's play the 30 minutes left.' They forget that they achieved only 90% of the target yesterday. Even if the team leaders worry about the delays in production, the shop-floor workers do not make efforts to reduce absenteeism.... If the same thing happens in Japan workers are called together and are severely encouraged by the manager. Here, encouragement does not work, generally.

Clearly this manager felt he faced distinctive problems of labour discipline and commitment at Telford, compared with the home plants in Japan (or even the American operations, where he believed improvements had arisen from the enhanced skills and commitments of a core of longer-service workers). Nevertheless, some Japanese managers noted that they had revised some of their negative expectations about the British workforce. Drawing on American experience and/or existing stereotypes, they had expected rigid job demarcations and resistance to overtime at Part-Co, but instead had found the workforce quite flexible and willing to work overtime when it was available.

Of course, the reference to 'severe encouragement' serves as a valuable reminder of the institutional framework within which worker effort and commitment is elicited in major Japanese firms, and especially the cumulative role of supervisory ratings and merit pay in rewarding and punishing employees. Furthermore, we will explore the character and basis of the scepticism and instrumentalism of many of the British employees of Part-Co in more detail later. Here we only need to note their widespread feeling that a combination of low wages, stringent production routines and work pace meant that they faced an unfair effort bargain, and this undercut any willingness to exercise additional initiative and responsibility beyond routine work performance.

British engineers as translators and innovators

The British engineers were generally appreciative of the skills and expertise of the Japanese managers in Japan and in Britain. One British engineer highlighted the prolonged and rounded training of the Japanese design engineers at the parent facility, described their knowledge of product design as 'very, very deep' and extolled the resulting expertise of the Japanese coordinator with whom he worked. This was the dominant emphasis among British engineers, despite some problems in communication between Japanese and British staff in English and some frustrations when product or process details were held in Japan because of commercial confidentiality. Furthermore, it was usual for such British staff to undergo intensive familiarization and training in particular production areas over a period ranging from one to three months in Japan, and to work with a range of Japanese engineers and specialists in implementing such production in Telford.

In this context British and Japanese staff shared similar perceptions of the distinctive features of the British operation. Thus one product engineer reflected on similarities and differences in the following terms:

> The prototype phase is handled by HQ, so they will send us a prototype unit. What we tend to do is get all the senior specialists... and we will disassemble and reassemble this unit a number of times to see how we can improve it. So sometimes we have to make modifications to allow for our assembly lines and allow for our operators. Normally it's difficulty of assembly. When I say compensate for our lines, or allow for our assembly lines, basically it'll be the same wherever you go in the world. We're looking at a method which will make assembly easier, so though it'll make it easy here, it'll make it easy in Japan. But [the Japanese parent plant] utilize a very high level of automation because the volumes are much higher, much higher. By an order of magnitude, whereby they can justify having robots, they actually have a complete assembly line which is purely automated.... So they may design something with a view for it to be handled by a robot, whereas we don't use robots, so we have to change that design.

At the same time such local engineers emphasized that tailoring the production process to the needs of the widening range of European producers meant the manufacture of a broader range of smaller batches of distinctive products, many of which were not made in Japan. Furthermore, both cost pressures and the advantages of proximity encouraged the local sourcing of parts (including high value parts where they were procurable) and specialist equipment and in some cases the in-house production of prototypes.

Japan continued to play the key role in design and development because they had a massive concentration of very experienced and highly trained design engineers and relations with customer firms were mediated through these design teams and the sales organization. Such features placed limits on the extent to which the Telford factory would become a focus of engineering expertise. However, the production engineers at Telford had a wide range of responsibilities in modifying designs for manufacturability (DFM) in the United Kingdom context and responding to changing customer requirements, and emphasized that they exercised considerable initiative and responsibility in developing appropriate product specifications and production processes.

The British engineers, like their Japanese counterparts, also regarded the attitudes of workers as an important influence on how they implemented production arrangements. Thus, several contrasted the motivation and commitment of workers at the mother factory in Japan with those in the United Kingdom in terms which paralleled those of Japanese managers, again spelling out some of the implications for work design:

> I've just put a machine in that originally we were going to be looking at very basic, we were going to rely on the skill of the operator to do the job. And

> we've actually done a lot of head banging with the management here to actually say 'no, we don't want to do this'. . . . I've actually put in a machine in which the skill is taken away from the operator. The machine does a lot for them. You've only got to load and unload. Even if he puts a wrong part in, the machine will tell him. If he's missed a part, the machine will tell him with a message, look you've done this. And even when he has to change the model to put a new tool in, he doesn't have to do anything. He just drops a tool in and the software in the machine will recognize I've got so and so tool and it'll load the part and it will tell him, now you are sort of running this product, you know. That's what we're sort of aiming for basically. And we've been allowed to do it.

Thus, while Japanese managers remained the senior and dominant influence in planning and production, there was also a shared recognition that production practices had to be tailored and modified to suit the distinctive product and labour market conditions within which the Telford factory operated, and this encouraged 'foolproofing'. Such solutions emerged from 'head banging with management', by which this informant meant a quite positive but lengthy process of discussion and justification.

The whole manufacturing process at Part-Co was organized in terms of teamworking, tight product scheduling, and rigorous QCCs. However, the implications of these underlying features of the production process were significantly different for different parts of the factory. One main area involved a series of short assembly lines involving fifteen to twenty-five employees, most dedicated to the production of a family of product variants for one customer. On these lines, cycle times varied between twenty-eight seconds and a maximum of two minutes, with outputs ranging from the low two hundred up to around eight hundred per shift. A kanban system of parts supply was in operation, 'andon' lights were used to signal problems, and deliveries were despatched at regular intervals through the day. Finally, there was a threefold inspection process, which involved the assemblers themselves, one of the team performing an end-of-line check and finally an inspector from the QC department.

Another area involved a combination of heavy machinery, such as presses, and testing equipment, which constituted a series of steps in the production of key sub-assemblies. This equipment required setting, loading, monitoring, and adjusting, operations that were performed by several clusters of workers on a three-shift basis. Output targets also operated in this area, and the design of operations had been informed by 'foolproofing', but the major machine-minding tasks were less tightly paced while the kanban system had limited impact, partly because of the scrapping of defective parts. However, there was a simple but systematic set of checks on both products and machine performance, in part tied to a preventative maintenance regime. In each case these production procedures were overlaid by teamworking arrangements which were translated into rather varied practices in terms of job rotation, and by procedures of individual appraisal linked to pay bands and policies for continuous improvement, in the form of QCCs and a suggestions scheme.

Thus Part-Co management, operating as we have seen in the competitive environment of components supply to a range of European car plants, sought to model their operations directly upon Japan. They used teamworking and 'andon lights' in assembly, and coupled teams with detailed procedure manuals and Statistical Process Control (SPC) techniques in the machining areas. However, the implementation of these techniques was significantly affected by difficulties of recruitment and retention. On the assembly lines one reflection of this was a rather limited rotation among jobs, despite management's theoretical commitment to extensive rotation, resulting in spasmodic redeployment of workers between teams or to provide overtime cover. In practice most workers had been trained and gained experience in just a few positions (compare Sharpe 1997), not only because many were newcomers and the work schedules allowed limited opportunities for training, but also because there were advantages to leaving experienced operators on jobs they had mastered, so long as they did not complain too much. Meanwhile, in the machining sections, the engineers resorted to more 'foolproofing' than was said to be common in Japan, while a simplification of procedure manuals into 'bullet point' job cards also reflected the proportion of inexperienced workers and the limited time available for their 'on-the-job training'.

The initial formation of personnel and employment policies

While Japanese managers dominated in the areas of production, planning, quality, and financial control, British managers were, from the foundation of the company, delegated primary responsibility for personnel matters. Thus, the senior British manager during the start-up emphasized that he was given a 'free hand' in organizing recruitment and personnel administration, with minimal direct guidance from Japan or the expatriate Japanese staff, as they recognized that they lacked experience of local conditions and practices. Of course, Japanese managers brought their own expectations with them. For example, some translated their experience of the structure of recruitment and career progression in their homeland into a preference for recruiting young inexperienced male workers to be shaped to suit the needs of the firm, while most were shocked and puzzled by the high rates of labour turnover. However, it tended to be the younger managers who had come direct from Japan who assumed that it would be best to recruit youngsters, whilst more senior and more internationally experienced managers were more open to alternative policies. In particular, those Japanese managers with American or Australian experience supported the inclination of the British managers to seek to recruit a wider mix of workers.

However, the relative autonomy of British managers in personnel matters did not mean an absence of constraints and guidelines. First, such key features as regular overtime and comparatively low wages were built into the original investment calculations of the firm and thus represented important constraints, though in regard to wages we were told that the calculations underpinning the continuing programme of investment and expansion did allow for some improvements, so long as levels remained below those in the nearby industrial conurbations. Second, the policies of existing Japanese firms also served as both constraints and guidelines. This cluster of plants had already set prevailing terms for pay and conditions, and it was expected that incoming firms would conform to these norms. This meant that managers at Part-Co were more or less locked into an existing pay norm that some of them, and especially the senior British manager, increasingly came to regard as an important obstacle to resolving problems of recruitment and retention, a theme we will return to later. Nevertheless, senior management at Part-Co, including the British personnel manager, were keen to draw upon the experience of these existing firms to inform their policies during the development of their own operations. The advice of other personnel managers reinforced their wariness about focusing recruitment too narrowly on young workers. They also took particular note of advice not to introduce a complete package of worker involvement and continuous improvement policies immediately, as managers in other firms felt that this made their eventual success less likely. As a result, the Part-Co managers pursued a staged introduction of QCCs and suggestion schemes, though these were supposed to be fully operational by the time of our main fieldwork.

The policies developed in the American sister plant, established six years before the British start-up, were another important influence on the development of employment policies at the Telford factory. For example, the preventative maintenance procedures were originally copied directly from the United States. Several of the Japanese managers at Telford, including the initial MD, had also played key roles in the United States, and they not only drew upon that experience but also regarded the policy documentation and training materials that had been developed there as an appropriate template from which to construct British practices. This did not mean the simple transfer of American policies to the United Kingdom, as local managers were left with substantial scope to 'anglicize' the policies and materials. Furthermore, as noted above, some of the Japanese managers became aware of significant differences between the workforces in the United Kingdom and the United States.

However, it was also evident from our interviews that this process of translation sustained a significant influence from the American plant. One example involved the training materials. These were being thoroughly revised by British managers in another, smaller, British Part-Co factory, which significantly was a brownfield site that had been taken over by the Japanese company and was thus more thoroughly embedded in established British employment practices. However, they were still being used in broadly original form at Telford. More significantly, the format and procedures of the Associates Meeting had been carried over directly into the Telford plant, supported enthusiastically by the Japanese MD who had been a senior manager in the United States. This institution did not mirror arrangements in the mother factory in Japan, but rather reflected the policies of union exclusion that have characterized much modern American management and that had evidently informed the approach of managers at the American sister plant. At the same time, this approach to giving a tightly circumscribed 'voice' to the new workforce was fully consistent with the preference for union avoidance that characterized the Japanese inward investors in Telford. Thus, it appears that the influence of the American experience arose partly from the latitude afforded to management by a greenfield site and partly from the fit between policies developed in the United States and the approach that had already been developed by other Japanese inward investors in Telford.

Of course, the effectiveness of this policy stance might have been challenged by the workforce or by trade unions. It will become evident later in our discussion that the Associates Meetings were experienced by most employees as an inadequate forum for articulating and pursuing their most pressing concerns. However, at the time of our research in the late 1990s such dissatisfaction had not been translated into any demand for alternative forms of representation. Apparently, two major trade unions had written to the management, early in the history of the factory, proposing discussions about union recognition, but senior management rebuffed their overtures and, somewhat to the surprise of our management informants, they had heard no more. Furthermore, despite some more recent union efforts to recruit members and pursue recognition through a strategy of union organizing, unions still remained unrecognized at Part-Co in 2004.

The struggle to manage recruitment, turnover, and discipline at Part-Co

As a non-unionized assembly plant with comparable wages and conditions, Part-Co was similar to the other large Japanese firms in the Telford 'cluster'. However, as a rapidly expanding car-components factory characterized by tight work schedules, extensive shiftworking and regular overtime, it was distinctive in ways that sharpened the problems of recruitment, commitment, and labour turnover experienced by all of the Japanese inward investors in Telford. There were particular difficulties in recruiting and retaining skilled engineers, but the major concern of managers was the recruitment and retention of semi-skilled workers. As our discussion of shop-floor views (in Chapter 11) will show, the frequency of job quits and the limits which employees placed on their commitment to such activities as continuous improvement were related to a widespread feeling that the work demands at Part-Co were greater than in most of the other Japanese factories. It was in this light that the wage rates were regarded as poor, as the work pressure was inadequately compensated by the going rate, so those with little to risk left for easier work elsewhere.

Some managers provided a more positive interpretation, suggesting that workers gained from their experience of a more complex but stringent work process but then had more scope to search for better pay elsewhere:

> They're confident, they've used skills they didn't even know they had when they walked in. They probably worked in twenty jobs where they used to put a screw in... and now they're using QC circles, graphs, they're filling in data. They feel part of something. You can sit in an interview then and you can say 'Oh I used to do this, I used to do that', and the guy says, 'he's quite handy we'll have him'. I think that the biggest problem we've got here is we do open people's eyes. They realize and they go off.

However, this still suggests that the firm continued to be vulnerable to the loss of its more experienced workers and not just disillusioned new recruits. This same manager also emphasized the stringent requirements of the production system and the extent to which it had been foolproofed for British workers. He argued that the Japanese production system was designed to operate with operators who exercised *disciplined* initiative, as Japanese workers exercised initiative within the defined parameters and stopped where they were told. However, British workers tended to just carry on or switch off, so 'we can't trust them, so some of the things we've fitted to prevent things, it's just crazy'.

This, then, was the context in which managers drew on a range of experiences, models, and advice to cope with these pressing problems and organize production and employment relations in the factory. British managers with responsibility for personnel matters were, however, sceptical about some of the solutions pursued at other Japanese firms in Telford (including Copy-Co). One such partial solution was to bus employees in from outside the locality, especially from the Black Country. However, this was seen as inappropriate for Part-Co because it would be difficult to reconcile with the complex shift system and the frequent but somewhat unpredictable overtime working that was integral to the operation of the factory. Furthermore, there was scepticism about the likelihood that turnover would be much reduced if those recruited had access to a labour market where better pay was likely to be available:

> Here it's more of a rural sort of lower wage area, and on that basis you know this commuting system, once something better comes along it falls down, and the policy of the company has always been to recruit locally.

Another widely adopted management response had been to recruit workers from 'temping agencies' (Elger and Smith 1998*b*) but again the managers at Part-Co remained sceptical, and had 'resisted the use of agency workers for a long time'. Though they eventually started to use them as they expanded production and recruitment, they still did not regard them as a solution to problems of commitment and reliability. Thus, they tried to keep the proportion of temporary agency workers relatively low and by the late 1990s less than 10 per cent of staff were temps.

The perceived inadequacies of such policies prompted Part-Co managers to consider more strategic moves. In particular it was evident early in our research, in 1996, that there was considerable debate within management about the scope, advisability, and potential effects of improving levels of pay, of breaking away from, or at least finessing, the going wage rate among Japanese firms in the area. Advocates of this policy, among them the senior British manager during that period, highlighted the extra demands placed upon their employees compared with those in other firms, and argued that higher pay rates could be legitimated by reference to the distinctive demands placed upon the car-components sector. At the same time, managers were wary about making such changes, not only because of the views of other firms but also because of the risk of destabilizing an established pattern of low wages. Furthermore, as we noted earlier, investment decisions had been based on these established wage levels, though the financial projections actually provided leeway for some improvements.

This meant that there were only minor changes to pay, rather than a more substantial departure from district norms. The main development was the award of modest service increments during the first two years of service, in recognition of the training undertaken over this period. A British manager claimed that other companies did not do this, so 'for the longer serving people this helped a little bit'. However, at the end of the 1990s a Japanese manager continued to identify a problem with pay levels:

> I asked the company to raise the salary after the appraisal, for the people that I want to stay... if the salary is not satisfactorily raised, they may move to another company. However as there is a company salary policy, the company may not necessarily be able to satisfy the employees.

In lamenting his inability to award more flexible, personalized increments, he drew on home-country recipes for a solution, but this was not one pursued by senior management.

Meanwhile, in the absence of decisive moves on the wages front, continuing attention was given to a range of more limited initiatives, especially concerning recruitment. The resulting changes in recruitment procedures were primarily ad hoc adjustments to changing circumstances, especially phases of expansion and the tightening of the local labour market, but the recruitment process was speeded up and also became less stringent. Both a maths test and a rigid requirement for previous job stability were dropped after a time, as the priority became to recruit routine assembly workers rather than key workers and it also became evident that the maths test was deterring applicants. At the same time the recruitment staff at Part-Co still saw themselves as more selective than some of the other expanding inward investors:

> We know a lot of the ones we've rejected are over there [at another Japanese firm]. . . . Anybody can get the numbers in . . . but we don't want that, we want to maintain the standards as best we can, take on people who are going to stay, otherwise your turnover's affected . . . So it's really been a move away from a narrow definition of manufacturing experience to a broader, more open-minded policy.

However, it remained difficult to facilitate recruitment without exacerbating turnover. As a consequence, induction and training were broken into stages, so that people were moved into production more rapidly and efforts were not 'wasted' on those who left after a short stay, but this also meant that later training was sometimes further delayed by the demands of production.

Team leaders: pivotal but troubled actors

In the absence of more substantial policy changes, it was the team leaders who were expected to play the pivotal role in mobilizing low paid workers to perform routine assembly and machining work. Managers emphasized that team leaders played a key part in handling employment relations, and saw action at that level as crucial to the reduction of turnover rates. In these conditions team leaders experienced considerable pressure. For example, one commented:

> Well, my idea of a team leader is to ensure that the product gets put out on time to the best quality possible. I mean that's the be-all and end of it as far as I'm concerned. But I think they expect a lot more than a team leader role should be. I mean we're all convinced that we're gradually getting like an under-manager job and we shouldn't be. We're getting involved with things like productivity. There's a lot of stuff we're actually involved in on the paperwork side of things that I don't see as our responsibility as such. . . . Something can go wrong there [on the line] and then we'll get told off for not keeping an eye on there, and then if we do that we get told off for not keeping up with the paperwork.

This tension between organizing the line and doing the paperwork could be read as just another instance of the cross-pressures which beset all supervisors or team leaders. It will become evident, however, that the pressures the team leaders faced at Part-Co were also marked by the specific conditions in which this factory operated.

Most of the team leaders we interviewed had been recruited as ordinary associates and moved up an internal job ladder, though they had been team leaders for periods varying from just a few months to many years.

They were generally enthusiastic about the opportunity for advancement (which reflected the growth of the factory and a management commitment to internal progression) but they also felt undervalued and underpaid for the work they did (a reflection of pay rates in the firm). Their views differed in emphasis but were in many respects consistent, partly because they had pooled experience and developed a shared outlook through day-to-day discussions among themselves. Thus four themes dominated their evaluation of their job, namely, good opportunities for advancement, real job security, the expanding and demanding range of their responsibilities and, finally, distinctly inadequate pay. While the first three were often seen as real attractions of the job and the firm, issues of pay combined with the demanding nature of the work to give a more negative tone to their overall outlook.

They were certainly positive about their opportunities to develop and progress through the ranks to become team leaders. This theme was well captured by an informant who had become a team leader after three years with the firm:

> I've never had a job in the past where I've had the opportunity to get on. So I didn't know whether I was capable or not I suppose. But I came here and I just tended to take an interest in different areas and I stuck in the business and it ended up I just got on with everything I suppose. Just sort of slowly worked my way up... I've learnt so much it's unbelievable. My whole life's improved. Because of the confidence I've gained from being in charge as it were.

Another commented that, though she had been concerned about how far her prospects for advancement might be curtailed, she had been reassured by the company's approach:

> They made sure that I was aware that, although I was female and thought I was in a dead-end type of job, they weren't intending leaving me [there]. They themselves are looking five years into the future. 'This is where we want you to go.' So I knew... earlier on that I was going to be going somewhere, you know. And when I did take on this job, the feeling to me is, if I do well at this, that obviously I've got to progress to a next step, which would mean I would be the first female supervisor.

This sense of progression was commonly linked with an appreciation of the company's approach to the organization of production and productivity. All these team leaders had experienced training from Japanese staff as operators or setters, while several had later visited Japan, though for shorter periods than the British industrial engineers, and they generally had a high regard for Japanese methods.

Both the interest and challenge of the job and some of its pressures arose from efforts to implement these methods. One team leader developed this point with particular enthusiasm:

> I mean every day of the week we have to look to make sure that we're following procedures. We have to always be looking to improve. That's the

> most important thing. If you want to stand still, you know, if you're the sort of person that likes your little circle, and you don't want to go out of your comfort zone, then don't work for a Japanese company. Because the Japanese, they like to improve and they do it on a regular basis. And there's nothing they like more than for you to take on something and prove yourself, and go to them and say 'look I've researched this. This is what I started with, this is what my conclusion is, and this is what the payback is.' And if you can show them every step along the line, and they think it's worth going for it, they'll do it.

These positive views about progression and innovation were generally accompanied by an appreciation of what was confidently regarded as substantial job security, often counterposed to earlier work histories marked by redundancies and competition to find work. Thus one team leader noted how repeated redundancies 'had had a hard effect' on him, while another felt that in contrast 'around here this has got to be the safest job around I should imagine'.

The third key feature of their outlook was an emphasis on the sheer range of demands and responsibilities that were placed upon them. When asked what the job involved the most experienced of our informants responded 'what doesn't it involve! Everybody must have told you that. It involves everything', adding that it would be 'a manager's job in an English factory'. In some respects this was welcomed, as an opportunity to develop within the firm. In this sense, both the variety of work and the satisfactions of exercising responsibility were appreciated. However, there was also a general feeling that too much was being asked of them. In this respect the language used by our informants was strikingly similar. Typical comments were that 'the pressure here is ridiculous, you are under too much pressure all the time', and 'being a team leader is very very stressful, extremely stressful, because a team leader here would actually be a supervisor level anywhere else'.

We will consider the character and sources of such pressures shortly, but first we need to emphasize that the arguments about overload were strongly linked to views about their level of pay. The consensus was that they were being paid low wages even for a team leader, while in reality they were being expected to perform the job of a supervisor. As one said 'I mean that's all we talk about between ourselves. We just say we just want paying what we are worth.' This view was buttressed by comparisons with conditions elsewhere, drawn from past experience, local knowledge, and information about the earnings of some of those who had left. One experienced team leader had, exceptionally, held line or group-leader positions in several other firms, and drew a sharp contrast with her role at Part-Co:

> A line controller at [an earlier employer], all we did was fill a line. That was it. And report if we were short of stock or not. But you got the money just for that. But here you get the money for just that. You don't get money for like being, you're a supervisor here. A line leader/team leader here is a supervisor.

Meanwhile, another informant highlighted the difference when someone moved to another firm away from Telford:

> At the time he were here we were on like nine and half to ten grand a year, ridiculous. I'm only on [under eleven] now, and he went to seventeen grand, eighteen grand a year. And I said, 'what do you do then? Do you have to do all this paperwork like we have to.' He says he goes down. He checks everybody's in on the check sheet. That's all he does, he just walks around all day making sure they do their job. He says he gets a bit bored though, but I mean he's on eighteen grand a year for that and that's the difference I think.

Indeed some argued that team leaders at Part-Co were poorly paid even in comparison with some of the other large Japanese firms in Telford.

Thus, the experience of team leaders at Part-Co differed markedly from that at Copy-Co, both because their progression in the internal labour market underpinned their high levels of involvement and because their pay was an acute source of dissatisfaction. Beyond this, however, the day-to-day pressures and challenges facing team leaders were also coloured by distinctive features of Part-Co's operation, such as a stringent production regime coupled with low operator pay, and high turnover during a period of continuing expansion. The most obvious pressures arose from the problems of recruitment and retention faced by the firm. In the words of one team leader, 'we're slowly running out of people to chose from. It's very difficult at the moment.' Labour turnover and recruitment difficulties meant priority was given to getting people onto the production lines with limited induction and training:

> Some of the lines are struggling. They've got a high turnover and it causes all sorts of problems . . . quality problems mainly, because you can't expect them to do the jobs to the same standard as someone who's been there a while. . . . We tend to get people in and they'll go on the lines and they'll sometimes be on there two or three months before they have an induction. It defeats the object really.

This placed added pressures on team leaders to train and monitor new workers and also had a direct impact on quality and delivery. Meanwhile, absenteeism jeopardized production targets and drew team leaders into working as floaters to cover for those absent.

In this context, several team leaders reflected on the changed character of recruitment and job movement compared to the the start-up period. In that initial period workers were selected more carefully (indeed potentially excellent workers were turned away) and they were given quite extended induction and rounded training, by building through whole sub-assemblies and practising each stage of production. This was how many of the team leaders had established themselves and moved through the grades to their current positions. However, the combination of rapidly increasing production and problems of recruitment had meant that both selection and training had been markedly simplified. Poorly motivated recruits were increasingly placed into narrow job slots and, in the context of an adverse effort bargain, such workers were more prone to limit their commitment or even leave.

These specific problems occurred against the backdrop of a broader worker instrumentalism, reinforced by low pay. One team leader who had visited Japan made an explicit comparison with Japanese workers: 'they're not as company oriented as the Japanese. I mean people just want to go to work and earn the money and go home basically.' However, others believed that pay levels at Part-Co were critical. One argued that 'substantially increased wages' would make a major difference to employee relations: 'looking back I think the associate's wage has increased, they've put little bonuses in here and bits in there for them, but it's not substantial enough for them, I don't think'. In this context it was particularly clear that associates were reluctant to become involved in QCC activities, which were seen as adding additional responsibilities. Thus one team leader told us that:

> It's hard work getting it done, and finding something that you're going to do that your associates are going to come in with and help you do. Because a lot of them say 'I'm not doing that, why should I', you know. Some of them can be really hard, because they don't want to be in the QC circles and they don't want to help you. . . . All the short-term ones and the young lads . . . they didn't want to stay over and help us.

Another characterized the input to QCCs in the following terms:

> I'd say 75 per cent team leader and 25 per cent other associates. It's very difficult to motivate the associates into wanting to join into it. We actually ask for volunteers to join the QC circle. If we don't get any then we obviously have to pick people, and they're not always keen to do it. . . . I've got one running at the moment and I've got, one of them's my sub-setter and he's basically doing all the mapping out of it, and getting a bit of help from one of the other associates, but it's not a lot of input from anybody else.

Thus it was notable that much of the effort put into QCCs came either from team leaders themselves or from experienced and upgraded operators, especially the setters. Another team leader reported that the QCC work 'was basically down to the setters. We've got a really good bunch of setters', while the team leader who registered the disinclination of the younger lads commented that 'it was all actually the long-term ones that did it'.

However, team leaders emphasized that this did not simply reflect a growing divergence between a longer serving core of experienced and committed workers (exemplified by the team leaders themselves) and a more volatile mass of less skilled associates. The low wage profile of the firm also meant that more experienced workers were lost, while those that remained often felt pressured and undervalued (as did the team leaders). As one said, 'what makes it difficult for us is, people that we have on the line, we spend time training them, six months down the line they go, so it starts again. Training again. Some good people we've lost. Basically they've gone for higher paid jobs.'

In this context, workers were disinclined to translate any shortcuts they may have discovered into codified job routines that would boost productivity. This was recognized by the team leader who commented that 'they work it their own ways don't they, "Oh it's a bit quicker doing it this way",... it happens all over the lines'. When asked whether such ideas could get incorporated into new job manuals she added 'Yeah, but it has to be proved and you have to go all through the system... so they probably do it, and then when they see you coming they go back to the old way'. Such tactics may also be linked to the way in which 'continuous improvement' sometimes resulted in more tightly paced work for ordinary assemblers. For example, after describing a substantial innovation in which she was a prime mover, another team leader noted that 'currently at the moment an associate on [this process], if they want to go to the toilet they can go. They say, "Oh, I'm just going to the toilet". The new system, they will have to be relieved. It's tighter, we're tightening things up.'

Such dynamics provide a fuller context for the tensions in the work of team leaders noted at the start of this section, between paperwork and being on the line. Day-to-day production problems, combined with absences and shortages of recruits, drew team leaders into the active performance of production tasks. This allowed them to retain familiarity with the details of the work process and strengthen their rapport with ordinary associates, facilitating such tasks as routine problem-solving and line rebalancing. However, it made it more difficult to perform the many other tasks they were assigned, especially those associated with wider coordination and record keeping: 'it got to the point where we were all stuck on the line all the time, so instead of them getting more associates in to fill they [managers] were saying "Oh you do it".'

This prompted the team leaders themselves to approach management about the disruptive consequences of the shortfalls in recruitment and training. In response to these complaints managers then urged the team leaders to step back from production and to concentrate on their other duties. However, for the team leaders this was more easily said than done. First, cross-pressures on their time and attention remained in place. Secondly, while some of the most experienced felt that they could move between the roles of co-worker and supervisor with relative ease, others were much more uneasy about this and felt it would jeopardize their relationship with their work team. For example, one team leader depended heavily on remaining close to, and actively involving, the workers in his relatively stable team. He characterized his approach to the process of line rebalancing in the following terms:

> The best thing to do is actually get everybody involved in it, because they're the ones who've got to do it... I'll get me setter and we'll come in at the

> weekend and we'll move everything around and say 'this is what we've done, but if you don't like it let me know and tell me what you think is wrong and we'll change it during the day'.

He also avoided watching his team from a distance, because 'I think it's a bit intimidating. I don't think they like that, because I know if I was on the line and people were watching me I wouldn't be very impressed [laugh]. So I tend to not do that.' However, another team leader was confident that her team:

> Know the difference, that if I'm there to help out on the line I'm one of them, but when... I've got to do something and it's got to be stern like, they know the difference in me. Because they'll say 'Oh no, here she comes!', you know. So they know the difference. There's a turning-off point. You can have a laugh and a joke and then you've got to put a stop to it.

Furthermore, this stance informed her approach to monitoring her team:

> I can be standing up in the hot corner and I can watch somebody work and the line's quite a bit away from me, but I know when they're doing something right and they're doing something wrong. Because you can watch by their hands. [It's] the routine.

Thus it was quite easy to spot operators who tried to take short cuts, given that the operations for every job and every process were tightly specified in manuals and key-point charts. Nevertheless, these different tactics reveal persistent tensions in supervising these teams, not just between paperwork and presence on the line, but also between empathy and surveillance.

A further twist to these tensions was added by the operation of the appraisal process. Grading points, and thus the related bonuses, were awarded within a framework of constraints on the proportion of staff eligible for each grade (a system rejected at Copy-Co). However, the team leaders found this difficult to operate and justify to their people. One commented that, though there was *some* scope to finesse the system, 'the hardest part is when they say to you "right, OK, that many can have a rise", and you've got, you can only give a rise to three of them and four of them are equally as good'. Another was more negative:

> There is a flaw in it really. The management say we should have, as a company you should have a strata, how many people go into which band. And it's very difficult when you're given the results before you've even decided what you're going to do, and you've got to fit that around how you're working it.

This was difficult to justify to employees, and in this context, too, the background of low wages had an insidious effect on the efforts of team leaders to mobilize worker commitment and involvement.

Finally, the team leaders coping with these difficulties also felt that the managers did not trust them. One reported that 'they [management] do like to know what's going on, but whether we get told the same, that's a different matter'. By way of illustration he explained that when team leaders had started to meet together senior management wanted them to produce written minutes of such meetings (which meant they did not continue), but when the team leaders requested a meeting with managers about the problems arising from labour turnover it was timetabled for just thirty minutes. Another commented that he doubted that they had the respect of management, reporting that if there are problems, they just tend to say, 'Oh it's your job. That's what you're paid for. If you can't hack it, you know, there's the door.' Thus the team leaders inhabited a classically tension-ridden role, but the form taken by those tensions also reflected some of the distinctive problems that beset Part-Co, as an expanding car components factory in the specific context of the Telford production space.

The persistence of instrumentalism and labour turnover

Despite the changes in recruitment processes and the efforts of team leaders, the problem of turnover at Part-Co worsened in the late 1990s, reaching a peak of 44 per cent in a year when the firm was rapidly expanding its operations and thus had to recruit many new staff (Smith et al. 2004). At the same time absenteeism also increased. One of the training staff captured the air of crisis in late 1998:

> The problem of turnover does not allow us to induct and train the new employees, as we would ideally do. They need people on the floor—even for a few shifts—to fill the vacancies caused by unexpected terminations.

At this juncture the original senior British manager, who had direct responsibility for personnel issues and had been a proponent of wider wage increases, left the company. He was replaced by another British manager, who had been a critic of the ineffectiveness of earlier policies and immediately established a 'project team' to re-address the problem of turnover.

Though there had evidently been continuing debate and disagreement within Part-Co management about the issue, this renewed attention was not only the product of internal management succession but also of external pressures (which may have contributed to that succession). First, senior management at the parent company had become concerned and actively involved, setting a target of 22 per cent as an 'acceptable turnover rate' for the Telford factory. Second, their main Japanese customer in the United Kingdom had expressed disquiet about the quality and delivery implications for their business and had become directly involved in addressing the problem within the plant. Thus, eight years after its formation, the managers at Part-Co continued to face major difficulties of labour turnover and worker commitment, that were exacerbated both by the stringent production demands of the motor sector and the continuing growth of the factory.

This prompted further efforts by the new personnel manager to reform the recruitment process, both through more careful selection (quite complex aptitude tests were under consideration) and by seeking to manage expectations by communicating a more 'realistic' account of the jobs on offer (especially by playing down the scope for overtime earnings). Alongside this, and in part influenced by the Working Time Directive, the firm was making some moves to reduce reliance on overtime and instead improve basic pay rates. Other changes included the development of a systematic database to monitor absenteeism and efforts to persuade more workers to join the company pension scheme.

However, most emphasis, at least rhetorically, was placed on changes in methods of communication and management style, with an ostensible move away from what was regarded as authoritarianism. Communication skills were promoted through management training and the reform of staff appraisal. However, the former was initiated first for team leaders and supervisors, against the preference of the personnel manager to start with managers themselves, while the second exposed tensions between management levels and resistance among managers, so their potential remained unclear and contested. Second, inadequacies were identified in established methods of consulting shop-floor employees and, partly prompted by EU legislation, this led to the formation of an Employee Consultative Committee. It was hoped that this would involve employees in company life, encourage commitment, and reduce turnover. However, its remit was limited, excluding terms and conditions, and only eight of the thirteen elected reps were to be drawn from the shop-floor, replicating some of the weaknesses that have been documented in such institutions in other Japanese firms.

Finally, the new personnel manager hoped to make promotion a fairer and more transparent process, arguing that past managers had favoured those similar to themselves ('clones'), while women had faced particular difficulties in moving into management (a point reinforced by the comments of several female office staff, one of whom noted the particular concern of some Japanese managers regarding pregnancy and family commitments). However, the extent to which these reforms would be carried through and how far they would alter the underlying employment relations at Part-Co remained unclear by the end of our research. Meanwhile, the existing problems and tensions associated with lean manufacturing continued to be addressed on a daily basis by supervisors and team leaders.

CONCLUSIONS

Our discussion of the two large assemblers in this chapter has revealed some enduring features shared by both factories but also demonstrated important differences in their operations, which we summarize and seek to explain in this conclusion. We have also charted significant changes in the character of employment relations over time, especially for the longer established firm, which raise important questions about how we should best understand such changes. In discussing these issues we will also draw comparisons with the research of Delbridge (1998) on Nippon CTV, as he provides a rare ethnographic account of 'life on the line' in a Japanese electricals subsidiary in the United Kingdom and the similarities and differences between Copy-Co, Part-Co, and Nippon CTV help us to explore the wider relevance of our findings.

Starting with the similarities between our two case studies: (1) Both establishments were characterized by the predominance of relatively low-paid routine machining and assembly work. (2) Ordinary employees had limited involvement in continuous improvement activities designed to enhance quality or productivity, which remained primarily the responsibility of team leaders and production engineers. (3) These were non-union plants which relied heavily on team leaders and the management hierarchy as channels of communication. (4) Workers in these workplaces had a fairly instrumental and often sceptical view of management and employment relations, evident in lack of enthusiasm to become involved in discretionary QCC activities and in significant labour turnover in both plants. (5) Relatedly, while Japanese managers remained pre-eminent in planning and technical functions, British managers had a central role in personnel policies, though there were important differences in the detailed operation and wider implications of this division of labour. (6) While employment relations in the two factories could be said to be unsettled, in the sense that they revealed significant criticisms and grievances that qualified worker commitment, in each case satisfactory levels of quality, productivity, and profitability appear to have been achieved, and the plants remained viable parts of their wider companies.

In some respects, these features may be reconciled with earlier research findings. In particular, earlier literature on the overseas operations of the Japanese electronics multinationals has sometimes recognized that relatively routine assembly operations and limited employee involvement in kaizen have predominated, and indeed a contrast has sometimes been drawn between the auto and electricals sectors in this regard. However, our research reveals a similar pattern in a major first-tier auto components manufacturer, suggesting that variants of this routine assembly pattern are more widespread and 'normal' than has often been recognized.

Our findings diverge more substantially from earlier research, however, in suggesting that managers in these large branch plants faced significant challenges in implementing even such routinized work regimes. In part these challenges arose from a need to redesign many production procedures to fit the production requirements in these workplaces, especially to accommodate rather more varied mixes but smaller volumes of production (and relatedly to reflect a greater reliance on labour inputs and less mechanization compared with arrangements in Japanese parent plants). In part, however, such challenges arose from the composition and conduct of the workforce, as both firms had faced substantial difficulties of recruitment and retention, and managers in each workplace were also concerned with the potentially idiosyncratic approach of employees to specified work routines. These concerns underpinned their interest in 'foolproofing' methods in each factory.

In these respects the production regimes in these factories were not a direct transfer from 'peripheral' or labour-intensive variants of Japanese production processes, as Delbridge (1998) drawing on Dedoussis (1994) suggests for Nippon CTV. Nor were they mainly borrowings from an indigenous British model of work organization. Instead, they drew heavily on the experiences of production in parent plants and sister subsidiaries, while being re-designed to address the specific requirements and conditions prevailing in the British branch plants. In turn, these conditions and requirements arose partly from the specific role of these firms within their parent companies and hence their relationship to regional product markets, and partly from their position in a distinctive locality and labour market.

Certainly the character of the local labour market and its implications for the management of the workforce were central and continuing preoccupations of managers at both of these companies and we have seen that this underpinned a central role for British managers in personnel matters in each firm. In this respect, our findings constitute something of a paradox because the relationship between management and workers at these greenfield, non-unionized sites appears more problematical than that reported for some unionized and even brownfield sites. Furthermore, British managers, at least, tended to see this in terms of an unresolved tension between the technical demands of production and the social organization of the employment relationship. In these respects Delbridge's (1998) work represents an instructive contrast to our findings, because he emphasizes that management power is quite pervasive on the shop-floor at Nippon CTV, so it is appropriate to compare his analysis with our findings at this point.

His main argument is that senior management had succeeded in implementing their chosen production regime more or less as they required, unhindered by formal or tacit negotiations with their workforce. This involved low buffer stocks between work processes (internal but not external JIT), team-based work, and a TQM regime that involved both direct operator responsibility for quality and peer monitoring. This meant the promulgation and enforcement of detailed and precise rules about work processes, quality procedures and work discipline, and in this respect represented a quite centralized and bureaucratic form of regulation. However, Delbridge argues that Nippon CTV management escaped some of the characteristic problems of such bureaucracy, especially the growth of informal and negotiated arrangements designed to circumvent the limitations of bureaucratic rules, because many sources of unpredictability were minimized, so the rules could be implemented in a regular and rigorous fashion. This meant that senior managers could pursue both the technical efficiency of the production process and the social control of the workforce, without these imperatives clashing in any significant way.

This appears to represent a very different pattern from the relationships we have analysed in this chapter. First, managers in both of our case studies confronted a variety of sources of uncertainty in their organization of production and employment relations; and second, there were important and explicitly recognized tensions between technical priorities and the social organization of production. However, Delbridge qualifies his own analysis in several ways that allow us to develop this comparison further. First, he emphasizes that management hegemony was primarily based on worker compliance rather than positive worker commitment, a point our research would strongly endorse and to which we return in Chapter 11. Second, he uses his own comparison study of a non-Japanese factory to emphasize the distinctiveness of Nippon CTV in terms of its capacity to minimize the intrusion of uncertainty into the production process. This capacity arose from the deployment of an established production technology to produce a mature product, the relative insulation of the factory from product market fluctuations, a dominant position in a weak labour market and a single-union deal with a conciliatory union.

Such features underline the potential importance of firm, sector, and locality dynamics in understanding the varied policies and practices at the subsidiaries of both Japanese and other international firms. In these respects, our own case studies suggest that many substantial Japanese branch plants have been less able to control potential sources of uncertainty that may generate tensions in (even though they may not disrupt) the organization of both the production process and employment relations. Copy-Co gained some protection from the vagaries of the product market because of the mediating role of the marketing organization, but it still faced some pressures and uncertainties from that direction. Head office decisions about the flow of new models also generated uncertainties, initially because Copy-Co failed to win a new model and later because of the challenges of productionizing the new line. Meanwhile, Part-Co was a very powerful first-tier supplier, but it still remained vulnerable to the demands of its major motor assembly customers, while being heavily dependent on Japan-based design and development offices when negotiating the introduction of new product lines. Thus, in terms of product market conditions neither of these subsidiaries was as insulated from sources of uncertainty and potential disruption as Nippon CTV appeared to be, though they were certainly less vulnerable than the other factories we studied and each faced rather different forms of unpredictability.

In pursuing the theme of uncertainty, Delbridge places more stress on the firm's management of its product market than on its management of the labour market, since this appeared to provide the strongest contrast with his comparator case study. However, it will already be evident that our research highlights sources of management uncertainty arising from the labour market, even in the context of greenfield developments, supportive local state policies and effective union avoidance. Of course, the problematical character of labour recruitment, retention and control in our two case-study plants varied in relation to specific phases in their development, with the most acute problems arising in periods of expansion and active recruitment. Thus, one might be tempted to attribute our findings in this regard to the relative newness of the Telford factories, a perverse 'greenfield' effect. We could then contrast the major difficulties that confronted Part-Co, as the most recently arrived and growing establishment, with the relative stabilization achieved at Copy-Co after ten years of operation, and with the highly institutionalized pattern of relations at Nippon CTV, where the Japanese firm's involvement dated back to a joint venture during the 1970s.

It is evident, however, that any such temporal effects are rather more complicated than a simple comparison of the longevity of the establishments would suggest. First, of course, phases of expansion (or contraction) are not a simple product of the age of the plant, but rather reflect broader product market circumstances and corporate investment decisions, while conditions in the local labour market may also fluctuate over time. Thus Nippon CTV had continued to expand (relatively slowly) over a long period (Delbridge 1998: 32) and Part-Co had already moved through several phases of expansion, while other major Japanese subsidiaries in the locality of our research had quite varied histories of expansion and abrupt contraction (Smith et al. 2004). Similarly, the pattern and extent of localization of different aspects of the operation of Copy-Co and Part-Co, such as the relative roles of Japanese and British managers or the extent of involvement in development work, should not be read directly from the period elapsed since the establishment of the subsidiary but again have to be seen in terms of a more complex evolution. In this context, the intractability of employment relations clearly provided a specific basis for local managers to claim a distinctive competence in both firms, while the centralization of major research and development work in Japan limited the role of local engineering specialists. However, within these parameters there was also scope for differences between the two firms in the evolution of the managerial division of labour.

Second, the existence of a cluster of major Japanese inward-investors surrounding our two case-study plants highlighted the ways in which newer arrivals to some extent learned and borrowed from more long-established firms. This meant that the sense of a problematical labour market, and also a variety of responses to these problems, were to some extent shared across firms, rather than simply being the product of the experience and learning of distinct enterprise managements. Furthermore, the leading firms in this cluster not only provided advice and experience but also generated common policy guidelines that significantly constrained policy options within each workplace. This is a point exemplified by the need for Copy-Co to account for its transport subsidies and by the reluctance of Part-Co management to move above the prevailing wage norms in the cluster. In addition, and crosscutting such cluster linkages, the experiences of sister subsidiaries also influenced managers at both Copy-Co and Part-Co. At Part-Co the longer established American plant played a particularly important role, not least because several senior and more junior Japanese managers had been involved in expanding production in America and key aspects of personnel policy were modelled on their experience. Meanwhile at Copy-Co, the most influential link appeared to be with another manufacturing subsidiary in Europe, though the American sister plant was also significant.

Thirdly, we would also emphasize that managers in both of our case-study firms continued to face significant and relatively intractable difficulties in managing their workforces. Certainly the form and extent of the uncertainties faced by the managers in each factory changed over time, and their tactical responses to these problems also made some difference. Nevertheless, neither the formation of a core of longer serving workers at Part-Co nor the broader stabilization of the workforce at Copy-Co produced the sort of management hegemony identified by Delbridge at Nippon CTV. Indeed, in each case the form taken by the relative stabilization of the workforce generated its own tensions. At Part-Co this took the form of considerable dissatisfaction about pay and the effort bargain, not least among the more experienced and promoted workers, and this represented a powerful counterpoint to the positive value they placed upon opportunities for experience and advancement. At Copy-Co it took the form of a growing criticism and disillusionment regarding promotion opportunities and the management of internal job ladders, notwithstanding a widespread appreciation of the avoidance of redundancies and a relatively relaxed pace of work.

Taking the experiences of the two factories together, this suggests that phases of expansion may have facilitated the use of internal job ladders to retain and develop a minority of employees, even as they magnified problems of labour turnover. However, it also underlines some of the problems that may arise in sustaining such a mechanism of relative integration. First, it is likely to be difficult to sustain in more stable periods, especially if (as at Copy-Co) managers seek to change the criteria for progression. Second, it is likely to generate expectations of patterns of training, rewards, and support that senior managers may be reluctant or unable to provide. In our case studies the views of the team leaders give particular credence to the importance of these contradictory aspects of internal job ladders in these types of Japanese subsidiary, while also underlining the pivotal role that these people were expected to play in the production process.

What also emerges from this discussion is the way in which our two case-study plants, though they shared important similarities, have also followed somewhat distinctive trajectories. At Copy-Co a period of consolidation had led management to highlight the theme of job security and the corollary of flexible redeployment in the context of a relatively relaxed work regime, but this had left management dissatisfied with existing patterns of worker commitment and discipline. However, their efforts to develop a more sophisticated approach to work and employment relations (through such techniques as merit pay, QCCs, and particularly the restructuring of supervision) had made only limited headway, and had often fed employee scepticism about management motives. Meanwhile, Part-Co managers had quite successfully implemented a more stringent work regime than Copy-Co, but continued to face substantial problems of labour turnover, and complaints about unfair appraisals and low pay. Employees complied with what many felt was an adverse effort bargain but refused to be drawn into discretionary problem-solving activities that went beyond the requirements of the existing work process.

Thus our two case studies highlight the ways in which such distinctive but unsettled trajectories may develop in relatively similar firms facing a common labour market, but we can also identify some of the particular features of the two firms that help to explain the differences between them. In particular, Part-Co had implemented a production regime that drew upon auto sector models and was constrained by the demands of the varied car assembly plants that it supplied, while the complex assembly lines at Copy-Co remained at one remove from a more differentiated range of customers, buffered by the intervening sales organization. Furthermore, Part-Co was central to the parent firm's effort to become a dominant presence in the European market, while Copy-Co appeared to have a more defensive role in circumventing tariff barriers and making profits from the production of a key consumable. However, we agree with Edwards (1986; also Edwards and Scullion 1982; Scott 1994) that we cannot simply read off specific configurations of management policy and work relations, or the trajectories of their development within such workplaces, from the broader pressures and contingencies to which they are subject. Rather, we have emphasized, the importance of the active, albeit sometimes reactive and contradictory, initiatives of groupings and alliances of managers, and in turn the responses of employees to such management actions, in constructing these distinctive factory regimes. In this way we have sought to explore and gain some understanding of the particular character of capital–labour relations in each of these workplaces and to recognize the active ways in which they have been made and remade within the constraints surrounding each subsidiary.

CHAPTER

8

Work and Employment Relations in the Smaller Component Subcontractors: Distinctive Pressures and Contrasting Trajectories

INTRODUCTION

This chapter provides a detailed analysis of the evolution of management policies and work and employment relations in two medium-sized Japanese subcontractors in Telford over the decade of the 1990s, and explores the ways in which these features were influenced by the distinctive and changing conditions of such subcontract production. In particular, it seeks to contextualize the developing patterns of workplace relations in these workplaces in terms of evolving relations between customer firms, competitors and the wider operations of parent companies, and the operation of local labour markets and the movement of workers within these markets. Our analysis of the evolution of management policies within these firms offers a very different perspective on 'transplantation', 'hybridization', and 'organizational learning' than is sometimes provided in the literature. This is because it highlights the uncertainties, contradictions, conflicts, and limitations that characterize management policy formation and enactment within such constrained and vulnerable organizations.

INTERNATIONAL SUBCONTRACTORS AS A FOCUS OF STUDY

Most of the debates about the character of Japanese production regimes, whether at home or abroad, have focused on the large plants of major manufacturers, rather than smaller supplier firms. At the same time it is widely recognized that manufacturing in Japan itself has been characterized by an unusually heavy reliance on an extensive network of subcontractors. This involves a hierarchy of workplaces that extends from large first-tier suppliers all the way to small 'garage factories', often employing members of a single family. Furthermore, the activities of some of these subcontractor firms have themselves been internationalized, with the establishment of substantial numbers of Japanese-owned supplier firms in the United States, the United Kingdom, and elsewhere, providing components to their Japanese customer firms in these areas. However, the character of the subcontract relations down such supplier chains in Japan itself, and the forms of work organization within the factories involved in these hierarchies, have remained controversial (Benson 1998; Chalmers 1989; Turner 1995; Whittaker 1997). Often the more positive characterizations of long-term subcontracting and upgrading draw upon features of the top tiers of the hierarchy, while more critical accounts of cost-pressures and vulnerability highlight experiences further down into the 'periphery'.

In any case, most of the debates about Japanese factories operating in Europe and the United States have focused on the operations of final assemblers and their major first-tier suppliers, comparable to the case-study factories discussed in Chapter 7, rather than smaller subcontractors. Indeed, when analogies have been drawn between the operations of peripheral firms in Japan and Japanese firms overseas (Dedoussis 1994; Dedoussis and Littler 1994), they have suggested that *all* overseas factories approximate the employment relations of the Japanese periphery, rather than differentiating between those variously located in the production chain. Furthermore, while commentators have often discussed the growth of clusters of smaller Japanese subcontract firms alongside the larger manufacturing 'transplants', and have highlighted the dynamic of successive waves of investment in such terms, relatively little attention has been given to the character of work and employment relations *within* such factories.

As we saw in Chapter 3, Munday (1995) provided a useful survey of so-called second-wave Japanese manufacturing investment in Britain, involving subcontractors drawn in to supply the final assemblers once they had become established. He looked especially at subcontractors supplying the electronics final assemblers, and highlighted the extent to which employment in such firms involved low paid, semi-skilled workers performing routinized tasks, with little scope for upskilling. Munday noted the continued dependency of these establishments on their original Japanese customer firms, but also identified important variations among the subcontractors, both in terms of ownership structures (more joint ventures than among final assemblers and also the involvement of Japanese trading houses) and in terms of areas of activity. In regard to the latter, the two main subsectors for subcontractors to electronics firms were the supply of electronic components and the supply of plastic components, while suppliers to the motor industry represented another distinctive grouping of firms.

Two important case studies of Japanese manufacturing subcontractors in the United Kingdom complement Munday's survey by providing more detailed accounts of social relations within such firms (Palmer 2000; Stephenson 1996; Webb and Palmer 1998). However, both were of quite large (400+) first-tier suppliers to the auto industry, so they may differ significantly from our cases, which are of smaller enterprises supplying electricals firms. Palmer and Stephenson each demonstrate in different ways that work and employment relations in such large subcontractors may be characterized by worker non-compliance and resistance. Stephenson documents the development of organized union representation and bargaining over working arrangements at Ikeda Hoover, but for us, Palmer's analysis of worker non-compliance with standard operating procedures in a non-unionized subcontractor is more directly relevant.

Palmer (2000; Webb and Palmer 1998) identifies several different forms of employee deviation from workplace rules and procedures. Some focused on evading identification as the source of faulty work while others were concerned with gaining free time. Some were organized individually but others were collective, in the latter case often with supervisory collusion. Palmer develops the argument that the very unpredictability of some features of the production process in his subcontract firm (arising from faults in components supplied to the firm and equipment failures on the shop-floor) encouraged and legitimated collusive non-compliance as a way of achieving cost and production targets. At the same time such processes opened up some spaces for employees to influence their conditions of work. Thus one of our concerns in this chapter is to explore how far such processes operated in our case-study firms.

Of course, subcontractors vary considerably in the scale of their operations and the size of their workforce. In Munday's (1995) study, Japanese-owned suppliers in Wales ranged from 15 employees to more than 1,100, with the largest firms among the suppliers to the motor industry. However, the majority of the electronics suppliers had between 100 and 200 employees. Thus one important feature of many subcontractors, even some of those supplying parts directly to final assemblers, is that they are relatively small enterprises, and it can be argued that smallness itself imparts an important distinctiveness to social relations within these workplaces. At the same time recent debates about the character of work and employment relations in small firms (Barrett and Rainnie 2002; Ram and Edwards 2003) have highlighted both the importance of differences associated with the operation of such firms within rather different product and labour markets and the extent to which emergent management policies represent active but contested responses to such circumstances. Thus, one of our concerns will be to explore the implications of workplace size, but only as this feature is embedded in other aspects of the environment and conduct of the firm.

INTRODUCING THE CASE STUDIES

A key argument in this chapter is that the role of these firms as subcontractors is pivotal to an understanding of the ways in which they operate as workplaces. However, this does not imply a simple homogeneity of experience across such subcontractor firms. First, our two case-study enterprises themselves differ in significant ways, and this provides a basis for considering some of the distinctive ways in which such subcontracted operations may be organized and institutionalized. Second, our research also highlights changes over time within such firms, as wider circumstances and management tactics have both evolved through time. Thus the chapter explores the rather different ways in which the managements of these two firms sought to cope with the uncertainties arising from their subordinate and insecure position as subcontractors, and the ramifications of these differences for the evolution of work and employment relations in these plants.

In one factory, PCB-Co, Japanese managers specified the targets and parameters of production as closely as they could, but this approach failed to reconcile the competing pressures for cost-control, quality, and delivery. This set the scene for considerable tensions between Japanese and British managers and for a crisis-prone organization of production. After eleven years, the factory was ultimately closed and production of their major product moved back to the Asian region. In the other factory, Assembly-Co, British managers were given considerable autonomy in their management of the production process and employment relations. This allowed them to develop a fairly coherent approach to production management that drew heavily on both historical (e.g. piecework payment) and recent (e.g. National Vocational Qualifications, NVQs) elements of a British production management repertoire. However, it did not allow them to escape from persistent dependence on a few key customers and the uncertainties associated with that dependence. Nevertheless, it provided the basis for quite cooperative relations between British and Japanese managers, relatively settled employment relations despite problems in the recruitment and retention of workers, and the continuing survival of the plant as a subcontractor.

In summary, then, the chapter seeks to understand both the micropolitics of management and the social relations of the work and employment in these two factories at three levels. The first concerns the shared pressures and dilemmas that characterized the experience of such subcontract firms, dependent upon final assemblers and paying relatively low wages in their local labour markets. The second involves the specific forms taken by these pressures in each factory, as they arose from specific ownership structures, evolving international divisions of labour, and the occupancy of particular niches in their local labour markets. The third is the cumulative path-dependent evolution of plant-level management–worker relations that has characterized each workplace over time.

PCB-CO: WORK AND EMPLOYMENT IN A PRECARIOUS SUBCONTRACTOR

The role of the firm and the uncertainties of subcontracting

PCB-Co manufactured printed circuit boards (PCBs) for seven Japanese companies with factories in the United Kingdom and elsewhere in Europe, almost all specializing in office equipment. The company had come to Telford on the direct request of one such office equipment manufacturer in the town, to supply both their British factory and later another in France. However, though they still did work for this company it was limited in volume, and formed only a small part of their portfolio of orders. At different times, over a six-year period, three different customer firms had each accounted for 80 per cent of the production volume of the factory. At the time of our research three companies accounted for the bulk of their work and each of these had a dedicated production line.

This pattern, coupled with fluctuations in the overall level of activity in the sub-sector to which PCB-Co was largely dedicated, underlined the volatility of the market within which it was operating. The order books covered three to six months, usually with firm orders about three months ahead and tentative orders projected a further three months. A further aspect of this market position was that the preference of Europe-based Japanese office equipment makers to source their production of PCBs locally, within the European region, remained subject to continuing reappraisal in the light of comparative production costs and changing regulatory regimes. The firm arrived in the United Kingdom at a time when the EU had imposed tariffs on the import of Japanese office equipment, designed to encourage local production and increased local content. However, by the end of the 1990s the changed tariff regime meant there was no longer such an imperative to supply PCBs from local sites, and thus the fate of the plant depended much more on comparative production costs across the world.

It is important to note that the parent company of PCB-Co was not directly involved in the manufacture of PCBs in Japan. Both domestically and to some extent internationally it had an established niche and reputation as an innovative, high technology firm specializing in components, equipment, and systems for factory and office automation. In this context, it purchased PCBs from its own associated subcontractors in Japan, rather than manufacturing them itself. However, in response to the expectations of final equipment manufactures it had undertaken the direct production of such products overseas, in subsidiaries in both Britain and China. While competition with the subcontracting factory in Japan was not a major threat to the British operation, especially during the appreciation of the yen, the Chinese factory appeared better placed to compete with British production. Not only did it utilize much more extensive manual production lines, but it was also reported to be investing in some mechanization, one of the features which was supposed to give the British factory an important advantage.

For managers, all these features meant that 'the subcontract market is very cut-throat'. This was dramatized by a powerful preoccupation among managers with the competition from China, and especially with the competition provided by their own more recently established sister factory there. It was widely felt that the larger batches of the simpler boards were increasingly being sourced from China. This meant that PCB-Co had to depend upon the production of smaller batches of more complex boards, a development which imposed fresh stresses on the system of production in the factory. Thus one Japanese manager emphasized the importance of the niche occupied by PCB-Co:

> They [China] are already very, very cheap. We can't compete, so we must find something we can compete with them on. For example, China can't make small quantities of product, they just carry on high volumes of product,... they are not interested in small quantities, many kinds of boards, because obviously it can cause a lot of change-overs which can require more, better control, which they can't do.

At the same time a British manager with direct links to customers emphasized the challenges this had posed for production at PCB:

> [In the past] you may have one line doing the same product day in day out... but it is a lot different now. We probably get at one time forty different products going through, so obviously we generate a lot more problems.

Overall, the awareness that work could be lost to production in East Asia, and more particularly China, fed a continuing sense of vulnerability and pressure among PCB management.

Changing priorities on the part of the parent company reinforced these features, especially a more rigid expectation that the British site should perform profitably. A senior Japanese manager suggested that this was not just a question of the maturation of the factory, but also involved changing priorities within the parent company over this period:

> Previously the branch in the world-wide [operation] was servicing... other Japanese companies. It was a method to produce profit in Japan. Today it is

> different. They can't keep paying negative profits on worldwide [operations] so they request us to produce purely profit, so it's been changed.

PCB-Co itself had moved into profit after an initial start-up period, but then began to make substantial losses as competitive conditions worsened, and these continued over several years. Under the pressure of the changed expectations of the parent company this generated internal management controversy and changes in management structure. Later, when the first Japanese MD went home, his replacement was a Japanese Production Manager with something of a reputation as a cost-cutter, whose prime objective was to deliver profitability for the parent company. These developments led to profit and volume targets which sceptical British managers regarded as 'completely unrealistic', but nevertheless the implications were clearly encapsulated in the harsh slogan that the new MD communicated to managers and workforce alike: 'no profit, no exist'.

Business strategy

Both Japanese and British managers envisaged short-term and also long-term strategies for survival in this context. Most immediately, these demands signalled the need to make the current machining and assembly operation as viable as possible, but it also raised questions about whether the factory could build its long-term future on the established but precarious role of a subcontract supplier to other businesses. In the longer term both Japanese and local managers looked towards the possibility that they might move away from this role, into the manufacture of some of the technology products associated with the parent company's core business in Japan. Thus one Japanese manager commented:

> At the moment we are just a subcontractor, but I must prepare for the future. I don't think we can survive, I don't think we can be profitable for ever as long as we continue this kind of business. I am interested in other areas or other markets for this kind of assembly, or I'm interested in refurbishing, remanufacture... or of course [the parent firm] in general has a lot of products, own brand products, so I wish to transfer some goods, products, over here. Of course to do so we must prepare our structure, our manning, our ability.

However, there were important differences in the ways in which Japanese and British managers viewed this latter scenario. For the Japanese the priority was to generate profits in the existing and closely related business. Only this would justify further investments, both to increase the efficiency of PCB production and then, perhaps, to begin production of alternative products. For the British managers, the emphasis tended to be the other way round. Only with more support from the parent company, in terms of investment and new product lines, could the factory escape from the multiple pressures of an increasingly competitive PCB market. Furthermore, the British were frustrated by the apparent unresponsiveness of the parent company in these respects, though they were aware that their past performance provided a weak basis on which to argue the case for a change in their role. Thus the most optimistic British assessment remained cautious:

> Twelve months ago the state of this company was no good, there was no way that [the parent company] would ever think of investing any money. But now we've turned the company round a little bit and have shown signs of profit and shown signs of improvement, I think that maybe we're in with a chance.

However, during our research, the existing MD emphasized that profitability would have to be sustained over a longer period to justify requests for further support from the centre. In the event, the factory continued to operate in this difficult market segment for another four years, before production was ended and the site was closed.

Management micropolitics and contrasting evaluations of Japanese techniques

At the time of our fieldwork there were only three Japanese managers on site, though Japanese advisers intermittently augmented the longer staying staff. The declared objective was to continue localization of management, but this did not prove to be a straightforward process and some time after our research the opposite process became dominant. Thus a Japanese manager who visited the factory in the late 1990s characterized the approach of the then MD in the following terms:

> When he came here, all British managers had not reached his expected level. The MD observed for a while and thought that the situation would not improve. Then he finally decided to change the personnel. . . . Coincidentally, the Japanese who came to fill the positions were the experts whom the MD had already known. I suppose it was easier and much more efficient to work together.

Thus continuing questions about the viability of the plant were eventually translated into a strategy which involved the dismissal of several long-serving British managers and the application of more direct Japanese management control, in retrospect a precursor to the later closure.

In the early history of the factory there was evident conflict between an initial Japanese enthusiasm for the enforcement of strict discipline on employees and attempts by British managers to institutionalize a slightly more indulgent regime. For example, workers wished to listen to radios on the line but the Japanese managers opposed this. A British manager proposed a compromise whereby radios would not play different stations but would all be tuned to the same one:

> This didn't go down too well with the Japanese, the idea of it, but OK to be fair they were prepared to look at it, accept some of the English factory ways, ... it was all set up, they were not very happy, but anyway OK.... What happened while I was away, my boss suddenly got it into his head not to have radios, so he promptly goes down the line, not saying anything, goes bang, bang, bang, turns all the radios off. That's it, off. They [workers] were all in the canteen, but [another British manager], he went down eventually and got it all sorted out.

Thus initial tensions and accommodations within management focused particularly on the viability and appropriateness of particular styles and levels of discipline.

Later, the conflicts and alliances within management began to cross-cut national origins. The expansion of the firm was accompanied by the appointment of a well-qualified British production manager who was given authority over British production staff and reported directly to the first Japanese MD. He was to provide the framework within which the expansion and improvement of production would proceed, but by the time of our research he had been eased out (demotion followed by resignation), and the remaining managers uniformly regarded his regime as a failure. According to the most jaundiced British management account, the combined failings of this British production manager and his Japanese sponsor created a lax disciplinary regime on the shop-floor:

> There was no discipline in this place at all. People could have sickness, they were never asked why they were sick... it was a holiday camp because there was no discipline... and even though we had got little work to do we didn't get it out on time.

It would be appropriate to discount the self-serving hyperbole of this account, but informants agreed that this period was characterized both by poor production organization and a degree of indulgency, though this was also interspersed with spasmodic impositions of harsh discipline.

The first Japanese MD continued to support the incumbent manager for a substantial period, but increasing pressure from corporate HQ for improved performance, combined with increasingly explicit criticisms from other British managers, eventually precipitated a change of policy. In turn, this change was consolidated by the arrival of a new hard-line MD and by the promotion of a British production manager who had been trained by him in Japan. This protégé was initially given responsibility for the assembly lines but eventually assumed the position of overall production manager. However, this did not involve an unqualified alliance to pursue the systematic implementation of Japanese production techniques. Tensions among British managers persisted, but British and Japanese managers continued to have different views on the most appropriate strategies for the management of the workforce and the organization of production.

In particular, a British production manager's understanding of management practice in Japan led him to qualify some of the claims of visiting Japanese managers. For example, he emphasized that the target figures for defect levels, benchmarked on Japan, were 'idealized' and anyway based on much longer production runs of each board design. He also adopted a pragmatic approach to juggling the competing priorities of day-to-day production, leaving a significant gap between his rhetorical commitment to continuous improvement and the minimal implementation of specific Japanese practices and techniques. Furthermore, all of the British managers tended to be critical of the role of Japanese staff in directly managing British employees, echoing their early reservations that had crystallized around the 'radios incident'. In this respect, Japanese staff were often characterized as insensitive and authoritarian (one had been nicknamed 'Genghis'), though this was not seen as a uniform characteristic of all Japanese managers. Another widespread feeling among British managers was that the Japanese were unwilling to give them more management responsibility because 'they have no confidence in British management . . . because of what happened when we first established. . . . They see us as very inflexible . . . there are a lot of trust problems.'

Nevertheless, there remained a marked contrast between the cynicism of personnel managers and the broadly positive perspective of production management. The former emphasized the inappropriateness of many Japanese production techniques. One stressed that many components had to be ordered and held over lengthy periods, making JIT links with suppliers unviable, and that an attempt to implement a kanban system to supply components to the assembly lines had been abandoned because there was too much wastage of stock:

> It was entirely Japanese. They just arrived one day without any warning . . . Kanban can be excellent, I'm sure, in certain types of business. But it's just not suited to ours, and of course it doesn't work together with the computer system.

He acknowledged that a visiting Japanese engineer had successfully reorganized the supply of parts to the automatic machines, using cassettes. However, he saw this (and anything else positive) as 'just common sense', rather than owing anything to specifically Japanese engineering expertise (we return to this theme of 'common sense' in Chapter 11). Meanwhile, a British production manager bemoaned the difficulty of developing a more thoroughgoing kaizen programme because of the immediate pressures of production deadlines, but tried to implement a stripped-down, management-dominated effort at problem-solving and 'improvement' based on liaison between production engineers and senior operators.

As might be expected, the perspectives of Japanese managers differed in important respects from those of all shades of British management. They were reluctant to defend any stereotypical version of Japanese management methods, emphasizing that the parent company had its own distinctive approach. Several suggested that it might be possible to combine Japanese and British strengths in organizing production, identifying the Japanese way with close analysis of the causes of problems and the documentation and rigorous application of counter-measures, and the British way with swift decision-making and clear lines of authority. However, such managers were unsympathetic to the stock British management explanation for failures in implementing improvement programmes:

> Yeah, busy is our big excuse, to them and to us, but we should break this bad habit. It's not a good excuse, because we are busy because we didn't improve. That's the truth, that's the Catch 22.

From this perspective neither the ingrained scepticism of the British administrator not the pragmatic compromises of the British production manager were legitimate bases for failing to involve employees in continuous improvement programmes, though this manager also acknowledged that he himself had been unable to orchestrate such involvement at PCB-Co.

Employment relations and the labour market: compliance, bitching, and quitting

The shop-floor workers at PCB-Co were clearly aware of the possible vulnerability of the firm. Not only had they been warned by the MD that without profits the firm would close, but their competitive position had been dramatized by a display in the canteen which was titled 'Our Competition in China and Japan'. This showed photographs of the Chinese PCB factory and a subcontract factory in Japan, with captions inviting comparisons with the British set-up and explicitly comparing hand insertion 'pitch times' (stated as two seconds, compared with three to four seconds). However, despite fears about the vulnerability of the firm and the cyclical pressures of the Friday panic, many workers at PCB regarded the pace of work as unexceptional. It was sometimes quiet fast, but nevertheless more relaxed than at some other factories ('we're not pressured as much as some factories I've worked at'). At the same time, most workers felt that the shop-floor work tasks at PCB-Co, especially on insertion but also on inspection, were highly routinized and often quite monotonous. Views on pay varied, but several people said bluntly that the pay was low.

This combination of features prompted ambivalent views. For example, one young woman commented that 'I had to just come to work. It's not something I want to do forever because really it's a dead-end job.' But later, when she compared her current work with that at another company she had worked for, known for the stringency of its labour regulation, she added 'I do enjoy this job. I could be working on a job I really, really detested. I don't get dirty, and it isn't really hard and it's good pay.' Another, a young man who had worked in several other Japanese factories as a temp but preferred PCB-Co, highlighted the avoidance of shift-working (but this was not an option for those on the machines) and relative cleanliness. For him, as for others, size was also important. 'It's the smallest factory I've worked in, where everyone gets to know each other a lot quicker, and it makes it a better working atmosphere, and it's not too bad.' It was widely acknowledged that the company did little formal training, and workers had to acquire the relevant skills by watching and asking other operators: 'It's more or less sit on the job, watch somebody, try and do the job.' Nevertheless, some people felt that there was scope for progression, even in this small factory. In particular, several women who had become, or hoped to become, senior operators or line leaders highlighted this possibility. Male shop-floor workers in positions of technical responsibility, however, often felt that the scope for advancement was rather limited, and more often talked of moving elsewhere to progress.

While some of the workers, especially among the women, had earlier worked in (generally more poorly paid) service sector employment, many had experience of working at other manufacturers. In this context, workers recognized that PCB-Co paid poor wages, but they moved to, or stayed with, PCB-Co mainly because it lacked some of the stringent controls found in some of the larger firms. The recruitment process itself was often based on established contacts—kin, workmates, and managers. There were several clusters of extended family members at the firm, and several people had been recruited through a manager who had earlier supervised them at their previous workplace. While these recruitment channels afforded managers some leverage in selecting workers, little attention was given to formal interviews or selection tests for shop-floor workers.

At the same time, the workforce at PCB was not very stable. Data for a typical six-month period showed that turnover was equivalent to 43 per cent per annum and, while some of those moving had only been employed for a few weeks, there were also leavers with much longer service, of three, four or five years. Managers regarded younger workers in particular as less reliable, but also suggested that turnover had recently become less of a problem as conditions in the local labour market changed:

> At operator level it is not as bad as it used to be when there were an awful lot of job opportunities in Telford. The job-hopping now has certainly been reduced as there's not that many jobs going.

Quitting as well as recruitment was influenced by kinship and friendship. At the same time recriminations surrounding issues of favouritism and 'bitchiness' could provoke several people to leave together while mates or cliques often left at similar times, sometimes moving to the same new employer. However, when people left this did not preclude returning to the firm:

> We've had a couple of girls gone across there, done three weeks and come back. And they said, the work here is mostly sitting down, but there you are standing up, and if you go off to the toilet or whatever, you've got to be quick because they don't stop the line... I don't know whether that's true or not, but that's the story we've got told.

When people did return, then, this provided other workers with further bearings on the opportunities and constraints characterizing the local labour market.

Alongside direct recruitment, PCB-Co also made use of temporary workers recruited through selected Temporary Employment Agencies. Managers linked the use of temps directly to the vulnerability of the subcontractor to upredictable fluctuations in orders. However, a Senior Operator noted that the use of temps also facilitated the selective recruitment of permanent staff:

> In the first place the temps were taken on because we did have a high workload. We were rushed off our feet basically, so they were taken on as a temporary solution, because the work was going to deteriorate so there wasn't the point in taking on full [permanent] staff. That was the first purpose. But while they use temps here, they've seen temps that have done a good job and they've actually asked them to stay, and that's got to the stage now where they do that quite often.

In turn, this reliance on Temping Agencies severely limited the options open to job seekers. As one of the temps at PCB remarked 'it's practically impossible to get a job in a factory unless you start with an agency first. They dominate the town.' At the same time the selection of some temps to become permanent meant this became an important job-seeking strategy. Thus one employee, who believed he had succeeded in this strategy, commented:

> I'm hoping to get taken on permanently.... To me it's better to go to an agency, earn a tenner less a week, work for them for three months and hopefully if you don't have days off and are reliable, you get to know the supervisors well, you get taken on. That's my attitude.

Nevertheless, the use of temporary staff to cope with peaks of production was viewed with some ambivalence. For existing staff it created extra stresses:

> We've got to show them what to do and it stops us from getting on with what we want to do, and they come to you with the slightest problem and you are trying to get on with your job. I mean, we don't mind helping half the time, but when you are real busy it does get a bit of a pain.

Moreover, senior managers tended to have a generally disparaging view of temps, notwithstanding the advantages of disposability and selection which they offered, because in general they regarded such workers as 'very unreliable' and unwilling to accommodate to such features as the shifts required in the machine section.

Management had developed a variety of financial incentives and disciplinary procedures in their effort to regulate worker behaviour. One of these was an attendance bonus, linked to the public display of attendance records and trends. However, it was evident from internal management debate, and warnings about the possible discontinuance of the scheme, that this had not secured the levels of attendance managers had hoped for. A standard system of verbal and written warnings operated at the company but had also faced problems, as it had been used in ways that sometimes caused resentment, for example when people were pressured to work overtime to cope with deadlines and backlogs of work. Another, more recent, innovation was a system of personal appraisal linked to the award of annual pay rises (a policy with echoes of elements of Japanese reward structures). This was deemed to 'encourage people to continually work hard.... You should continually be trying, improving more and more, and you should be rewarded for the effort you put in and the commitment you show.' However, this was still being implemented during our research, and had made little impact.

Needless to say, in the context of the broader avoidance of unionization among Japanese firms in Telford, this small firm was not unionized. It did, however, have a consultative body, termed the Works Council, which met at least quarterly, though this was a relatively recent innovation. According to British managers, more informal and indirect forms of grievance handling had proven difficult earlier in the life of the factory, occasionally leading to dramatic confrontations of the sort described earlier, while the daily line or section meetings provided no opportunities to air grievances. Eventually, the Works Council had been established at the prompting of British personnel manager, as a forum for giving information to employees and also to address grumbles and grievances. According to the somewhat self-interested account of this manager (who evidently encouraged the voicing of some grievances) the Council was quite effective at first:

> When it first started there was five years of pent-up discussion, you know, the usual things... [but] once we got the rubbish out of the way it started to be quite good... and it was an opportunity for the people themselves to explain the problems that they had endured through total bad management.

However, this pattern had not been sustained. Apparently, the MD had adopted an increasingly defensive and critical stance, representatives became 'frightened to ask things', and eventually 'the reps didn't actually want to represent their people because they got too much hassle out there' from their sections. In important respects, this outcome, if not the evolution, was corroborated by the comments of employees. Thus one said of the Works Council: 'that's just issues like... we need more chairs in the canteen, that's nothing to do with the work'.

In practice, grievances were either suppressed or handled very informally, even when they assumed an explicitly collective character. In this context, the Senior Operator was often a pivotal figure and one worker caught the ambivalences of this relationship in the following comment:

> Well she was more of a friend to start off with anyway, but they do change when they get in a position like that, the pressure begins to build. It helps if they are friends beforehand though.

Furthermore, such personalized relations could sometimes be effectively mobilized in forms of sectional collective initiative. This was illustrated by another informant who described how shift patterns (an issue of substantial tension) and access to overtime had been informally negotiated in the machine room. On the one hand the formal 'open door' policy had few attractions:

> Everyone says it's OK, you can go and see [the MD] and so on, but it doesn't really work that way, because you know that there is going to [be] something coming back, and your name is, you are on the block then.

On the other hand, however, informal representations could sometimes gain concessions from key managers. When asked if people had acted individually or collectively the response was:

> It was definitely a collective thing, well it was a collective thing but there is one person in the machine room, [name], who is quite a loud voice in there, and [it] tends to be what he says goes. As far as, [manager's name] listens to him quite a lot, although he doesn't admit to it he goes his way quite a lot.

Thus informal relations could involve low key forms of collective representation, but these were rather sectional and self-limiting forms, which might secure advantages for one section at the expense of another. Furthermore, concerns more often seemed to remain muffled or unarticulated, as in the case of reactions to changes in the work routines on the insertion line discussed later.

The social organization and regulation of production: coping and crises

Production at the PCB factory involved two main processes, the automated picking and placing of components on boards and the manual insertion of components. Surrounding these processes were an initial design and pre-production phase involving close liaison with each customer, the procurement and supply of components, and a series of processes of inspection, testing, and rectification at various points in the process, then final quality assurance and despatch. There were twelve or thirteen workers in the machine shop, but around forty on the four lines involved in hand insertion, with four to six involved in each of the other areas: pre-production, purchasing, stores, inspection and repair, and quality assurance. The division of labour was strongly gendered: all the managers were men and there was only one female in the machine shop, while just four out of the forty assembly-line workers were men. A young semi-skilled male worker underlined the implications of this for his own pattern of varied work experience:

> With it being ninety per cent female, the lads they have in the factory they use to the full, so that, you know, the women stay on the line and the lads that are here tend to get moved around, which is good really.

The machines involved in the automated construction of PCBs were run on a continuous shift system to cope with the volume of work, and the machine shop formed something of a production bottleneck. Different managers put different glosses on this: one suggested that 'the machine room is the area that historically has always been the most unsupervised. It's always been the biggest problem. It's never been managed properly', while another commented that 'sometimes I think we're on continental shifts purely because we're running inefficient, outdated machines'. Difficulties arose not only because of the volume of work but also because the process generated a substantial number of quality defects. Experienced workers attributed this to a combination of working with short runs on ageing machines and the inexperience and limited training of many of the workers. Some of the machines had been secondhand when installed, and funding constraints meant that replacements would also be secondhand and consequently relatively slow and inflexible:

> We're now working continental shifts, doing twenty-four hours a day, and we still can't get through the day, and really it's foresight, what we should have is more machinery. We need the machinery so that you cannot just build but maintain more.

Meanwhile, unskilled workers made loading and setting errors, which were compounded because the shift system meant work could accumulate unchecked overnight, while only a few skilled workers were able to check and repair the machines. Furthermore, plans to provide more training were themselves compromised by the work loads and time pressures, as the person with training responsibility noted with some despair: 'I've done a training schedule for all the operators and technicians but none of that's been started because I haven't got the time.'

Past disputes about the performance of quality checks and shift-work arrangements in the machine shop had apparently been exacerbated by the heavy-handed approach of one of the Japanese managers. 'There were lots and lots of written warnings and verbal warnings being thrown around, and it got to the stage where there were *so* many people on a final warning.' But while this episode had prompted the removal of this manager from the machine room, this did not alleviate the underlying production pressures. Thus the manager who had identified the machine shop as under-managed also recognized the cross-pressures to which these workers continued to be subjected:

> They are being pushed. Changeover times, part shortages, machine breakdowns, deadlines to keep. They've short-circuited the procedure. Everybody's happy until it goes wrong. They've actually been told to short-circuit the procedure sometimes. It's not a problem until it goes wrong, then they get a warning.

In response, managers tried to enforce a more rigorous checking of first-off boards from each batch and redeployed some of the inspectors onto shifts to catch defective products early. However, through-put in the machine shop remained under pressure, while many of the workers remained untrained, and these features set limits to the effectiveness of such policies. The outcome was graphically captured by an employee who was involved in the inspection which occurred between the machine shop and hand insertion:

> There is a lot of quantity talk, but at the same time as they want the quantity they want the quality as well, and you just can't do that in the short time that you're here. Because most often as not the machines are eight or nine hours behind schedule, which makes us nine hours behind schedule which makes the line nine hours behind schedule, which makes the customers get on the phone. So all they're really bothered about is to get the work out fast. So fast, so they make sure you concentrate on that.

As this implies, pressure to meet schedules was a pervasive feature of this workplace.

The four adjacent assembly lines accounted for half the factory workforce. These people inserted components, monitored the solder bath and inspected the completed boards. Each line was generally dedicated to a specific manufacturer, in part because workers became familiar with the particular style of board design, 'used to the way [firm-name] builds the boards, and they'll be very, very quick at it. If I give them to [another] line they haven't the experience.' Thus experience was crucial in sustaining both speed and quality of manufacture, while redeployment threatened both:

> When we had the flu epidemic . . . then I think we went down to about 84 per cent [of the production target], the quality went up to about 23 per cent [defects] . . . because you are pulling people from pillar to post trying to keep the output high.

However, despite the salience of tacit skills acquired through practice, most of the work was highly routinized and boring:

> You get used to the boards that well, you could probably do it in your sleep.... It gets boring, but you've got to live with it, you think of the pay packet at the end of the month.

Nevertheless some of the jobs were more complex than others:

> You don't need any experience for hand insertion, anybody could do hand insertion.... The inspection side is a bit trickier because anybody that we employ on inspection we like them to have some soldering experience, and a lot of the people that are on the inspection side might have moved from hand insertion.

Thus, experienced workers were sometimes able to move down the line into positions of greater responsibility.

The lines were not mechanically paced but regulated by production targets that were set by the production manager. These targets were based on the original standard times used to generate the price for the customer, modified by his experience of past work-rates for particular types of board design. The targets for each day were broken down into sub-targets for specific periods, and were also used as the benchmarks for the visible assessment of line performance. These sub-targets provided a framework of accountability in relation to performance throughout the day, and Senior Operators were expected to explain any marked failure to meet such targets. Charts at the end of the shop indicated the pattern of such performance through the week, alongside defects, repairs, customer returns, overtime, and the like. Line leaders or senior operators had the responsibility of balancing the line, both by moving operators between task clusters and by the reallocation of specific tasks among operators.

The social regulation and negotiation of work-rates on the basis of these norms was evident from our interviews. For example, the production manager described how he hoped to engender rivalry among the lines to gain the best performance rating ('we're trying to get competition between the lines'), while he sometimes deliberately inserted the wrong rating to make sure they were paying attention to the chart ('every now and again I'll try to keep them on their toes'). Another manager captured the mixture of personal relations, understandings, and threats by which production was managed on the shop-floor:

> He's much more capable than [the previous incumbent] ever was of actually getting the place running and motivating people or kicking people. Because that's when I was talking about him being a bit dangerous, you know, because you can only kick people so much. You've got to motivate them really... but a kicking is necessary sometimes isn't it?

However, a senior operator played down the pressure to compete:

> The girls know how well they're doing. It's not a competition if one line's got an A and one's got an F. They're not going to say 'Oh, God'... it's just purely for

> their information so that they can see how they're doing. If they're not told about their batch rejects they're not going to know the problems they are having.

Thus the grading given to any line was never treated simply as an unproblematical rating of staff performance. Instead it was read through a knowledge of the surrounding circumstances, such as problems with supply from the machine section, the difficulties of particular board designs, shortages of staff and redeployment.

There was significant surveillance over job quality and worker errors, though this didn't have the formal rigour emphasized by accounts of the surveillance 'panopticon' in some large Japanese electronics companies:

> Final [inspection]actually sit down with a piece of paper and write down the mistakes, and at the end of the day it's written on paper... how many has been made, and they come down and tell you how many you've made, but like most of the time it's temps that make more than anyone.

Persistent faults were taken up by Senior Operators and highlighted in line briefings but, as this quote implies, did not represent the main pressure on permanent staff. There was also a degree of informal negotiation about sociability on the line. Thus one informant remarked that: 'we do get told off occasionally but it's not that bad, we do talk, we're women, we talk... [But] after lunch everyone's quiet, because everyone's tired, you just want to get on with your job and go home.'

The tasks of operators were assigned according to comparable job times, but there was also some leeway for the senior operator to modify these task-clusters at the margins to accommodate individual capabilities, so long as operators were regarded as making an effort:

> If you've got one person that's putting ten parts in and you may have to take off one of them, it might be just that they're just that little bit slow. Some people are faster at some things than others, and it's not that they're trying to pull wool over your eyes and get away with doing less, it's just that they're slower.
> [*So there's a fine judgement there to be made?*].
> You can usually see the difference. If somebody, you know, is really casual putting their parts, you know they're not trying, but if somebody is using two hands and they're going as fast as they possibly can you can see it, but they're still struggling to put their parts in, then you know that something's wrong.

In these respects Delbridge's (1998: 91, 116) discussion of the moral imperative of being seen to be 'trying' was pertinent to this work environment, but this also opened up issues of favouritism in the relations between operators and seniors or line leaders. This was highlighted by the comment that:

> A lot of the people here don't get the chance to be in them [preferred jobs]. It's like, it's as if your face fits, ... if you're friendly with your line leader then you get moved on fine. But if you are not over them like, they'll leave you there.

It was also evident that accusations and counter-accusations of favouritism played a role in decisions to quit the firm, though 'bitching' could also focus around other issues too.

The pace of the line varied depending upon the production schedule. As one operator remarked:

> We know if they're not needed desperately and we've got nothing else on that day, then we will probably all take our time, but half the time they need them desperately, or we are just waiting for the machine room to send us some boards out.... But it can be really fast, really, really fast sometimes.

Indeed, a central feature of the pacing of the assembly-line was the heightened pressure associated with the approach of the end of the week and the intended despatch of completed orders on Friday afternoons. Often there was a rush to meet the deadline, either because of bottlenecks in production or because of defects on some of the completed boards:

> Friday is a bad day because Friday is shipping day. So it's a mad rush Friday. If for instance you're behind during the week,... then it's a mad rush on a Friday... to make sure the boards are in their boxes waiting to go out the door.

This often involved pressure to speed up the work, or requests to work overtime on production or rectification, but it could also involve managers in a re-negotiation of delivery schedules, with a portion of the original batch delayed.

It was in this context that the production manager exercised subtle judgements about the distinctive priorities of different customers, in terms of the relative priority of delivery and quality criteria:

> Various companies, Japanese companies have very different policies. One customer will say that their quality is the first and only option, but you get [another company] that they are only interested in making sure that when they ask for the board, you've delivered on time. Quality's second, delivery is first. So it's very different with different Japanese companies, different concepts.... I've got in my mind how does that company think. Right, delivery. We must get those products out the door quickly then. If quality comes at the same time, hopefully that's a bonus. It's usually there. If we know this company have had a quality problem in the past, we can say hold on... let's ship 3000 [instead of 4000] and make sure we get 3000 of real good quality and keep them happy.

In this way he sought to finesse the activities and decisions of those in the Quality Assurance (QA) office when he felt they were placing constraints on his management of production.

One of the obvious consequences of this approach to the juggling of quality and delivery was that QA employees were subject to contradictory pressures. A manager at one remove from the resulting conflicts commented that:

> We've sacrificed quality, you know, and [QA manager's] people have said 'this is wrong', and [he] has had to say 'Well, let it go through anyway', because he is under pressure.

Meanwhile, one of those most closely involved underlined the ways in which the need for cost savings had been seen to force this situation:

> We were making quite big losses before, so we really had to make a profit, so therefore circumstances were, you had to be more lenient shall we say. In fact I came in for a lot of criticism from my own people. I don't blame them because you tell them 'you must do this, you must do that', and they say 'bloody hell, what are you doing now, you told us [so and so]'... [You have to] explain to people, circumstances change, the world is changing all the time.

He hoped that, as conditions improved again, with more customers and less pressure to cut costs: 'hopefully people will really concentrate on the quality side now we are in profit, we can afford to, whereas before we couldn't do that'.

However, the immediate pressures of subcontract production were also manifest in the organization of inspection and repair activities on the shop-floor. Rectification was the responsibility of one cluster of workers who inspected and repaired PCBs after they had been through the machine section, and another couple of skilled staff who diagnosed and tried to repair faults after the completion of manual assembly and soldering. In each case, records of the pattern of defects were kept, which could inform more proactive problem-solving activities. However, in each case much of this data remained unused because time and resources were not available to act on it, 'We go and collect lots and lots of this data but... we never get a chance to do anything with it.' As a result some of the workers involved in collecting data on defects had become very sceptical about the likelihood of change:

> When we've finished the fault sheet goes to somebody that puts it into the computer, but from where we can see, it just goes into that computer and stays there. It's not used.... So basically it's going from us to nowhere. So there's really no point in us.... We filled in about three [suggestion forms] saying that the fault sheet is just doing no good because they're not getting back to machine room to what's going wrong.... Because nothing was done when we put the last one in we're just basically wasting our time.

There were some attempts to solve production and quality problems. Managers drew on the expertise of Senior Operators and technicians, and sometimes individual operators made suggestions. However, such suggestions were rare, and managers recognized that their occasional efforts to involve more shop-floor workers in problem-solving had also been undermined by time or resource constraints:

> It really comes back again to being a subcontractor, our resources are limited... you can't give [problems] works time because the line is going flat out, so then it's only a matter of trying to get people working overtime.

At the same time, operators found that management initiatives actively constrained their efforts to make their work easier. For example, workers were instructed that they could no longer separate out a preforming task from the main task of insertion, but had to do each sequentially on each board. This encouraged a strategy of low profile compliance rather than active problem-solving:

> Just keep your mouth shut basically and get on with it, you can't get into trouble that way... we just get told what to do and we do it, we might mumble but we still do it, it's like, it's our job to be told what to do.

Thus, in the day-to-day running of the factory, there was a substantial gap between the rhetoric of continuous improvement (embraced in principle by the production management and also projected as something which was soon to be implemented), and the realities of crisis management and pressured efforts to meet deadlines in the context of short-batch production and investment constraints.

The fate of subcontract operations

As we noted earlier, PCB-Co continued in business for about four years after our main fieldwork, before it was closed. It was clear during our research that the production of PCBs for office equipment represented an increasingly precarious niche for the firm, especially because of the competition from production in China, once local production requirements no longer constrained global production decisions. At the end of the 1990s the parent company was also forced into a general corporate restructuring because of a sharp downturn in overall profitability following falling sales in recession-hit Japan. This led them to sell some operations and develop a multidivisional structure designed to focus on the performance of specific businesses. In this context, the levels of worker effort and forms of qualified commitment delivered by the mixture of limited training, crisis management, calculative involvement, and personalized appeals which were outlined earlier were deemed insufficient to sustain the operation. Thus the closure reflected both the long-term precariousness of the subcontracting operation in Telford and a broader process of corporate restructuring.

However, this did not mean the withdrawal of the parent company from manufacturing in the United Kingdom. Rather, the closure of one small factory was paralleled by the opening of another small subcontract site, employing slightly fewer workers and this time producing components for the car industry. By the time of the closure of PCB-Co the management was largely Japanese, but these managers were themselves replaced in the new plant by managers from the auto components division, several of whom had earlier international experience in an American subsidiary. The new factory was also relocated in another part of the West Midlands, in part to avoid the tightening labour market in Telford by moving to 'where the unemployment rate is higher'. There must be some doubt, however, whether this will allow management to escape from the limitations of labour commitment and stability documented earlier, unless a very different pattern of investment, training, and effort bargaining is institutionalized in the new factory.

ASSEMBLY-CO: OLD FASHIONED FLEXIBILITIES AS THE BASIS FOR THE GROWTH OF A SUBORDINATE SUBCONTRACTOR

The role of the firm and the uncertainties of subcontracting

Assembly-Co, like PCB-Co, had been established in Telford at the behest of a larger Japanese customer firm, a final assembler of office and consumer electronics goods. In this case, however, the company was characterized by a more complex pattern of ownership and corporate management: the parent company of Assembly-Co was a joint venture between a large Japanese trading company (Trading-Co) and a small American design and development specialist. The latter had developed and patented the specialized mechanism which was Assembly-Co's core product, while Trading-Co provided the resources and contacts to facilitate the production of this component for the Japanese final assemblers who dominated the market for the product that incorporated this device.

Assembly-Co was established as an overseas arm of this Japanese-based joint venture, initially to meet the needs of a specific Japanese final assembler that had located production in Britain, but it later developed to serve a wider range of such customer firms. It also expanded its operations from assembly of the specialized mechanism to a wider production process. Initially, it was little more than an assembly 'warehouse'. However, it soon developed beyond this to incorporate the production of plastic mouldings, the construction of large sub-assemblies around the core device, and finally additional lines of work involving the assembly of other plastic components. At the same time the bulk of the workforce continued to be involved in routine assembly work.

This pattern of developments was the result of evolving management policies intended to expand and sustain production activity at the factory in the face of considerable uncertainty. At Assembly-Co, as at PCB-Co, managers were concerned about the viability of the factory in the context of changing customer demands and growing international competition. However, the specific character of the pressures experienced by Assembly-Co differed from those on PCB-Co.

First, alternative production sites were a potential threat to the Telford factory. However, the latter had established itself as a major supplier not only for the European market but also for a major American customer, and was seen as the flagship production site. One index of this was that production had increased nearly three-fold in terms of sales value over the first six years, though this had not been a smooth process but punctuated by two downturns in output.

Second, however, Assembly-Co remained more heavily dependent upon their original major customer than had PCB, though that customer had encouraged them to seek work from other firms. At the time of our research Assembly-Co had produced work for fifteen customers at one time or another, with a current commitment to ten. However, production for three factories of their original customer firm (located in Britain, France, and the United States) had never accounted for less than 68 per cent of their sales value and was back up to 84 per cent at the time of our research. Furthermore, the web of relations with this major customer went beyond being a direct component supplier, because the subcontracting process also meant that Assembly-Co received work from this firm for further processing. Some managers were exercised by a longer-term search for areas of work that would reduce their dependency on their dominant customer and provide new product lines to replace the original patented device that would ultimately become obsolete. However, these were not immediate priorities.

Thus the British factory sustained its order book in a variety of ways: partly by adding new customer firms (though none of these accounted for large orders), partly by their primary customer finding new markets for the old product lines and partly by moving into plastic parts production for a new generation of products, again for their main customer but without the leverage of a patented device. One implication of this pattern was that, while a substantial amount of the production activity in the factory continued to involve the original product assemblage, a changing range of additional production activities had been added, creating a continuing and somewhat unpredictable reconfiguration of production processes.

In responding to these circumstances and in developing their work and employment policies, the managers at Assembly-Co enjoyed considerable operational autonomy from the joint venture parents. The American parent played only a minimal role, while Trading-Co played a somewhat more active role. They provided successive MDs, who worked under and reported to Japanese staff at Japanese and later European head offices, the establishment of which meant more frequent meetings, once a month rather than once every six months. Nevertheless, their role was also relatively limited, with an emphasis on financial transactions rather than substantive policies: they guaranteed loans and monitored investments, but a senior British manager characterized them as 'very patient' in regard to returns. This probably reflected the fact that Trading-Co itself had limited production experience, as evidenced by their recruitment of the key Japanese manager for the British plant from outside their own management cadre.

Thus this factory was characterized by considerable operational autonomy from the joint venture parents and also by a very predominantly local management team. The Japanese MD underlined the distinctiveness of the company in this respect, in terms that were echoed by British managers:

> Most of the Japanese companies, Japanese are very similar because they came from head office and they stayed five or even seven years, and most of the design, and how to produce, and all operations, are coming from Japan. But for us nothing is coming from Japan, only they ask for profit, so it is a big difference.

The MD concentrated on liaison with the Japanese parent and winning orders from Japanese customers, while a Japanese technical specialist acted as a production engineer in the moulding shop. However, all other management posts were filled by British managers, including production, finance, and personnel.

Relations with the dominant customer were evidently close and long-term rather than distant and short-term, and in these respects approximated to the 'obligational contractual relation' discussed by Sako (1992) and others. Thus the MD of Assembly-Co observed that when he had faced a downturn in orders he had gone to his dominant customer and asked for more work, and they had responded by contracting out work they had previously done in-house. Nevertheless, the factory was not immune from pressures from lower cost producers in South-east Asia. The management sought to gain orders by emphasizing the strengths of the company, including new equipment and quality standards, but cost reduction remained a continuing pressure, especially when customers considered sourcing components from South-east Asia. However, the British Operations Director also emphasized that sourcing from a distance was not always an easy option for the final assemblers:

> It's very difficult to try to compete with China, Singapore, in the end, in some cases now it's like, 'No. This is what we can do it for and I'm not going to take a loss on the job. If you want to get it from Singapore, get it from there then'.... But of course they don't want it done over there anyway. Long lead time, they're not so good actually, anyway... it's obviously advantageous if you've got people around you that are going to supply you at a moment's notice, you can pressurize them to supply it at a moment's notice. But pick up the phone for someone half way round the world, and they're having to fly it in.

There were, of course, local competitors for some of the work, which also gave the assemblers some leverage over their suppliers, but they did not have the obvious cost advantages of the East Asian competitors.

Management micropolitics and contrasting evaluations of Japanese techniques

The senior management at Assembly-Co were not riven by disagreements in the way that managers at PCB-Co were. Instead, there appeared to be a fairly comfortable division of labour between the various managers, Japanese and British, in commercial, administrative, and production roles. This did not preclude differences of emphasis in their approaches to corporate and employment policies, but it did mean that overt conflict was rare and policy disagreements did not threaten a broadly agreed strategy, especially in regard to production and employment practices.

In part, this may have reflected the limited presence of Japanese managers, but it also arose from the degree of operational autonomy granted to the whole management team and from the strong commitment of the Japanese MD to the local operation. His career pattern was quite different from that of the majority of Japanese managers in overseas manufacturing subsidiaries, even those at the other subcontractor we studied. His earlier work experience had been as a manager of a third-tier subsidiary in Japan, supplying plastic parts to component manufacturers for a major motor company, and he had experienced the early 1990s downturn in that sector, one of the factors that had influenced him to accept a job offer from Trading-Co.

He had some pre-existing personal and commercial links with Trading-Co, partly through an old college friendship and partly through the purchase of raw materials, and was eventually attracted by their invitations for him to join the firm. However, he was not assimilated into their management structure, but was recruited specifically to work at the British subsidiary, spending only a matter of days in Japan after he was recruited before moving here. Furthermore, he identified himself with the British subsidiary rather than the Japanese parent company, and envisaged remaining in Britain for a longer period than was usual among those Japanese managers who hoped to continue their careers with the parent company on returning home. As Assembly-Co grew, his main role became gaining orders from existing and potential Japanese customers.

The senior British manager was the 'operations director', and he worked closely with the manager of finance and administration, the most senior female manager we encountered across our research in Japanese-owned companies. Their collaboration focused especially on the development of a distinctive array of policies to stabilize and regulate the workforce, prompted by the difficulties they experienced in the recruitment, motivation, and retention of labour. In turn, these policies were implemented and interpreted by more junior British managers who also emphasized their local provenance. Two features of these policies are noteworthy. Firstly they involved an idiosyncratic combination of reward and training policies, involving a piecework payment system, an attendance allowance, awards for task flexibility, and the use of NVQ accreditation, representing an ambitious, but not entirely successful, formal apparatus of employment regulation. Secondly, unusually, the firm had resisted the use of temporary employment agencies characteristic of the other Japanese firms we studied, but instead used a small pool of outworkers and had established a satellite factory in a location where labour was more readily available.

Employment relations and the labour market: the scope and limits of formalization

As we have noted, the British management team at Assembly-Co had developed a distinctive set of personnel policies. A central feature of these policies was that they sought to address what managers experienced as problematical features of the local labour market, especially problems of turnover and absenteeism. Labour turnover was a major preoccupation, with especially high levels in the mid 1990s, running at 201 per cent in 1993 and 190 per cent in 1994 among the assemblers who constituted the bulk of the factory workforce. However, the turnover rate for the whole workforce had also oscillated markedly, between quarterly peaks of over 50 per cent and troughs below 10 per cent. The highest peaks of turnover followed large-scale recruitment, suggesting that substantial numbers of recruits moved on quite rapidly, but length of service data also suggested that longer service workers contributed to the pattern, with another peak at around two years. Managers were also aware that both external circumstances (such as the availability of alternative jobs) and internal developments (such as plans for expansion or the introduction of the NVQ programme) influenced these fluctuations in turnover. At the time of our fieldwork, in a period of limited recruitment at the main site, the annualized figure was down to around 50 per cent, but this was still a cause of some concern, especially as the rate in some areas remained higher, for example among the operators in the moulding shop, predominantly young men on shift work.

Furthermore, it remained difficult to recruit new staff, something workers themselves were aware of, as suggested by the comments of one person about her induction:

> I did about a twenty-minute interview with [personnel], and then they took us out to the mainframes and we had to do fifteen of the frames in thirty minutes, . . . but from what I can see everyone who has been for an interview has got the job. So whether it's just because that many people aren't coming that they can't be choosy.

Much of the administrative effort at Assembly-Co had been devoted to the development of a complex, multilayered, payment system, intended to deliver attendance, effort and commitment to the firm. One of the architects told us that 'the benefit I think is that... it's making people do what you want, and combating the Telford disease [high turnover] and rewarding people who make the most effort'.

A key feature of this system was that the starting pay was comparatively low, even for this relatively low paying labour market. This meant that when new recruits started, they experienced this low starting rate, and it was some time before they began to improve on that figure. One manager's characterization of the pay rate was that 'if I'm truthful initially it's low, but eventually no, we're just above average'. She also suggested that, during recruitment, the scope for such progression was emphasized, in an effort to retain recruits over the period before they accumulated bonus payments. Nevertheless, it was evident that a major source of initial dissatisfaction and early leaving was the low starting rate. The overtime premium was also modest, at twenty-five pence per hour, so this was not really an alternative means of boosting pay, and this was also a source of complaints, though many workers, especially women with family commitments, were not keen to work overtime.

Against this background, the most important component of the payment system, in all areas except the moulding shop, was the productivity bonus. According to the HRM coordinator, 'that is what makes your money up... that's what feeds your salary', with bonuses averaging above fifteen pounds a week and a potential to earn thirty pounds. However, managers still found that their hopes of racheting up production through the piecework system gained only limited success, and (as Baldamus (1961) showed) the dominant effect was rather to stabilize worker effort and output around an established norm:

> I mean base plus ten which is the top, you're talking, last year it would have been twenty pounds, this year it's thirty pounds in a week. So there is an incentive there to move them on. But then, what we found was they're consistently producing at or about base and not really pushing themselves to go above base.

Nevertheless, according to employee testimony the piecework system certainly led to a preoccupation with hitting production targets, 'making the count'.

> I mean every break you can hear other girls say, how many boxes have I done, oh my God I'm two under, I'm not going to do it... sixteen boxes is a lot, it doesn't sound a lot but it is, I mean there's quite a few fast workers and they are only just getting their sixteen a day.

One important feature in this respect was the way the productivity bonus interacted with the active policy of job flexibility and rotation operated at Assembly-Co. This policy was designed to provide flexibility for management but also to relieve the boredom associated with such routine assembly work. However, it could threaten workers' immediate earning potential because of their level of experience or the varied difficulty of the tasks. This meant that some senior operators tried to share the good and bad jobs across the assemblers.

However, despite such tactics, the piecework system was widely experienced as exerting an unfair pressure on employees, especially in the light of demands that they perform their own inspection and quality control. This led the assemblers both to criticize the system and to cooperate in the development of covert shortcuts to make the work more manageable. For example:

> On the grease... you've got to put one, two, three spots of grease, whereas I just go swish with it there, and everyone does it because if you do it like that, you just can't make any money... if you see someone struggling, like that girl who is facing me, she has put the collets on one at a time then checking them, I said no, collet the box first and then check them, it's a lot quicker.

Occasionally, on unpopular jobs, employees might resort to making deliberate mistakes or oversights, which resulted in batches of rejects being returned while allowing the saboteur to move to more acceptable tasks. This could also lead to semi-formal renegotiations of the times or tasks for some jobs; especially if they involved altered procedures or were seen as particularly tight. We were told that the use of time and motion study had at some point been effectively opposed on the shop-floor. Instead, synthetic times were used (as for generating the costings), subject to the possibility that senior managers could be asked to reconsider and compromise in particular circumstances. In this context, senior operators were important in articulating the views of the work group.

Attendance levels were also a major concern for Assembly-Co management. Indeed one senior manager exclaimed that 'absenteeism around in this area is diabolical, diabolical' and another recollected that 'when I finally put the figures together it was frightening'. This prompted an increase in the attendance bonus, coupled with sanctions against 'bad attendees'. In this area, as in others, Assembly-Co management pursued a process of formalization and standardization of practices within what remained a relatively small firm, making the policies less dependent on individual action and discretion. Nevertheless, the attendance bonus also prompted criticism from some workers, because it could actually be experienced as harsh and unfair.

A further layer of the payment system was built around learning to do a variety of jobs, to satisfy the requirement, written into the contract of employment, that 'total job flexibility is an essential condition of employment':

> The way they get their increment is a system they call "points make prizes". ...Every job has a base rate to it, some jobs could have three parts to it, some two, some four, but each part of the job has got a base rate. Once you've achieved base rate three times on a part of a job [in moves back and forth

> between jobs] you then qualify for a point, and that point makes a pound, which makes sure that the training is done on each job and that you are qualified to do it. And you then become multiskilled within the job.

On this basis assemblers could eventually earn a maximum of fifteen pounds a week for full task flexibility.

Beyond this workers could also gain payments for successfully completing NVQs. There were some complaints among employees about a rather long gap between fulfilling the requirements and gaining formal accreditation and payment, and there were also rather varied views among employees about the broader worth of NVQ certification. Nevertheless, some junior managers certainly believed that NVQs were having a beneficial effect on staff retention and development, not least by acting as a stepping stone to promotion. In some respects this involved the formalization of an established practice, but it also strengthened this practice. Production pressures often limited the time available for training, and some workers remained sceptical. Nevertheless, for a relatively small subcontractor, this firm had put significant efforts into an organized policy on training, a feature celebrated by the junior HR 'coordinator':

> The training and development, that is the one thing Assembly-Co has got in its favour and I've always applauded it since the day I came here. They have good training and development programmes here.

One aspect of this policy was that, in the context of the expansion of output and employment, most of the senior operators, inspectors, and even supervisors were 'home grown' within the firm. Often, such promoted workers were particularly appreciative of the firm's training policies and some of them formed a nucleus of long-service staff who had worked for the company since it started. However, this pattern of internal promotion could also encourage expectations that were disappointed, as in the case of one worker who had been promised advancement from 'off-line assistant' to 'not quite senior operator', but this did not happen because of the postponement of a new line. In consequence, he was instructed to return to work as an operator, but refused and threatened to resign, until coaxed and cajoled into staying on.

Alongside such personalized counselling and cooling out, the work of the HRM specialist primarily involved the elaboration and extension of existing arrangements, though she had been very critical of an appraisal system that was directly linked to merit pay. As a result, she had eventually persuaded the senior management team to separate these two elements and to establish an explicitly developmental appraisal scheme. Meanwhile the merit payments were assimilated into other elements of the wage packet, including a profit-related pay element. This clearly represented a move away from a merit payment system similar to those used in Japan, and the adoption of an approach to appraisal directly influenced by professional personnel practice and debate in Britain, though the payment system itself seemed more like a throwback to earlier British payment-by-results systems.

The concerns with attendance, retention, and training also informed the development of several further layers of policy. These included the development of a profit-related bonus scheme (which was also geared to attendance) and the pursuit of 'Investors in People' accreditation, both intended to foster a sense of 'ownership' among the employees and boost their commitment to the firm. However, at the time of our research, managers recognized that their whole complex array of payment and training policies had not accomplished these ambitious objectives. Thus the HRM specialist lamented that:

> I don't think that they [employees] understand that they are part of Assembly-Co. They perceive themselves as the workers and there's an 'us and them' situation.

Similarly, more senior managers recognized that their policies had done little to change an underlying instrumentalism on the part of the workforce. This was a repeated refrain in an interview with one of the senior British managers:

> We get people in, we try and look after them, we try and involve them with what's going on. But there is a little bit of a brick wall there, we feel, that we have been trying to knock down from the day we opened.... People are still very withdrawn [about] asking questions and being involved. It's still an 8 to 5.15 job. You can't break through that. There isn't a lot of company feeling, if you like, from the day-to-day employees. A lot of people here do put themselves out, but there isn't that family feeling.... We've tried very hard but it's still very difficult.

It was notable, however, that the multilayered formalization of the regulation of employment relations, outlined above, provided little scope for employees to voice their concerns to management, and certainly no means of collective expression such as a consultation committee or works council. Trade unions were not recognized. While management saw their commitment to Investors in People as a potential route towards enhanced 'communications' in the workplace, it was evident that this was an aspiration rather than a reality. It was anyway intended to enhance lateral communications between people in different departments and sections rather than providing a forum for concerns about pay and employment issues. To the extent that these were being addressed at all, the tendency was to highlight the established disciplinary and grievance procedures as forms of 'communication'.

Informality and counselling in HRM

In the absence of any more formal process of worker consultation, the HRM specialist had developed an informal practice of being around and engaging in conversation on the shop-floor. In this way she emphasized empathy, confidentiality, and counselling but this could develop into an active but informal and personalized form of grievance handling. This style of being an involved, personable manager involved a lot of individual counselling, to help people cope with circumstances arising outside work (particularly with an awareness of the pressures facing women workers, about which male members of management could be less sympathetic). It could be used to cool out or smooth over grievances arising in the workplace. It could also mean sympathizing with the problems of groups of workers, such as those involved in coping with defective components or mastering a new work process:

> Yes I'm management, but I'll go on the shop-floor. If they've got a new job I'll ask them to explain the new job to me. Or can I have a go then, I can see what they're doing and I'm there making a mess of this job because I can't quite do it as well as they can. What's it done? "She knows what's going on." "She'll have a go."... I've just broken down a barrier which is what [Assembly-Co's] all about.

However, while this could result in quite supportive responses to employees who brought problems into work from outside, the alternatives in regard to work-related problems were construed rather narrowly:

> If it's on-the-job then the remedy's in our hands, and it's easily rectified. Any on-the-job problems that cause it, either is simply rectified or the person doesn't suit Assembly-Co, it's really like that. If it's on-the-job it's so, so easily sorted out. Perhaps they haven't had sufficient training. Perhaps they weren't listening. Perhaps they were away when that job was coming on line. Perhaps they don't really understand why the rejects have come back.

Thus the alternatives envisaged seemed to be more communication, explanation, and training, or otherwise employees should seek their solution outside Assembly-Co.

Perhaps not surprisingly, several workers expressed the view that there was little opportunity to voice grievances over such issues as the piecework system or the attendance bonus. This even prompted one of our informants to raise the issue of union recognition and to muse about the positive role that a trade union might play in such circumstances. Interestingly, this was a relatively young worker, but one who was able to draw comparisons with work elsewhere, where a union had not only encouraged a more responsive stance by supervisors but had also helped to improve redundancy payments for relatively short-service workers when the firm closed down.

The satellite factory

As mentioned earlier, Assembly-Co, unlike our other case-study companies, had not made use of Temping Agencies, though they issued their own temporary contracts for workers during their probationary period of three to six months. One manager reflected the broader management view, that 'agencies charge an awful lot of money just to maintain people here, and they're only getting [people] from the same market aren't they. It doesn't pay.' This clearly reflected the tight cost constraints faced by the firm, but it also reflected the determination of the senior managers to develop their own distinctive employment policy, which could have been compromised by delegating extensive recruitment and selection responsibilities to an Agency. They had also rejected the policy of bussing-in workers from a wider area, again because of the costs involved. Instead, they developed another approach which sought to escape from the constraints of the local labour market, through the development of a satellite factory situated in a more depressed labour market.

Capacity constraints at the main factory, and the availability of appropriate premises within a reasonable travelling distance influenced their decision to open this satellite factory. However, the fundamental concern was labour supply:

> Our customers were saying that they were going to need us to take on more work, there would be this work which would have necessitated taking on another fifteen to twenty people...and we had previously experienced extreme difficulties in recruiting quality labour in large numbers.... We did a feasibility study and sent somebody out on the road looking.... Where there was labour available, talking to the job centres, talking to economic development units of the councils and what have you.... There was a reasonable pool of unemployed female labour and a history of work, of similar work if you like.... [A large employer] had closed down, and created a little unemployment blackspot if you like in the county.

Initially, the new unit had no difficulty in recruiting: apparently there were over 150 applicants for the first six posts. However, turnover was initially high, as the new recruits experienced assembly-line pressures on low starter wages. In turn, the opinion of those who left influenced potential applicants and, in this small local labour market, recruitment became more difficult for a time, before the reputation of the firm began to improve, just as they embarked on a new round of expansion.

At the time of our research, different managers offered interestingly varied accounts of the potential of this new factory. One suggested that in some respects their performance could be regarded as a model for operators at the main plant: '[Satellite] have got a very, very good team. They're very, very fast and they're very, very high quality. They're very good. But they're only small.' Another was also positive but argued that it needed to grow to be effective: 'they are producing faster than I expected them to, so probably it's just about breaking even now in terms of covering the costs, so it needs to grow to justify its existence really'. Finally, however, the Operations Director emphasized that the satellite operation was yet to be fully integrated into the tighter control regime of the main factory. It was shortly to acquire several senior operators and an inspector, and he believed that this would limit what he regarded as the rather cosy relations at the site, suggesting some move away from a temporary indulgency pattern.

The social organization and regulation of production

Clearly, the payment system, and especially the 'payment-by-results' approach, directly structured the organization of the production process at Assembly-Co. Much of the assembly work was performed on benches or tables without any mechanical pacing, with the work replaced in boxes or passed to the next operator by hand, though in some areas assembly was also paced by the movement of a conveyor belt. The main rationale for this pattern was the variety and frequent change of products, which required the flexible reconfiguration of production arrangements, and the comparative cost and rigidity of moving lines. In this respect the changing pattern of assembly work, with an increased variety of other tasks alongside the long-running assembly of the core device, reinforced the rationale of bench assembly.

These production pressures represented a potential threat to quality, especially as managers sought to devolve responsibility for quality to the operators, rather than resort to extensive in-process inspection. Certainly operators often felt caught between the twin pressures for quality and quantity, caught on the need to make the numbers to gain their bonuses. However, management appeared confident that they had achieved a reasonable balance in this respect. They remained strong advocates of quality assurance rather than inspection and believed that they had contained the pressures of the piecework system in a way which did not jeopardize current quality:

> In terms of quality suffering because we're rattling the thing out too fast, I think we've pushed it as far as we can now, in terms of the proportion that the productivity bonus is of the total wage, and if it got any bigger I think that's where we'd really start to suffer.

As a result most quality problems occurred in the production of new items rather than with established lines, though sometimes errors were not discovered until later, disrupting production elsewhere in the factory or even, occasionally, at their customer plants.

Managers regarded other aspects of the prototypical model of Japanese production with considerable scepticism. Some approaches, such as 'continuous improvement', were seen as 'common sense', not as specifically Japanese. This was also the case with the training and development policies adopted by the firm. As one manager emphasized, these policies, though they might have some Japanese parallels, were 'British-owned, they've been in Britain for years and years'. Furthermore, it had been the local staff who had developed them at Assembly-Co, sometimes in ways which would not be replicated in Japan. However, several managers argued that other ideas, especially JIT, did not work as they were claimed to do, but rather represented 'a form of [the] customer taking advantage of a supplier'.

This did not mean that Assembly-Co could escape from the pressures of customer demands, but rather that these demands were not generally organized through a JIT system. Production schedules for supplying customers were tightly defined, but they were set up on the basis of information from customers supplied a month in advance, rather than through a JIT shuttle system, though such orders were also subject to late modifications that forced Assembly-Co to redirect resources from planned targets. A telling example in this regard was the moulding shop. The manager characterized the pressure of customer demands as acute: 'you usually find that they wanted it yesterday. "You've got to make X number of thousands of these components or our lines stop tomorrow".' Nevertheless, he argued that it was inappropriate to give priority to small batches and quick changeovers to serve JIT requirements. Rather:

> This is a company based on rapid response. We do try to respond rapidly, but JIT is a system which in moulding is not practical because it means that you are going to be changing tools more often, your down time is going to be greater, and Japanese customers tend to be delivered on price. So we are a rapid response company, not a JIT company.

In this context, he also argued that quality should be given priority over delivery when production problems occurred, because that would both be cheaper and sustain the firm's reputation with customers.

Thus at Assembly-Co, Japanese management techniques were not ignored, but British managers selected those aspects they regarded as most appropriate for the business and production conditions they worked in, and Japanese provenance was not pivotal to their decisions.

CONCLUSION

Both these subcontract firms occupied subordinate positions as suppliers to large final assemblers. They were both vulnerable to persistent pressure to minimize costs and sustain the timing and quality of delivery, both to maintain their relations with customers and to fund their operations to the satisfaction of their parent companies. Furthermore, they both depended on a capacity to recruit and control a low paid workforce to perform routinized labour-intensive production in a way that responded to these pressures. These are the key features of the substantive circuits of capital and labour (see Kelly 1985) with which the local managements of these branch plants had to operate.

However, there were also significant differences in the intensity of these pressures on the two establishments. PCB-Co faced a more volatile pattern of demands from a shifting customer base, against a background of growing vulnerability to competition from East Asian factories and increased pressure from their parent company to minimize costs and generate profits. Meanwhile, Assembly-Co retained a more sheltered dependency on its major customer and faced less pressure for immediate financial returns from its joint venture parent firms. In neither case were these branch plants even partial replicas of 'mother' or 'sister' factories, and in both cases their owners were centrally concerned with financial indicators of performance. Here again, however, there were important differences. The ownership structure of Assembly-Co meant that the parent companies had little specialist expertise in subcontract assembly work, and this reinforced the localization and relative autonomy of the factory management team. At PCB-Co, however, senior corporate management linked localization with a more active and interventionist approach, drawing on broad Japanese management competencies rather than specialist expertise in overseas branch management, and this gave a distinctive inflection of frustration and mistrust to evolving management responses to the persistently precarious position of the plant.

In many respects, work and employment relations at the two factories were similar. In each case, the production process combined the semi-skilled servicing of capital-intensive machinery with a tightly defined set of semi-skilled labour-intensive assembly procedures, and in both cases managers confronted the practical instrumentalism of a semi-skilled, low paid workforce. However, the organization and evolution of these relations differed in the two factories in ways that reflected the distinctive pressures on these branch plants, but also involved different patterns of management-micropolitics and 'organizational learning'.

At PCB-Co constraints on investment and moves towards shorter production runs intensified a sense of crisis management, in which aspirations regarding operator training and initiative remained persistently at odds with practical coping strategies. In this context, the collusive finessing of formal procedures identified by Palmer (2000; Webb and Palmer 1998), together with informal pressure and tacit bargaining over the pace of work, were standard parts of organizational life (and features which Japanese managers found difficult to handle without appearing too soft or, more often, too draconian). As in Palmer's research, the scope and limits of these patterns of informalized cooperation and bargaining were influenced by efforts to cope with problems that recurrently threatened to disrupt production and delivery targets. However, it was also evident that the positioning of employees in the wider local labour market also influenced the terms of the resultant effort bargain, partly because there were limited choices of alternative employment and also because experienced but dissatisfied workers were prepared to quit despite this.

Against this backdrop, the tightening demands placed upon the factory, both directly from the parent company and indirectly from alternative sources of supply, appeared to feed increasing controversy and distrust within management, but no obvious recipe for the sustained viability of the factory. The practical applicability of Japanese-inspired forms of process innovation and quality assurance was debated and contested, in a way which involved disagreements among British managers as well as between Japanese and British staff. There were related controversies over the appropriate methods for securing labour discipline and the stringency of such discipline. Finally, there were contrasting views on the rationale for any further parent company investment or alternative product lines. While head office and their local Japanese representatives regarded improvement as a condition of additional support, British managers regarded such support as a prerequisite for escape from deepening crisis. Thus, management policy formation at PCB-Co was characterized by piecemeal and contested innovation in a context of crisis management, an absence of formalized employee involvement policies (but informal collusion in coping strategies) and the entrenchment of conflicting diagnoses and policy responses within management.

At Assembly-Co, greater branch management autonomy and a somewhat more stable form of dependency on a dominant customer provided the basis for a more cohesive management and a more coherent policy trajectory. This trajectory sought to entrench an idiosyncratic but decidedly old-fashioned basis for labour flexibility (compare Ackroyd and Procter 1998), based on combining a piecework regime and the formal bureaucratic regulation of attendance, discipline, and training. In this context, distinctively Japanese management techniques played a minimal role, though the dominant customer sometimes intervened to define operating procedures in some detail. However, while the relative stability and growth of the factory facilitated and encouraged the formalized regulation and disciplining of labour, informal processes that qualified the impact of such controls accompanied these developments.

One aspect of the informal modulation of formal procedures was apparent in the personalized performance of empathy, counselling, scolding, and cooling out practised by the HR Manager. Moreover, it was evident that the recruitment and retention difficulties faced by management not only influenced the structuring of the formal procedures but also the sorts of leeway provided by this less formal pattern of control and accommodation.

However, the operation of the piecework payment system was the crucial site of such informal dynamics, involving both the informal contestation and subversion of intensive work norms and the collusive adjustment of work loads and procedures to improve equity across work groups. In these respects this workplace reproduced well-documented patterns of informal cooperation, rule bending, and tacit bargaining, which accomplished some reconciliation between the achievement of production and quality targets for management and a tolerable wage and effort bargain for workers.

Thus collusive rule-bending to facilitate task completion and target achievement (documented in modest form by Delbridge (1998) where external sources of turbulence were minimized, and in a more florid form by Webb and Palmer (1998) where employees had to cope with significant disruptions) was also an important feature of this work-setting. As at PCB-Co, this involved an implicit and bargained reliance on worker competencies and experience rather than any formalized apparatus of involvement or continuous improvement. What is also evident is that such practices were intertwined with tacit processes of effort bargaining and moderation of work effort, once more influenced in their scope and limits by wider labour market options and the potential to quit.

Unlike PCB-Co, the managers at Assembly-Co had pursued a modestly incremental policy of bureaucratic employment regulation. Over time, this involved financial rewards and penalties for attendance and performance, and also basic on-the-job training linked to increased labour flexibility and some promotion. At the same time this policy repertoire coexisted on the one side with more informal patterns of cooperation and bargaining, and on the other with management efforts to escape the constraints of a relatively volatile labour market, especially by establishing their satellite factory. This represented a trajectory of policy development which owed very little to Japanese management approaches, but for the present allowed survival and modest growth within the constraints constituted by the dominance of their major customer and the relative volatility of semi-skilled labour within their local labour market.

Thus, in this chapter, we have demonstrated how the evolution of management policies and work and employment relations in these two subcontract firms were influenced (i) by evolving relations with their parent companies, customer firms, and competitors, and (ii) by conditions in the local labour market and thus the options open to employees. While the two companies faced the same local labour market, differences in their positions as subcontractor branch plants also generated different pressures on each firm. However, we have also shown that the evolution of work and employment relations within these firms cannot simply be 'read off' from these broader conditions, but involved tortuous but cumulative processes of cooperation, conflict, and accommodation characteristic of each firm, both among managers and between managers and employees.

CHAPTER

9

Computer-Co and Electric-Co: The Pursuit of Design and Development Capabilities

INTRODUCTION

The extent and limits of R&D activity by Japanese manufacturing investors in Europe and North America has been a topic of considerable controversy. While some commentators have highlighted the growing number of workplaces where some R&D is conducted, others have emphasized the relatively limited resources involved and a concentration on a limited range of customization activities. Furthermore, it is unclear how far the contemporary restructuring of Japanese manufacturing firms may reinforce a strategy of retaining high value-added activities in Japan or involve the relocation of R&D close to international competitors in pursuit of foreign expertise. In either case, there are likely to be important implications for the character of work and employment relations, not only within centres of research, design, and development but also for those engaged in production.

To address these issues this chapter seeks to analyse the rescue, restructuring, and recent closure of Computer-Co by Electric-Co, a major Japanese multinational keen to develop stronger capabilities in networked PC applications. In 1990, Electric-Co purchased Computer-Co, the struggling hardware design and manufacturing arm of a British computer company, which employed about 360 people. The Japanese company provided the capital necessary for Computer-Co to continue to design and develop computers and servers for the business market, and invested in new technology at the factory in Scotland. Computer-Co was increasingly integrated into the Electric-Co corporate structure by becoming its PC

Division, but retained a British management, with the British MD as the only non-Japanese Director of one of its divisions. However, Computer-Co never gained a strong position in its various markets and continued to make losses through the 1990s. In 1999, Electric-Co announced that it was pulling out of this market and that Computer-Co would be closed. The closure took place in 1999 with a loss of around 500 jobs.

This chapter is based on extensive interviews at all three sites of Computer-Co—the HQ and the R&D facility in the English Midlands and the factory in Central Scotland—and situates our findings within a broader discussion of patterns of expertise and competitiveness in the Japanese IT industry drawn primarily from Fransman (1990, 1995, 1999). On this basis we first reconstruct the logic of the initial purchase of the company, both for Electric-Co and for Computer-Co, highlighting their vulnerable positions in global competition and managerial assessments of their distinctive corporate competencies. We then explore the implications of these initial conditions for the processes of internal restructuring of work and employment relations in the British R&D and production facilities during the 1990s. This provides the context for an analysis of the evolving relationships between Japanese managers and British managers, and also between management and employees, over this period. In particular, we examine the interplay between the methods and approaches of managers and specialists from the Japanese company and from the British company, both in the design and development process and in work reorganization in manufacturing. This demonstrates the continuing centrality of British management and sector recipes in this company, and the relatively modest role of the Japanese parent company in the active reworking of existing corporate and sector approaches to product development, work organization, and employment relations. Finally, we outline and assess the timing and character of the closure.

Research, Design, and Development in Japanese Manufacturing Subsidiaries

Computer-Co represented a distinctive form of inward investment, not only as a takeover of an existing company but also as an operation characterized by a substantial British-based design and development capacity. Japanese companies, even more than other international firms, have tended to retain the bulk of their R&D operations at home (Dicken 1998: 211–14). Nevertheless, Japanese firms have established a variety of forms of research, design, and development capability in Europe, leading some commentators (such as Papanastassiou and Pearce 1995) to argue that their overseas R&D trajectory has converged with that of other international companies. However, as we reported in Chapter 3, there has been a slowdown in Japanese R&D investment in Europe over the last decade.

In interpreting the significance of such trends it is conventional to distinguish particularly between factory-based design and development work and research institute based fundamental R&D (Lauchlan 1993). The former generally involves product modifications and developments related to local markets, regional supplier networks and European standards, and related process engineering. Such units are usually quite small, though there are some exceptions with a broader remit and larger staff. The latter are generally separate from factories, often having links with University research groups, and are concerned to tap advanced research expertise in such areas as pharmaceuticals or materials science, as part of a global R&D effort (Lam 2003).

Papanastassiou and Pearce (1995) also differentiate between those factory-based R&D activities which focus largely upon the adaptation of existing products and production processes (characterized as 'support laboratories' for 'truncated miniature replica' plants or possibly for 'rationalized product subsidiaries'), and those that embrace a more extended and distinctive product development role for the international firm as a whole (a 'locally integrated laboratory' for factories with a 'regional or world product mandate'). They hypothesize that Japanese companies might have a bias towards the latter rather than the former. Their data, however, suggests that the adaptation and development of products and processes to suit local conditions, rather than a more global remit, remains central to the *factory-linked* R&D activities of Japanese firms in Europe (ibid: 279), though the free-standing labs in Europe may play a more important role in basic research than those of international firms from other countries. A similar pattern was also evident in the postal survey of Japanese manufacturers in Britain by McCormick and McCormick (1996: 141), albeit on the basis of a fairly low response rate. First, they found substantial variation in the presence of both Japanese and British engineers across their respondent firms (about one-third had no Japanese engineers on site and less than 10 per cent had more than five, while a quarter had no local engineers and only 13 per cent had more than twenty). But, second, it was primarily the *acquired* plants that had an established engineering capability, and the one firm with a heavy concentration of over fifty engineers was such a brownfield acquisition.

These findings therefore suggest that many Japanese manufacturing investments in the United Kingdom have had relatively *limited* research, design, and development capabilities (ibid: 296). Among our own small portfolio of five Midlands-based Japanese-owned manufacturers, none of the greenfield sites had such a broader role, and their product and process development roles were narrowly circumscribed. It was only at the brownfield takeover that research and development was more central. Electric-Co/Computer-Co had by far the largest concentration of design and development engineers.[1] Thus our case stands out as distinctive in being neither a greenfield transplant with a highly circumscribed (or non-existent) design and development role, nor a free-standing research institute designed primarily to tap basic research for corporate R&D activities still concentrated primarily in Japan. However, it clearly represents an important form of Japanese R&D investment in the United Kingdom.

Our case is similar to one other intensive study of the R&D operations of a Japanese inward investor in Britain, Lam's (1995) account of relations between British and Japanese engineers in a 'technology partnership' between a Japanese and a British firm, following the purchase of a majority stake in the latter by the former. We therefore develop a comparison between the two cases in Chapter 10, in the context of a broader discussion of the social formation and interaction of British and Japanese managers in all our case-study firms. However, in this chapter we focus on the distinctiveness of the Electric-Co/Computer-Co case in its own right, both as a brownfield takeover and ultimately as a failure. This allows us to analyse the rationale of this overseas R&D operation and the implications of this for British and Japanese managers and engineers (and also for employees in the Scottish manufacturing plant).

Analytical Themes

In seeking to address the experience of takeover and restructuring represented by Computer-Co and Electric-Co we need to extend our analysis of the specific roles performed by overseas subsidiaries beyond our earlier discussion of final assemblers and subcontractors. In examining the relationship between two existing firms, the buyer and the bought, we need to consider the distinctive technical and organizational competencies possessed by these firms, and the ways in which these competencies influenced both the process of internationalization through takeover and the consequent operation of the brownfield subsidiary.

In this context Fransman's (1990, 1995, 1999) evolutionary and institutionalist economic analysis of the technological and commercial trajectories of Japanese information and communication technology (ICT) firms is helpful in explaining why Electric-Co was interested in taking over an apparently failing British designer and manufacturer of PCs. For our purposes, the attractions of this analysis are three-fold. First, it understands the development of particular productive and competitive capabilities in firms and sectors as embedded social processes of organizational innov-

[1] Our sixth, ongoing, case study, unreported here, was the only other example with a (small) stand-alone development facility, and this also involved the purchase of a British design and development company as a going concern.

ation. These are influenced by legacies from earlier phases of corporate history, by the networks of support and constraint represented by enterprise groupings and state agencies, and by the strategic moves of competitor enterprises on both local and international terrains. This approach meshes with other studies which have registered important differences between Japanese firms from different sectors, and with the broader literature on 'sector recipes' (Smith et al. 1990; Spender 1989). Second, it highlights the ways in which established and evolving competencies represent both sources of competitive power and advantage *and* sources of weakness and vulnerability. Third, it offers an important resource in seeking to understand the opportunities and dilemmas which confront specific international corporations and encourage particular trajectories within their broader national and sectoral contexts.

We are not arguing that Fransman's conception of corporate competencies is complete in itself. As his analysis developed over the 1990s, in the context of the prolonged recession of the Japanese economy, it became more concerned with the vulnerabilities as well as strengths of the trajectories of these firms. However, it has also become clear that the analysis of specific firms and whole sectors in such terms cannot be abstracted from broader accounts of economic turbulence and crisis, but in themselves cannot pretend to offer a rounded analysis of the political economy of crises and restructuring. They may, however, illuminate the ways in which particular firms and workplaces experience and mediate such processes.

THE TAKEOVER

Computer-Co began as the hardware manufacturing arm of a pioneering and successful British computer software and servicing company. Manufacturing began in the early 1980s, at the beginning of the boom in demand for office PCs, and was initially very successful. In the mid-1980s, Computer-Co was described as 'the UK's leading manufacturer of high performance work stations' (financial press, 11/88). However, it then faced major problems which flowed from being small and independent in a period of increasing corporate rivalry between larger players, which both squeezed margins and enforced the expensive adoption of industry standards defined by the dominant firms. In this context, the original Computer-Co continued to demonstrate its design capabilities but was forced into niche production of office systems, while their factory apparently ran at around half of its capacity (financial press, 1/90). It was reported in the financial press (4/90) that 'Computer-Co's difficulties in turning a profit on hardware illustrate the hazards of competing in the top end of the personal computer sector where research and development costs are high, profit margins are slim and competition intense'.

By the end of the 1980s, the British parent was shifting back to its original emphasis on software and maintenance operations, while seeking to divest itself of its loss-making computer design and manufacturing operations. This move was famously underwritten by a John Harvey-Jones (1990) television programme, where he recommended that, despite his ostensible commitment to British manufacturing, this was a case where the holding company should quit manufacturing in favour of developing its service sector business. Thus, by early 1990, Computer-Co were reported to be searching for 'an overseas partner to share development costs and open new markets' (financial Press, 1/90).

During our interviews at Computer-Co we were told that five or six companies in the sector showed serious interest in buying the company, including several major sector players. In the end, Electric-Co purchased Computer-Co for £39 million and, with assets valued at £16.4 million, the Financial Press, suggested that the remainder of the sum represented Electric-Co's payment 'not only to extend its influence in Europe but to gain access to Computer-Co's expertise' (4/90). A key part of this expertise was their capability in developing IBM-compatible computers as this was becoming the industry standard. From the vantage point of the factory workforce, Electric-Co offered more by way of continuing employment than some of the other contenders, who already had existing production capacity in the sector. But from the vantage point of R&D employees there was some disappointment that they had not been absorbed into the design and development side of one of the leading PC producers, which was felt to offer more resources and security for their activities. Nevertheless, Electric-Co promised substantial financial support and stability for both the development and manufacturing activities of the British firm.

Sector Dynamics of the ICT industry in Japan

Fransman's (1990, 1995, 1999) analysis of the strengths and weaknesses of the Japanese computer sector is built around a fairly conventional periodization of three key phases in the global development of the sector. The first, the mainframe era, covered developments up to the end of the 1980s, when IBM remained the hegemonic firm. The second, the PC phase, covered the end of the 1980s and the first half of the 1990s, when Microsoft and Intel become dominant players. Third, the period since 1995 is characterized as the Internet era, during which a wider range of mainly American specialist firms have vied for position.

Several consortia of Japanese electronics firms with interests in computers and telecommunications were initially encouraged by the state to develop their mainframe capabilities to compete with IBM, and they were relatively successful in so doing. 'By the early 1990s, four of the world's ten largest computer companies were Japanese' (Fransman 1995: 127), a position they had gained from relative weakness in their original forms in the early post-war period, though this success remained heavily dependent on their dominance in the Japanese home market. However, these companies, and indeed the whole Japanese sector were slow in realizing the importance of the reorientation to PCs and networks. Their greatest success was to 'catch up with IBM', an achievement celebrated in Fransman (1990). However, as Fransman (1995, note the *mea culpa* on 131–2, footnote 6) emphasizes, their pursuit of the IBM mainframe vision left them poorly placed to participate in the reorientation of the sector around networked PCs, which was led by the newer American companies.

Thus the Japanese computer and related industries developed particular strengths in some areas of technological capability but they also manifested distinctive weaknesses. In hardware the Japanese firms became strong in the production of microcontrollers and memories—relatively standardized products, which became thoroughly commoditized—but weak in the global microprocessor market, where the branded products of particular innovator firms such as Intel continued to dominate the market. In software, Japanese firms gained only a small share of the burgeoning packaged software market, as they largely remained committed to the production of bespoke software, which was a declining sector of the world market though it remained a major share of the Japanese market.

Fransman (1995) traces the multiple roots of this configuration of competencies, in the preoccupation with rivalling IBM, in close links with the telecommunications sector, and in the distinctive character of the Japanese domestic market. However, the global competitive context for these developments was largely constituted by the dominant American firms. Thus the changing terrain of competition among international ITC firms meant that Japanese companies faced sharpening competition in the early 1990s. First, they had been outflanked in the global market place by the PC revolution, so they were left heavily reliant on their domestic market. Second, this protected market was also becoming vulnerable by the early 1990s, as new software innovations made it increasingly viable to use the cheaper and more powerful IBM-compatible American computers.

Strengths and Weaknesses of Electric-Co

Where did Electric-Co figure in this pattern of competencies, competitive strengths and weaknesses? It is a massive manufacturing company with diverse engineering interests. It has enjoyed a particular dominance in capital goods, but it has also had a long-standing involvement in heavy electrical equipment and consumer electricals. From the 1970s this has involved a presence in mainframe computers but only as a minor player. Thus it was not among the big four Japanese computer companies of the early 1990s (Fujitsu, NEC, Toshiba, and Hitachi). Indeed, Fransman (1995: 126) suggests that Electric-Co had 'exited' from the mainframe market in the 1970s, along with several other firms, though this actually meant retaining a limited role in supplying machines to Electric-Co group firms so that the company still retained 'substantial capabilities in the computing area' (Fransman 1990: 213).

A senior British manager at Computer-Co later construed this history in the following terms:

> Electric-Co was a heavy industry company. In the 1960s, their heavy industry customers said, 'we need some computers to control us', so of course they said 'we do everything else, we might as well make computers'. So they started making computers for heavy industry customers.... These had to be designed to be rugged systems, so the computer business has come from a rugged engineering background with huge amounts of engineering into it. So that's their history, so when they design a mini-computer, it's a robust mini-computer, not an office mini-computer... it takes decades, fives to tens of years for them to change their way of thinking. So they go a little bit over the top by selling the engineering side.

As Fransman (1999) emphasizes, the growth of the PC market during the early 1990s left the mainframe-oriented Japanese companies, always highly dependent on their home market, increasingly vulnerable. Like all these companies, Electric-Co had found it difficult to establish a successful presence in PC manufacture in Japan. Even NEC, despite its early dominance of the slowly growing domestic Japanese PC market, was eventually forced to accommodate to the international standards set by the dominant American players, and they responded by purchasing the American company Packard Bell, though this failed to revitalize their role in the sector.

Electric-Co's venture into the PC market was never as successful as NEC, and its relatively small mainframe business remained of greater significance. It was, thus, vulnerable both to the further erosion of the mainframes market and to the increasingly harsh competition characteristic of the growing PC market. As one of the senior Computer-Co management team remarked:

> Certainly at the time when they started to look at us they were very interested in our R&D because they were quite open about the fact it was more efficient then theirs. It was taking them eighteen months to get a product to market, and when they did, it was already past it. It was taking us probably twelve months and we were just hitting the crest of the wave. So they saw that as important. They saw that our products were innovative and that there were a

lot of people... that had got a lot of value and a lot of reputation within the industry that would add a lot of value to them.

This was the context in which Electric-Co purchased Computer-Co. It was an attempt, on a smaller scale than NEC's purchase of Packard Bell, to enhance its capabilities and reduce its vulnerability in what appeared to be a pivotal growth sector.

Computer-Co within Electric-Co: Investment, Relative Autonomy, and Restructuring

After Electric-Co acquired Computer-Co, the Japanese firm funded significant investment and expansion in the British company. This was initially most obvious in the factory but also occurred later in R&D, despite continuing losses and one of the sharp cyclical downturns characteristic of the industry. The biggest investment was to build a surface-mount (SMT) PCB unit at the factory, which not only signalled the commitment of Electric-Co to the manufacturing facility but allowed Computer-Co to draw most of this production in-house, instead of continuing to rely upon what management regarded as 'unreliable' Singapore-based subcontract suppliers. The development of their own SMT facility was preferred on both cost and QC grounds, though Computer-Co continued to be heavily reliant upon other component manufacturers.

During this period of restructuring, the British MD was quite successful in championing the repositioning of Computer-Co as the core of Electric-Co's global PC operations, but also retained considerable operational autonomy. These developments were signalled by his appointment as the only foreign Company President of an Electric-Co business division, with management responsibility for certain operations in Japan, Germany, and elsewhere outside the United Kingdom. The company continued to incur losses, but these were on a 'planned basis linked to substantial investment'. As a senior manager stated in 1996 'we'll lose quite substantial sums of money again because of our big investment and rapid growth in the Japanese market... we budget to make a loss, we budget to invest'. Thus, through the 1990s, Computer-Co occupied a very unusual position as a Japanese-owned firm, not simply because it was a takeover rather than greenfield operation but more because of the distinctive sectoral capabilities which this involved. We will now consider what this meant in terms of the organization and reorganization of R&D and the factory respectively.

RESTRUCTURING R&D

The relative autonomy of Computer-Co R&D

Electric-Co's lack of success in its own venture into PC design and manufacture, together with the continuing pressures on even its mainframe business, provided a basis for Computer-Co's management to enjoy considerable autonomy and initiative. It meant that Electric-Co HQ recognized Computer-Co was operating in a different sector and commercial environment to that of the parent firm, with differently tailored expertise, particularly in regard to PC design and development. Thus, British managers emphasized that Electric-Co had largely left Computer-Co management to run the division in the way they regarded as appropriate, and this was particularly the case in relation to R&D.

Certainly British managers believed that Computer-Co's very distinctiveness as a design centre, and indeed its attractiveness to Electric-Co, lay in its capacity for rapid and necessarily risky design and development decisions. These allowed effective competition in the PC market, and this was very different from the balance of quality and risk involved in building mainframes for the heavy engineering customers of the Electric-Co group. A Japanese informant, with experience in Electric-Co's own PC venture, powerfully endorsed this assessment:

> Electric-Co is a big enterprise, too big. What this industry is, is very quick moving, from the point of view of competitiveness and pricing. . . .Like Computer-Co, we need to move quickly—quickly means three months . . . Electric-Co wanted to have such kind of capability. Of course, they had a lot of engineers, fundamentally, technically, they are strong, strong, but the decision making process in Japan is very hierarch[ical], even if an engineer had a good idea. . . . Electric-Co enterprise is not so quick moving, Computer-Co, phew [very quick].

These differences highlight the ways in which Electric-Co had to learn from Computer-Co to match the dynamics of the PC sector: 'this industry is moving so quickly, and moving so quickly means we have to introduce or we have to buy something from vendor, software, hardware, we have to . . . try with not matured things at that time, and we have to assume . . . if I didn't do it Compaq will do.'

Thus the distinctiveness of the role assigned to Computer-Co underpinned the considerable autonomy given to the British subsidiary compared with the branch plants of many Japanese multinationals. This meant that, while a small number of highly experienced Japanese engineers were seconded to Computer-Co, Japanese managers played a relatively limited role, and the relationship was largely mediated through the development, modification, and ratification of business plans. As a British engineer explained:

> Electric-Co acquired us and allows us to run semi-autonomously as a business, so we forecast our sales; we forecast our profits and loss. We forecast our own investments and have to justify our own investments and at the end of the year answer for our performance against what we said we would do.

The idiosyncratic approaches of Computer-Co and Electric-Co engineers

When design and development engineers from Electric-Co Japan and Computer-Co did work together, this highlighted major differences in their experience and priorities which were grounded in distinctive patterns of professional formation and different configurations of design, manufacturing, and marketing (Lam 1995, 1996*a*, 1996*b*). On the relatively rare occasions when they were involved in joint projects these differences became quite evident, as a British informant emphasized:

> The people here aren't inclined to sit down and write specs, they want to get on and do things. There's been a management laxity there which, OK, we've lived with it and that's the way it is. But the Japanese have this traditional, long winded, quality approach to things and the PC market just won't hold that. You can't have three month schedules for a disc drive, you've got to do it in a month.... They are a very well-established long-term company that have real, very clear views on what they think the customer wants and the market wants, and there is quite a lot of inertia in that system. The QC department in Electric-Co is very much the ruler of the roost in relation to changes of specs and what you can get away with, what you can't get away with, whatever, and it's just massive inertia to change that culture, that perception. I think that the stuff that they do, though, on the other hand is very good, it benefits the customer ultimately because the products are much more stable, much more mature; but you lose one, two months on the window, other people are in there, products just aren't as competitive when they are released as they ought to be.

Indeed numerous informants contrasted the systematic but cautious approach of the Japanese engineers, with their heavy emphasis on engineering foolproof systems, and the adventurous but unsystematic approach of the British engineers, who emphasized speedy incorporation of current innovations.

However, as we show in more detail in Chapter 10, such differences were not merely embedded in broad differences in the social organization of manufacturing in Japanese and British enterprises or the related processes of professional formation and careers of engineers in the two countries. Rather, they were reinforced by more specific contrasts in the enterprise and sector logics of Electric-Co and Computer-Co. While the former was a massive engineering conglomerate used to heavy engineering contracts with large corporate and state customers, the latter was a small 'entrepreneurial' company producing for a volatile and rapidly changing market.

Such differences were highlighted when, as a result of the squeeze on their Japanese computer business, Japanese engineers with mainframe experience were offered for involvement in joint projects with Computer-Co. The context here was precisely the vulnerable position of Electric-Co in the computer sector, including the mainframe market:

> Electric-Co are downsizing as well, and they have lots and lots of departments where they are looking for work for those groups, whether it is disc drive evaluation or hardware design, whatever. And so they keep coming to us and saying 'look, Computer-Co, you are short of resource, we've got the resource, let us do some for you.'

This meant that the Electric-Co mainframe group secured an important role as Japanese partners in one of the few joint design projects which were undertaken at Computer-Co, and they brought the specific preoccupations of mainframe engineering with them. However, Computer-Co managers clearly recognized the specificity of the clash of skills and priorities during the resulting efforts at collaboration. As the same informant commented 'it [joint project work] would potentially be a lot different if we dealt with the PC sections rather than the mainframe sections'. Indeed, a crucial feature of the practical implementation of this joint project, as well as broader liaison between Computer-Co and its parent, was the central mediating role of a leading Japanese engineering manager whose background *was* in Electric-Co's Japanese PC business.

Matrix management and the pursuit of system integration in R&D

Such collaboration in R&D projects between Computer-Co and Electric-Co engineers was rather rare, and Computer-Co's R&D activities remained very much an arena of British management and technical skills. Nevertheless, the semi-autonomy that Electric-Co granted to Computer-Co, and its orientation to learning from Computer-Co, did not simply translate into continuity in the organization of R&D at the British plant. In the mid-1990s, R&D moved to a new site, much closer to corporate HQ and this move was accompanied by the recruitment of additional staff. Even before the move there had been a series of changes in the configuration of the specialist groupings—software engineers, hardware engineers, mechanical engineers, test engineers—in relation to specific design and development projects, and these were carried further on the new site. This reconfiguration involved different variants on 'matrix management' and culminated in a deliberately more project-focused form of organization which made project managers more pivotal. This reflected increasing senior management attention to the integration of design, development, and manufacturing, with the objective of subordinating these processes more strongly to the cost, delivery, and performance features which were required by the rapidly evolving PC market.

The increasing emphasis on the role of project manager was designed to alter the relationship between work on discrete design elements of specific products and their integration and testing, and reduce the extent to which design limitations were only picked up at the end of the verification process or even after customer complaints. In the earlier structure, functional groupings were dominant and the existing project managers had a rather limited role:

> The nature of R&D in Computer-Co, it has been very much functional in the sense that you had each of these functional groups... that all worked independently of the product. You had a project management thread which has been pretty weak.... If you've talked to the project managers they may have commented that they were impotent to a greater or lesser extent, because they had no real direct reports, they had no power to influence the way that product was developed or projects were moved, and they really just served this primary policing role, to blow the whistle to senior managers, who would then go and assert their wills on the staff. So it was a fairly circular, tortuous route for getting decisions made. Quite effective for all of that, I mean we have delivered lots and lots of products, but the successes we've had have been pretty much technology-focused successes, where integration has been pretty minimal.

As this implies, the established tradition at Computer-Co, at the time of the takeover and beyond, gave particular weight to technical innovations developed by specialist engineers.

The reorganization challenged this pattern by pushing system architecture and integration responsibilities back up the project design timetable, rather than leaving these issues to be picked up through testing procedures in a way which created a bottleneck (and scapegoats for delays) at the end of the design process. Thus an R&D manager described his enhanced role in the following terms:

> It just gives each project group a little bit more control over their own destiny.... Now the persuasive skills available to me are a little bit more managerial as we both work for the same guy; me saying to him 'I think we need to do this and you need to do that', there is a little bit more weight behind it. So it does change subtly the style of management, but really that is the only change.

Top management's rationale for these organizational changes at R&D was that, while the lead time between new designs and delivery to customers continued to fall dramatically, the cost and serviceability of the product, rather than its sheer technical innovativeness, were becoming increasingly important. This was conceptualized in terms of both a maturation of the market and the growing importance of individual/domestic rather than business customers.

Electric-Co's indirect influence on the restructuring of R&D

Given the distinctive role of Computer-Co within Electric-Co, how far was the parent company a direct influence on these developments? A widely shared view among British managers was that Electric-Co's concern with quality was an influence, but could not be directly transposed into Computer-Co because of the very different markets within which they operated. Thus a senior Computer-Co manager involved in quality said:

> I think within Computer-Co, as a British company, we are not natural quality thinkers. It's not the first thing we think about; and here's a contrast between ourselves, and our Japanese parent. It is quite plausible for Electric-Co... to have a strong quality group and that's all they do, that influential role. And they can do that and get away with that because everybody within that organization has a natural aptitude towards quality... very often they'll push for a project or an improvement when there is very little financial justification for doing that.... Despite the fact that they will never recoup that investment in terms of improved sales or customer awareness. We think our view is pragmatic in the sense that if we can see a good return on the investment we'll make it... that is one of the differences, and I would say it's a continuing difference of opinion between ourselves and our Japanese parent. Not one that we are going to fall out on and stop doing business on, but one that we are going to continue to question each other's motives and operations.

Such assessments were explicitly grounded in arguments about the specific character of the PC market and the mix of risky innovation and robustness appropriate to that market, and in this regard there was a continuing debate within Computer-Co.

As the above comments imply, however, few of the participants in this debate saw much scope for direct borrowing from Electric-Co because their approach, grounded in the production of specialist goods and mainframes, was seen as too constraining and cumbersome. Nevertheless it was recognized that, while Electric-Co had not intervened very directly, they had come to exercise a more diffuse influence, what one informant termed a 'soft push'. He summarized this situation in the following terms:

> There is an awful lot of influence from Japan for more formalizing and testing processes. More formalizing of design processes. But at the same time the whole organization is learning the lessons themselves and there is no formal communications, no formal edicts that come from any space that could remotely be considered to be Japan or Electric-Co... [It is] the soft push of 'have you done this?' Makes you think that next time you do a project, better do that, because I know what the question is going to be. But at the same time, we don't *have* to do it because we can turn round and say 'we haven't done it; we are not going to do it.'... There is no forcefulness... They are a customer, and we will negotiate with them... and that is basically what it comes down to. It's that commercial pressure that we have basically.

What this brings out is the indirect influence which Electric-Co wielded through its role as the major customer for PCs (shipped to Japan), but also the extent to which this influence converged with the priorities espoused by senior British management, rather than cross-cutting their objectives.

The significance of resource constraints at R&D

While the reorganization of R&D to strengthen the role of project teams began in the early 1990s, limited resources constrained the extent of this reorganization at least until the mid-1990s. It was widely agreed that in sector terms the design and development staff at Computer-Co were under-resourced for the work they did, and the product designs they delivered. However, while many of the technical employees highlighted such staffing constraints during this period, senior managers had an ambivalent attitude to these constraints. They acknowledged their existence, but they also emphasized that R&D had nonetheless proven capable of delivering the product in such pressured circumstances. Thus a senior manager reflected that:

> They would probably say that they are world class designers in their segment, and they definitely are, and if you could measure output in designs per person, number of lines of code per person or whatever, I think you would find in the sector they are world leaders. We do get more out of R&D than we have a right to expect. Having said that, that's the way R&D has always been managed. It's always been expected to do more than is reasonable, and always delivers more than is reasonable to expect. That, if you like, contributes to this sort of tech room mentality that 'the world is on our back and they're trying to squeeze a quart out of a pint pot', but having said that they always have and always achieved it.

The pressures on staff were also registered by an experienced Japanese manager, who discussed the implications of different staffing levels in Japan and at Computer-Co for the levels of documentation accompanying design and development work:

> Five engineers here for instance and ten projects, [they are] just always busy, so I can't ask them for redundant, reluctant documentation. But in Japan, 100 engineers... [there are] more 'redundant' people always, that means insurance, that means always overlap. That is not just difference between the Japanese way and the western way. Just Computer-Co scale company, not so small, but medium, [contrast with] not Electric-Co [as such], just a big company. That's the difference between them that we need to understand.

Furthermore, he saw this difference of staffing as closely related to the much tighter control over staffing levels arising from Computer-Co's attempts to survive in a quite narrow and turbulent market sector. By comparison Electric-Co's operations across a wide range of markets meant that the effects of upturns and downturns were often offset across the firm as a whole.

Thus one preoccupation of Computer-Co management was to manage resources in the context of the overall small size of the R&D operation, measured against the range of tasks and products it was involved with. This tight staffing was seen to underpin recurrent tensions over task allocation, as people were switched between competing priority projects:

> Because of the resource aspect of it . . . the company never wants to have too much resource and we often, in my opinion, perhaps run a little bit too lean; it's a constant resource balancing issue of what is the important problem each day, this week, this month; but also the risk analysis of 'We have a date to hit, do we *really* need to do this? Which are the important items?' And those really are the difficult aspects of the job.

As a senior R&D manager commented:

> There are some good reasons for doing this and some bad reasons. The bad reasons are we have a group of ninety-five people which in the scheme of things is pathetic compared with what other companies are doing. However, it is pretty much as we have always been.

Such managers sometimes made a virtue of this situation, by arguing that continuing organizational change and pressure kept people 'on their toes'. Nevertheless, by 1996 they felt able to make an explicit case for more funding from Electric-Co to augment the design team.

This led to a modest increase in staffing and provided the basis for further efforts to integrate the project teams in R&D by again recasting relations between functional specialists and project managers:

> I feel that you need to keep the barriers down all the way through the product development cycle. . . . One of the things I've seen is that the project manager needs to be put in that position where all he is doing is managing and leading, rather than actually getting down and doing the technological side of things. . . . So that we can afford for the functional specialists to actually remain functional specialists, and we will just keep them on track with the [managers]. Now, its not going to be perfect, ideally you know, I believe we would have an organization of functional specialists who were [product] oriented but we are not going to have that in the short term.

As this final comment emphasizes, the continuing reorganization which accompanied the expansion and relocation of R&D did not serve as a panacea to overcome persistent tensions in the design, development, and manufacturing process. Rather, senior management continued to juggle resources and organizational arrangements in pursuit of a set of objectives—of innovativeness, rapid productionizing, and cost control—which themselves remained somewhat contradictory.

One further aspect of the constraints within which Computer-Co R&D operated was their location in relation to the market for qualified technical labour. First, there were few comparable establishments in Britain, let alone the West Midlands (most comparable operations were in the United States). This meant that Computer-Co rarely recruited established engineering specialists directly from comparable firms, but rather drew employees from a wider spectrum of software, electrical, and mechanical engineering backgrounds, most particularly from older military-oriented engineering companies and small software houses. Second, as a small and unprofitable company they offered only average salaries compared with firms competing for similar labour. Third, against this background their location in the West Midlands conurbation meant that it was often difficult to attract people from the south and especially from the M4 corridor. One senior R&D manager remarked that:

> The Midlands is a difficult place to recruit computer, high tech oriented people in the PC manufacturing business. So it's a little difficult actually getting the calibre of people in from the companies we would really like to recruit from.... I mean nobody would, one, move to Birmingham, two, the salaries we could offer probably aren't attractive enough for them... I say that just purely from the fact that I came from a company where we were paying a hardware designer £44k, and here we pay our designers practically about two-thirds if that.

They certainly could not recruit from their international competitors, but instead lost experienced people to such companies, including to the United States: '[it's] a bit of a problem that we had, because we've actually got quite a lot of good people here and they obviously get great exposure to these companies.... So we actually do get poached at'.

The key implication of all these features was that the R&D operation was primarily reliant upon capturing people from a variety of engineering backgrounds and developing their specialist expertise in-house, while seeking to retain them through the interest and technical challenges of the work rather than through highly competitive salaries. Indeed, in this context there were some suggestions that the reorganization of R&D had been less radical than it might have been, as there had been a tempering of plans to fit sensitivities and established ways of doing things, to facilitate the retention of experienced and valued staff.

RESTRUCTURING AT THE FACTORY

The relationship between British and Japanese engineers and managers was rather different at the factory than in R&D. This can once again be placed in the context of the logic of the takeover for both Electric-Co and Computer-Co. Electric-Co was particularly dependent upon tapping the design and development expertise of the Computer-Co R&D team, and the manufacture of PCs was also influenced by the distinctive character of the design and marketing of computers. However, Electric-Co management saw the factory as closer to some of its own existing operations. Thus they believed that their production engineering skills as well as their financial investment could contribute to the refurbishment of the Scottish production facility, though they recognized that there was no simple analogue to be transferred from Japan. The influence of Japanese managers and engineers was therefore rather more evident and extensive in Scotland than in the Midlands, but it was still mediated through the distinctive features of Computer-Co's PC operation.

A key figure in this respect was an experienced Japanese engineering manager who had worked on small business computers in Electric-Co in Japan, and on that basis had been involved as an engineering specialist in the parent company's assessment of Computer-Co before the takeover. After the purchase he was then despatched to become a senior Japanese manager at the factory, where he played a central role in engineering process innovations. He saw his specific remit as to draw upon the parent company's manufacturing expertise:

> Mainly my job was so we could get the infrastructure. It was difficult, [Computer-Co was] a very young company. From the manufacturing point of view not so strong compared with Electric-Co. At that time Electric-Co [had] already decided to import the Computer-Co product to the Japanese market and sell their product through Electric-Co channels. That means that the product should [must] be very reliable. That means Computer-Co needs to create good manufacturing process.

This meant overcoming substantial differences between the approaches of the two companies. However, as will be shown later, the implications of these features varied in different areas of the factory.

Direct transfer and its limits: the SMT story

So far as the SMT line was concerned, the initial investment decision was designed to address quality problems arising from distant production in Singapore, and was strongly led by Electric-Co. In the words of a British manager:

> When you've got something like a week between when the board is manufactured and the fastest you can get it into the UK, your cost and flexibility start to suffer. So you end up with lots of work in progress... lots of rework... lots of commuting backwards and forwards, all of which got very expensive and quite difficult to manage.... The first thing they [Electric-Co] said was 'right we are a manufacturing company, we are going to have circuit board manufacturing next to where you assemble the computers. It's all under control.' They'd got a great deal of experience and expertise in this area, and said 'OK we can support Computer-Co to reduce its costs and

> previous flexibility problems by making this investment', so... the planning started in [the year of the take-over].

The introduction of an automated SMT line at the factory, together with its associated manual insertion and testing operations, was intended to make the Scottish plant self-sufficient in PCB/motherboard manufacture. Since the parent company already had experience of operating such facilities in Japan this was seen as involving a more or less direct transfer of a full manufacturing process from Japan to the United Kingdom, with only minor modifications which related to such matters as shift working arrangements.

Senior British managers emphasized that, once the team of Japanese managers got the line up and running, it was then taken over by local management. Meanwhile, the experienced female workforce on that section saw the initial input of the Japanese engineers as important, both as trainers in soldering techniques and in implementing new procedures for testing and rectification which had improved quality. However, they also emphasized that the older production pressures remained paramount. This underpinned their scepticism about the way work was organized in SMT and elsewhere in the factory, because of the constant pressure and also sudden switches in production to meet priorities. One consequence of this was that moves between jobs were experienced as being shuffled around to meet production crises, rather than as any form of rounded training:

> That's what's wrong with this place I would say lack of training... I don't know how many jobs I've done through there. I could be two or three weeks on one job and then I am pushed on to another job, and I'm on that for a few weeks and then I'm off that. 'Flexible [Name]' that's what it is.... It's like working on the line here, this company, quantity not quality, and I always said that from the day I came in—it's quantity.

Thus the SMT facility, which had been funded by the parent and involved processes which were common to many of their other factories, saw a heavy involvement of Japanese engineers in installing the production process, training the operators and later troubleshooting various production problems. However, local management emphasized that the continuing management of the work process was now in their hands, while employees suggested that neither Japanese nor British managers had moved far to enhance worker expertise or product quality in this area.

Hybrid innovation in production methods: the new line

While the SMT facility represented an addition to existing manufacturing capabilities, the other major area of process engineering innovation involved a radical reorganization of the bulk of the existing operation. This sidelined the established range of separate and dedicated flow lines, each involving a classic sequence of highly fragmented assembly tasks, and replaced them with one interlinked assembly process, organized in a sequence from kanban (kit-assembly), through 'common build', then 'cell build', and finally tests.

The senior Japanese engineer played the dominant role in the development of this new production line, aided by some briefer visits by other Japanese engineers. Thus, in explaining the distinctive production rationale of the new line, a British production engineer emphasized that:

> That idea for that method of manufacture came from the senior Japanese manager... The process that we do now I would say has been his baby.... We try to go for as much common elements as possible, like common elements within the system, and then 'what do we need to do to configure it for the customer'—which is usually software, drive size, and motherboard type, so that is how this thing has been set up.... What we tended to be good at in the past [was] doing things in batches. Again, [the senior Japanese engineering manager] was very interested in being able to do it on a one-off basis. Because [if] we [can] do it as a one-off thing, we [can] do batch products as well.... We've also got material planning for a system which looks at a 10-day rolling forecast and looks at shortages of material. The idea is that this common assembly is good as a repeatable thing, the quality level should be repeatable.

At the same time, managers at Computer-Co, including the lead Japanese engineer, also stressed that the new line had not involved a direct transfer of established manufacturing engineering solutions from Japan. Instead it was 'our own concept', original to the Computer-Co factory. It drew on ideas gleaned from other Electric-Co factories but, more importantly, from visits to some of the computer companies which were in direct competition with Computer-Co in Europe. While access to the latter had not been easy, 'in this country many engineers move to other companies so our people have some relationships', and contacts had also been made through equipment vendors (compare Smith et al. 1990).

Indeed, top management at Computer-Co emphasized the importance of these domestic and sectoral influences, rather than the specific expertise of Japanese advisers, despite the secrecy engendered by competitive rivalries:

> We go off and visit... where there is competitive plants.... Go and have a look at the American plant, as to what is the most successful manufacturing recipe for the PC industry and we've actually got those companies coming back to us now. We've had Compaq trying to get in to see our facility, because we think we have now probably got the most flexible semi-automated facility going today.... Openness is what the PC industry is about. What does that mean? It means relationships with as many people as is required to get the job done. Don't believe you know anything any better than anybody else. Copy

> wherever you can. Utilize and plagiarize is really the only thing we should be about in the PC Industry.

Given the differences between the products and markets of Computer-Co and those of most of the Japanese parent's factories, it was perhaps unsurprising that the senior Japanese engineer had spent over two years investigating the requirements of PC production, trying out ideas on a small product line and planning and developing the new line itself.

In the end this resulted in a *hybrid production line*, which sought to embody three key features. First, different labour requirements and work tasks were deployed along a single line in contrasting 'common-build' and 'cell-build' sections. The short-cycle routinized tasks were on the early 'common build' part of the line. The longer cycle (initially 12 minutes), more varied, partial build-through, and testing routines were in the later 'cell build' area, where individual operators had the responsibility to complete the assembly by adding the customized elements to each machine to order. Second, the persistent line-balancing problems of building small batches on conventional assembly lines were avoided by taking the more complex build-throughs temporarily offline. However, the maximization of through-put with such varied production still relied heavily on tight work scheduling and effective QC on the single line. Finally, a version of a 'kanban' supply system was implemented, based on holding one day's stock of most components. However, the variety of models and the power of dominant suppliers to ration vital high-value parts made a classical internal kanban system, designed for mass production, inappropriate.

This innovation had major consequences both for the relationship with R&D and for the character of employment relations in the factory. First, the universal line placed a premium on 'design for manufacturing' (DFM) so as to maximize the scope for 'common-build'. This increased the leverage of the manufacturing engineers in pushing DFM up the design process, with the backing of Computer-Co's top management ('The factory has to be more and more powerful, say "I am sorry, we are not going to build that product if you design it like that" '). Second, factory managers interpreted the contrasting labour requirements along the new line as an opportunity to differentiate the workforce more systematically into permanent and temporary workers:

> The cell-build operators, because of the function they are doing now, have got more product knowledge.... There is a common assembly area, I suppose you can see what they've done by bringing in lots of temps, it's the temps that's gone into those areas.... So with minimal training they go in and do whatever part of the job... I dare say, if the production drops, what we can do is move people back, [move] full-time operators back into the common assembly but you've still got those skills.

In practice the allocation of workers to positions on the new line appeared more haphazard than this, but we will return to the implications of this differentiation for employment relations shortly.

This move, to single-line cell-build from the older dedicated flow lines, was intended as a basis for a substantial growth of output which would also have to accommodate an extended model mix. It represented a major reorganization of the main production area and involved substantial Japanese engineering input, but in a form that was also heavily influenced by sector recipes, rather than mirroring established practice in Japan. In particular, the way in which the combined team of British and Japanese production engineers addressed this distinctive set of production requirements was strongly informed by a range of visits to other electronics factories within 'Silicon Glen'.

Testing in quality *and* building in quality

Japanese concerns about product quality also had an influence on the way the production process was operated. However, this was mainly through the role of Electric-Co as a customer, rather than directly through the presence of Japanese staff at the factory. This was because Electric-Co imposed stringent standards for the large volume of machines being produced for the Japanese market, which led to continuing negotiation over the balance of cost, durability, and innovation appropriate for the PC market worldwide. Quality standards continued to be met primarily by rigorous and repetitive testing procedures (and rectification) rather than a sophisticated enforcement of 'building in quality'. Interestingly, the senior Japanese engineering manager on site was rather more relaxed about this than the British quality manager, who bemoaned the inadequate commitment of production management to quality procedures.

A common thread in our management informants' accounts, not only at the factory but also at R&D and HQ, was that Computer-Co had devoted significant attention to improving product quality in recent years, compared with the fairly cavalier attitude which prevailed in the early years of PC production. A key informant on such issues, a senior quality manager, certainly found the general orientation towards QC at Computer-Co more congenial than some of his earlier experience as a quality engineer in other manufacturing firms:

> [Elsewhere] there was very little regard for people in that category. I was always fighting production. Production had their agenda; quality had their agenda. Completely different agendas and I thought, 'I can't work this way'. Coming in here that is not the case. I have no one to fight. Production people here, we both have the same agenda. We both have regard for quality and production targets, as it should be.

However, he also suggested that the scope for systematic quality activities at Computer-Co remained limited by staffing constraints, especially when compared with Electric-Co's Japanese plants ('We are lucky if we have one engineer to cover a problem, they could have ten. We haven't the luxury of this.... You need to rely on experience, gut reaction a lot of the time'). When he talked about his current responsibilities it was also evident that building quality into the process through documented procedures remained an uphill task. This was partly because of the pressures of production volumes, partly because of the added complications of implementing the new production system and partly because of the stringent quality standards imposed by their main customer, Electric-Co's marketing arm in Japan.

The first feature emerged in a discussion of the role of QCCs:

> When I first came here the QCCs were very successful... but getting the time from management was difficult. They saw it as taking production operators away in what was prime build-time... I had a fair bit of battle there... [But] they agreed eventually and each line sent along a leader and some members for their meeting and they would come along with their problems.... We had a lot of success fixing some serious problems on the production line.... But for various reasons that fell apart. And then about a year ago, tried again and.... that worked for a while, and then it sort of fizzled out.... In the case of QCC it needs a regular injection of something, some kind of incentive programme, and it's not always money they are looking for... and I think senior management should have been more involved.... What's missing is this regular injection of something. Still working on that one.

Thus QCCs had fallen into abeyance in the mid-1990s, in the face of the usual round of production pressures and crises.

Meanwhile, managers were involved in debate and experimentation concerning the relationship between self-inspection, sampling, and comprehensive post-production inspection. The implementation of the single production line, coupled with complaints about quality from the Japanese sales organization, had stimulated an alliance between senior Japanese engineering staff and British quality managers in pushing for an extensive resort to separate intermediate and end-of-line inspection. In 1996 this remained the interim response of factory management to the main source of pressure for improvements in quality, namely the Japanese parent in its guise as customer. However, the dominant view at the factory was that this reliance on final inspection and rectification to achieve quality would be a transitional phase. The hope was that, once the initial phase of productionizing the new line had been completed, and as the target levels of output, three or four times the volume accommodated on the old flow lines, were pursued, it would be developed on the basis of on-line QA. But for the time being, end-of-line testing and rectification remained the dominant feature.

Top management at HQ shared this perspective though with an important qualification. It was certainly claimed that:

> Those [tests for Electric-Co sales] are slowly decaying away. As our product gets better they are going away. We are building it onto the line. ... These people as the customer are pretty ruthless when it comes to any failure, so Electric-Co can't afford to have a product that fails at any sort of frequency, therefore they put the pressure back on us to deliver a product that totally works and is 100 per cent reliable.

However, it was also argued that even for this market (which was expected to take between 40 and 50 per cent of Computer-Co's production) reconciling quality standards remained a two-way process because:

> The Japanese market is beginning to realize that PC quality may not be allowed to come up, be as high, as they would have liked because its cost then goes up. They can't have both. Quality is not for free. ... We've put lots of pressure back [on Japan] in our discussions.

This captures the persistent interplay between Japanese—and specifically Electric-Co—models of robustness and quality engineering, and sector-led preoccupations with the competitive features of the PC market and their implications for design and production, which structured much of the discussion among British and Japanese engineers and managers at Computer-Co.

This informant also summarized a widespread senior management gloss on this debate. For him it was part of a process of maturation out of a highly autocratic, seat-of-pants style of management, characteristic of a small high-tech company, as it grew and became part of a bigger organization in a somewhat less turbulent technical environment. From this perspective, Electric-Co's influence ran parallel with wider trends within British manufacturing management, in a context of more diffuse flows of influence, both from innovating European and American firms, and through the professional dissemination of versions of Japanese manufacturing techniques and practices. What remained particularly obscure from this vantage point, however, were the conditions under which shop-floor employees, both temporary and permanent, were to be incorporated into this management trajectory.

Employment relations on the shop-floor: the costs of flexibility

Computer-Co, as an established but financially vulnerable British company, had been bought because of its distinctive technological capability, but its personnel policies also remained home grown and were again strongly coloured by sectoral practices and current fashions. The need to manage local and specialist labour market conditions apparently reinforced this pattern. One notable feature, congruent with the pattern in other new electronics firms in so-called 'Silicon Glen' (Findlay 1993), was that the management had successfully avoided unionization in the factory as well as at the R&D centre.

The original pattern of management at the British company was that of autocratic rule by the founder entrepreneur, coupled with the uncodified delegation of personnel responsibilities to line managers. This was the pattern that had been inherited by the incumbent British MD. However, while he retained considerable personal control of corporate policies, he had established a personnel department even before the takeover, and had begun to limit the discretion of line managers over personnel matters, not least because of problems that had arisen under the old policy. Such a movement towards the codification of policy was reinforced by the concern of the new parent to be informed of procedures, but the substance of policy remained entirely under the control of British management.

Thus, notwithstanding the increased formalization of personnel policy, Computer-Co continued to conform to sector recipes in having a lightly staffed personnel office, which remained clearly subordinated to the servicing of line management. Meanwhile, the influence of sector fashions and contemporary British management debates could be seen variously in the enthusiastic use of agency temporary workers at the factory; the development of a customized MBA programme for management development; a somewhat superficial revamping of supervision in the guise of team leaders; the formalization of health and safety and equal opportunities policies; and the limited activities of the exquisitely named 'One Goal Committee' (and also the idea that this might be tweaked into a shape which could pass muster as part of a European Works Council). Electric-Co appears to have had minimal involvement in any of these policies, but conversely Computer-Co management believed that they had some indirect influence on aspects of personnel policy within other Electric-Co factories in Europe.

Here we only have space to comment particularly upon the substantial use of temporary contract workers, who came to constitute about half the manufacturing workers at Computer-Co during its reorganization and expansion in the mid-1990s. The firm had employed temporary workers for some time, primarily to cope with seasonal peaks in production, but only moved to the use of 'agency temps' in 1994 on the additional ground that this was a cheaper way of employing temporary labour. First, Computer-Co sought to avoid the costs associated with the administration of recruitment, selection, training, and wage payment, as the Agency had taken on all these functions. Second, they had also bid down the price they were willing to pay to the agency, a feature reflected not only in the lower pay of these workers but also in the cavalier way in which they were treated. Management justified the expanded use of temporary labour in terms of the significance of seasonal fluctuations in production more than the design of the new line, and used the terminology of core and peripheral workers to rationalize the terms of their deployment. The 'training' of these workers was usually fairly rudimentary, confined largely to testing manual dexterity and ensuring that recruits could get up to speed on basic assembly operations, and many temps performed the most fragmented assembly tasks.

However, temps were not only used on such tasks, but were scattered unevenly across production and inspection areas. Hence, sharp functional and even spatial divisions between permanent and agency temporary workers (of the sort implied by the management comments quoted earlier) did not operate in any rigorous fashion. In some respects, such extensive use of agency temps also appeared to contradict other aspects of management's rhetoric, which emphasized the wider development of a more skilled and responsible workforce. As we have seen, however, such moves were also constrained by production pressures, as workers' comments, such as these on team meetings, suggest:

> We started off with great intentions. We should get a meeting every morning, and then we got a brief every month, and now I think [we] never see a visit, since last year. . . . That's one thing in this place the communication is terrible, even between shifts. Something will happen on day shift and they'll not think to leave word to the next shift. . . . Every year they get a review and they asked us all these questions and nothing is ever done.

Moreover, in the mid-1990s the policy on the use of agency temps was a substantial source of discontent on the shop-floor, not only among agency workers themselves but also among the established workforce. The latter not only expressed sympathy for the way the temps were treated but also believed that this treatment reflected badly on Computer-Co's own record as an employer ('The agencies, terrible, some of them even haven't got their right wages. They even got [threatening] letters, horrible letters. It really is giving the place a bad name, the way that agencies are treating the people').

In the mid-1990s, then, Computer-Co factory management not only followed a fashionable British personnel management nostrum in pursuing the use of agency temporary labour, but in so doing threatened to destabilize employment relations at the factory. Furthermore, while they later explored such other fashionable 'alternatives' as the use of zero-hour contracts to manage the seasonality of production, the extensive use of temporary workers continued until shortly before the announcement of the rundown and closure of the company.

THE CLOSURE

Senior management were notified of the closure of Computer-Co in February 1999, and it was was announced in March. At one level, this decision was clearly grounded in the failure of Computer-Co to attain profitability throughout the period from the takeover, and the way this reflected the vulnerability of a small producer in an intensely competitive PC market. In this respect, it reflected a failure to escape from the limitations which had faced Computer-Co before the Electric-Co takeover, though the ways in which these limitations manifested themselves had changed with the evolution of the sector and the company.

At another level, the decision was not so much about the performance of Computer-Co as about the broader crisis facing Electric-Co, its parent company. In this respect, a whole set of developments, ranging from a particular crisis of overcapacity in the semiconductor sector, through to the broader stagnation and wider crisis of the East Asian economies, precipitated an unprecedented lurch into large scale losses (financial press, 5/98). It was this that triggered a systematic reappraisal of the performance of all parts of the corporation following a top management succession in June 1998. The pressures and crises at each of these levels, and the manner in which they intersect, form an essential background to the decision to close Computer-Co.

Competencies, vulnerabilities and crises

As we have seen, Fransman's analysis emphasized the distinctive lines of technological and organizational 'competence' development pursued by the various Japanese ICT firms. However, he also recognized sources of vulnerability and crisis which cross-cut such configurations of corporate competence. First, as the argument about the pursuit of the IBM vision implies, new innovations could radically rewrite the bases of corporate competition. In this regard, the relative weakness of the Japanese ICT firms was later reinforced by the emergence of the Internet as the locus of communications innovations, with the associated growth of specialist American Internet and European mobile phone firms. Second, Fransman also recognized that the implications of these technological/sectoral transformations cannot be analysed separately from broader patterns of crisis and restructuring.

In this regard, he highlighted the implications of three overlapping sources of crisis facing the Japanese economy and thus Japanese ICT firms. The first was the bursting of the bubble economy in the early 1990s and its continuing stagnation subsequently. The second was the Asian financial crisis of late 1990s, which cut market demand in Asia. The third was the particularly acute overproduction and price collapse of semiconductors, exacerbated by price-cutting driven by the Asian financial crisis. As he noted, all these aspects of crisis constituted 'pressures and incentives for important organisational and strategic changes' (Fransman 1999: 318), especially through quite new demands for enhanced profitability just at the moment when long-existing low but stable rates of return had been replaced by substantial losses.

However, Fransman insisted that these crises were 'primarily cyclical in nature', while:

> the negative effects of the three crises must be distinguished from the internationally competitive competencies that the firms have accumulated over the last few decades. It is these competencies, and the knowledge they embody, that will determine the ability of the Japanese firms to bounce back and regain their growth and profitability once Japan and the Asian region more generally resume an upward path and once semiconductor prices pick up (Fransman 1999: 318–19).

In this context, he noted that the Japanese ICT firms themselves claimed that, in contrast to the specialist American and European firms, they had the capacity to capitalize on a broad range of competencies, in computers, electronic devices and telecoms, to provide 'multimedia solutions'. However, he also noted that this remained only an 'article of faith' (ibid: 223).

Finally he recognized that the interaction between such corporate vulnerabilities and the broader dynamics of economic crises was prompting some corporate restructuring among ICT firms, though this was usually rather 'minimalist' (see also Lincoln and Nakata 1997). However, there were some 'more radical attempts at corporate restructuring' among the more diversified 'general electronics and electricals firms', such as Toshiba, Hitachi, and Electric-Co, who faced 'difficulties [in] finding the economies of scope and synergies among their wide range of businesses and technologies that would compensate them for the additional costs of managing highly complex and diversified companies, technologies and markets' (Fransman 1999: 330).

The Crisis of Electric-Co

Thus the lack of profitability of the Electric-Co PC division became critical in the context of a wider crisis in parent company performance. Electric-Co was particularly exposed to the consequences of overcapacity and price competition in the semiconductor market that developed dramatically in the late 1990s, leading to warnings that the company would make an operating loss in 1997–8 (financial press, 2/98).

These developments precipitated the unprecedented decision to close part of one of their American semi-conductor plants, together with an 'obsolete'factory in Malaysia in 1998 (financial press, 1/98). The firm also shut down factories operating in another highly competitive market, colour televisions, again in the United States and Malaysia, though it was also reported that there had been resistance to change among senior management and 'domestic restructuring had yet to begin' (financial press, 3/98*a*). Meanwhile the stagnation of the Japanese economy in the late 1990s intensified the company's difficulties, as it harmed most sectors of its business and made it increasingly difficult to cross-subsidize to support vulnerable areas (financial press, 3/98, 9/98). The Asian economic crisis intensified the pressure both by reducing demand and by precipitating price reductions by Korean competitor firms.

As the decisions to close factories indicate, some restructuring was under way at Electric-Co before the arrival of a new company president in June 1998. The scale of the losses incurred in these conditions led the outgoing president to argue that 'further restructuring is needed both overseas and in Japan, not only to cut back operations but to strengthen those businesses where we have strength and to halt businesses that are no good', implying the closure of further overseas factories (financial press, 3/98). On his arrival the new man immediately announced such a policy of 'selection and consolidation'. One of the earliest casualties of this more ruthless policy was an Electric-Co television factory in Scotland, defined as a loss-making plant in the context of the sharp drop in prices in the mature and highly competitive standard colour television market. The closure of this factory was announced in April 1998, with the loss of 400 jobs, together with 25 more jobs at Electric-Co's British Head Office. Meanwhile the Japanese parent company warned that the 1998–9 financial year would produce another massive loss ((financial press, 11/98, 2/99), as the underlying problems, especially of economic stagnation in Japan and vulnerability in key product sectors, continued.

The Vulnerability of Computer-Co and Alternative Strategies for Survival

Against this background it was widely recognized at Computer-Co that they were vulnerable, as the PC division continued to be unprofitable, though there was some hope that a case could be made concerning their longer term viability. As one of our management informants at Computer-Co reported:

> [The new President's] view of Electric-Co was, that it had to be profitable, was that he was going to review all non-profit making parts of the business, and we knew that that would mean us, but we also believed that we could get

> through to 'break even profitability'... I would say the lack of profitability was definitely there, but we were heading in the right direction.

However, the recent history of the company suggested that the conditions in which Computer-Co was operating left little scope to demonstrate such potential.

This brings us back to the growing intensity and the rapidly evolving character of market competition in the PC sector. Computer-Co was always vulnerable to competitive pressures in their established specialist market, where they sold high performance networked PCs and servers to business users, because several much bigger companies were also competing in that market. In particular, Compaq and Dell were engaged in a price war based on substantially higher volumes than Computer-Co. One way of responding to this was to seek higher volumes by expanding sales in the home computer market. However, Computer-Co entered this market by selling through high street retailers and found that this was a very tough market in which to make profits. Not only were the retail chains able to make heavy demands on manufacturers for price discounts, but the costs of servicing the warranties in the domestic consumer market proved much greater than management expected. Furthermore, in 1997 only 10 per cent of its PC sales were for the home, while the business market continued to account for 90 per cent of sales (financial press, 2/98). Thus expansion via the home computer market had proven an illusory escape route, and in February 1998, before the new edict on profitability from Japan, Computer-Co withdrew from that market. Meanwhile the competitiveness of the business market had also been exacerbated by smaller businesses themselves turning to the high street retailers to meet their IT needs, as computers became increasingly standardized off-the-shelf commodities. Once again, Computer-Co remained a small and vulnerable player in a rapidly evolving market arena.

As Fransman's (1999) commentary highlighted, the rapid evolution of new strategic alliances formed around Internet service provision squeezed many less specialist firms like Electric-Co, whose PC divisions were only minor players on this turbulent terrain. This nevertheless remained the chosen territory on which Computer-Co management still hoped to develop their business, and there had been some areas of relative success, primarily in the Japanese market where Electric-Co/Computer-Co could build upon the home brand. However, the recession in Japan combined with the strength of the pound to cut back the orders from Japan, which was their key market. Thus none of the escape routes pursued by Computer-Co management allowed them to transform the financial fortunes of the business in the late 1990s.

Organizing the Closure

Against this background, the managers of Electric-Co's PC division had little scope to finesse the assessment from Japan by demonstrating convincingly that their losses were temporary. As one of the senior management team remarked, 'it was a fait accompli', and the only room for manoeuvre which this left to the management was the task of seeking to sell off or spin off some parts of the business and close the remainder. Efforts were made to sell several significant parts of the business during the period between the announcement and final closure. Apparently, there was even some prospect of selling the factory to another inward investor at one point, not as a going concern but to manufacture a telecommunications product, with the possibility that 'a lot of the staff' would have been taken on. However, this possibility never materialized, and the sale of some of the other parts of the business also fell through.

In the end, only two relatively small parts of the business were sold off, and staff transferred to the new employer through a Transfer of Undertakings (Protection of Employment) (TUPE) transfer. One was the service division, which had to be sustained to honour the warranties and service agreements, and this was sold to an existing warranty operation. The other was a specialist provider of 'software solutions' for businesses, which became a management buyout. Beyond this a cluster of motherboard designers (there had been a team of around thirty-five people) were recruited by another firm, almost as a team, having been made redundant, but this fell outside the TUPE framework. The rest of the staff at both the offices and the factory was made redundant over a period of ten months.

CONCLUSION

One way of understanding the Computer-Co experience might be to see it as an example of the failure to transplant Japanese management best practice to the British subsidiary. It should be clear from the above account, however, that this would be an inappropriate interpretation. First, it is evident that Computer-Co management was explicitly granted considerable autonomy in their management of the factory and (especially) R&D. Second, the terms of this relative autonomy were clearly grounded in the technological competencies and innovative capacities which the management of Electric-Co regarded Computer-Co as possessing, and providing for the whole company.

As we have seen, both the purchase of Computer-Co and its projected role in Electric-Co's international operations were underpinned by a perceived complementarity between the strengths and weaknesses of the subsidiary and parent companies. Not only was Computer-Co seen as valuable because of its established technological track record, even though this had not been translated into sustained commercial viability, but the perspectives of Electric-Co's management were also informed by the limitations of their own venture into the PC market. In part, this echoed the broader weaknesses of the whole cluster of Japanese ICT firms that produced computers, and it also arose more specifically from the particularly marginal positioning of Electric-Co's computer business within that cluster.

Thus, our main argument is that analyses of the relationship between Computer-Co and Electric-Co, and thus of the relations between Japanese and British managers, must explore the implications of the distinctive competencies developed within and mobilized by the Japanese parent company and the British subsidiary respectively. Electric-Co granted Computer-Co management considerable autonomy to develop its own activities within the framework of an approved business plan, because Computer-Co was better placed to match design and development trends in the PC sector in a way the parent company had found it difficult to achieve. This was particularly evident in the orientations of the small number of Japanese engineering managers who played a central role within Computer-Co. They drew upon their knowledge of the different contexts and competencies characteristic of the two organizations to mediate between management cadres and negotiate the parameters of relative autonomy. They also shared Computer-Co management's judgement of the relevance of sector experience and recipes drawn from British and American firms. In this context, Computer-Co management were able to continue to draw on sector recipes provided by contacts with the branch plants of other electronics and computer companies, while the direct influence of Electric-Co remained quite limited and selective. Indeed, where it was most influential, in relation to manufacturing quality, this owed more to the role of one of its divisions as a major customer than to the activities of the Japanese managers and visiting advisers.

Such an analysis of the distinctive competencies mobilized by Computer-Co and Electric-Co also helps to illuminate the vulnerability of the subsidiary. First, it underlines the limitations of the resources provided by the parent company, since their embedded expertise had only partial and problematical relevance to the problems facing Computer-Co. Second, it suggests that, whatever the technical competencies possessed by Computer-Co, they were vulnerable to the competitive pressures that had beset the company before it was purchased, especially as the pressures exerted by the dominant players in the sector intensified in the 1990s. The continuing precariousness of Computer-Co bears the marks of a takeover that was developed from a position of relative weakness, both for Computer-Co and also on the part of Electric-Co. Thus Computer-Co continued to occupy a competitive position which was inherently relatively vulnerable, despite the additional investment provided by its parent, since it remained a small player in terms of its technical and organizational capacities, facing several major and well-entrenched competitors.

Of course, despite these insights, an analysis in terms of organizational competencies only provides part of the picture. While we have sought to analyse the work and employment relations through which such competencies were developed and sustained, both in R&D and in the factory, the level of analysis developed by Fransman does not explore these features in any detail. Furthermore, the story of Computer-Co provides only partial leverage on the character of the turbulent market competition that these firms confronted. In part, this is because it can only address *post hoc* the emergence of new constellations of technical and commercial capability which altered the terms of existing competitive relations. And it is also because broader patterns of crisis and restructuring involved a wider dynamic, and can only be treated as exogenous conditions in analysing experience within specific firms and workplaces.

Clearly, we cannot simply extrapolate from our analysis the Computer-Co experience to generalize about the role of R&D activities in Japanese manufacturing FDI in recent decades. However, drawing on Fransman's broader analysis, we have shown that some of the more extensive investment in R&D on brownfield sites reflected a defensive strategy from a position of relative weakness. This provided a distinctive context for an engagement between Japanese and British managers and engineers (which we return to in Chapter 10), but also underlined the precariousness of the organizations in which such an engagement took place.

Finally, our focus in this chapter has been on the relationship between Japanese and British managers and engineers, with the experience of the shop-floor workers at the Scottish factory very much in the background. However, we hope we have written enough to indicate that their experience of production and innovation bore strong family resemblances to those of the workers in the Telford factories, discussed in other chapters, though with a more persistent sense of insecurity underlined by the eventual closure.

III

REMAKING WORKING LIVES: MANAGEMENT AND WORKERS

CHAPTER

10

Japanese and British Management: Alliances and Antagonisms

INTRODUCTION

The overseas operations of international manufacturers represent a specific context in which managers from their home countries have to operate and managers from quite distinctive backgrounds in home and host countries have to work together. Thus 'transplant' research provides an opportunity to explore the nature of management in the *distinctive setting* of the subsidiary. Our concern in this chapter is to investigate the experiences and outlooks of our Japanese and British management informants, and their relationships within the subsidiaries we studied. Earlier chapters have outlined the varied evolution of management policies and practices in our different case-study factories. From these accounts it will be evident that Japanese and local managers often had different perspectives and priorities, but it should also be clear that the relationships between them varied across the different companies and also over time. Managers within these foreign subsidiaries clearly drew upon aspects of the distinctive management repertoires of both home and host countries, but the resulting policies often differed from both to produce hybrid or experimental features. Our case-study accounts also underline the significance of active processes of management debate, conflict and uncertainty within these enterprises, rather than any smooth and straightforward process of either transplantation or hybridization. In this sense they also suggest that 'management learning' is a more fraught and problematical process than is often envisaged in the prescriptive literature.

These points set the agenda for this chapter, which seeks to interweave four themes. The first concerns the ways in which Japanese and British managers each participated in management career pathways and worked with perspectives that were rooted in their distinctive societies and employment systems. Our discussion of these features draws upon the societal effects and national business systems literature but underlines the ways in which distinctive experiences of economic dominance and decline have also helped to shape the professional formation of manufacturing managers in each of these societies. The second theme concerns the ways in which our informants were deployed or recruited to work at our case-study sites, and the implications of these processes for their conduct as managers. On the one hand this involves discussion of the assignment of expatriate Japanese managers to these overseas subsidiaries and on the other it involves consideration of the recruitment of local managers to work for Japanese inward investors. The third theme reviews some of the main ways in which Japanese and British managers interacted and understood one another in these workplaces, with particular attention to the varied character of these relationships and some of the differences in approach *among* British managers and *among* Japanese managers. Finally, we compare our different case-study enterprises by mapping the differences between them in these terms, and seek to explain the distinctive patterns of dominance and accommodation revealed by this comparison, in part by reference to the constraints that flowed from the distinctive roles and resources that characterized these factories.

On this basis we seek to develop a better understanding of the 'micro-politics' of management (Burns 1961) in these workplaces, and the varied roles of Japanese and British managers in the active but also circumscribed construction of their distinctive work and employment regimes. In pursuing this objective our prime focus is on relationships and processes within each of these factories, though we also comment on the importance of the wider field of relations within which each factory operates. Thus the roles of management actors elsewhere in the international firm, at head office or in 'mother' or 'sister' plants, are only touched on briefly, though their significance will be evident from our earlier case-study chapters. Similarly, shop-floor workers only appear in this chapter as targets of management policy, but will re-emerge as more active protagonists in the next chapter. Finally, our analysis suggests that in such places as Telford, with a substantial cluster of Japanese firms operating on greenfield sites, the interplay of management approaches takes place in local networks beyond the enterprise as well as at company level. In part these firms were responding to the policies of the Development Agency that administered inward investment and marketed the area by emphasizing the availability of labour, comparatively low wages and pacific industrial relations. In part they were developing forms of cooperation and policy coordination designed particularly to manage the mobility and intractability of labour in the local area, though these efforts to regulate the local labour market were only partially successful. Thus, though our analysis in this chapter will focus on relations between Japanese and British managers within the factories, we also recognize that management discussions and policy formation also took place on this wider terrain.

DISTINCTIVE SOCIAL FORMATIONS OF MANAGEMENT: THE STRENGTHS AND LIMITS OF SOCIETAL SYSTEMS ANALYSES

The formation of management, the nature of the enterprise, and the identity of individual managers are all substantially influenced by national institutional arrangements (Armstrong 1984; Gallie 1978; Maurice et al. 1986; Sorge 1991; Whitley 1992*a*, 1992*b*). Managers may face similar problems, and engage in similar processes and activities, which are identifiable as managerial, but managers are also creatures of particular environments, which produce distinctive ways of being a manager, place emphasis on different bases of expertise and construct careers in contrasting ways. Japanese managers who work in overseas subsidiaries have generally gained substantial managerial experience in Japan, while their tours of duty overseas may vary from a short visit of a few weeks or months to a longer posting of between three and five years. This is the norm even for senior managers, who very rarely remain overseas beyond eight years, though some may move between overseas subsidiaries during that time. Thus we would expect Japanese institutions and career pathways to remain dominant influences on their formation as managers.

Similarly, many British managers, whether recruited directly by Japanese firms or working in enterprises bought by Japanese companies, were formed by the institutions and career pathways characteristic of the British employment system. While some may have worked for other non-British companies in Britain or abroad, or may more recently have visited or worked in Japan for varying periods, they will have learned how to be a manager in Britain. However, the extent of international investment and the relatively unregulated character of the British labour market is likely to have generated a quite varied experience within this framework. Furthermore, the recruitment of younger British specialists with little prior experience might mean that the influence of existing British institutions and practices is more attenuated among this category of local managers.

Thus we can locate the experiences of our managers by reference to national business systems and 'societal effects' analyses of the distinctive ways in which management and employment are organized in Japan and Britain. However, much of the research that examines cross-national institutional differences in the formation and organization of management is an exercise in comparative *statics*. As a result it overstates supply side or input influences on the nature of social action within the firm and understates the tensions and shifts which characterize such action, together with associated patterns of sub-national diversity within sectors, companies and regions. As was noted in Chapter 4, such research underestimates the increased mobility of capital, which may in turn increase the mobility of labour, not least through internal movement within the international organization. Thus comparisons of societal business systems often emphasize cultural cohesion or institutional isomorphism in ways that overstate the coherence and stability of such national systems. As such they cannot account for non-trivial changes within such national business systems and are of limited use in understanding the dynamics of management policies and labour processes in international companies.

In particular, attention to the distinctive home and host country systems of professional formation and the ways in which they impinge upon the operations of international firms needs to be accompanied by discussion of the configurations of power that influence relations among managers. The most obvious manifestations of such power relations are the leverage of HQ, afforded both through direct instruction and via decisions to invest or disinvest, and the distribution of managers from home and host countries within the management hierarchy and across management specialisms. However, we wish to highlight two further features that also have a significant influence on policy formation within overseas subsidiaries.

The first of these is associated with the relative dominance or decline of national economies, which respectively bolsters or undermines the competence claims of managers from these economies. For much of the 1980s and 1990s there was a widespread assumption among commentators that Japanese inward investment would carry with it the transfer of Japanese methods of production and their diffusion and adoption by other manufacturers (Elger and Smith 1994). This underlined the strong international reputation of Japanese manufacturing management, not least in management thought and writing. Thus, during the period of our research, Japanese managers in internationalizing Japanese manufacturing firms could readily claim the superiority of Japanese techniques of production management, while British managers were well aware of the retreat and rationalization of British manufacturing. At the same time our research shows that the precise implications of such claims often remained contested, while the experience at Computer-Co, in particular, provides a valuable reminder of the extent to which the plausibility of such claims remained firm and sector specific.

The second feature is that the contrasting ways in which careers have been organized in Japan and Britain have generated sharply contrasting power and dependency relationships for Japanese expatriates on the one hand and British recruits on the other. In particular, British managers may seek to progress within the subsidiary but rarely have the opportunity to advance beyond it. However, they may well be able to enhance their chances in the wider British labour market on the basis of their experience of working for a Japanese firm, though their labour market leverage may also be weakened by a depressed demand for managers in the declining manufacturing sector. Meanwhile, very few Japanese expatriate managers are likely to benefit from open labour market mobility, but rather depend upon using their overseas experience to advance further within their existing firm. In this sense the substantial dependency of almost all Japanese managers on their existing employer is carried over into the operation of the subsidiary, and access to this pool of organizationally dependent, reliable and controllable labour is a powerful resource for senior executives within these firms.

Kenney and Florida (1995: 797) provide an example of this contrast. They quote an American manager of a Japanese telecommunications transplant in the United States who noted that 'the turnover of American managers was the single biggest problem facing the plant' and wanted 'more Japanese managers and engineers because they were more reliable'. As a result the number of advisers from Japan increased rather than diminished, apparently because senior management felt they could control the problem of local management turnover by using internal reserves of labour from the home base of the parent company. Such patterns of dependency and commitment are also reinforced by the legal status of expatriate labour, which deepens the contrast with the position of local managers. For example, the employment of Japanese managers within the United Kingdom is legally dependent upon the organization, as they only have a work-permit to work within their current organization. Our own case-study findings show that the role and character of overseas operations may sometimes support deviations from these patterns. Thus a Japanese manager could pursue an occupational rather than organizational career (Assembly-Co) or a British manager could gain a senior management position 'above' the British subsidiary (Computer-Co). However, they also suggest that such developments are quite exceptional.

THE SOCIAL FORMATION OF MANAGEMENT IN JAPAN

Despite significant recent changes in the social organization of employment and labour markets in Japan, it remains the case that many male Japanese managers enter and build their career inside one firm, and this was certainly the case when we were conducting our fieldwork. Almost all of the managers we interviewed in our five case studies had worked for a single company. The obvious exception was the MD for Assembly-Co, our subcontract joint venture company, and his career pathway was more typical of the small firm sector where petty employers and managers are more mobile (Chalmers 1989). This commitment to a single firm was the greatest contrast between Japanese and British managers. It signalled greater economic stability and reciprocity between the organization and the individual in the development of an organizational career (Dore 1973). Further support for our findings was provided by a more recent survey of twelve Japanese managers across six companies in Telford. This found that eleven had only worked for a single company, while the exception was a manager who had worked in only two firms, the first for two years and the second for fifteen, while the tenure of these managers averaged twenty-one years and ranged from thirteen to thirty years (Igarashi 2000).

Most commentators also suggest that management careers in large Japanese firms have been structured through regular rotation between different functions and across different divisions according to company needs (Dore 1973; Lam 1996*a*, 1996*b*; McCormick and McCormick 1996; Shirai 1983;). Integration into a 'company consciousness' rather than an occupational consciousness has therefore been the norm. Those Japanese engineering managers we interviewed confirmed aspects of this practice, which gave them varied combinations of broader management expertise arising from experience as supervisors or plant managers and/or as personnel or quality specialists. This sometimes meant movement across divisions of their firm, but in other cases movement was accomplished within one division. Some managers without engineering qualifications, such as a manager in a personnel department who had a psychology degree, had rotated only within administrative functions. However, others had been drawn into technical management, underlining the importance of the development of expertise within the company. For example, one manager in business planning had studied Arabic at university, but began his career in the company in production control, while another, an unusual character who studied literature at university and had travelled and married in Europe, had worked within engineering and production departments in his subsidiary.

As this implies, engineers in Japanese companies have historically had a strong production or manufacturing focus, a practical engagement with both the organization of work and production machinery, without the negative status connotations found in Britain. As Fruin (1992: 137) notes, from the 1920s onwards 'engineers showed up on or near the shop floor in ever larger numbers, and an engineering approach to manufacturing gradually permeated the workplace'. Furthermore, while many engineering managers possess university training, there remains more fluidity between manual and technical labour in Japan compared with other countries. Thus one informant insisted that:

> my manufacturing section [in Japan], usually they start from operators, usually after high school they enter the company and start in manufacturing and [are] gradually promoted to manager in twenty to twenty-five years, while graduates of university usually don't enter manufacturing section but the staff section, like engineering, business production control, but the possibilities of operators and staff are the same.

In our Telford studies most dispatched managers were engineers and most managers had an engineering educational background, common features in manufacturing in Japan. However, this relative fluidity was also evident in the experience of our Japanese informants, both in terms of the work experience of graduates and through the presence of several managers with lesser qualifications who had started as production workers, and progressed into management. At the same time there were suggestions that different Japanese firms had somewhat different approaches in this regard, with some (like Copy-Co) giving more emphasis to advancement from the shop-floor and others (like Electric-Co) placing more emphasis on recruitment from elite universities.

The other side of this pattern has been the insignificance of accountancy and marketing as functions separate and distinct from production management, and the low status accorded to non-productive services that are seen as adding no value to the product. Again Fruin (1992: 26–27) notes that standardized accounting systems did not figure in Japanese corporations until the 1950s and 1960s. This meant Japanese management had long been used to managing without detailed financial indicators of performance over the short term, and hence, developed longer-term time horizons for judging success. He suggests that this, together with slower promotion ladders for executives, represented internal organizational factors behind the more strategic outlook of Japanese companies.

This pattern may have been reflected in the integration of technical and financial data in the activities of the planning departments in our larger case-study firms. However, strategic decisions about such matters as new models and large-scale investments were largely made at HQ, while even the details of design and development were often settled in Japan. In this sense these were 'reproduction factories' (Kenney et al. 1998) rather than sites of strategic innovation, though we have also seen that even 'reproduction' involved considerable modification and tailoring of Japanese production systems. Of course, Computer-Co was an important exception where British senior management played a more strategic role, until company-wide strategic decisions driven by financial crisis precipitated the closure of the factory. More mundanely, the dominance of Japanese manufacturing expertise in these factories, coupled with the claims of local managers to expertise in personnel and employment matters, left Japanese personnel specialists with a rather marginal role. The few people who were in this category found it quite hard to develop a substantial role for themselves (as a British personnel manager in one of our firms remarked 'he doesn't interfere') beyond administering the details of the employment relations of their fellow expatriates. They also appeared particularly anxious about the implications of their overseas tours of duty for their career prospects on their return to Japan.

For certain specialist technical functions in Japan, such as information technology, university specialization has been a requirement of entry, and these have been the areas where recruitment of experienced experts from the external labour market has developed furthest. Some commentators on the post-war Japanese employment and production system have drawn an optimistic picture of the R&D capabilities of core employees in Japanese high technology industries (Kenney and Florida 1993: 50–86). Others, however, have argued that Japan would have to increase technical and scientific specialization of labour if it was to compete in world markets in 'knowledge industries'. Thus McCormick (1996: 220–3) diagnosed a problem of 'under-specialization' and a deficiency of individual inventiveness in Japan. Meanwhile, Okimoto and Nishi (1994: 200) highlighted the 'conservatism' of Japanese R&D managers, their unwillingness to 'take risks' and tendency to follow established procedures ('stick to what is known and bulldoze ahead') when encountering problems, rather that thinking laterally or afresh, in contrast to the more innovative approach of American R&D managers.

The point this underlines is that the social formation of management cadres in different societies is likely to produce distinctive sorts of individual expertise and organizational capabilities. However, we would also argue that these distinctive configurations are unlikely to deliver unproblematical superiority of performance across all aspects of management and all sectors of the economy. This is partly because managements face intractable problems that pose persistent dilemmas, a systemic feature underlined by many critical histories of evolving recipes in the management of the labour process. However, it is also because the strengths of management strategies devised to suit specific national or sectoral conditions may become weaknesses in other contexts, especially when such specific arrangements are exposed to new sources of competitive pressure. This implies that systemic dilemmas are mediated through changing patterns of national, sectoral or enterprise dominance.

Thus in our computer case study the inventiveness, flexibility, and risk-taking of the British engineers and designers was consistently contrasted with the slower, more bureaucratic but robust R&D conducted in the Japanese parent company. This contrast was partly framed in terms of national stereotypes, of the individual serendipity of British computer engineers compared with 'group think' amongst the Japanese. But it was also seen to reflect the contrasting organizational and market settings in which these R&D teams operated, and thus the different design and product knowledges they deployed. In turn, a recognition of these nested contexts allowed both Japanese and British staff to acknowledge the differences in their backgrounds and orientations in ways which did not automatically lead to conflict or mutual incomprehension (compare Lam 1995). Instead it could also frame debate about the salience of different sorts of expertise and alternative solutions to technical and organizational difficulties. This was evident at Computer-Co, where we have seen that Japanese inward-investment was premised on a recognition that the parent company lacked certain design and development capabilities. However, it also emerged in a low key in some of the other cases, such as the discussion of appropriate quality procedures at Copy-Co.

It should also be underlined that management pathways in the large Japanese manufacturing firms are male pathways, as the Japanese large enterprise employment system is highly gendered. It is premised not only on the 'organization man' having a wife at home supporting him and his children but also on the short length of tenure (seven years on average) of young female workers, whose insecurity of employment underpins the security of male manual workers (Gottfried and Hayashi-Kato 1998). Exceptional women have forged careers in education, medicine and some other areas of service employment (Liddle and Nakajima 2000), but despite recent gains in formal equal opportunities legislation women remain strongly disadvantaged even in the emergent multitrack promotion systems, especially in manufacturing (Hanami 2000; Lam 1992. Thus Japanese manufacturing management remains overwhelmingly male, both at home and in overseas postings, while the presumption has been that local managers will also be male, with little scope for women to become managers (Kenney and Florida 1993; Fucini and Fucini 1990). However, this was not quite the pattern of *local* management recruitment in our case-study factories, as women had gained some access to work in personnel and administration (see pp. 288–9).

INTERNATIONALIZATION AND THE ALLOCATION OF EXPATRIATE JAPANESE STAFF

So far we have registered some of the ways in which the experience and orientations of Japanese managers in our case-study plants echoed major features of the distinctive social formation of management cadres in the Japanese business system, and we have also noted some of the variations around this pattern. Now we need to address the conditions under which Japanese managers were selected and deployed to overseas subsidiaries. As we have seen, the surge of North American and European investment by Japanese manufacturing capital in the 1980s was both new and concentrated, so that most Japanese companies had little comparable experience on which to build. This meant that many of these companies were still in the process of developing systems for training and managing the managers they despatched overseas. Thus one manager from PCB-Co reported that he had been involved in a cumulative three-year programme, but this had been heavily focused on language training:

> [The company] has educational system for international persons.... It is up to me and the boss, we can discuss 'are you interested in international

> business or not'. I was interested, so I said 'yes'. So I was an international trainee and then I entered this system, then I had a lot of training for three years. Like a weekly English course and a one-week full English conversation course, twice yearly exam, and then my [score on the language test] was getting better, then I reached the level to graduate this system. I must graduate within three years, or the company gives up spending money. Then soon I was nominated to this position. Previously there was no procedure, no training and we had a bad experience, so [the parent company] training personnel have learned from this experience, then they have created this system.

Another informant suggested that his company had now moved beyond language training, though too late for him to benefit from recent developments:

> I had language training... and they sent me on the management course for assistant managers. Since then they [have] started a special management training programme for the people who are going abroad, but the five years I was there, there wasn't such a training course.

By the mid-1990s some of the larger companies, and especially those with a longer history of international operations, had created specific management development programmes for their expatriate managers, but few of the managers in post had participated in such programmes.

Turning to the personal experience of the Japanese managers we interviewed, they generally suggested that they had little choice over which part of their company's overseas operations they would work in, though the overseas posting had an element of mutuality. There was a certain bemused fatalism connected with their submission to their company's requests. As one Copy-Co manager explained:

> I was talking to my boss and suddenly he asked, 'Do you mind going to the UK?' (laughter). I don't want to [but] I said 'No' (laughter). In Japan—maybe it is difficult for British people to understand—usually we don't change our company, we don't move companies, and if company say 'Go there' we go there (laughter).

Sometimes the overseas posting came as a surprise. Thus a manager at PCB-Co remarked that:

> Although I thought [I would go] at some period, I had completely forgotten [about] it when I was actually *assigned*. Honestly speaking, I had not prepared at all when my boss told me.

Thus relatively limited preparation was sometimes accompanied by short notice of assignment to the United Kingdom.

Even in larger firms the experience was still of a rather involuntary move, though with somewhat more preparation, themes expanded on by a Japanese manager from Part-Co interviewed in the late 1990s:

> This is my first foreign assignment. Although I did not necessarily wish [to go] I was interested. The company asks employees' willingness, and the employees are assigned when they agree.... The company has a human resource database for international operations. It is updated every year, checking the employees' preference and qualifications. Basically, expats are supposed to be chosen from that [database], but the current expats were not necessarily chosen from that. Many expats are assigned to management positions. Therefore, the candidates are not always young. An important condition is whether they are suitable for the positions. The requirements depend on the position. In each section in the parent company, it is discussed who should be assigned. The selection procedure is not necessarily very clear, and qualified human resource is rather short, because the speed of expanding business to foreign countries has been very fast. Therefore, the company is promoting localization as much as possible.

This captures the extent to which, during the period of fastest growth in foreign investment, the large firms with growing experience of internationalization made greater efforts to plan overseas postings. However, it also suggests that the very rapidity of expansion compromised these efforts and heightened the unpredictable character of the experience for those involved.

Rapid internationalization also meant that most of those who were sent to the new subsidiaries were working abroad for the first time, though it was possible for these firms to redeploy some managers with existing experience of overseas operations to work in newer foreign ventures. Several of the more senior managers we interviewed had already done a tour of duty in another subsidiary, but it remained the case that most of the Japanese managers in the Telford factories had only recent and limited experience of working abroad. However, although working abroad is a recent development for many Japanese companies and managers, training abroad and learning from the West has a long history. Japanese industrialization was built on an active utilization of foreign technology and production methods and an active passion for learning from, re-engineering and improving upon Western management practices (Tsutsui 1998; Westney 1987). There is therefore a history of learning from others within the Japanese management tradition, as well as more recent proselytizing of the capacity and strengths of their own management approach.

While the process of assignment was experienced in similar ways by many of our Japanese informants, it will have been apparent from earlier chapters that they joined rather different management structures in which Japanese managers played somewhat different roles. It is difficult to provide a simple numerical summary of the patterns across the companies, not only because management structures varied considerably but also because titles such as 'coordinator' or 'adviser', which were often used to characterize the roles of significant numbers of Japanese staff, were rather ambiguous in terms of their real authority (see below). As we have seen,

Japanese managers played a quite limited role in some of the subsidiaries. In both Computer-Co and Assembly-Co most managers were British, and British management played a key role in policymaking. In the former case this reflected the mandate retained by the existing British management after the takeover, though a small number of senior and experienced Japanese engineering managers played important roles within the British operation and other Japanese staff made shorter visits connected with particular projects. In the latter case the two Japanese staff played very different roles, as one was the MD who focused on finding and liaising with customers while the other was a specialist technical adviser.

Japanese managers were much more prominent in the remaining subsidiaries, but still there were substantial differences in their presence. Part-Co was strongly dominated by Japanese management. In addition to the MD, seven of the nine senior managers were Japanese. The most senior British manager was responsible for personnel management and communications while Japanese managers ran finance and business planning and there was one British production manager alongside four Japanese production engineers. At lower management level there were twelve British and fourteen Japanese, but twelve of the Japanese (including ten engineers) were defined as 'coordinators' reporting directly to the most senior Japanese managers, while four of the British were 'assistant managers' at the base of the organization chart. At Copy-Co, as we have seen, the ratio of Japanese and British managers was more balanced. In addition to the Japanese MD there were three Japanese and three British senior managers, with the most senior British manager definitely second in command. Below them there were twelve British and two Japanese department managers, but also an additional thirteen Japanese managers or 'advisers'. While Japanese managers were more prominent in engineering and monopolized business planning, local managers had a significant engineering presence and dominated personnel, purchasing and logistics. Finally PCB-Co, with a much smaller management cadre, had similar numbers of Japanese and British managers during our research, with a Japanese MD and two Japanese 'technical advisers'.

In part the particular predominance of Japanese managers at Part-Co can be read as a result of its relatively recent arrival. This would fit with the reduced numbers and interventionism of dispatched Japanese staff at both PCB-Co and Copy-Co in the period before our research. At Copy-Co the 'localization' programme involved a fall from fifty in the early 1990s to thirty-five in 1993 and twenty-one in 1995. However, after our research the Japanese presence at PCB-Co grew again, as management struggled with the difficulties we discussed in Chapter 8. This serves as a reminder that the particular position of the subsidiary may promote growing Japanese management intervention, just as in the cases of Assembly-Co and Computer-Co it supported a more limited role. Indeed it is plausible to suggest that the continued dominance of Japanese managers at Part-Co reflected the role of the subsidiary as a key European 'reproduction factory', as well as its relatively recent establishment.

THE VARIED AND CHANGING ROLES OF JAPANESE MANAGERS IN OVERSEAS SUBSIDIARIES

As we have already suggested, the Japanese managers working in overseas subsidiaries are not a homogeneous group, but vary in terms of specialism, age, rank, and experience. The Japanese managers we interviewed were clearly formed by the Japanese employment system, but the implications of this for their experience of work in an overseas factory varied quite considerably. Important factors were the role they were allocated in the British factory, the stage of their career and also the character of the branch plant itself.

Our comparison of management structures in the previous section suggests that some areas of management were likely to remain Japanese in almost all cases and thus continue to be established career pathways for expatriate staff. One of our local Copy-Co informants captured this in the remark that 'the Business Planning Division will always remain Japanese, as the key link to Japan and the MD's "leg man" '. As this implies, the planning of activity and monitoring of enterprise performance represented fundamental linkages with the parent company, even when Japanese staff played a limited role in employment policy or, more unusually, relinquished a central role in the organization of production. Thus it was usual for a core of technical and planning activity to remain dominated by Japanese personnel, and the Japanese MD (and in the larger organizations, the business planning department) played pivotal roles in this regard. Such staff maintained close and continuing relations with their colleagues at the HQ or in parent plants in Japan. However, the contrasting cases of Assembly-Co and Computer-Co demonstrate that there were wide variations in the scope of this core range of activities. At Assembly-Co the MD concentrated heavily on liaison with existing and potential customers, while at Computer-Co monitoring of performance was primarily mediated through the agreement of production and investment plans submitted by the British MD.

Other areas of activity were subject to a more complex and changing division of labour between Japanese and British staff, as policies of partial localization were implemented through the movement of increasing numbers of Japanese staff into 'advisory' or 'coordinating' roles. Almost by definition such roles involved quite sensitive and negotiated relationships with local managers and employees, and these were discussed in a particularly revealing way in interviews at our research companies conducted by a Japanese researcher (Igarashi 2000). Thus one Japanese manager at Copy-Co remarked on the differences between the roles of the Japanese staff employed in business planning, who were engaged in frequent communications with Japanese managers at home in the parent company, and the technical advisers who were working directly with locals. He then noted the complexity of the latter role:

> Many of the Japanese in Telford are advisers, then they have no authority to evaluate the locals directly. Therefore these Japanese can't expect the locals to follow them. It is difficult to say whether the Japanese should manage them directly, or should advise them, staying beside [them], it [this arrangement] has been developed by trial and error.

Another informant, from Part-Co, drew on a generational terminology which was shared by others in the firm to underline the way in which such changes might affect successive cohorts of Japanese managers:

> Localization is proceeding year by year. Then the role of expats in the second generation is supposed to be 'coordinator', then [the job of] the second, third generation will become more difficult. Because the conflicts with locals will gradually occur, if the second expats are not far better qualified than the first, the locals will not accept it.

Together these comments highlight the way in which such Japanese staff were affected by a loss of authority grounded in positioning in the managerial hierarchy, though they often sought an alternative basis of legitimacy by emphasizing their expertise.

Some of the complexities and potential sources of conflict faced by such Japanese staff were spelt out more fully by another Copy-Co adviser who highlighted the way in which the loss of direct authority altered his relationship with both local managers and workers:

> The organization is difficult because the Japanese 'adviser' is 'kuroko' [an assistant hidden in the background in traditional Japanese theatre genres such as Noh or Kabuki] and does not have any authority. There was a case that a worker worked very hard and was good enough from adviser's viewpoint, but the local manager did not necessarily evaluate him as good. The worker came to me and complained about his evaluation. I suppose he expected me to take some action, but I had no authority to do anything. In that case the worker left the company with complaints. After the organization changed the Japanese feel [it is] difficult, but I think the British feel frustration as well.... On the surface the Japanese do not have the authority, but in reality the business does not move without the Japanese.

Both the note of frustration and the analogy with the hidden assistant in traditional Japanese theatre underline the tensions embodied in this role (especially in the fraught context of management–worker relations that we have outlined in earlier chapters and will discuss further in Chapter 11). In these circumstances some Japanese informants suggested that they had become more circumspect in the way they responded to problems on the shop-floor, whether breakdowns, quality problems, or employee complaints, so as not to overtly challenge the authority of their British counterparts. In turn the dominant response was to focus on cultivating an effective relationship with British managers, specialists and supervisors to develop a common approach. Thus one Part-Co 'coordinator' emphasized his role in offering advice and support so as to 'bring on' the key specialists in his department, though ideally this meant 'creating copies' of himself.

Where there were efforts at extended localization, this also had implications for those more senior staff who retained their line management positions, though under these circumstances Japanese managers could retain more control of the process. This sometimes translated into a relatively smooth transition, as is suggested by a senior production manager at Copy-Co:

> I communicate mostly with the [British] technical manager. Basically, he and I work together very closely. I try to work so he can work effectively, and so he can use me well. I feel I have transferred most of my techniques to him. I am thinking that I can go back to Japan, I feel that the British can manage on their own.

However, as we saw in discussing the restructuring of supervision at the same firm, this process could be much more beset by misgivings, and as the example of PCB-Co shows, conflict could throw the process into reverse.

At this point we should note one further complexity in the roles played by Japanese staff in these British factories, and this concerns the activities of project groups on short 'business trip' visits to address particular problems or complete specific tasks. We met accounts of the activities of such visitors in all the factories we studied, but we did not interview any participants (though several of our Japanese informants had been involved in such activities at other factories at some time in their careers). On this basis we wish to register just three relevant points. First, such visits were evidently fairly commonplace, especially to facilitate the establishment of new processes or to seek solutions to recurrent problems. Second, expatriate Japanese managers were often wary when this involved a unilateral initiative from Japan, because such 'hit squads' were taken to imply that HQ was dissatisfied with the performance of the managers on the ground, though visits 'by invitation' were a different matter. Finally, however, there was a widespread perception, among both Japanese and British managers, that such interventions tended to be ineffective because, as one Japanese Copy-Co manager commented 'they did the activity and they didn't transfer their knowledge to local management'.

AGE AND EXPERIENCE

Clearly the ways in which Japanese staff were located in transplant management structures and experienced these tensions and conflicts were strongly related to age, experience, position, and power. At one extreme were the very experienced older managers who were appointed as managing directors in the larger firms. For example, a resume of the career of one of these men emphasized his accumulation of a deep and rounded experience in the relevant area of manufacturing over a thirty-five-year period with his company. This involved ten years as a production research engineer at HQ after graduation, fifteen years as a production engineer responsible for production lines and then six as general manager at the Japanese parent plant. During this time he also had a major role in planning three sister factories in the United States and Australia, before coming to the United Kingdom. Thus such men generally had experience of managing a substantial factory in Japan and had often been involved in the establishment of new factories at home and abroad. Indeed their appointment often involved a matching of their experience to the priorities and problems faced by the branch factory at the time of their appointment. For example, the first MD at Part-Co had gained previous experience of starting a new factory, while the MD during our fieldwork had the expertise and the remit to 'ramp up' production during a phase of expansion. Again the new MD who arrived at PCB-Co was clearly perceived as a strong man sent to 'sort out' a troublesome business. The MDs of the big factories were clearly part of the senior management cadre of their parent companies, and were likely to move on to further senior positions back home, or in the developing super-structure of international management. For example, an earlier MD from Copy-Co had moved to the European regional HQ, where he continued to be a valued ally of the current senior management. Meanwhile, the final MD at PCB-Co, though less powerfully positioned in his parent corporation than the heads of the bigger factories, was reportedly able to recruit Japanese replacement staff from among managers and specialists he already knew back home (and this facilitated his dismissal of most of the existing local managers).

As this last example suggests, the distinctive preoccupations and personality of different MDs were also felt to have an important influence on life in each factory, albeit often filtered through translation and interpretation by more junior managers with a better command of English. A senior British manager at Assembly-Co, who had been a close observer of patterns of management succession in the major Japanese firms, claimed that 'it has been a general trait within most [of our] customers that they've started off with a very nice diplomatic, sincere person, and the next time they send somebody who is a little bit more ruthless, shall we say'. British managers at Copy-Co, however, provided a more nuanced view of successive MDs.

The first was said to have been 'a very competent man, but very set in his views' and 'very authoritarian'. The second was a 'completely different character', likened to a 'classical British PR Chairman or a sort of Japanese Executive or President', with less involvement in operational matters and a commitment to 'localization'. Finally, the third, newly arrived when we were interviewing and more of an unknown figure, was nevertheless perceived to be more reclusive, with a financial background and none of the bonhomie of his predecessor. These characterizations again suggest a succession of different patterns of expertise tailored to the condition and performance of the factory, but also emphasize the potential ramifications of differences of style, reputation, and character that may also colour the experiences of those who work in these enterprises.

At the other extreme to the powerful MDs were the younger technical managers in the large companies, whose main tasks were to use their expertise to facilitate production operations and to act as channels of communication between Japan and the United Kingdom in terms of information and problem-solving. In general this also meant that they were the carriers and advocates of parent company priorities. Thus in discussing Copy-Co's venture into design and development as a way of enhancing the position of the plant (outlined in Chapter 7) one Japanese manager remarked that

> We Japanese, we also belong to Copy-Co HQ, and we have to pass the jobs which are given by Copy-Co Japan, and therefore, whether we want to or not, we have to put priority on that business which is transferred from Copy-Co Japan.

For such managers an overseas posting was another phase in their movement through specialist functions, building upon their existing technical and systems expertise. As we have seen, their preparation for an overseas posting often appeared quite limited, though some had been involved in shorter 'business trips' to work for brief periods at a foreign subsidiary. Younger British managers and engineers seemed to take a pride in trying to 'Anglicise' these younger dispatched Japanese managers—exposing them to the 'hot spots' of Birmingham being one such predilection. However, several British managers also commented on the superficial nature of changes in their social behaviour, even when they appeared to break the mould of 'conformity'. Meanwhile, the Japanese managers themselves often remarked on the difficulties they continued to have in interpreting the language and social cues of locals in the workplace. A characteristic comment was that 'it's very difficult for me with local people, because I don't understand their feelings completely, therefore I already give to local managers responsibility [for people management]'.

These managers usually remained in close touch with specialist colleagues back in Japan, through a combination of e-mail, faxes, phone calls and occasional visits, liaising particularly with the factory or section with the most relevant experience. Thus one reported that 'I communicate with them every day when it's necessary, for example when the new product starts up . . . e-mail, telephone is used every day'. However, they also faced the challenge of tailoring Japanese expertise and guidance to suit the distinctive requirements of the subsidiary. As we have seen in the case-studies, both the contrasting scales of production operations and the differing orientations of Japanese and British workers were important in this context. In the latter respect these junior Japanese managers often had preconceptions about the United Kingdom but they also revised their opinions in the light of their growing experience in the British plant. On the one hand this often involved jettisoning established prejudices, such as the supposed reluctance of British workers to work overtime, but on the other hand it nurtured fresh stereotypes. For example, one such manager told us that when he arrived he was convinced that better communications would minimize labour turnover, but he eventually decided that such turnover was 'natural' in the United Kingdom.

The expectation of most of these younger managers was to return to Japan for the next phase of their management career, though where they would be moved to generally remained unclear. In this connection several commented on the distinctive character of their experience of working overseas in terms of their wider and more integrated responsibilities in a smaller workplace compared with the narrower specialist roles of their counterparts back home. For example, a Part-Co manager in his early thirties contrasted the wider but more shallow knowledge he had developed at the British plant with the narrower but deeper expertise he would be expected to apply on his return to Japan. A similarly aged Copy-Co manager positively enthused about the wide overview he had gained from his relatively junior position within the Business Planning department, commenting that his vision oscillated between that of an operator and an MD. However, he was uncertain whether he would be able to build on this when he returned home:

> Talking about the job in Japan, it's very difficult because I'm covering so large a responsibility, so large an area here, and in Japan, because the company is so big, there is no section which has a function like I have.

Thus for junior staff a period working overseas could be part of the wider process of career development and progression, but there was little sign that the distinctiveness of this experience had been actively integrated into the management of career progression at this level.

However, it was evident from the biographies of several of our informants that the larger companies were increasingly able to draw upon a cadre of managers with some international experience in manning their overseas operations. It was not uncommon for experienced managers to have worked at an overseas factory for several months 'on a business trip basis' before coming to the United Kingdom, while several middle-ranking managers had more substantial experience at foreign subsidiaries. One reported that in a career spanning thirty years he had worked at an American plant for five years and had returned to Japan for another five years before his current job in Telford. The normal expectation at all levels was for a tour of about five years. In the British context this reflected not only parent company policies but also taxation and contractual arrangements for expatriate staff, as they generally remained employees of the parent company with exemption from British national insurance contributions for this period. Very few of our Japanese informants expected to stay longer than this, though some felt that a longer stay would suit their families who had settled with them. Again the MD at Assembly-Co was the exception who proved the rule: his plans to stay matched his earlier experience of working in subcontracting and his non-participation in an extended organizational career.

The other senior and experienced middle managers remained oriented to resuming their careers in Japan, though they were often uncertain about what this would involve. Thus a man who had worked his way up from operator to manufacturing manager at Copy-Co reported that he would be returning:

> Maybe next year, but I have no idea [where I'm going]. Of course I can request, but I don't know if they accept this or if they have a job for me.... I'm here a General Manager,... I've already passed General Manager test in Japan, so I [should] get similar position when I get back to Japan, I hope so [laughter] but I don't know.

At the same time there was a concern that being based overseas made it more difficult to sustain contact networks and awareness of developments in Japan. A British manager at Part-Co drew on conversations with his Japanese counterparts to highlight such anxieties:

> Things are probably moving maybe quicker back in Japan, so if they go any longer than that [five years], when they go back they're just so far behind that it's very hard to catch up, certainly to go back and do some sort of managing over a department that has now advanced beyond what he was expecting.

Meanwhile, the future scope for building careers by gaining international experience, or even moving between overseas operations, will remain constrained by the degree to which these firms sustain, expand or contract their international operations.

THE SOCIAL FORMATION OF BRITISH MANAGERS AND THEIR RECRUITMENT BY JAPANESE SUBSIDIARIES

The deployment of expatriate Japanese managers to overseas sites is a relatively expensive business, and thus in terms of cost alone there are attractions to the recruitment of local managers. However, other considerations may outweigh such costs. First, Japanese managers are already familiar with company products and procedures, they have appropriate expertise without major investments in training, though limitations in communicating with a local workforce, developing language skills and appreciating the peculiarities of local social cues may shift the balance of advantage. Second, Japanese and local managers tend to have contrasting orientations to the firm and the labour market, which have implications for the patterns of control exercised by senior managers and the forms of commitment displayed by workplace management. This reflects the contrasting patterns of firm-specific career progression in Japan and the (growing) importance of movement between employers in building management careers in the United Kingdom.

Thus locally recruited managers may be expected to have lower levels of commitment to the Japanese firm, both because their access to the internal labour market is likely to be truncated and because their market opportunities are likely to be enhanced. The Japanese managers we interviewed frequently lamented not only the turnover of factory workers but also the difficulty of recruiting and retaining managers and specialists. From this vantage point Japanese expatriate staff represent a secure management resource, while top managers have fewer levers over local managers, who are likely to be harder to control, retain and manage. The company may increase wages, but though this was contemplated by some middle managers it rarely found favour with senior management. For example, when engineering managers at Copy-Co faced shortages of staff they were allowed to pay overtime for longer hours to help to retain people, but they were not permitted to increase salaries. In this context the firms tended to recruit local managers with less labour market leverage, either older managers who had experienced job insecurity or younger, less qualified staff who could be rewarded through internal promotion.

As this suggests, the British managers and specialists who worked in our case-study factories had a variety of backgrounds that in different ways reflected the complex and changing character of the social formation of management in Britain over recent decades. For senior and middle managers university study was rare, while the dominant pattern, whether in production, quality assurance, purchasing, finance, or personnel, was accruing vocational and professional qualifications through part-time study over a number of years (see also Storey et al. 1997: 68–72). The most common pattern among older managers was craft apprenticeship followed by multiple moves between employers, accumulating supervisory and management experience, and sometimes qualifications, in a varied range of specialisms. The most senior British managers in the large firms were exceptional in having university degrees, and one was unusual in having developed his previous career wholly within one leading international firm, a pharmaceuticals company with whom he had completed a Ph.D.

Some of the other managers in our sample had also worked for a substantial period for leading British companies, but most had also experienced a number of job moves, partly as a route to career advancement but partly driven by worries about job security or actual redundancies. Quite typical were the following career histories which underline the importance of practical experience and relatively open access into manufacturing management. The first was recounted by a senior manager at Copy-Co:

> I started as a Craft Apprentice. I did a typical 12-month off-the-job and another two years on-the-job training. I went into the Quality Control Department.... I moved round in the Quality Department. I was promoted to Quality Control Supervisor for a small group of people on two shifts and progressed from there basically through the Production area. I was promoted to a Production Superintendent, which was looking after a group of foremen for a month. The position changed, we got rid of all the foremen, got rid of all the superintendents and went to supervisors. From then I spent my last 12 months as a Production Manager within the Company, and then I was made redundant and I came here.

The second summarized the experience of a senior manager at Part-Co:

> At twenty-five, having served my apprenticeship and got a little experience under my belt I looked to move. I joined [company name] as a work study engineer. I acted in that capacity for about five years, and then started in the personnel department. Well I was termed at that stage deputy personnel manager. But over a period of time then my company was taken over and I was moved as a personnel manager to [another] company, and as a consequence stayed with those until ... four or five years ago when I transferred here. It was as a consequence of the company closing down, they closed the company down and transferred the production ... to a plant in Scotland. I was made redundant. In truth I've never been unemployed, so I count myself very fortunate in that, and particularly with the last move [to Part-Co]. Because at that stage I was 48 years of age and jobs within the personnel function were few and far between, because of basically the recession within the manufacturing industry that occurred in the 1980s.

These work histories capture the range of experience that such managers had gained in pursuing career advancement, moving both within and between firms.

As the first example suggests, some careers had developed within large, well-established firms in a way that had echoes of Japanese company careers. Furthermore, experience in these firms often remained a significant and relatively positive point of reference for such managers, though this example suggests that progression within such an organization could still be rather haphazard. More often, though, management careers were built through movement between companies, through open labour markets. One of the older managers had worked for five firms during his earlier career, averaging five years tenure with each, and he regarded all these moves as deliberate 'career moves'. As these work histories suggest, however, recession and restructuring meant that many managers had also made moves to escape growing insecurity or even as a result of actual redundancy. For example, one manager recalled that 'there were redundancies [at his existing firm] and business was poor and I thought it was a matter of time before they actually closed'. Another reported that, by the time he was offered a job at Copy-Co, 'the company I'd worked for had gone under and was in receivership and we knew we were all going to be made redundant'. Such a combination of chosen and constrained moves had nurtured more of a commitment to sector, profession, and geographical location among these British managers, compared with the company orientation of the Japanese expatriate managers (see also Storey et al. 1997: 66–93), though it had also underlined the potential insecurities involved.

This, then, was the context in which the new Japanese inward-investors sought to recruit British managers, starting with the most senior and moving quite rapidly through the ranks. The Telford Development Corporation (TDC) played a major role in recruiting the early senior staff, in cooperation with top Japanese managers. British managers often saw the role of the TDC as quite positive: providing the necessary resources and advice were seen as supportive of appropriate selection procedures, and also as an incentive for firms to invest in Telford. Nevertheless, there were also some criticisms of what, in retrospect, were seen as unsuitable appointments, perhaps made because particular candidates were readily available because of redundancy. Later, management recruitment was taken in-house, but remained fairly elaborate in the large firms. British managers tended to filter and recommend applicants for management jobs, but senior Japanese managers usually retained at least a formal role in the final interview. However, Japanese managers used to internal corporate careers remained somewhat wary of British managers recruited in mid-career. As one remarked:

> The people who enter Japanese companies in Japan after graduation from junior high school don't have any skills and stay in the company for 6 or 8 years [and] become a very skilled worker; and usually some of them make manager in the future. But here it is different. A manager is [a] manager from the start.

Indeed, among Japanese managers there remained a preference for recruiting younger specialists where possible, as people who could be groomed as future managers (and were also less expensive in terms of salaries). This echoed the findings of Kenney and Florida (1995: 798), who found that Japanese managers were keen to recruit young managers who were more likely to embrace Japanese methods and 'were not "polluted" by American management ideology and techniques'.

BRITISH MANAGEMENT ORIENTATIONS AND ENCOUNTERS WITH JAPANESE MANAGEMENT

In comparing their past careers and their contemporary situations experienced British managers drew out a number of themes which underlined both the character of their managerial formation and the distinctiveness of their new position. An obvious theme concerned the increasing precariousness of earlier jobs compared with the apparent security of their new employment. In this respect their biographies were marked by the contraction and near continuous rationalization of the British manufacturing sector, especially during the 1980s, characterized by redundancies, takeovers and the reduction of management hierarchies. Even if managers stayed in the same workplace the process of takeovers and rationalizations could mean experiencing several different ownerships and styles of management (Marginson 1994). Thus one manager noted of his old firm that 'in the seventeen years I worked there I think for the last ten years we had redundancies every year', and also that 'there were six takeovers while I was there. It looks as though I've worked for six different companies on my c.v. but it's the same company, but I think a different direction every time it was taken over.'

Another feature of these career narratives, drawn out most explicitly by one of the Copy-Co managers who only just escaped redundancy, was the importance of practical but unsystematized experience in building a career in the engineering sector in Britain. In moving from toolmaker to development engineer and production manager, he saw himself as developing 'not [as] a manager of systems, but a manager of people, and very practical hands-on, which in that metal bashing industry was the right thing'. When the widespread experience of the crises of British manufacturing was combined with a sense of the pragmatic but ad hoc and limited character of much British management expertise, this opened up particular possibilities for a positive appreciation of Japanese management systems among experienced British engineers. Furthermore, this interest was often reinforced by their awareness of the growing professional debate about new forms of management and work organization in this period, in which Japanese models and exemplars played a prominent role. It will be evident from our case-studies, however, that the terms in which these managers actually engaged with the philosophies and practices espoused by Japanese managers were quite complex and equivocal, and the character of these responses will be analysed more fully later in this chapter.

Many of the younger British managers recruited by our case-study firms had followed analogous but less extended career trajectories, starting with a craft apprenticeship (or for the small number of women, secretarial training) and moving between employers. A few of the youngest managers and specialists had gained a degree before starting work. Even in the latter case, however, their engineering qualifications were often seen as of limited relevance to the work they were engaged in once recruited by their current employer. Thus one remarked that 'from what I learnt at university I don't think there's anything [specific] I use within my job, and so everything I've learnt that I use here, I've learnt here'. In either case, however, they tended to be less steeped in British management assumptions and particularly attracted by the systematic approach of Japanese managers in such areas as project planning, process design and, especially, QC.

While these younger managers had less experience of different employers than many of their older counterparts, they were very aware of contrasting routes of career development in Britain, involving progression within the firm's internal labour market or movement between companies. One commented that:

> There's always two ways to advance your career. One is you can hop around and change jobs and what not and hopefully achieve your target that way, and the other way is to stay within one organization and try and progress.

He had enjoyed advancement at Part-Co so he felt that staying with the firm was attractive:

> My theory was I'll stay with the company as long as I'm learning and I'm happy with the environment, and as long as I feel I've got a future in the company. Clearly I joined as an engineer, I was progressed through senior engineer to assistant manager within a period of four years.

Thus, unlike his Japanese counterparts, he *chose* to stay because of the current attractions of internal promotion. First, he contrasted this with the obstacles to internal promotion in what he called 'typical British industry' where 'it's very difficult to progress because there's always somebody there ahead of you'. This involved an implicit contrast between static or shrinking management hierarchies in British firms and growth and movement within an expanding inward investor. Second, he believed that staying with Part-Co actually improved his ultimate marketability, illustrating this with reference to several fellow managers who had left to work for competitor firms:

> Part-Co is growing so quickly and it's so popular and the training you get is very good, so when an external company looks at Part-Co they know that the engineer they're going to get has got a load of experience or has gained some very valuable experience. So consequently in some cases I guess they're willing to pay over the odds.

However, these remarks perhaps overemphasize the immediacy of the trade-offs in the thinking of such managers. First, some were more sceptical about enhanced marketability in the climate of the times, making reference to past colleagues who had moved but had then been disappointed at their lack of progress in their new firms. Second, others gave a stronger emphasis to the attractions of their current job:

> Because of the variation in my job at the moment it's not too bad, I've got room for development and I'm doing different things, plus after being in the same job for 13 years I'm not a job hopper, I've come into an environment that's very stable.

Thus concern for stability combined with the possibilities of career development encouraged younger managers to stay with the firm.

It was against this background of wider career possibilities and constraints—often experienced directly during the decline and restructuring of British manufacturing but also experienced vicariously through the experience of past colleagues—that both older and younger British managers sought to build their careers within the transplant firms. At the same time it is important to emphasize that the orientations and responses of these managers continued to develop in ways that were also influenced by developments within their own organizations. Much of the character of these developments, including similarities and differences between the different firms, will be evident from our earlier case-study accounts, and will not be reviewed again here. However, we wish to take one example, namely British management visits to Japan, to underline both the continuing accumulation of distinctive forms of management experience by British managers working in these firms, and the rather varied character of such personal career development.

One of the potentially formative influences for British managers was visiting parent company factories in Japan. We have seen that this took a variety of different forms. It could be just a brief trip characterized by an itinerary of social and organizational meetings. Thus a senior manager at Copy-Co reported that 'I have only been to Japan once and that was an ambassadorial duty to go and meet the President of the company and shake hands'. Often, however, it meant direct training and sometimes substantial involvement in production activities. Understandably, such extended visits made the most lasting impressions on British managers. For example, a production engineer from Part-Co recalled that:

> I started with the company on the Monday and I was off to Japan on the Friday. . . . So I spent seven weeks intensive training. . . . And the main idea was to actually look at how things were done over there. Look at, understand the individual process and actually get to know the product, and how it's actually put together, and what sort of on-stream problems you could have. And then I was also trained in terms of [the] actual project, how to manage the project and actually bring the equipment on-stream.

At the same time they could also alter the balance of expertise between British and Japanese staff, as another Part-Co engineer suggested:

> The [new process] line was something brand new for our [Japanese] manager and our coordinator, they had never dealt with these [products] before, so consequently that was why I'd gone to Japan. I've been trained in all that, so normally, if there's a problem... it comes to me. To be handed that responsibility is, I suppose, quite flattering really.

Furthermore, as we saw in the case study of Copy-Co, such visits were central not only to the transfer but also the modification of production processes as subsidiaries took on new product lines.

Occasionally, such visits assumed a more strategic importance, both for the firm and the individual. A senior manager from one of the smaller firms, PCB-Co, recollected that:

> I've been to Japan twice. In the early days, initially, anybody in a sort of supervisor or manager role would go to Japan for up to four weeks. But after the initial problems we had here... in fact four weeks was not enough to learn the real true quality aspects, the manufacturing aspects and the human aspects and how to deal with Japanese customs. Four weeks wasn't enough. And from the early problems we had they decided to send the next person for three months [chuckle] and that ended up being me. So I went for three months initially to Japan.... I was on my own, so it was sort of thrown very much in at the deep end.

This was a formative experience because it provided an opportunity for close observation of production practices in Japanese firms. On this basis he developed an enthusiasm for Japanese manufacturing methods, but also critical insights into gaps between rhetoric and reality that informed his role in mediating between Japanese advisers and British staff. His visits were also important for two other reasons. First, they established a link with a Japanese mentor that was of continuing significance, especially when the mentor himself was seconded to the British subsidiary. Second, one of these trips involved visits to factories in Japan and China that were direct competitors with the British operation, and this again informed his tactics in the factory. Finally, however, we should recognize that some visits to Japan failed to provide the experience and insights that the visitor had hoped for. This was particularly evident in the comments by a senior manager at Assembly-Co:

> They [large customer firms] don't let you tour round their factories. You can see subcontractors, the customer will instruct the subcontractors (laughter) 'they are going to come and see you', but it is unusual for [the parent company's] customers to allow you to go round their factory. They are quite secretive, really... going on a trip like that, you'd think that everything would be scheduled down and this is what you are going to do. Not really, no... it's all very informal, it's really an exercise of saying 'hallo', so they know who you are, to phone them up. It's a good thing but in effect you don't actually learn a lot from it. You only pick up what you can.

Thus the limited leverage arising from his position as a manager of a subcontract operation, combined with a pattern of rather fleeting and informal contacts, curtailed his access to relevant workplaces and production processes and, for him, the value of his visit.

Our discussion so far has concentrated on British managers with an engineering background, though some then moved across into other functions. It is widely recognized that in British firms finance and marketing executives have tended to dominate the higher reaches of management, even in manufacturing. Furthermore, in the mid-1990s, 20 per cent of all British graduates entered accountancy, while Britain had more accountants than the whole of the rest of Europe (Hantrais and Walters 1994). There was, however, little scope for such specialisms to play a dominant role in the management of our larger Japanese manufacturing subsidiaries. The business planning function involved almost exclusively Japanese staff, while British finance managers were given a relatively narrow remit and marketing was often the prerogative of a separate sales company. Senior managers with a professional training in accountancy were more conspicuous in the small subcontractors, as in the absence of an elaborate planning office they came to combine the roles of 'financial controller', senior administrator and potentially 'company secretary'. Nevertheless, in each case senior production managers were more powerful than these administrators, though the relationships among the small teams of managers were also markedly different from firm to firm.

THE BRITISH CLAIM TO EXPERTISE IN MANAGING BRITISH WORKERS

Against this background we can now explore the extent to which these British managers responded in similar or distinctive ways. It is evident that they occupied a variety of distinctive positions in these firms. In particular we may compare older managers with wider experience of British management and younger recruits with little such experience, and we can compare those involved in technical and engineering functions with those involved in personnel or administrative activities. At the same time it is evident from our case-studies that the strategies and structures of management differ in quite substantial ways across the enterprises. Thus the responses of British managers will have been coloured in important ways by their distinctive career trajectories and experiences before joining a Japanese subsidiary, but they will also have been influenced by developments within their specific enterprise.

As will be evident from our case-studies, there was one ubiquitous theme in the discourses of British managers across specialisms and enterprises, namely the importance of British management expertise in addressing the problems of managing a British labour force. Of course, personnel management and industrial relations have generally been subordinate functions within corporate management in British firms. Moreover, despite increasing professionalization, it has remained relatively easy for managers to move into personnel work from other specialisms during their careers. Nevertheless, personnel management became of increasing importance at workplace level from the 1950s to 1970s, as tighter labour markets and then stronger workplace trade unionism gave these functions increasing leverage within management (Blyton and Turnball 2004: 111–21). More recently, however, the role of personnel specialists within management has became more actively contested and in turn defended, as both senior managers and line managers have made increasing claims over the territory of 'human resource management' (Bacon 2003).

Against this background one of the striking features of the role and rhetoric of British managers in our Telford case-studies was the emphasis they placed on their pivotal role in managing British labour. This was particularly true of those managers who had primarily administrative and/or personnel responsibilities, but it was also an important aspect of the specific expertise claimed by factory and production managers, especially those with significant experience of management in British factories. One aspect of this argument was that Japanese managers arrived with assumptions about personnel management that were inappropriate for British conditions. An obvious example concerned the common Japanese preference for the recruitment of young, inexperienced workers, particularly evident in the efforts of British managers to persuade Japanese managers to accept changes in the basis of recruitment at Copy-Co. A related example was the initial commitment of Japanese managers at Part-Co to the rigid use of a measure of previous job moves as an indicator of likely worker commitment, when this ignored age and the state of the local labour market.

Sometimes such arguments were supported by suggestions that differences of culture and problems of language had made it difficult for Japanese managers to negotiate the nuances of shop-floor relations. A senior Copy-Co manager evoked a picture of past difficulties based on such a diagnosis:

> We had riots among people, we had people crying, we had people doing all sort of things. They [Japanese managers with reservations about current policies] can't remember that.... The Japanese view is, you don't see anything in relations skills because of the culture, you don't have to be sensitive to people. [That] doesn't work in this culture.

In turn this could be portrayed as the basis for an ill-judged imposition of discipline (banning radios at PCB-Co or attempts to enforce the uniform regulations at Copy-Co) or conversely an inappropriate relaxation of rules (the relaxed 'indulgency' relations that prevailed at one time at PCB-Co or on the night-shifts at Copy-Co). Often British managers also deployed their view of the greater discipline and commitment of Japanese workers (sometimes citing their own experiences in visits to Japan) to suggest that this explained why Japanese managers were ill-equipped to cope with a more sceptical and instrumental British workforce. A production manager at PCB-Co drew these features together in extreme terms:

> The point I'm trying to make is, in fact I think generally because of this self-discipline [among Japanese workers] you don't tend to need the same management techniques as you would in a Western country where there are more individuals. ... If they've got problems with the human side I have to deal with it, because the Japanese, they just don't, they can't. And I've found the[ir] human man-management appalling, it really is appalling.... They don't understand the British person, how they tick and how they think and how they react. They can't understand why you make the same mistake twice. In Japan that doesn't happen.

A more specific illustration involved the need to persuade Japanese managers at Copy-Co that British workers were unlikely to commit themselves to solving quality problems in their own time, so QCCs would have to be run during paid time.

At the same time British managers often suggested that the problems posed by the Telford labour market were more challenging than those that they themselves had experienced elsewhere. This part of the shared discourse of British managers was articulated in typical fashion by experienced managers at Part-Co (but for comparable comments see also Chapters 7, 8, and 11). Thus one contrasted Telford with his earlier experience in the nearby conurbation—'my experience has always been within the Black Country area, Wolverhampton, and it's a different experience [in Telford], a totally different experience'—while another drew out the likely implications for Japanese managers:

> I found Telford a difficult place and I worked fifty miles away. Coming from Japan must have been horrendous. When we started in the early days it was almost an inquisition [when someone left] ... they were not used to the fact that people made their own decisions and left companies of their own volition.

This suggested that Japanese managers would understandably face greater difficulties in managing what British Managers saw as a particularly problematical labour force. In turn this placed British management expertise at a particular premium. At the same time it suggested that even such expertise would not yield easy answers, but rather warranted a continuing and pragmatic search for more effective policies. This was the broad approach that British managers tended to adopt as they engaged in debate among themselves and with Japanese managers in each of the Telford factories. However, as we have seen, the ways in which such debate developed were nevertheless rather different.

MANAGING LABOUR AS A PIVOTAL FUNCTION FOR BRITISH MANAGEMENT: DIFFERENT PERMUTATIONS IN DIFFERENT FACTORIES

At Assembly-Co British managers were given responsibility for both personnel policy and production management from the start, while the Japanese MD concentrated on customer relations and liaison with Japan. This meant that there was little need to articulate these arguments to alter personnel policy. In the words of a Senior British Manager:

> Here [the Japanese presence is] one man and his dog, and really, the UK management, it was much easier for us to influence what was going on than it would ever be for the UK managers, even the senior UK managers, in [large company] . . . In terms of management style, the way the company is run, the day-to-day decisions that we make about the people in particular, most of it wouldn't be referred back to the MD. If it is, I've never known him disagree. He's very receptive and he's very open to what's going on.

This, then, was the context in which the Senior British Managers worked closely together to develop their own distinctive solutions to problems of labour recruitment and labour discipline at the factory. However, it should be added that this relative autonomy was not interpreted in quite the same way by the main British protagonists. A Manager with direct responsibility for personnel policy emphasized the influence that they wielded in this sphere through a combination of delegation and active debate (and sometimes disagreement) with the Japanese MD. Meanwhile, a senior British production manager at the factory recognized the advantages of their relative autonomy, but was more critical of the strategic vacuum within which he felt they operated, which inhibited meaningful debate ('[we] don't know what the parent company wants to achieve, apart from a target . . . you ask the main man [for guidance] and he'll say "not my problem, I've said yes, go and do it" ').

By comparison the founding Japanese managers at Copy-Co had clearly started with a strong influence on personnel policy. However, Chapter 7 showed that British managers had been relatively successful in using arguments about their expertise in labour management to develop their influence over policies in the workplace. First, they had persuaded specific Japanese managers to alter specific elements of personnel policy, and later they had developed an alliance with senior Japanese managers that carried this case into the reorganization of supervision and other aspects of work relations. At the same time British managers had come to appreciate some of the advantages of a job security policy for permanent staff, despite significant initial scepticism. Thus in this case there had been a process of debate and mutual learning through which British managers had gained a more central role in company policymaking, primarily on the basis of their competence in 'person management'.

There are, however, two important reservations that we should make to this picture of a benign process of alliance formation and organizational learning. The first is that this process involved confrontations and leverage as well as debate. Thus, at one critical juncture, a senior British manager sought to establish his authority in relation to a Japanese top manager by refusing to facilitate the implementation of a policy on individual employee assessments which he claimed was 'likely to cause a riot on the shop-floor'. He refused to sell the idea to other British managers 'because I felt so deeply about this and I could not convince the managers [of] something I felt so deeply against'. However, the Japanese manager backed down on this proposal and the British protagonist judged that 'I think he then realized that anything was open to discussion and there was give and take'. The second reservation, which will be evident from the narrative in Chapter 7, is that the policies championed by the British managers themselves raised difficulties on the shop-floor. In turn, such unresolved problems fed into continuing reservations among Japanese staff, who questioned such features as the shift away from promotion of team leaders through internal job ladders to recruitment from the external labour market.

The later arrival of Part-Co, and their discussions with managers in established companies like Copy-Co, helped them to avoid some of the initial problems that earlier companies had experienced as a consequence of the implementation of personnel policies by Japanese staff. There was still scope for difficulties, misunderstandings, and arguments, as the example of the index of job changes suggests, while the rapid growth of the factory continued to exacerbate problems of recruitment and retention. However, as we saw in Chapter 7, a top British manager emphasized that from the start British managers were given the major role in formulating personnel policy:

> I was pleasantly surprised by the degree of autonomy we were given . . . and to be fair to the Japanese they did come in with an open mind.

Furthermore, he saw this as learning from the experience of other firms in the cluster:

> They invariably have a local personnel person in from the start, basically because the realization is that they cannot set realistic terms and conditions that are based on experiences outside the UK . . . so in general my task was to set the agenda.

At Part-Co, then, British managers did not have to deploy an argument about the distinctive features of the British and local labour market to establish their remit in dealing with personnel issues, because this case was already broadly accepted.

However, the implications of this remit remained problematical, both because of the range of constraints surrounding this autonomy and because of the apparent intractability of some of the labour management problems. The constraints within which British managers developed their personnel policies included the subordinate position of personnel policy in relation to a range of Japanese-dominated policy arenas, the implications of a commitment to 'cluster norms' for policymaking, and the propensity of experienced Japanese managers to look to American experience for policy guidelines. Taking the last of these first, one of the supports for a rapid delegation of personnel responsibility to British managers was the international experience of leading Japanese managers. However, a corollary was their inclination to import American policies instead of Japanese ones, as exemplified by the form of the consultation machinery. Consultation with other Japanese companies in the locality was also paradoxical in its implications, as it provided a warrant for learning lessons about localization from other firms, but it also tied Part-Co to cluster wage norms that British managers judged inappropriate for their distinctive operations. Finally, the observation of a senior British manager, that localization of management was a very partial process, deserves reiteration:

> The engineering side, the purchasing side, the system side, they are very much done by Part-Co in Japan . . . so I would say [personnel] were the only function probably in the company that were given reasonable freedom to do things the British way, but influenced by Japan.

Thus Japanese managers continued to dominate all other aspects of policymaking, while personnel policy remained quite narrowly defined and subordinated to broader strategic policies.

Finally, at PCB-Co British managers also deployed the argument that Japanese managers lacked skills in person management and should leave this to British managers, as the colourful comment of a production manager quoted earlier illustrates. However, in their case this argument had not been even partially resolved through an agreed division of labour or alliance of the sorts found in our other cases. Instead it remained a continuing source of tension and even conflict between British and Japanese managers, and also among British managers themselves. The British protagonists in post at the time of our research shared a common account of the failings of initial personnel and production policies in the factory. In this account a powerful alliance between a Japanese engineering manager and a well-qualified but relatively inexperienced British production manager marginalized other British managers but presided over chaos on the shop-floor, as the coordination of production failed, labour discipline was eroded and production targets were missed. In this account the Japanese manager was criticized because:

> There was just no discipline, nobody was brought into line... so we started hinting quite strongly that it was very difficult for a Japanese person to control British people, he's got far too much to do anyway, and he's an engineering manager not a production manager.

Meanwhile, the British manager was castigated because

> There's nothing worse than having somebody who talks a good story but doesn't really know what he's talking about, because the members on the line they're not stupid and they'll pick it up very quickly.

Thus in each case theoretical expertise was counterposed to practical sense and on this basis the remaining British managers eventually persuaded the Japanese MD to demote both of these men and themselves gained more leverage over factory policies.

However, as we saw in Chapter 8, this did not provide the basis for a coherent coalition of senior managers, partly because of the contrasting roles of the two key British figures, one as company secretary and the other as senior production manager. The production manager was able to build upon his links with the new Japanese MD to consolidate his influence in production and set the tone for managing workers on a day-to-day basis. At the same time he acknowledged that the legacy of the earlier years was 'a big lack of confidence between Japanese hierarchy and the British management style', from which he was only partially exempt. He also felt that an essential focus on manufacturing was being compromised by departmental divisions, not only between administration and production but also between QC and production: 'they're like the Gods, quality control, they are quality control aren't they, and you're production'. Thus what he appeared to look for from other 'departments' was a willing subordination to the imperatives of production and delivery as he interpreted them, and as we saw in the case study this precipitated continuing tensions with quality staff in particular.

In contrast, however, the senior administrator felt thoroughly marginalized and was sharply critical of Japanese management:

> I don't believe in operating like the traditional accountant in his nice office, you know, insulated from all the happenings of the world. We actually want to be involved and participate, we don't just want to be a service to them. We want to understand what's going on and we want to be involved in the decision-making. But if people don't want [us] to be involved we're stuck out on a limb anyway,... if people chose to isolate us we're isolated. Because after a while you just get to the stage where there's no point in interfering. You don't get any thanks for interfering.

Furthermore, he felt that the resulting conflicts were grounded in the failure of Japanese managers to appreciate his contribution to the firm:

> He [the MD] actively would like to lose me, because I'm the highest-paid person here, British-wise. And he thinks that you can break down admin jobs

> into clerks' jobs, which you can to a certain extent, but only to a certain extent. . . . So I think when they're talking about admin in Japan they're talking about a very different kettle of fish to the function that we're fulfilling here.

This meant that the obvious advocate of a somewhat more systematic personnel policy remained on the sidelines and deeply disgruntled, while the British production manager pursued the tactics of personalized pressure and encouragement of workers common to many small enterprises. In consequence he was seen by the administrator as highly capable but also, as we saw in Chapter 8, 'dangerous' if, backed by his Japanese superiors, he were to overstep the mark. Distinctive career orientations and personalities fed into and were reinforced by these conflicts between the various Japanese and British managers at PCB-Co. However, the precariousness of the subcontracting operations performed by this firm (and the limited scope for escaping from such precariousness by implementing refinements in either production arrangements or personnel policies) certainly fuelled these antagonisms.

In this section we have suggested that most British managers shared broadly similar views on the value of British management expertise in managing British workers. These views underpinned their arguments for a central role within the management of each enterprise, both as individuals and as collectivities. It suited British managers to highlight the problems posed by British workers, and the failures of Japanese managers in coping with these problems, as this gave them a legitimate claim to manage what they knew best. It therefore provided a basis to limit the influence of Japanese management and increase their own power, though as we have seen there were significant differences in the extent to which these claims were successful.

The wide currency of such arguments did not mean that there were no differences of opinion on these matters, especially when it came to the appraisal of specific policy options. For example, British managers at Copy-Co and PCB-Co made substantial use of temporary workers supplied by Temping Agencies, though with some reservations, while British managers at Assembly-Co and Part-Co were more sceptical, even though Part-Co had found it necessary to employ some temps. Furthermore, younger British managers, in particular, were often sympathetic to the Japanese emphasis on internal development and promotion, while older managers were often more sceptical and inclined to look to outside recruitment. Nevertheless, these differences represented variations around a dominant and widely shared theme, which served as a major focus of mobilization and source of leverage in relations between British and Japanese managers.

One final comment in this regard concerns the role of women as specialists or managers in our case-study companies. The small number of women who were employed at these levels almost all worked in personnel, an area that has been increasingly feminized in many areas of British employment in recent years. However, the senior administrator at Assembly-Co, who dealt with a wider remit including personnel, was also a woman. She was the most senior woman we met and worked in the firm with the most limited Japanese presence. The promotion of a woman as personnel manager at Copy-Co marked the consolidation of the localization policy by the alliance of British and Japanese senior managers, and had successfully challenged existing expectations within the cluster of Japanese firms. At Part-Co, however, the younger women who played an active role in personnel administration at the time of our research remained outside the ranks of management, and some felt that this pattern would be difficult to break. One remarked that 'I was once told that you couldn't become an assistant manager unless you are thirty, although we've got a twenty-eight-year-old male [assistant manager].' Thus our evidence suggests that Japanese managers have found it hard to accept women managers in these roles. However, the emphasis of British managers on the centrality of British expertise in personnel matters has provided some qualified openings for women, and it was in this context that they were able to deploy their professional expertise.

THE ENGAGEMENT OF BRITISH MANAGERS WITH JAPANESE TECHNICAL AND SYSTEMS EXPERTISE

We now turn to a discussion of British management responses to claims for Japanese pre-eminence in the organization of production systems and technical expertise. British managers were certainly influenced by the powerful claims that were made for the efficiency of such Japanese systems in wider management debate, as well as within their own enterprises. They were aware that the distinctive conditions of subsidiary operations, involving such features as length of production runs, levels of automation, workers' attitudes and patterns of technical support, necessarily raised questions about the interpretation and implementation of Japanese production models. However, there were quite marked differences in the ways in which British managers responded to these circumstances, especially between younger and older managers. It will also be evident from our case-study accounts that there was a dynamic and evolving character to these responses as innovations were undertaken and reflected on within specific firms and as managers developed in their own careers. With these caveats in mind it is possible to map a spectrum of British management attitudes ranging from real enthusiasm and advocacy to sustained scepticism coupled with the appropriation of any valued features as 'just common sense'.

The most positive responses tended to come from the younger specialists and managers who had joined a Japanese firm quite early in their careers and had developed much of their technical expertise under expatriate Japanese management tutelage. This was especially the case for those with opportunities to broaden their expertise and progress within internal job ladders, features that were especially characteristic of the larger firms in their phases of expansion (see the earlier comments on the advantages of staying with such a firm, rather than moving on). Like some of the Japanese managers these people were also aware that, by comparison with both Japanese parent factories and many British establishments, their jobs required the development of a broad and varied expertise, echoing the point made by younger Japanese managers. Thus a Part-Co specialist commented that in Japan 'a new product will be split between different people, here I do everything, I do the lot for that particular project', while an assistant manager reported that 'the job we handle here is very, very wide and it's very varied'.

In this context younger managers whose main professional formation was within the transplants were often converts to the promise of the 'Japanization' of British manufacturing and champions of Japanese management practices, forming alliances with Japanese managers against more sceptical British senior managers. When language barriers and formal hierarchies were overcome the expertise of such mentors was very highly valued. For example, an assistant manager at Part-Co remarked that:

> Our coordinator, he has gone through that nine-year training period, so he's an absolute genius. I don't know whether he's a genius or not but, in design, basically any question I ask him he can answer.

As we saw in the analysis of developments at Copy-Co in Chapter 7, some of these younger managers themselves adopted the language of 'mentors' and 'protégés' in characterizing their relationships with Japanese managers or advisors. At certain junctures they also saw themselves as guardians of good practice in the face of pressures to modify and compromise the principles and procedures they had learned.

Older British managers were often more ambivalent about Japanese approaches and procedures. Against the backdrop of the crises of British manufacturing they were often willing to recognize key strengths in Japanese management systems. In particular they were acutely aware of the reputation for poor quality amongst British firms, both from their employment experience and in dealing with British suppliers to Japanese companies. Thus one manager contrasted his experiences at a previous employer and at Copy-Co:

> Quality and dedication to quality improvement [is the hallmark] of Japanese companies . . . I can't remember a machine ever coming back. I can't remember in my other company [where he worked for 17 years] a lorry not coming back at least once a week. That's the difference.

Others expressed embarrassment at the poor quality of machinery and parts supplied by British firms during the equipment of the factory or during the localization of parts supplies:

> [During start-up] we had horrendous problems with suppliers of equipment, all English unfortunately. Horrendous! Unbelievable! The machines they delivered didn't work and they said they'd tested on their factory site. It was a nightmare.... In the metal-bashing industry, if a customer had got a problem, English companies go out to the customer and convince them it's *their* problem.

At the same time they usually had considerable experience and expertise of their own, and shared misgivings about the capacity of Japanese managers to manage the social relations of the workplace. Thus they were more often critical of Japanese management techniques and better able to draw on a reservoir of alternative ways of managing from their wider work experience. They tended to be more pragmatic than idealistic or ideological, and more likely to push for alternative policies that enhanced their own authority.

This meant that their discussions with Japanese managers were often more robust than those of their junior colleagues, though again much also depended on the extent to which Japanese staff were prepared to engage in debate. Thus an experienced British manager at Copy-Co, the person who was earlier quoted as 'a manager of people and very practical hands-on', drew a strong contrast between different Japanese superiors in characterizing what he had learned since joining the firm:

> So I knew really nothing of the science of management and really [Japanese manager] was my mentor, really taught me the way to approach problems, and we had many an argument. He would say 'you don't look at problems, you just fly by the seat of your pants'. He didn't use those words, but that was what he meant, 'you are just going along fire-fighting'. And he said 'no, you have got to sit down and start to look at problems and plan ahead.' I'd never done any planning. I'd never even seen a budget.... So he went through that with me, and really developed that side which the Japanese are really indoctrinated in... and really it was a very great training period for me, although it was particularly difficult because we still had to run a factory and I was learning, and I now realize at times they must have had severe doubts about whether this guy was going to make it.... And then I had another Japanese boss, who was more detached. In fact I didn't have a lot of in-put from him. With my previous boss, we had rows, we had heated discussions... because I would also criticize his management style. I said, 'You are too Japanese.... You are not bending anything; you are not taking any flavour on board and I can understand there is nothing we can teach you in that respect, but please learn to accept our culture.' And he did, whereas [later Japanese manager] he didn't. Very good chap, he knew all his stuff and he was on the ball in that sense, but he couldn't pass it on.

This nicely captures the way in which mentoring and mutual learning could develop even between older British and Japanese managers, but it also suggests that this was by no means guaranteed.

It also indicates that some British managers saw themselves as having a quite sophisticated and active, but by no means uncritical, engagement with Japanese approaches and systems. This was exemplified by the same informant, who celebrated the way in which Japanese approaches to problem-solving had been effectively disseminated through the organization but also argued that this had come to involve a more critical debate rather than obedient copying, with a move away from simple conformity to Japanese prescriptions. At Copy-Co, in particular, such an approach was codified by the senior British manager on the site by deploying the contemporary management language of 'ownership'. This led him to contrast areas where British managers had been successful in drawing upon and adapting Japanese ideas by thinking through their implications in their own terms, and less successful areas where Japanese managers had insisted that they be carried out in the Japanese way. For him this was a contrast between departments where the initiative came from the British staff and they had developed and had 'ownership' of their own procedures, and areas where methods had been imposed from 'outside' and the British were not committed to them, even when they shared common objectives. He also argued that some of the Japanese managers also recognized the effectiveness of such British 'ownership', reporting that in policy meetings one had commented that '"yes you've moved [forward] because you've done it your way, [but] over there [in another department] they either can't or they don't".'

It was perhaps significant that the key sponsors of this variant of localization included some of the few British managers who had also worked abroad and for major multinational firms. Such managers seemed most attached to a pragmatic and contingent view of production practices, and most sceptical of claims for distinctive national ways of managing, whether Japanese or otherwise. Thus their attitude was more calculative than directly hostile to Japanese methods, implying that there was 'nothing new in manufacturing' and everything is 'case by case' even in Japanese companies. For example, one manager who had worked for multinationals in both North America and Britain consistently emphasized the importance of a pragmatic approach and illustrated this in relation to long-term subcontracting:

> Every relationship we enter into we want to be long-term, but it's no good having a long-term relationship unless you're getting something out of it. . . . We've actually stopped business with [some] Japanese companies. Long-term relationships are okay, providing you benefit.

He also highlighted the persistent salience of the relationship between the head office and subsidiary as an influence on management conduct, whatever nationality was involved:

> I personally don't see any difference [in working for a Japanese company]. I've worked for multinationals and I've worked in the satellite office, which is what this [plant] is, and I've been in the head office, and the same things happen, there's no difference. I don't think there is any difference. When you work for a multinational it's the same, you get the same problems.

Thus such managers tended to see the *form* of the multinational, rather than the *nationality* of the firm, as the dominant influence structuring opportunities and action.

The emphasis of senior British managers on critical engagement and adaptation had important implications for the more unqualified enthusiasm of the junior British protégés of Japanese management, as it implied that such zeal would have to be tempered by pragmatism. Japanese managers looked to the protégés, who had developed their expertise and advanced their careers under Japanese sponsorship, to champion Japanese approaches, but the expectations of older British managers were that they would compromise and adapt. The resultant tensions and changes were evident in several of our case-studies, but they were particularly obvious at Copy-Co in the context of the strategic alliance of top Japanese and British managers favouring localization.

The most dramatic account of the resultant reorientations was provided by the young quality manager whose change of position—from strict enforcement and castigation of production to active discussion and support—was highlighted in Chapter 7. He had developed his expertise under the guidance of the senior Japanese quality manager and with the direct encouragement of the first MD, but had then to adapt to the new management coalition:

> The first MD... got very involved with all product planning matters, financial matters, etc. And he did expect my department, which is seen in Japan as a very important department, to be very strong, to be critical, and he'd often come to me after a quality meeting and put his arm on my shoulder and say 'excellent report'.... However, things changed [with] localization to the management style. That was the big shock for me. I was put forward for promotion to assistant manager. I expected to get it as a matter of course. However, there had just been a change of MD and I was very surprised to find that I was not accepted. I was then asked to go away and make a plan for the next six months and it would be reviewed. I had to think very long and very hard.... Look at myself and think how I could turn this thing around. Obviously at that point, with a view to, if I couldn't, having to leave the company. It was such a radical cultural change that I was being asked to make. Not only myself, some other key people, we had had very strong Japanese mentors, who were technically without equal, but in management style terms were not what you would expect to meet.... Happily I was able to give the right answers and come out with a number of projects I was looking to support as a departmental manager.

Even at Copy-Co the narratives of young British managers rarely involved such a clear process of conversion from Japanese protégé to British pragmatist, but others experienced similar tensions and uncertainties.

At Part-Co the hegemony of Japanese engineering management and technical systems was more secure, and senior British managers had little influence on such matters. As at Copy-Co, junior British staff were directly influenced by and learned lessons from their Japanese superiors. For example, one recounted how he had come to appreciate their systematic and professional approach to buying-in components, involving cost reduction through demands for detailed cost breakdowns but also positive guidance rather than condemnation, very different from his earlier experience at a British firm. However, the relationship between mentor and protégé was not always straightforward. One young Part-Co engineer outlined the vicissitudes of such a relationship:

> We were not allowed to express our opinion, and that led to quite a few battles I think between [him] and me early on. It was a case of him getting used to me and me getting used to him. In my views I suppose I'm quite stiff in certain cases. I'm willing to learn many things, but it's as if he made a decision, that was it, he wouldn't explain it. 'You will do it', and I couldn't cope with that.... 'At least tell me why that is the best way, or else how am I going to learn'.... So it was a case of how am I going to learn if he doesn't tell me, so we used to butt heads quite regularly.... Now he knows me and I know him, we'll still disagree and he knows I have a certain look and he'll go 'Oh you do not agree'. And I'll go 'OK, you want to do it this way, I'll do it this way', and he'll sit there and think and he'll be up on the board then, and he'll try and explain it. And then you'll say 'yeah OK, but', and you maybe throw something back in. But I step back, I don't butt heads like I used to. We've both learnt in the time... we've learnt a lot from each other. His English is still not brilliant, but you can communicate with him.

Once the language barriers and formal hierarchies were overcome, however, the expertise of such mentors was highly valued, while the enthusiasm of the younger British staff was encouraged by their growing responsibilities and promotion prospects.

At the same time the process of localization still had significant implications for junior managers and specialists. In particular several of them discovered scope for greater autonomy and initiative in liaising directly with non-Japanese providers of machinery and parts. One of the engineers drew out this implication of pursuing such local suppliers:

> The problem we found is, although we've got a very strong link with Part-Co in Japan, we find that information flow isn't always, we don't always get the right information or the right time. So we're looking if we can actually work with a local equipment supplier, then we buy the knowledge and know-how with that and we don't have to go to Japan. We find that actually it's first-hand knowledge.... For me as an engineer I prefer local because I can work much closer with a supplier, and actually if I need to know anything I can pick the

> phone up. Whereas I find from Japan sometimes you have to go 'round the Wrekin' to get the information.

Thus the adoption of Japanese systems and protocols was still negotiated and modified at Part-Co. But this was accomplished in a more piece-meal and low key way by junior British staff, rather than under the rubric of the localization of management and British 'ownership' that had been championed by top British managers at Copy-Co. In both cases, however, British managers were not simply the beneficiaries of localization but could actively espouse it as a source of additional leverage and autonomy. At the same time, the character and extent of such localization clearly remained strongly influenced by the policies of Japanese managers at HQ and in the subsidiary itself.

BRITISH MANAGEMENT PRAGMATISM AND THE DISCOURSE OF COMMON SENSE

Among more experienced British managers, however, a more sceptical and resistant strand of thinking about Japanese production systems coexisted with the language of localization and adaptation. This sort of response was more conspicuous among administrators than among engineers, but it also had more general currency, particularly in the smaller subcontractors. In those firms, especially, a frequent refrain was that the useful features of Japanese management were really just 'common sense'. For these managers this served as a persistently potent vocabulary, not only because it was central to a wider discourse justifying pragmatic management strategies but also because it provided a language which resonated with some of their distinctive experiences as managers in small subcontractors.

A senior British production manager at Assembly-Co articulated a pivotal feature of the notion of common-sense management shared by all the small-firm managers we interviewed, namely that management was about obvious good practice and had little to do with any specific national provenance:

> It's all the same thing, whatever name you call it, common sense. All down to training and appreciation, communication, it's been around for donkey's years. Whatever they call it, whichever name they pin it under, it all comes down to the same thing, is that everybody's got to understand why they're doing a job, what they're going to achieve, it's going to be done in the most efficient way.... They're thinking 'oh it's Japanese, it must be a new concept'—rubbish, absolute rubbish.

When asked to elaborate on such a claim these managers acknowledged that Japanese firms had sometimes prompted British managers to think afresh, but suggested that this was about a return to 'the basics' rather than anything new. For example, a Senior manager at PCB-Co suggested that:

> The big difference is that they've picked up all these common-sense ideals ... all these little things that British companies pick up and have a go at for a while and then forget about, the Japanese keep bringing them forward all the time and reminding people about them... and I don't take that away from them at all, I think it's good, but I still stick to the fact that it's common sense, but common sense you need reminding about all the time.

Thus it was acknowledged that the application of 'common sense' was not automatic, and that there had been failures among British managers, but the distinctiveness of Japanese management ideas was still challenged.

This theme was often reinforced by the argument that apparently Japanese innovations had roots in earlier western approaches. While it was usually conceded that they had then been developed more systematically in Japan, it was also argued that this reflected a more docile and disciplined workforce. Again a production manager at Assembly-Co exemplified this theme by drawing on the wider mythology (Cole 1989: 113) about the Japanese borrowing rather than innovating management techniques:

> Ludicrous to say that all these ideas are Japanese, because they were American in the first place. Japanese just ripped off the American concepts and changed them because it fitted that well into their culture, because the Japanese generally do as they're told.

At this point the argument about common sense converged with the British management rhetoric about contrasting competencies in managing workers and employment relations. Thus, while 'good management is the same the world over really' (Assembly-Co manager), 'with regard to managing people, I still think [the Japanese] they're useless, absolutely useless' (PCB-Co manager). These arguments provided one powerful warrant for the selective appropriation and, even more, the pragmatic reconfiguration of Japanese management ideas, and they were most strongly voiced by the managers in the subcontractors. Thus in these firms the notion of common sense underpinned pragmatism in handling both problems of production under intense commercial pressures and problems of recruitment and retention of labour arising from their subordinate location in the local labour market.

A second major strand in the discourse of common-sense management involved scepticism about the relationship between the *rhetoric* and the actual practices of Japanese firms and managers. For example, the senior administrator at PCB-Co remarked that:

> They have lots of things which they espouse don't they, [but] whether they actually do them I don't know. So I believe that all management styles at the end of the day have to be common sense.

In both of our subcontract cases British managers developed this argument by reference to their experience of the demands made upon them by their Japanese customer firms. Thus PCB-Co managers pointed particularly to the differences between the expectations of their different Japanese customers, with their different emphases regarding cost, quality, and delivery. Meanwhile, Assembly-Co managers highlighted the tensions between long-term supplier relations, sudden changes in supply schedules and the offloading of risk by final assemblers.

Such arguments helped to legitimate an emphasis on pragmatism and 'practicality', especially when pressures to adopt Japanese management practices were limited (as at Assembly-Co) or unsystematic (as at PCB-Co), though there were also weaker echoes of such claims among British managers in the different circumstances of the larger assemblers. One important feature of this discourse was the very elasticity of the concept of 'common sense', which meant that it could be deployed to explain and appropriate successful Japanese innovations whilst criticizing developments that were judged to be failures. For example, one manager at PCB-Co argued that kanban had been a failure because it had been imposed without proper consideration of its limitations, while a new kitting system that had also been introduced by visiting Japanese engineers had been successful because it was an 'obvious thing', just common sense. The only problem was to explain why such common sense 'regrettably came from Japan', but this was attributed to a lack of common sense on the part of *specific* British managers! Thus successful and acceptable innovations were 'normalized' while glossing over their Japanese provenance, but those judged to be inappropriate were portrayed as alien impositions.

Another key feature was the way in which arguments about a gap between rhetoric and practice could open up space for negotiation around the adoption of Japanese ideas. This was highlighted by a senior British production manager at PCB-Co, who drew upon his own experience of working in Japan to gain such bargaining leverage. At one level he embraced some of the principles he had encountered in Japan, such as the underlying idea of constant improvement. However, he also entered a series of caveats when he discussed such matters as quality:

> The concept of their quality is superb, [but] it's not *that* superb. . . . They won't admit they make problems. We get batch outs from customers where they've found a problem with our [products] in Japan. . . . 'No that wasn't a problem, it was design error'. . . . Well afterwards I had my own argument and said 'you're not telling the truth'. [The response was] 'I know, but we can't be seen, because we've got to keep people on their toes'. . . . I see both sides of it so I know their little ways and faults [laugh].

Thus he used such challenges to legitimize what he regarded as his own pragmatic approach, whether it meant involving individuals rather than groups in problem-solving or balancing quality and delivery according to different customer profiles. In such small enterprises, then, the very flexibility of the notion of common sense meshed with practical management experience of certain aspects of the operations of parent and customer firms to persistently reinforce a traditional British management language of pragmatism and practicality. Furthermore, the very uncertainties and inconsistencies they experienced in such firms reinforced such responses in a more thorough-going fashion than was generally the case in our larger case-study firms.

BRITISH AND JAPANESE DESIGN AND DEVELOPMENT MANAGERS AT COMPUTER-CO: A CONTRASTING CASE?

Our discussion of the interplay of Japanese and British managers has so far concentrated on experience in the greenfield sites, where research and development activities were limited or non-existent. One of the young British managers at Part-Co underlined the way in which the social formation of Japanese managers and the specific production remits of the British subsidiaries generally defined the role of British engineers in such circumstances. In particular he emphasized the sheer size of the Japanese R&D facility, with 'four or five hundred design engineers purely concentrating on [one type of product]', so:

> The reason why I say it's not really feasible to have a design centre here is their training programme, I was really amazed! They have a nine-year training programme which is very structured, which goes from the basics of design right through, and the only way they can do that is because Part-Co is so big. When they get the graduates from university, they start at the age of 21 or 22, and they stay there. And they stay with the company until possibly they retire, so they develop along with the company. They fully understand their design policy and so it's not really possible to teach anybody [from outside] design [to that level].

This highlights the significance of long-term career development and an associated induction into distinctive corporate design philosophies as powerful constraints on the internationalization of advanced research and development activities by Japanese enterprises.

As we discussed in Chapter 9, however, there have been a variety of circumstances in which Japanese manufacturing companies have become more involved in overseas research and development. This has been most common when takeovers of existing non-Japanese firms and the operation of existing brownfield sites have been motivated by efforts to complement or extend the existing competencies of the Japanese parent. Our Electric-

Co/Computer-Co case study represents one variant of this experience and thus throws light upon the specific character of the relations between British and Japanese managers in such circumstances. We will therefore give brief consideration to the features of the distinctive outlooks and interactions of the British and Japanese managers who were involved in the design and development operations of Computer-Co, without revisiting the relationships between Japanese and British staff in the associated manufacturing plant.

There have been few analyses of the micropolitics of management in such firms. However, Lam (1995) provides a pioneering account of relations between Japanese and British engineers involved in collaborative R&D projects and technical exchanges in another Japanese-owned but British-based high-tech electronics company, allowing us to compare our findings with her analysis. She found that, though the two firms sought to exploit complementarities in technical expertise, joint R&D activity was largely confined to a limited form of 'arm's length interface collaboration', fraught with uncertainties and mutual suspicions. In particular there were major differences in the perspectives and priorities of the British and the Japanese managers and engineers, which proved difficult to reconcile and helped to sustain this hierarchical and limited form of collaboration. However, Lam did not rest her explanation at the level of such cultural contrasts. Instead she quite properly emphasized that differences in attitudes and practices were embedded in wider institutional matrices, both within the two firms and beyond in the broader social organization of education and employment in Japan and the United Kingdom. In emphasizing the structural constraints involved she remained sceptical about facile recommendations for 'reciprocal acculturation' but outlined several ways in which organizational arrangements might more or less effectively mediate between distinctive approaches to R&D engineering in Britain and Japan.

This analysis was grounded in Lam's (1996*a*) own discussion of the contrasting institutional formations of Japanese and British engineers. There she argued that engineers in Japan generally pursued their careers by developing their expertise through job rotation within multifunctional teams within one enterprise, developing a broad competence that embraced process and product engineering but remained embedded in a fund of tacit knowledge. In this context project leaders were engineers with long and varied experience, who remained 'player managers' and continued to concern themselves with the details of technical developments. In Britain, meanwhile, engineers generally followed their careers across several firms, placing a premium upon responsiveness to the dominant management specialisms of financial control and marketing and the accumulation of specialist knowledge within a formally organized division of engineering functions. In this context, young engineers expected to be granted considerable technical autonomy and responsibility, while project leaders assumed a managerial role that involved disengagement from technical work.

The salience of such institutional differences between internal organizational careers and external market careers was recognized by several of our own informants. Thus a British engineer from the Computer-Co factory remarked that:

> I came up through a recognized apprenticeship scheme, and you've got broad-based training, departmental training and . . . I was moved around within the company—GEC. But I have also gained a lot of experience by moving through companies, whereas Japanese personnel don't move from company to company. So they tend to get a lot of experience going within the different . . . divisions within Electric-Co. . . . I think they get their experience from going from division to division.

This comment, however, also suggests that such differences should not be overstated. In particular such comparisons between national patterns of professional formation also reveal that Japan and the United Kingdom shared certain features, such as a focus on company-specific training. In both Britain and Japan the role of the firm has been critical, and often engineers in Britain have defined themselves partly by reference to their firm and not simply by reference to their occupational specialism. Furthermore, design has often been firm-specific, especially within larger firms or more specialist areas (Smith 1987: 169). This suggests a potential layer of similar understanding among British and Japanese engineers, which may not exist between their more academic continental or managerial American counterparts (Meiksins and Smith 1996).

THE IMPORTANCE OF SECTOR AND CORPORATE FEATURES FOR MANAGEMENT MICROPOLITICS AT COMPUTER-CO

More conspicuous from our own research, however, are the ways in which the experiences of engineers at Electric-Co and Computer-Co could diverge from apparently national 'norms'. In particular, specific features of scale and market position added further layers of distinctiveness to being a Computer-Co or Electric-Co engineer, and these features appeared particularly significant in defining interactions between the two groups at our research site. As Chapter 9 implies, the contingencies of specific market positioning and particular corporate and sector histories mediate and modify the salience of the broader institutional frameworks of professional formation highlighted by Lam (1995, 1996*a*). This suggests caution in identifying distinctive 'national' patterns of consciousness and action among the engineers at any specific Japanese-British R&D venture. We saw in Chapter 9 that Electric-Co had a large and sophisticated cadre of production engineers and managers, but a central feature of the takeover was a recognition that the relevance of this expertise in the PC sector was not unproblematical. At an organizational level this recognition underwrote a pattern of autonomy in which the Japanese presence was limited to a deputy manager at each site, a few juniors performing quite narrowly defined tasks, and infrequent visits by task groups. At a more interpersonal level it meant an active dialogue between British and Japanese engineers, though this developed in different ways in the distinct arenas of the R&D facility and the factory.

In R&D most of the work was only minimally influenced in any direct way by the parent company, largely through the inclusion of specifications relevant to the expanding Japanese market. There was, however, one major attempt to develop more ambitious joint activity in a design and development project intended to pool the differing expertise of British and Japanese engineering staff, and there the engineering expertise and cultures of the two organizations were more directly engaged. One aspect of this joint project was the involvement of eight Japanese engineers in the design activities in the United Kingdom (together with other people visiting from time to time) and the other was the placement of a key sub-assembly design in Japan.

The British and Japanese managers who were directly involved in this joint project agreed that this collaboration had been very difficult and had considerably overrun its time schedule. Echoing Lam's (1995) analysis, the British project manager identified major differences in the ways in which the Japanese and British engineers approached such design projects:

> That comes back to the way they expect to run projects and the way we run them. Basically they spend a lot of their time designing on paper exactly what the product is going to be. Doing a very dirty prototype, doing bigger build, to prove everything goes together, and then going to production. Whereas we kind of fall into the project, have done in the past. Basically 'it's a damned good idea let's start guys' and develop the spec as you are going along.

Furthermore, such differences were seen as embedded in distinctive patterns of professional formation, either through mobility between employers or through internal career paths. As a result a leading British engineer emphasized the *limitations* which he believed could arise from the more varied and generalist engineering experience of some of the Japanese engineers:

> Oh, it's perfectly normal for . . . Japanese engineers to move around within their organization to completely different groups and we suffered at times from that, especially on the software side, as they'd got guys who had never written this kind of software before and were now writing software for us, and we are going to have support issues from that because their code is bloody awful.

However, a leading Japanese engineer emphasized the relative rigidity of engineering roles in British firms, including R&D, and their corresponding limitations. In particular he noted that jobs were 'defined as a very narrow career path: job A means drawing something, job B means design something, not overlap'. In contrast to Japan, this meant that the responsibility for the overall product and its delivery was not really shared, despite any rhetoric to the contrary: 'if another guy failed that is not my responsibility'.

Despite such contrasts, however, a British project manager believed that the activities of the integrated design team had eventually been relatively successful, though this involved a painful process of mutual learning:

> I think that bringing them in as contractors to work within a team worked quite well. There was a large learning process for them as well as for us because their background was mainframes. Completely different set of design criteria, completely different way of running projects.

What he highlighted, though, was that these difficulties were related to specific sector and corporate dynamics, rather than simply national professional formations. This was evident right at the start of the joint project, when the contrasting preoccupations of engineers operating with mainframes versus PCs became evident. The same manager recalled:

> They gave us a spec of what they wanted which we, once we'd got back up off the floor, said 'you've got to be joking, there is no way we could possibly attempt that'. It was just a huge project—huge box. So much mainframe orientated we couldn't possibly sell it in the PC market. It would have been no good to us.

Moreover, the importance of the sectoral contrasts in this assessment was underlined by the judgement that joint project work 'would potentially be a lot different if we dealt with the PC sections rather than the mainframe sections'. For the Computer-Co engineers, operating in the PC market rather than as a mainframe builder involved fundamental differences of orientations and ways of doing things. Furthermore, working with Electric-Co engineers involved engaging with an engineering bureaucracy that was, by Computer-Co standards, inflexible, hierarchical and slow moving.

As might be expected from our earlier argument, the PC experience of the leading Japanese engineer was therefore crucial in intermediating between the different organizations and sets of engineers. One British engineer commented that 'his PC market background helped me talk to him, and him back to me, and then him ensuring the mainframe engineers were going in the right direction'. He also argued the case for less extensive documentation than Electric-Co expected, because it would anyway be overtaken by design changes. His orientation in these respects reflected both an understanding of the contrasting market environments for PC and mainframe R&D, and an awareness of the limited number of staff at Computer-Co compared with the surfeit of engineers in R&D at Electric-Co.

Those British engineers who worked on the joint project did concede that the quality preoccupations of the Japanese engineers had had some influence on the British designers, but they also sought to downplay any such influence by emphasizing the continued importance of different operating environments:

> Obviously their proposals of how to solve particular problems would have been biased towards the quality side of it from their experience and therefore we are learning from that point of view. I don't believe there is anything that they have brought to the project that said 'that is a good way to monitor quality' or 'that is a good way to improve quality'. We know what they all are, it's just that we constantly, our seesaw of balance between quality and the commercial aspect, whether that be time-scale or cost, is a different pivot point to theirs.

For such British engineers Computer-Co's very distinctiveness as a design centre, and indeed its attractiveness to Electric-Co, lay in its capacity for rapid and necessarily risky design and development decisions. This allowed effective competition in the PC market, and this was very different to the balance of quality and risk involved in building mainframes for the heavy engineering customers of the Electric-Co group. However, it was striking that this assessment was also strongly endorsed by the senior Japanese R&D manager mentioned earlier, reflecting his own distinctive experience in the Japanese PC group, and in turn this influenced how he performed his intermediary role.

Three themes can be drawn from the interactions of the British and Japanese staff involved in the joint design and development projects at Computer-Co. The first is that there was a distinct difference of approach between the British and the Japanese engineers. Numerous informants contrasted the systematic but cautious approach of the Japanese engineers, with their emphasis on engineering in foolproof systems, and the adventurous but unsystematic approach of the British engineers who emphasized speedy incorporation of current innovations. The second is that the pursuit of the joint project was a fraught process, which, from the British management perspective, produced a good product but well behind schedule—an experience they did not wish to repeat too often.

The third theme is that the differences in approach between Japanese and British engineers set up a quite complex pattern of negotiation which did not simply entrench these contrasts. This did not mean a convergence upon a mutually agreed mix of 'system' and 'flair', but rather the establishment of an increasingly shared vocabulary through which responses to engineering problems and the day-to-day work of professional engineers could occur. Finally, however, both the differences in approach and the bases of negotiation were heavily influenced by the specific corporate and sectoral traditions of the two companies. One was a massive engineering conglomerate used to heavy engineering contracts with large corporate and state customers but facing serious problems in the PC market, and the other was a small 'entrepreneurial' company producing for this volatile and rapidly changing market.

As in Lam's (1995) study we found that the British design and development engineers had experienced mobility in the external labour market, emphasized criteria of cost and time to market and tended to exclude manufacturing engineers from the development process. Meanwhile, the Japanese engineers had built their careers within one company, tended to emphasize systematic testing and quality, and sought to involve manufacturing in design and development decisions. In other respects, however, our findings differed somewhat from Lam's. In particular she contrasted the more specialized, sequential and heavily documented organization of British engineering activities with a Japanese emphasis upon teamworking and the deployment of shared 'tacit knowledge'. By contrast our respondents suggested that the Japanese engineers were more concerned with tight procedures and extensive documentation. Meanwhile, the British computer sector's emphasis on innovation and ad hoc initiatives, marked on one hand by a fluidity and creativity in problem-solving but on the other by rushed and unsystematic decisions, often ran ahead of proper documentation. Furthermore, Computer-Co relied quite heavily upon on-the-job learning among its design and development staff, partly because the firm was unwilling to bid salary levels up to attract those who had accumulated the most expertise through interfirm mobility.

In these respects our research qualifies Lam's contrast between 'organic' teams of Japanese generalists and the fragmented activities of British specialists, and instead highlights differences between different sorts of collaborative groupings, with different priorities and different styles of problem-solving. These were rooted not just in contrasting national patterns of professional formation but also in different sectoral dynamics and related differences in specific corporate traditions. One consequence was that the process of reorganization in R&D at Computer-Co was not an attempt to transfer a Japanese form of teamworking onto the British terrain. Rather, it was primarily a home-grown senior management programme, pursued against a background of substantial resource constraints. This sought to modify the balance and form of integration and specialization among R&D staff, to increase the visibility and accountability of the design process to senior management, and thus to reposition the firm in relation to evolving market circumstances (including the Japanese parent as customer).

In Computer-Co, then, the active reworking of existing corporate and sector approaches to product development, work organization and employment relations involved a difficult process of negotiation between contrasting approaches. Different corporate, sector and national experiences and traditions were all in play. The influence of the Japanese parent, coupled with changes in the sector, did give notions of 'robustness' and 'manufacturability' increased salience in the design process. However, sector recipes associated with the perceived dynamics of the PC market appeared dominant. In essence this meant a continuing emphasis upon the mobilization of a relatively poorly rewarded collectivity of technical specialists/enthusiasts to deliver risky, state-of-the-art innovations.

CONCLUSIONS

One recurring motif in the literature on the relationships between Japanese and local (British or American) managers has been that resistance to the implementation of Japanese methods has come more from local managers than from local workers. Broad (1994) develops this argument on the basis of a British case study, while Florida and Kenney (1991*a*: 389) suggest that American managers were 'the source of recurring adaptation problems at the transplants', partly because of their resistance to full job rotation or promotion from within. An underlying premise of such accounts appears to be that Japanese models of production and involvement will generally prove attractive to local workers, creating the conditions for a productive alliance between Japanese managers and local workers that is put at risk by the short-sighted calculations of local managers.

Our case-studies certainly document a variety of conflicts between Japanese and British managers and they *sometimes* provide evidence that local workers compare British managers unfavourably with Japanese managers. However, they also suggest that this emphasis on limitations and problems arising from local management resistance represents a thoroughly inadequate basis for understanding management micropolitics in Japanese manufacturing subsidiaries in Britain, because the emphasis on *nationality* obscures other aspects of the relationships involved.

First, it glosses over the extent to which local management claims to expertise in personnel management are grounded in the distinctive social organization of labour markets and worker expectations in particular countries and localities. A recognition that such claims are also self-serving, underpinning the leverage of local managers in policymaking and career building, does not negate the real uncertainties and debates regarding personnel policies among both Japanese and British managers. Second, it treats Japanese management competencies in the organization and management of production systems as readily transferable, without addressing the specific market and production exigencies characteristic of many overseas subsidiary operations. However, we have seen that such exigencies again open up areas of ambiguity, discussion, and innovation in the process of production and manufacturing processes, and these can again cross-cut the national affiliations of the managers and specialists concerned.

We agree that the claims of Japanese firms and managers to internationally superior management practices were of particular significance through the 1980s and 1990s, and coloured the character of management thinking and debate within these firms. However, we have shown that the salience and implications of such claims varied from company to company and subsidiary to subsidiary. We also recognize, indeed emphasize, that the distinctive national social formations of Japanese and British managers, and the distinctive stakes they had in building internal versus external management careers, were important influences on how these groupings related to one another in the subsidiaries. However, our claim is that both Japanese and local managers in these subsidiaries also shared common problems. These related to the specific role of the plant in broader corporate strategies and structures and to specific forms of class relations in the production process, and these shared challenges strongly mediated and modified any direct dominance and societal effects.

CHAPTER

11

Shop-floor Consent, Accommodation, and Dissent

INTRODUCTION

We saw in Chapter 10 that the management of labour was claimed as a key competence by British managers, providing a basis for legitimacy and leverage within the Japanese subsidiaries. In this chapter we explore the experience of employees more directly, by focusing particularly on shop-floor workers in the two larger assembly plants among our Telford case-studies. As we have seen, these were the firms that stayed closest to Japanese production arrangements, albeit more modified and localized in Copy-Co than at Part-Co. They also occupied similar positions in the local labour market and were leading members of the local cluster of Japanese inward-investors. At the same time the details of management policies in each firm, and thus management–worker relations, had developed in distinctive ways over time. Finally, as the largest factories they were also the ones where we interviewed a substantial number and broad range of shop-floor informants. As such they provide the basis for a detailed analysis of shop-floor experiences, viewpoints and responses to management initiatives in these workplaces.

Our discussion of the perspectives and responses of our shop-floor informants in these two factories is designed to advance our understanding of the contours of consent and dissent within such Japanese subsidiaries. In so doing we also seek to contribute to more general debate about the contemporary scope and limits of management hegemony and the current character and implications of employee survival strategies in the workplace (Ackroyd and Thompson 1999; Thompson and Ackroyd 1995). In this regard our research is particularly relevant because developments in Japanese 'transplants' have represented an important resource on which such larger debates have drawn (Elger 1999; Ferner 2003; Grant 1996).

In outline these broader controversies have centred upon the implications of a combination of new, more sophisticated policies of human resource management in the workplace and the wider 'deregulation' of the labour market and erosion of trade union organization. For some commentators these developments have radically recast management–worker relations in a more cooperative or compliant mould, so that worker dissent and deviation from management expectations are virtually eliminated from the workplace. In this view the realities of shop-floor life have converged increasingly with unitarist management prescriptions, while the hegemony of unitarist ideologies has itself reinforced this convergence. By contrast the critics of this perspective have insisted on the persistent significance of underlying sources of antagonism between management and workers. On this basis they have discussed the ways in which scepticism, instrumentalism, and dissent arise from and in turn influence employee strategies of survival, negotiation, and accommodation in the workplace (Ackroyd and Thompson 1999; Scott 1994). At the same time the critics have acknowledged that the boundaries and contours of such scepticism, dissent, and accommodation have changed in significant ways in response to new management strategies and wider social and political changes.

Over the last two decades commentators on the character of management–worker relations in Japanese manufacturing 'transplants' in the West have developed a series of overlapping but distinctive interpretations of the relationships between managers and employees, and these resonate strongly with core features of this wider controversy. The next section provides a brief overview of this literature as a more immediate point of reference for our own findings and analysis.

RECENT ANALYSES OF MANAGEMENT–WORKER RELATIONS IN JAPANESE MANUFACTURING SUBSIDIARIES

Early commentaries often emphasized the importance of the distinctive, more inclusive, and involving character of the new work and employment relations to be found in Japanese transplants (Florida and Kenney 1991*a*; White and Trevor 1983; Trevor 1988). Such accounts mirrored those of 'soft' human resource management in 'high involvement, high commitment' workplaces (Legge 1995). They placed primary emphasis on the shared benefits for managers and workers that emerged from these novel features, so that sources of antagonism were eroded from within. These bland accounts of joint gains were, however, challenged by analyses that highlighted the 'dark side' of lean production methods, and this led to a changed understanding of the bases of cooperation in the work process. In particular, greater emphasis was placed upon the capacity of management to actively engineer consent through processes of selection, training, surveillance, and incorporation (Delbridge et al. 1992; Garrahan and Stewart 1992; Oliver and Wilkinson 1992; Sewell and Wilkinson 1992). These mechanisms ostensibly acted as 'functional equivalents' of the Japanese employment system in the distinctive conditions of crisis-ridden British manufacturing decline.

One significant qualification to the 'functional equivalents' analysis was developed in the late 1990s in some of the discussions of 'hybridization', especially in the United States (see in particular Adler et al. 1998; Adler 1999*b*). This involved the argument that the distinctive expectations of American workers could encourage the implementation of a modified and more acceptable management regime, especially when they were mediated through the presence of a trade union but even if they influenced management efforts to avoid unionization. However, a more substantial challenge to the earlier arguments was mounted by other North American writers on unionized Japanese auto subsidiaries (Babson 1995, 1998; Fucini and Fucini 1990; Reinhart et al. 1994, 1997). They acknowledged the importance of management policies of plant location, recruitment and training, alongside job security, in encouraging worker cooperation. However, they also argued that the stringency of evolving production regimes generated substantial grievances that, coupled with increasingly active union challenges, fed a dynamic of worker disillusionment and organized contestation. In turn this placed real, though limited, constraints on the exercise of managerial prerogatives, so that such 'contentious hybridization' (Babson 1998: 181) produced a more negotiated (and potentially more resilient) accommodation between managers and organized workers.

A final twist to these debates has been provided by detailed ethnographic studies of management–worker relations that have recognized the salience of shop-floor discontents but have nevertheless re-emphasized the hegemony of management (Delbridge 1998; Graham 1995). These researchers have argued that, in the factories they studied, the survival strategies of ordinary workers were generally subsumed and coopted to meet management priorities. This created something close to what Burawoy (1979, 1985) terms 'hegemonic despotism'. For example, Graham's study of a non-unionized auto transplant in the United States documented a growing disillusionment among workers, fuelled by increasing production pressures and a gap between management rhetoric and practice, and analysed the varied ways in which employees informally opposed or distanced themselves from management requirements. Graham provides a subtle discussion of the interplay between individual survival strategies and wider networks of shared action and informal support, including telling attention to the distinctively gendered character of such features (see also Gottfried and Graham 1993). The intensity of work, overtime demands and industrial injuries all became foci of dissatisfaction and low-key contestation. Nevertheless, she argues that, in the absence of a trade union and with increasing reliance on vulnerable temporary workers, management prerogatives remained entrenched, team-working continued to elicit self-discipline, and protests were marginalized.

Delbridge (1998) argues that workers at Nippon CTV, a large Japanese electrical subsidiary based in the United Kingdom, expressed considerable scepticism and even resentment towards management. They were not ideologically committed to the enterprise, but retained an instrumental attachment to work as a basis for earning a living. They did not believe that managers understood the realities of work on the shop-floor and were critical of the harshness of the monitoring and disciplinary regime. However, he characterizes the dominant mode of worker response as one of resignation and survival through distancing, signified by refusals to engage in discretionary work, the discarding of company jackets and a rush to exit at the end of the day. Thus there was worker antipathy towards management but, paralleling Graham's account, this did not result in an overt challenge to management prerogatives, and management sustained a practical but pervasive control within the labour process.

Nevertheless, management–worker relations at Nippon CTV involved more than mere calculative accommodation between a subordinate labour force and a powerful management. Thus Delbridge explores the role of effort norms in the day-to-day conduct of workers on the line, in ways reminiscent of Baldamus's (1961) analysis of relative disparities and effort bargaining on the shop-floor. This leads him to examine the significance of inter-worker recriminations in the governance of the shop-floor, for example when co-workers judged that someone was a 'lazy cow', slacking in ways which also disrupted the work routines of contiguous workers. Such rivalries could be harnessed by management as peer pressure to conform to production and quality targets, and they were exacerbated by the personalized allocation of blame for quality defects (Delbridge 1998: 117). However, such norms of reasonable effort also underpinned certain resistances that set limits to the unrestricted application of managerial prerogatives. In particular, the recurrent efforts of team leaders to nudge up line speeds were sometimes undermined by a rise in uncompleted boards, as even the 'best' operators failed to sustain production. Furthermore, workers had apparently earlier defeated a management effort to introduce faster, 'two-handed' insertion (Delbridge 1998: 99).

A strength of Delbridge's analysis is his exploration of some of the nuances and paradoxes of the resulting tacit negotiation of workplace social relations, within the broader framework of entrenched management prerogatives and worker preoccupations with getting by. An important example was the willingness of workers to cover for the mistakes of co-workers, by rectifying those mistakes while leaving them unrecorded. This breached the formal regulations and protected co-workers from sanctions, but it also accomplished effective online rectification and kept production flowing (Delbridge 1998: 91). Such processes also had further layers of complexity. First, the rectifier could herself become vulnerable to monitoring and punishment for failing to adhere to procedure, so tacit negotiations also developed around the circumstances in which informal rectification was tolerated. Second, team leaders themselves became implicated in this residual informality by neglecting to enforce the recording of incompletes or errors, or by relaxing the threshold for the administration of 'counselling' to those failing to meet performance targets. Similar dynamics arose in the context of line rebalancing and speed-up. This sometimes involved a tacit recognition that a more systematic imposition of sanctions would itself be disruptive. Such processes helped to sustain continuing production at the expense of a failure to secure work intensification.

Delbridge argues that these processes served to manufacture a situated and qualified 'consent' through a basic adherence to quality and effort norms, despite an absence of positive commitment to management objectives. Informal negotiations served more often to augment than to mitigate management control (Delbridge 1998: 181). What this did not deliver for management was any active cooperation in the discretionary exercise of added effort or initiative. Thus Delbridge's study offers unrivalled insights into the day-to-day experience of workers and the forms of control, resistance and negotiation that developed within a tightly disciplined and stringently controlled production regime. However, it also raises questions that he himself acknowledged regarding the extent to which such processes have been replicated in other Japanese 'transplants'. Furthermore, his work, combined with that of Graham, poses important questions about the extent to which management hegemony and worker compliance may be challenged by the informal coping strategies of ordinary employees, even in non-unionized workplaces.

In this regard our case-studies in Telford appear to have documented a rather different picture to that of pervasive management control, despite the arrival of greenfield investors in a relatively isolated local labour market with an abundance of labour in a period of supportive national and local state policies and minimal union leverage. In particular we have shown that the managers in all of our Telford firms faced recurrent problems of labour recruitment and retention and remained preoccupied with issues of worker attendance and cooperation throughout the 1990s. At the same time investment and production were sustained at Copy-Co while Part-Co expanded substantially, suggesting that top management regarded each factory as playing a satisfactory role in the corporate strategy of its Japanese parent despite their concerns about the problematical features of labour. Thus it becomes appropriate to consider, more fully than we were able to do in Chapter 7, how shop-floor employees experienced the production and employment regimes in these factories. What options did workers envisage for themselves within the workplace and in the wider labour market? What were the contours of consent and dissent on the shop-floor? How were the survival strategies of workers reconciled with this overall pattern of 'good enough' production? More generally, what may experience in these factories tell us about the limits of management hegemony and the relationships between cooperation and conflict at work?

To address these questions we cannot draw upon direct observational material gained through participant observation studies, as did Graham and Delbridge. However, our programme of intensive interviews with a broad range of shop-floor workers allowed them to reflect at some length upon different facets of their day-to-day experiences of work. In this context our informants talked about their grievances and satisfactions, their informal survival strategies, and the dilemmas they and their fellow workers faced in responding to management policies and production pressures in different ways. This provides a rich resource for addressing the questions outlined above. We will start by considering views from the shop-floor at Part-Co before discussing the experiences and responses of Copy-Co employees. The rationale for considering Part-Co first is that, as the more recent arrival, more of its employees had been recruited relatively recently, while its continuing expansion offered more possibilities for internal promotion. In these circumstances workers had an acute sense of the trade-offs between leaving and staying with the firm, which formed a backdrop to their responses to the character of the production regime. By comparison Copy-Co, as a longer-established and stable plant, had many workers who had worked for the company for a substantial period, while the reorganization of supervision (discussed in Chapter 7) had posed particular questions about the scope and limits of internal progression. In turn this provided a rather different backdrop to the responses of workers to the social organization of production at Copy-Co.

VIEWS FROM THE SHOP-FLOOR AT PART-CO

Perspectives on wages and labour market options

As we have already documented, the inward investors were characterized by relatively low wages and were part of a low-wage local economy. This was highlighted by many of our shop-floor informants at Part-Co, as it was by the team-leaders discussed in Chapter 7, and this set the scene for widespread discussions of the financial trade-offs between moving or staying at the firm, especially as unemployment in the locality declined.

Some of the more skilled workers noted that Part-Co wages were similar to those at many other employers, though clearly inferior to the best rates in the district:

> If you take the shift allowance off we're on roughly the same hourly rate as an electrician would get. So comparable... I mean they don't pay as much as some firms, some firms do pay an awful lot of money. But I mean there's like so many Japanese firms around here, they sort of set the wage for the area. It's only, I think it's a couple or three [non-Japanese factories] that actually pay silly money, and of course everybody tries to get in there.

Such views underpinned the judgement that the chances of gaining employment at the few well-paying firms were slim (not least because they had been reducing their employment), while the new arrivals increasingly (and, as we have seen, in a quite organized way) set the going rate. Another informant, a less-skilled worker, drew out the practical implications of such labour market conditions, though not without an ambivalence that characterized the comments of many of those who expressed relative satisfaction with their position:

> Some people come in and run the company down terrible, and they're not that bad. I'm not saying the company's brilliant, you know. How many companies do you get are brilliant? I mean work conditions are good, so you have to check things in perspective as they are, and say 'well yeah, it's all right', you know. I mean it's the real world we're all living in, and ideally everybody would like more money, wouldn't they?

Such accounts suggested that relative satisfaction reflected the limited labour market options facing most workers, as much as the positive attractions of working for Part-Co.

Others, however, were more critical, both in terms of earnings and the work pressures that characterized Part-Co's production regime. Thus one of our assembly informants emphasized that:

> The basic is very low, I think that's another factor why people don't stay here, it's because of the money. [Elsewhere] they're probably on shifts and they are getting more money, not being treated like they are treated here, because they are constantly on your back all day and want more, pushing more and more, whereas [other] places they're not.

Such criticisms were reinforced by other grievances, not least when there was a loss of the overtime opportunities which had helped to compensate for the low basic pay:

> I used to do a lot of overtime and I used to take home that much, whereas this year the overtime has been really cut down.... It's just that the company seems to give it you when they need you to do it, but if, say, like one month you need the money and you ask the supervisor... they'll turn around and say 'no' straight away. They won't accommodate you, but they'll expect you to accommodate the company, which I don't think is very fair.

In the context of a tightening labour market, and dissatisfaction with Part-Co wages, movement between the various more or less comparable factories in the district responded to quite subtle differences in wages and conditions. One of our shop-floor informants emphasized that the arrival of new investors increased the scope for such moves, but also spelt out some of the complexities involved:

> All the new ones [factories] that opened . . . one good thing is you don't have a problem getting a job now really, it's a lot easier to get a job now. You can get a job somewhere else straightaway, as long as it wasn't Japanese. . . . They won't pinch [poach]. . . . They also have big meetings between themselves and they discuss what pay rises they're giving . . . because they don't want to step on each other's toes. . . . [company] at the minute are paying 16p an hour more for the assembly-line staff. So quite a few are going from here, on the dole, to there, just so they can get through the system. But then come April when we have our pay rise they'll all be coming back again . . . there's a lot of that. But I mean it's all roughly the same job, assembly-line working.

As noted earlier, Japanese firms set similar wage rates, shared a preference for non-unionism and operated an unofficial but widely recognized non-poaching policy by refusing to accept people direct from another Japanese factory except for promotion. Thus one complication to movement for the worker was that a gentleman's agreement existed which strengthened the hand of Japanese employers in relation to labour. Nevertheless, this informant not only recognized this, but also noted that there were recognized ways of circumventing such policies. A further complication, however, arose from the small differentials in pay rates between most factories, as the rationale for moving could easily be undermined by shifts in these differentials.

As an alternative to such quitting, however, the threat of leaving could sometimes be used as a modest bargaining counter to gain improved conditions. Thus one process operator emphasized that, in the circumstances of high turnover and recruitment difficulties, the threat to quit could be used as something of a lever by experienced workers:

> You could say 'we're a bit fed up, I think I might leave'. They go 'Oh don't leave. We'll put you on another job.' There's that many people leaving it's unbelievable. There must have been about five thousand people through this place since I've been here, you know. That's not including temps. . . . You have to do a lot of overtime at this place to get a decent wage basically [and] they want to cut the overtime. People say, 'right I'm off', you know, so they all jack in and they're like leaving. So they're continually replacing people . . . [so] they usually bend over backwards [to try and keep you].

For some, then, the existing effort bargain was under threat, but the very volatility of labour meant that there was also some individual leverage to limit such deterioration. In particular it was possible to press for a move to an area of the factory with more autonomy or a section with more overtime opportunities to compensate for the low pay.

However, not all employees saw their wage–effort bargain in such a negative light. In particular some of those who had worked for worse wages, especially within the service sector, saw the pay at Part-Co as distinctly more attractive. This experience was not uncommon among older women. For example, one middle-aged woman suggested that pay was fractionally better than at some other places:

> Here tend to pay a few pence more than most, I think, from what I've looked at in the papers, unless you're really [a] specialist, you know. Just bog standard factory workers, it's just a fraction higher... [and] office work isn't very well paid, not in Telford anyway.

At the same time she perceived a variety of perspectives on such issues among her fellow workers, which she linked to different patterns of household commitments. In particular she felt that what was acceptable to many older women was seen as unsatisfactory by many men because 'it was not a living wage, while for youngsters without commitments "they just say, oh, I'll try there, or we'll try there" '. Furthermore, another woman suggested that:

> Women seem to get promoted more I would say in general here. Whether that's because they think they're probably going to stay longer than others, because it's not a living wage... most women are on a second wage, so they tend to stay longer.

Thus both labour market options and family circumstances were seen to underpin variations in the experiences, priorities and orientations of employees who were working on the shop-floor at Part-Co.

Returning to the experience of poor wages in the service sector, this was not confined to older married women but was also highlighted by several other employees with service sector backgrounds. For example, one young woman commented specifically on the problems of working in retail:

> I loved it but it was part-time anyway. I was on a twelve- to twenty-hour contract, but after Christmas we were knocked down to twelve hours a week. I couldn't really afford to work twelve hours. I mean before that my part-time job was [in the] market. So I was in the retail anyway. I loved it. But there isn't any money in it. I mean, although you want job satisfaction you've got to be realistic about a well-paid job.

Again, an older man recognized that many fellow workers regarded wages as poor compared with elsewhere, but compared *his* wages and hours more favourably with his previous job:

> Well from what I can see it ain't that much different. Others are better obviously. ... [But] it was just rubbish wages all the time... van driving, you'd work all day and Saturday night. It was terrible. So [here] I was feeling

> a bit ill so I had last Saturday off and it was like heaven. And the wages are superb compared to that. That's the way I look at it.

This suggests that direct personal comparisons of poorer wages and conditions, especially in the service sector, often underpinned a relative acceptance of the wage–work bargain on offer at Part-Co.

Finally, another distinctive pattern of responses was articulated by those older male workers who came from better paid industries, such as engineering or coal-mining, but had experienced redundancies and/or unemployment. These men generally felt rather grateful for obtaining a job after such experiences in their former employment, but were also sharply conscious of their changed circumstances. Thus one ex-miner reported that in terms of wages:

> There was no comparison really, still no comparison now, years on like. I'd say half the wages maybe. But at the same time money wasn't the motivation, it was the work.

Another man reflected on getting his current job:

> I was quite pleased actually because I mean I'm [late forties].... One grey area that I would like improving is the wages, but like I say, I accept the fact that I wouldn't perhaps have the same wages.... So then, when you say you're grateful I mean one shouldn't moan about the wages too much. But after a while you do, don't you? At first you're grateful, 'they'll do me', and then after two years you think, well I'd like a little bit more.

As this comment suggests, 'gratitude' can be a somewhat perishable underpinning for *relative* satisfaction. As we will see later, this set of employees may have more or less reconciled themselves to the lower wages and often found the work itself reasonably acceptable, but they were among the most sceptical or critical of management in other respects, such as the unfairness of appraisals. They were also acutely aware of the lack of any effective collective voice in the workplace.

In summary, then, the firm was generally seen as paying quite low wages, especially in relation to the pressures and demands of the work, but the pattern of responses varied from rather stoical acceptance to grumbling compliance to active consideration of leaving for another job. In seeking to understand these responses we can make three main points. First, each of these options could be seen as appropriate by fellow employees, depending on the circumstances, while being linked to different patterns of experience within the local labour market. Second, each also appeared to be coloured by a sense of the dilemmas and uncertainties that attended all of these options. None was seen as a simple choice flowing from an unequivocal judgement in the circumstances in which these workers found themselves. Finally, these responses were not simply cold calculations, but were often coloured by normative judgements about what was fair or reasonable.

The pattern of influences on the ways in which employees might choose between these alternative responses cannot readily be captured in simple dichotomies, not least because they were combined in many different ways in the lived experiences of these workers. Nevertheless, it is possible to draw out some contrasting configurations from the comments and reflections of our respondents, while recognizing that they were rarely found bundled together so neatly as many workers combined contradictory experiences. Among the influences reinforcing *stoicism* appear to have been being an older worker, having worked in the service sector, awareness of a slack external labour market, being part of a two-earner couple, being in a relatively less pressured area of production (such as process operations), having been promoted and, linked to some of the above, being female. Among the influences reinforcing *criticism* appeared to be being younger, having experienced better-paid manual work, awareness of a tight external labour market, being an unpromoted 'associate', working in a more pressured part of the plant (such as assembly), earning what was seen as the main wage for a household and, linked to some of these, being male.

Shop-floor views on appraisal, promotion and the internal labour market

Assessments of wages were not only embedded in comparisons available in the external labour market, but were also coloured by the construction and management of internal job ladders. While 'associates' across the production areas shared the same basic pay, a central feature of management's gearing of pay to performance was the use of an appraisal process which was also linked to internal promotion. The appraisal was initially separate from pay, but it was later linked to a grading process that had consequences for wages. This involved the assignment of points for such features as attendance (penalizing absenteeism and lateness), teamwork, quality and 'attitude to work', and provided the basis for progression within the associate category and on to higher grades.

Some employees regarded this quite positively, as a way of encouraging and rewarding associates on the shop-floor. Thus one commented that:

> It works quite smoothly. Sometimes if you get assessed and you get told where your shortcomings are... you don't like it at first, but then you get over it. Yeah, I think it does work, because everybody wants to do a little bit better.

Another argued that:

> If you're willing to work then you will get somewhere eventually.... If you're willing to help out when need be, whenever there's overtime, say 'yes', you're

> willing to do it to help them out, rather than say 'yes, I want it because I want the money'. They want enthusiasm, I think, rather than 'can I have some more money'.... But yes, I said to them that I didn't want to go for the setter's job because I was too stressed out, but I'm willing to go up in the associate level.

Furthermore, it was evident that the firm did seek to promote to setter and sometimes team-leader grades from within (and we saw in Chapter 7 that team-leaders generally valued the resultant opportunities). For example, one process worker we talked to was then a setter and hoped to become a team leader. This was a prospect she thought realistic because she had been actively encouraged to become a setter and the factory was continuing to expand. She had worked for several other Japanese and non-Japanese manufacturing firms in the locality, which she compared unfavourably with Part-Co. This was partly because working in process production was less constraining than the assembly work she had generally done elsewhere, but relations with management and especially promotion opportunities were uppermost in this comparison.

Set against such broadly positive evaluations of grading and promotion, however, were a series of much more critical assessments, especially of the appraisal system. These highlighted the constraints within which the scoring system operated and the often divisive outcomes. Thus one associate echoed the comments of the team-leaders, emphasizing that the weighting given to time-keeping and attendance, coupled with constraints on the award of higher grades, meant that:

> You're marking people down on their team work and their attitude to work and the quality of their work because you've got to meet this magic figure. ... Every April you upset everybody.

Another man rehearsed an argument we met several times, namely that the operation of the assessment and grading process crystallized resentment on the shop-floor, precipitating both antagonisms among workers and decisions to leave the firm:

> They'll say 'well we've got four people here that are worthy of assessment', like going up a grade, 'but we can only let two do it this year or this six month period'... really they should be paid the grade but they're not getting it. This is something I disagree with... and it can actually work against you because you can get people with ill feeling towards one another.... 'I'm doing the same input and I just ain't getting it'. So that's why, then, you'll see a job in the paper, 'stuff them, I'm going somewhere else'.

Quitting and grading could thus be closely connected, as exiting became an active protest against perceived unfairness and inconsistency in the way the system operated. This was underlined by another associate who claimed that 'If you looked at when people disappear, they're dissatisfied with their appraisal in general'. Thus sometimes the perceived unfairness evidently acted as a spur to leaving, but for our (non-quitting) informants it served more to reinforce a pattern of grumbling compliance rather than active commitment to the firm.

One important reason for this preoccupation was highlighted by an older man with long experience of working in manufacturing, who emphasized that such policies fostered competition and division among employees:

> They always appear to set worker against worker. That's my opinion.... You can call it competitiveness between associates if you like, but they seem to set up a system where in order to get on, improve the grades, you've got fellow workers prepared to cut your throat if you like.... And where it's caused a deal of animosity is, people that have been on there the longest seem to be overlooked.... You get an element of distrust, you know.

Thus, while a minority of workers embraced the appraisal system with some enthusiasm, many saw it as operating unfairly, both because it left reasonable claims unmet and because it encouraged favouritism and antagonism between fellow workers. In these ways it helped to structure worker responses in ways which encouraged largely individualized coping strategies, rather than any form of organized or collective opposition, though this was also influenced by the very structure of consultation that we will discuss later.

Experiences and responses within the production regime

So far we have considered worker orientations at Part-Co from the vantage point of job options within and beyond the factory and from the wages side of the wage–work bargain. Next we need to explore the demands of the production regime, which constituted the other side of this bargain. First, we will outline key features of day-to-day production arrangements, both in the 'process' area and on the assembly line. These defined the basic requirements to which workers had to accommodate, though there was some scope for tacit bargaining over the precise character of these requirements. Then we will turn to features of the production regime that made additional demands on workers but also offered additional opportunities for some. In particular we will consider responses to the 'QCC' programme. While some employees saw such developments in a positive light, most expressed criticisms or reservations, not least because these initiatives were seen as imposing additional burdens in the context of an already unsatisfactory wage-work bargain.

At Part-Co there were two main production areas. The first was characterized by assembly lines that produced families of major components, each for a specific customer. The second was talked of as the 'process area' and involved a series of highly mechanized processes, interspersed with sub-assemblies and testing stages. Employees occasionally moved between these areas, for example if they were redeployed to cover rush jobs during overtime. However, workers more usually stayed in one part of the plant or the other and the organization and experience of work was recognizably different in these two areas, so we will deal with them separately.

The assembly lines

The assembly lines involved teams of workers (usually between twelve and twenty-five including associates, setters and team leader) working on a specific family of products, with daily switches between different product variants. They varied in terms of the volume of products and the typical cycle time. For example, one produced a relatively light and simple assembly and made up to 800 a day, with tasks fragmented down to twenty-eight seconds. Another made 200 or so of a more complex and bulky assembly, with cycle times of up to two minutes. In each case, though, changes in volume meant adjustments to line balancing and cycle times:

> Our numbers of [units] we've had to build has been going up. So what they've had to do is actually change the line around, split some of the stages down to make it so you can do that stage quicker, like add two or three extra stages in . . . so that they can get the numbers out, and then speed the line up. . . . I mean it's not so bad, because when they actually started speeding the line up they did it slowly, perhaps a second at a time, to actually get used to it. I suppose over time now it's been sped up I've adjusted myself to actually do the job in the time limits, even though it's quicker than it was before.

Thus different lines were characterized by different work cycles and levels of work fragmentation, but incremental adjustments and increases in work rate were shared features across the assembly lines and workers generally accommodated to these features.

One important management concern in allocating workers to tasks on the line was that they accumulated experience of different tasks to facilitate job rotation. Thus one worker commented that:

> What I find with this company is, once they've trained you on anything they like you to move around so that you can get trained on everything. So you're more universal to them, you're not just a static person in one job.

In the early days, when the assembly lines were first being developed, the aim was to train 'associates' on each of the stages for their line, and there was also scope for assemblers to practise off-line. However, this concern for extensive job rotation had become compromised in the context of major increases in production volumes combined with substantial labour turnover. One experienced assembler suggested that the doubling of their production target had meant that 'there's no time to do any training . . . you've got to give them a quick twenty minutes is what you actually do', though weekend overtime was sometimes used to show new people how a complete unit went together. Another worker remarked that she had arrived:

> At a very good time because I was one of the first people that started on the line and the line actually wasn't running at the time, it was still being built.... So I actually learnt to build the whole [product], you know, in the space of a couple of days. Whereas people now, they learn one job and then when they've mastered that job they go on to another job, so it takes much longer to do it.... I mean they do ask for flexibility here, so that you can move around if people are ill or away or whatever.... But there again, if people are away, then you have to stay on the stages that we know best. That's a bit of a pain really.

Thus a basic feature of the working lives of these employees was that they had to accept and cope with the exigencies and pressures of highly routinized assembly-line production, while the scope for learning and moving between different jobs varied according to production priorities. Furthermore, these priorities were rather contradictory. They extolled worker flexibility but they often depended on holding workers on a given task. Workers often had little influence over whether they were moved around or kept in the same place, but as we saw earlier, experienced workers could sometimes gain sufficient leverage to bargain a change between sections or positions.

There was also some space for informal coping strategies and tacit negotiation in regard to other aspects of the work on these lines. The flow of the assembly process was regulated through a kanban system of component supply and batch control, and by the use of 'andon' lights to signal problems and bottlenecks. Meanwhile, the quality of the products was controlled through a threefold inspection process, involving assembler self-checking as products moved down the line, an end-of-line checker who was part of the assembly team, and lastly a quality department inspector. These procedures enforced stringent output and quality targets, but not without an element of negotiation surrounding their implementation. For example, the formal recording of faults was moderated by informal guidance, especially when it involved inexperienced staff. An inspector commented that:

> They always get a bit funny when you send things back, but some things, if there's a little bit of a loose screw, you won't book it straight away, because you give them a chance. But if it keeps on happening you book it.... If it's only like a little gap I send it back, because if you book it there's no point. We're still only human and everyone makes mistakes, but then if they keep doing it all the time then you know that they're not doing it properly or it's a machine fault. But the majority of things you will book.

This comment, coupled with those of assembly-line workers themselves, suggests a rather fine balance between informal guidance and formal notification about faults, underpinned by somewhat fluid (even contested) conceptions of what could be regarded as an understandable mistake.

Either way, of course, fault identification and rectification took place, but the penumbra of informality appeared to lend humanity and hence legitimacy to the process.

However, there were suggestions of a more overt conflict over the use of the 'andon' lights as a potential means of mitigating work pressures, especially in the context of manning arrangements which limited the relief available. An assembler outlined the tactics that could result:

> You're supposed to turn that [light] on to yellow if you're behind, which is a good thing if the setter, or whoever's off-line, will answer it straight away. But like on our line, they don't answer it straight away, you're usually waiting for a while, and then you just get fed up with it and you think I'll turn it straight to red. And then you get told off for having it on red [and stopping the line], so you can't win really.... Because the more you try and rush, if you've got it on yellow and you're falling really behind and you're trying to catch up, you just can't do it. You fall more and more behind. That makes it even worse then.

This suggests that the efforts of team leaders to keep up line speeds and stress the line were to some extent resisted. In turn team leaders sometimes responded by forbidding most assemblers from using the red light, so as to limit line stoppages. From this account such tactics indicated a persistent source of tension, but one in which team leaders continued to have the upper hand.

Talking on the line could also become a point of contention in the process of regulating and negotiating effort, but in this case, as with issues of job rotation, different team leaders adopted rather different tactics. Thus one assembly-line worker remarked that, whereas some supervisors were definitely stricter about talking on the line:

> On our line they don't seem to mind. Because sometimes if you're chatting to somebody next to you or opposite you, you sometimes get the setter or team leader come down and join in.... I think it's better where you can actually talk because you actually want to do the work more, knowing that you haven't just got to stand there doing the same job all through the day without talking to anyone.... You can have a quick chat with somebody, and you don't even have to look up really to chat to anyone. If they're next to you, you can just carry on doing your work and chat as well, as long as there's no problem with your work and you're getting it done... they don't mind.

While this highlights the somewhat different styles of different team leaders, it also suggests that all team leaders were engaged in a balancing act. Often they offered some leeway to workers to mitigate the tedium of work on the line, but only within the limits set by stringent productivity and quality targets (compare pp. 171–2).

Such tensions surrounding the effort bargain were not only characteristic of the relations between workers and management but, in the context of the overall pressures of the production process, could also involve animosities between workmates, a theme also discussed by Sharpe (1997) and explored at length by Delbridge (1998). Thus the associate who had highlighted conflicts surrounding the 'andon' lights claimed that the employees on her line were very friendly with one another, but nevertheless noted that:

> Some people have got an easy stage and they see someone else further down the line struggling to keep up with their stage, and they say 'Oh no, I don't want to do that, I'm going to stay on this one because it's easy for me'.... People don't turn up for work... which lets everybody else down you see, they can't move on to another stage. And then you've also got three or four that don't like moving around, and it all sort of builds up on those that have got a hard stage. They get fed up with it and they say 'why have we got to do this every day. How about putting somebody else on here and let them have a go.'

Certainly there was considerable evidence that, as in Delbridge's (1998) research, assembly workers operated with notions of what were reasonable effort and attention. Moreover, these involved comparisons between workers and the effects of their work on fellow workers, rather more than any direct challenge to management-defined objectives. Sharpe's (1997, 1998) ethnographic study of an analogous factory, with a similarly heterogeneous workforce in terms of age, gender, and labour market experience, suggests that such evaluations were often implicated in the emergence of distinctive age-related sub-cultures on the shop-floor. By comparison our interviews did not suggest that there was one dominant axis of such lateral comparisons among the line workers, but they did support the view that such comparisons and tensions were an important part of the lived experience of these employees. Notions of reasonable effort and attention particularly came into play in workers' responses to the juggling of tasks in the process of line balancing or the movement of operators between tasks. In such contexts they represented a form of peer pressure not to let down fellow workers, and helped to sustain levels of worker effort and attendance, so long as team leaders did not push things too far.

The mechanized process lines

Turning to the mechanized process areas of the factory, the pacing of work there was somewhat less relentless than on the lines, because associates were loading, adjusting, and monitoring machines, though there were some stages of assembly work interspersed between the machine processes. This meant that for the more experienced workers in this area:

> The best feature is you're your own person. You're on your own, you decide your own rate, you do more or less, within the constraints [of the production targets].

This appeared to be coupled with more scope for learning a variety of tasks, generally clustered around one major part of the overall process:

> We do all the jobs. I've been moved around and trained on everything like. So I haven't been stuck on one job.

In these respects process workers generally saw themselves as better placed than the assembly-line workers.

Nevertheless, the procedures involved in the processing and testing of components and in checking the machinery were tightly specified and monitored. For example:

> You've got a big checklist and you have to tick everything off, that's Total Preventative Maintenance (TPM).... And then, whichever shift you're on, you have a disc. ... That's so they can just walk past and if they see it's not done, have a closer look. 'Oh, they haven't done the maintenance check.'

Furthermore, production mistakes could be traced back, at least to the team:

> They can always trace anything back, if there's any faults, trace it back to the shift, maybe not the actual person [but] they know who's responsible for it.

As this implies, that the effective operation of the machinery depended to some extent on the knowledge and experience of the employees:

> The lads who've been here two or three years, they're the ones, they seem to know more than the actual setters and team leaders actually... there's a guy on our shift, and he's been there from the first day and he knows everything, and he sorts things out.

However, engineering management placed substantial emphasis on reducing their dependency on such skills. From a maintenance worker's perspective this meant that:

> They try to make it as foolproof as possible. But then again it takes a lot of the skill factor away then.... They don't want to pay for skills or whatever, to train people, so they're trying just to be able to get somebody off the street, put them on a panel for a day and like, they're safely operating the machine.

Indeed, this informant argued that, though TPM had been implemented when the machinery was installed, it hadn't been followed through consistently, whilst other informants noted that the original detailed specifications for process checking had been progressively simplified into a series of 'bullet point' instructions.

Such features apparently resulted from the pressures of ramping up production, combined with staff turnover and the use of temporary workers. These conditions diluted the pool of expertise among the operators, and also limited the scope for movement between tasks, as the most experienced people had to stay on the critical processes. Thus a process worker remarked:

> I was here about four months and I was the most experienced one [on night shift]. I didn't know what I was doing really. When it came to a machine

> breaking down it was completely and utterly hopeless . . . if you're good at it you're stuck with it, because they get no mistakes, well, one or two, and the others [operators] are terrible, so you're stuck with it really.

Here, then, any explicit management rationale for 'job rotation' in the process of job allocation was compromised by management expediency in conditions of expansion and high labour turnover.

Several process operators nevertheless saw their work routines as distinctly preferable to those of the assembly-line workers, often suggesting that they would not be willing to work permanently in assembly. From the vantage point of the setters in the process areas, especially, variety and responsibility were attractive features of the job:

> I'd rather be moving around doing things like we do here with it being process . . . the setters get together and discuss what we're going to build. They look at the computer and see what needs doing and we sort it out among ourselves. . . . It's quite a responsible job actually. If someone's messing about then you have the authority to tell them 'Get on with your work'.

As this last comment implies, however, tensions still surrounded the implementation of the wage–work bargain in the process areas, as team leaders and setters pushed workers to meet quality and, especially, productivity targets. This was nicely captured by the comments of another nightshift worker:

> At the end of the day the company's paying you to do a job . . . so I do believe that you've got to be prepared to work when you go in, but it's just an atmosphere in the way they pressurize you all the time. They don't need telling 'this is what you've got to do tonight', and then coming back half an hour later, and [another] half an hour later, 'how many have you done?'

In this account, recognition of the obligations of wage labour was combined with an emphasis on the experience of the operators, to question the detailed directives of the team leaders.

Again, though, this left significant scope for different views on what was reasonable among the operators themselves. As another observed:

> On [this process] you just work as a team and have a good laugh . . . when we're working we're just laughing and still working at the same time . . . [but] further up the line they just stop. . . . They're stood around talking all the time, so *they* get watched all the time.

Once more, though, the team leaders were engaged in a balancing act between capitalizing on the capabilities and mutual support of the operators, and exerting pressure to increase production. This could be glimpsed in the reflections of another experienced process operator, responding to a question about the relationship between management control and worker autonomy:

> We work well as a team . . . like, if there is a problem we would get it sorted, but the managers go into a flap. They actually make things worse, get us into a flap too. We would get on fine without them actually. When they are away we actually turn out more product. We can have a laugh and get the job done as well.

In this context an important aspect of the interventions by team leaders and setters was an attempt to orchestrate competitiveness between sections, and more especially shifts, but this also elicited rather varied responses. First, it was recognized that this could draw upon some of the 'games' which operators played in their work ('there's competition there even between us like. You know what I mean, they've struck seven hundred, I'll beat that'), and this could make it easier to get through the work ('I mean he keeps us busy, time seems to fly when you're doing that'). Second, however, it was also clearly recognized that it was their superiors who pushed such competition ('all the shifts, they're doing about six hundred . . . and he likes to hit the thousand a day') and this prompted a certain distancing from the process:

> We have a laugh about it actually. There is a bit of competition there, yeah. I think the team leaders take it very seriously, and the setter. If there's scrap, 'Oh blimey', you know. But there again it's them that's getting the responsibility ain't it. We won't get told off, they probably will in the office. I can understand that they've got the pressure on.

As we will see in the next section, however, such scepticism was selective. It was one element in shop-floor responses to pressures for increased output. However, it was much more widespread in response to the efforts of Part-Co to involve 'associates' more directly in process and product improvement, primarily through the mechanism of QCCs.

Shop-floor views of quality circle rhetoric, ritual, and practice

This firm, as a late arrival, had taken advice from other Japanese firms about how to implement their production regime, and one feature of this advice had been to wait several years before implementing a QCC programme. They had followed this advice, but by the time of our research this programme had become part of the firm's repertoire, though significant numbers of workers (e.g. some new arrivals, some night shift workers) still had little contact with it.

Of those who had participated there were some who were quite enthusiastic and, though setters were disproportionately likely to be such enthusiasts, this also included some associates. For example, a relatively new young assembly-line worker reported that:

> You just volunteer for them . . . you just define something and try and sort it out like, and you're just each given jobs to do to help them along. . . . And then at the end of it you do a presentation to the management. . . . That was just a lad off the line, he was quite good. . . . While we were doing the QCC our investigation sorted it out anyway, so by the time we'd finished the problem had disappeared.

However, it was much more common to express scepticism or cynicism about quality circle activities. This scepticism was grounded in a combination of resentment that the firm was making extra demands on hard pressed and poorly rewarded employees and a feeling that the company was not really serious about worker involvement either. For example, another assembly-line worker commented that she, like many others, was so fed up with her work that she wasn't interested in voluntary participation in QCCs. However, her reluctance was compounded by her judgement that 'weren't going anywhere', especially because in her experience neither the engineers nor the operators had sufficient time to pursue corrective improvements during usual working time:

> Originally it was a couple of the [engineering] guys . . . doing that, but apparently they didn't have time to do it this year, so [the team leader] organized a meeting with our line and says a couple of people like to do it, off our line . . . [but] we don't have time to do it. Like last week was the perfect time to do it but we never got the chance, we just got sent on other lines . . . you just don't get the time and you give up in the end.

There was little dissent from the idea that employees could contribute to process improvements. However, there was a widespread feeling that it was unreasonable to expect enthusiasm for such activities in the context of the overall wage–work bargain on offer.

Moreover, such views were reinforced by a perception that the programme often assumed a ritualistic character. QCC activity was often perceived as going through the motions without much real purpose. Characteristic comments were:

> If it was to improve things, yes, I could agree with it. But the more I see it the more it doesn't improve things. It's doing something for the sake of doing something, but it doesn't come about in actual improvement.
> [*and*]
> We've come up with something, I mean to keep our manager happy. It won't go any further, and then they'll say, right, another one now.

As these comments imply, such judgements were not uninformed, but were often grounded in substantial experience. One sceptic elaborated on this in the following terms:

> We've had one or two battles over that I can tell you. . . . Basically we were informed that we were going to do it. . . . The presentation was very good [they won] and we thought, well, at least at the end of doing the QCC

> something's going to come out of it which is going to benefit the department. And it just disappeared . . . we got to the presentation and that was that. We've heard no more of it since. . . . They came for another one and, of course, I said 'the last one was a blessed waste of time'. . . . It didn't go down very well, and a couple of the younger chaps on the job, they pressured them into starting another one. Of course they went two weeks, and I think the general consensus was that the rest will follow. But the rest didn't follow, and so they stopped doing it . . . I think the basic idea is good obviously, and I mean new ideas always have got to be good for any company. But the end result I do feel, obviously they can't implement everything, but I do feel there should be a reason why.

The way such disenchantment could spread was also evident in the comments of another informant, an employee from the process area who had become a 'one-man' quality circle:

> I've had to do a lot of work myself and I haven't had a lot of help, so I don't think too much to it. . . . The whole section isn't interested basically. Somebody else started it and he said 'no I'm not doing it now, I don't want to do it'. So then they said 'right, well, you'll do it then'. Yeah, cheers for asking me, OK then. So I've had to do most of the work and I haven't done anything on it for two months, and I've got a presentation in about two weeks, and I don't know when I'm going to do it . . . I might just be sick on that day, I don't know. It's hassle you don't need.

Thus, many employees viewed quality circles with some disdain, both because of the extra pressures that were involved and because there was little sign of positive outcomes from the vantage point of the shop-floor.

One of the sceptics quoted above also argued that, despite the rhetoric, such activities actually failed to tap the tacit knowledge of the workforce in any meaningful way, and he had captured this apparent paradox in a couple of verses. One of these, called 'Useful item?', was apparently hung in the appropriate place on the machine line, and read in part:

> Do we really have to have a tray,
> For stopping dripping on the floor,
> Positioned in a place
> Where oil has never dripped before?

Another verse, titled 'The Unconsulted Working Man', reiterated a theme articulated by many workers in other workplaces, but given curious poignancy by the rhetoric of continuous improvement:

> It wouldn't take a lot to ask
> The person who performs the task.
> Would these problems have resulted
> If this person we'd consulted.
> I don't know, it's hard to say,
> He only does it every day.

For this man, at least, the ritual was seen to have displaced the rhetoric in a thoroughgoing fashion. Thus, the scepticism about quality circles was partly grounded in a dissatisfaction with the prevailing effort bargain, but it was also reinforced by this gap between rhetoric and practice which itself was read as a reflection of management's own priorities in the organization of production on the shop-floor.

Worker discontent and the scope and limits of challenges to management

We have already seen that dissatisfactions with the wage–work bargain at Part-Co were variously expressed through searching for alternative jobs and quitting; seeking to mitigate some of the most onerous features of the production regime, sometimes against and sometimes in cooperation with team leaders; and limiting involvement in such additional activities as QCCs. Grumbles and grievances, especially about wages, grading and work demands, appear to have been widely articulated among fellow workers, but only rarely addressed directly to management.

It was also evident, however, that some individuals, particularly some of the older workers with extensive industrial and trade union experience, had voiced criticisms of aspects of management policies directly to their superiors. One such worker, one of the vocal sceptics about QCCs, emphasized that he was quite positive about some features of his employment relationship but that he still spoke out when he thought it justified:

> In some ways I think of myself as a company man and I like to think I won't just say things for the sake of being against the company. If I see a good idea I can say it's a good idea, but I can't go along with things that perpetuate the bullshit system if you like. That's what I don't get on with, what I can't do with.

At the same time he felt some vulnerability as an individual critic, remarking that 'I mean, that's why I'm surprised really I'm still here, because I fall out with them over [such things as QCCs]'. Similarly, another such employee, pleased to have been taken on at his age but very critical of aspects of management policy and practice, said that on a series of occasions he had openly questioned aspects of management policy, but he also reflected, 'do you know where that's got me? I'm on the same grade as [when] I came here'.

Such comments raise questions about the opportunities that workers may have to articulate their grievances in a more collective and public fashion. As we have noted, none of the Japanese companies in Telford recognized a trade union, but Part-Co, like several others, did have an 'employee forum' where workers could raise issues and put questions to management. Some employees were quite positive about this meeting.

Indeed, in contrast to many of the other older industrial workers, one ex-miner told us that:

> They have regular [employee forums], and well, the only thing you cannot mention is wages, so by and large everything else, as far as I know, is brought up. And the problem, whether they get done or not, well, you know, is besides the point. But they are there.... I mean obviously things like that have to go to higher discussions, don't they. I don't know whether the unions do any better. They could cause you more trouble in the long run.

This man had experienced the 1984–5 strike and had returned to work after eight weeks, and he was deeply critical of militant trade unionism. In this case, then, a deep disillusionment with traditional trade unionism underpinned a willingness to accept what was recognized as a quite limited form of consultation.

More often, however, this consultative meeting came in for considerable criticism. One common theme was that all the important things, such as wages and grievances about appraisal, were excluded from the meetings, leaving only rather trivial items to be dealt with:

> You can talk about anything bar money, and that's the only thing you want to talk about really. Because the rest of it is just, well you're going through the motions.

Another worker, an assembler who had worked at the factory for several years, summarized a widespread view of the superficiality of these meeting:

> A lot of the time when associates come for the meeting, and they go back, [other workers] say 'Oh, have you asked this question... what answer did you get?'. And they say, all the time, all you'll ever get is, [management] say 'yeah we're thinking about it. We're looking into it.' That's the only answer you'll ever get... You don't get anywhere, and I think it's a waste of time having them.

However, it should also be noted that this did not entirely negate the possibility that employees could use these meetings to gain some leverage. Another of our informants explained:

> There's certain things they won't discuss, like money and things.... They'll discuss overtime but it depends how you ask him... if you ask them nicely you can get a bit of a discussion going and you can get a bit out of them. ... You have to be careful how you do it, because if you raise an issue and it gets back to the manager, they don't know who raised the question... and they'll jump up and down, saying 'why didn't you come to us first?'... [Sometimes you can get something done] by approaching them and saying 'well if you did something about it now, we wouldn't have to be ready for the [employee forum]'. Then they do something then.... You have to use it to your advantage as much as you can.

Thus there were some ways in which these meetings could be used, either directly through careful use of questions, or indirectly to pressure section management.

The scope for such skilful opportunism was, however, severely limited, not just by the exclusions from the agenda but also by the way in which workers were selected to attend by management on a roughly rotating basis. Thus the experience of the employee forum raised questions about the role that a union might play as a more autonomous representative structure within such a firm. This issue arose more or less automatically in discussions with those workers who had fairly extensive experience of unionized workplaces elsewhere, though it had limited salience for many of the younger employees. In general, older, experienced workers felt that union organization could improve their situation in the firm (though as we have just noted, there were significant exceptions). Thus one remarked that 'I think if we had unions, yeah, we'd be worker representatives if you like, [have] worker representation', while another asserted that:

> If this place was unionized they'd be on strike more times than who knows what, just because [management change things as they want].... If you had a union, that would never have happened.... Because unions being unions, they won't stand for any messing, you know. Anything silly, it's like they'd be out.

However, while there were substantial shop-floor grievances that a union should be able to address, there was also a recognition among such experienced and sympathetic workers that union organization would face major obstacles.

Not only would a trade union have to overcome management hostility but it would also have to transform the perspectives of many of the employees. Thus one worker remarked that non-unionism 'was something a lot of them accept when they come here now', in part because many youngsters had no experience of trade unions. However, he also felt that there was no real sense of solidarity among the older workers either, including those with previous union experience, in part because of the apparent powerlessness of unions:

> If you've got no unity with your workforce, you're all singled out. I mean you can get cases in the department where actually somebody's been, not picked on but unjustly accused of doing something, and they're just getting roped in the office or whatever, you know. Like they haven't got any backing really.... Like they won't stick up together. So you're wasting your time anyway.

Such employees confronted some of the real difficulties of developing any concerted or collective way of articulating and pursuing grievances at Part-Co. While there were widely shared and often deeply felt grievances in this workplace, there was also a substantial variety of experiences and outlooks among the workforce. Meanwhile, management policies served to contain, diffuse, and fragment grievances, and there was a widely shared belief that management opposition and union weakness would make moves towards collective organization arduous.

VIEWS FROM THE SHOP-FLOOR AT COPY-CO

Leaving, staying and job security

Most of the shop-floor workers we interviewed at Copy-Co had relatively long service, having worked there for between four and ten years, reflecting the composition of the workforce there. Thus most were experienced workers who had decided to stay at Copy-Co, and many of them juxtaposed this decision to the high turnover going on around them in earlier years. One recalled that in the early days:

> A lot of people could get jobs in Telford, so if you came for a week here and then you got a job over the road . . . that was more money, they just left for that job. There were that many jobs about. Some people said 'well sod it, I'll move to that one'.

Another agreed but charted longer-term shifts:

> It was like a drop-in centre, they would just come. There was so many jobs about and they'd say 'I don't like this job', just go over the road and get another job. But since the recession they just stay in their jobs, they get to know people and it makes it harder for them to leave. . . . [But he added] but lately there has been quite a few people leaving. Jobs are coming up.

Thus the pace of recruitment had fluctuated as the initial wave of recruits (and high turnover) was followed by a period of consolidation, as the labour market slackened but the firm adopted its job security policy. This had been followed by a modest recent phase of renewed recruitment, often via Temping Agencies in the first instance, but the bulk of the workforce were quite settled. This was emphasized by a recently recruited agency worker who herself hoped to become permanent: 'I think most people are happy here, most of the people I work with have been here for years, you know, so it proves it's quite good.' Thus our research primarily addressed the orientations and concerns of these relatively settled workers.

Initially, as we have seen, there had been a strong preference for young recruits, making it difficult for older people to get a job:

> I had a hell of a game to get in because when I came here the average age throughout the company was twenty-two I think or twenty-three, and I came here [a short time] before my fortieth birthday. And my first couple of applications were refused, so I wrote them a letter saying please don't dismiss

me out of hand, please grant me an interview and then decide, but don't decide on my age.... So I came here and got the job.

As the recruitment policy changed the workforce became more diverse in this respect. However, throughout the life of the factory, but especially in periods of active recruitment, managers had tried to recruit through kin or friends, and almost half of our informants had gained their jobs partly through recommendations from relatives, though many of these relatives had themselves later moved on. At the same time, recruitment difficulties at times of expansion had encouraged the firm to recruit across a wider hinterland, running buses from several surrounding centres, and this had also increased the diversity of the workforce, in terms of age, experience, and ethnicity.

Against this background our informants often recalled that their decision to seek work at Copy-Co was a mixture of the sheer availability of a job at the time and a reasonable reputation in relation to terms and conditions. One man remarked that:

> I wouldn't have actually come here, but the job I was in before, they were doing a lot of cutbacks and there was no way of getting on there because the jobs were getting so scarce, and the money wasn't very good either.

Nevertheless, many continued to offer a broadly positive view of working for the firm, albeit tempered with important reservations about the conduct of day-to-day management. Thus one informant, who made many criticisms of the social organization of production and the relations between management and workers, also commented that:

> I'm happy with the pay, the pay isn't the problem. I like to come to work to earn and I come here because I do love coming here... and there's more positive things about it than negative, it's a very good company.... There's things that they could do to make it better, [but] it's only simple things that are wrong, there's nothing major wrong here.... It's just simple things that are never addressed, and things just fester and fester and fester.

This mixture of goodwill towards the firm and frustrations about important features of shop-floor relations was widespread at Copy-Co, and will be a focus of our discussion below, though it should also be noted that many workers were rather more critical in their overall responses than this particular employee.

Wages were clearly an important part of the mix. They were often viewed quite positively, especially in comparison with earlier experiences of casual and unskilled work. Thus one man who had been a Youth Training Scheme (YTS) trainee in the building trade commented that:

> Moving from site to site, different areas, it was quite nice, I used to enjoy that. But I was on a YTS scheme there, and the money wasn't that much. That's why I applied to Copy-Co, the money was better.

Similar comparisons were made by women who had worked (often part-time) in shops or offices, and they often presented the move to full-time factory work primarily in instrumental terms: 'I just want to come to work, earn my money, go home, basically forget about work.'

However, such comparisons did not sustain an uncritical view of wages at the firm. For example, when asked about negative features of the job some people highlighted the relatively low pay:

> I know someone who's in the same situation as me, who works for [a similar] department, but for a British company. He's on something like fifteen thousand pounds, compared to what we do, what we're on, our pay is nine thousand, eight hundred.

There were also significant criticisms of the structuring of the reward system and the perceived effort bargain in the firm. As one informant commented:

> Oh, it's better than my other jobs, but for what you do, you could get paid more. I find it hard to believe how a senior op gets more money than an operator. . . . I find it totally wrong, I think they should pay the operators basically nearer to what the senior ops are getting, because they have to stand there all day.

Nevertheless, reservations about wage levels were often placed in the context of the attractions of relative job security. As one person said:

> It pays in a way because people are loyal. People leave for better-paid jobs, but even then you think well, is it worth leaving and going to an English company, where you might get more money for a year and a half and then, the first time they lose an order, you're out. Whereas here you're safe, it's not brilliant money but you survive.

As this suggests, for many workers job security was one of the particular attractions of employment at Copy-Co during recent years.

Security had rarely been a primary motive for applying to the firm, but was rather an advantage that people had come to appreciate, sometimes with some surprise after initial scepticism about management's commitment in this regard. Typical shop-floor comments were:

> They don't believe in getting rid of people, no. They made that very obvious in the beginning. There were rumours going around the factory saying 'Oh, we're going to be made redundant', and in all fairness the managing director got up and gave a speech and said there were no redundancies.
> [*and*]
> They said we've got a job and secure even if there is a recession, and they just stuck by it. When we had the recession we had people walking around doing nothing at all, just waiting for something to do, jobs to pick up. It was quite good that was.

In this way Copy-Co's avoidance of redundancies was seen as a distinct modification of usual British employment relations. Furthermore, workers often accepted management expectations of a quid pro quo for this policy, though not in a way that was felt to transform their relations with management. As we saw earlier (p. 147), one worker remarked that 'none of us like to admit it, but I think they've done us a favour, so you tend to do them one good favour like', but he also explained his equivocation in very standard terms: 'it's us and them isn't it, everywhere I've ever worked at it's always like, there's the bosses and there's us.'

The restructuring of internal job ladders and the theme of favouritism

The early growth of the factory meant that many of those we talked to had participated in some movement through the operator grades. Furthermore, the possibility of such advancement had often encouraged them to stay with the firm. However, as we saw in Chapter 7, the restructuring of supervision by the dominant management coalition had dramatized the uncertainties associated with such progression. Some people believed these changes had made little practical difference, and this could be seen quite positively when it was felt that relationships continued much as before. However, even continuity was often regarded quite critically, by emphasizing the superficial and cosmetic character of the innovations. A particularly pithy comment was:

> It's ridiculous isn't it... why they think of these silly stupid ideas about team leaders, we're not a team, we're working. It's a supervisor at the end of the day. It's just another fancy term for doing all that.

However, many ordinary workers thought more was at stake and they were often sharply critical.

One theme of shop-floor criticisms was to question management's judgement. In particular the competencies of people who had lost out in the process were defended, while the inexperience of the outside appointees was emphasized. However, the most consistent theme was the perceived erosion of promotion possibilities:

> It's caused more trouble with the senior operators. I mean there's been a lot of trouble about that because, as they say, they're going nowhere.

Such sentiments were particularly significant because they formed the basis for criticisms of a specifically British management policy by those workers who had stuck with the firm, people who had benefited from the no-redundancy policy and progression within internal job ladders. One commented that:

> When all the Japanese people started to go back to Japan, I think personally [and] what other people who have left think, that the British managers are

going backwards in the way they think.... It says on these posters 'team spirit' and all this, but it doesn't seem to be there from above.

Thus some felt that the growing role of British managers was undermining better relations between workers and managers and actually motivating people to leave.

These criticisms were also coloured by widespread charges of favouritism and patronage. A typical remark was that promotion was difficult 'unless your face fits or unless you know somebody that's a little bit higher'. Another informant claimed that a team leader who was much disliked had got her job through family connections and concluded:

Well, nepotism exists and it's a fact of life and if you're going to have a stranger in the family you're going to always come down on the side of your family rightly or wrongly aren't you, [but] that makes a very very bad aspect.

Again, in this regard, some people drew an explicit contrast between Japanese and British managers:

I think people are more recognized for their accomplishments under the Japanese. You're recognized for your own merits under a Japanese manager. It seems to me that if you work for a British manager it depends who you play golf with.

This argument was voiced by an informant who was actively contemplating leaving the firm. As a skilled worker he felt there were definitely alternative jobs available, and if limited promotion prospects left little scope to compensate for the relatively low pay rates then moving became more attractive. Indeed he claimed that several recent recruits in his skilled section were also 'actively looking for another position' as they felt that 'they've been employed under false pretences'. [It should also be noted that in this context he was vehement in condemning the apparent effort of Japanese companies to restrict movement between their factories: 'you're selling your time and skills to someone else and I think it is totally wrong that you should be discouraged from going from one company to another'.]

Operators often contrasted their own experience of being stuck on the line with the patronage afforded to some:

You just get really pissed off with it, just working on a line, just working five years putting screws in, it just got really boring, and I think well I ain't going nowhere in this company. So if you ask most of the operators, it's who you know not what you do... and most of it's drinking buddies.

Similarly, an Asian worker felt that his opportunity to progress had been curtailed compared with other employees, and detected racial undertones:

I've been in the same job since I've been here, I mean I would like a change. I did try [to move] but unfortunately I think if your face fits or you get along with management then there's a point where you might be able to progress

> further.... At that point I felt as though I was like really left out, and that to me was a racial thing, from my point of view anyway.

Again his cumulative experience had led him to think seriously about leaving the company. Such examples show that the ways in which job ladders operated at Copy-Co often generated criticisms of management framed in the language of favouritism, and on occasion such grievances informed thinking about quitting.

Another aspect of the scepticism about promotion prospects was a feeling that progression depended on sycophancy. Thus on the one hand we were told that 'sometimes if you've got an opinion you've got to keep it to yourself if you want to get on'. On the other hand, however, it was claimed that people had rejected promotion because 'I won't, I can't suck up to the system... I can't lick a backside, I have to tell the truth'. Such sentiments focused attention on significant shop-floor cynicism and distrust of the ways in which managers made decisions about promotion and progression. These views reinforced a sense of a division between managers and supervisors and the shop-floor. This was captured in such remarks as 'basically the theory on the lines is, if they tell you something wait till it happens, don't believe what they tell you, wait until it happens' and the suggestion quoted earlier (p. 140) that 'operators are treated as the lowest of the low'.

By the time of our research, then, established workers at Copy-Co had often become sceptical about the operation of the firm's internal labour market, though many remained appreciative of the job security on offer. Some of those who felt they had lost out were contemplating leaving, and there was more evidence of such moves than in the recent past, but most of our informants expected to stay despite their criticisms. However, the experience of the restructuring of supervision and associated management policies had clearly eroded earlier expectations and commitments among long service workers, so that shop-floor workers felt more at odds with management.

Attractions and limitations of the work regime

How, then, did shop-floor workers experience and respond to the daily work regime, the demands of the labour process and patterns of work discipline, at Copy-Co? First, in positive terms, it was fairly common to compare Copy-Co favourably with earlier work experience in terms of the overall feel of the place. Some informants talked of a 'better atmosphere' and some even felt that it was 'more relaxed' in comparison with other workplaces. For example, one man who was by no means uncritical drew a sharp contrast with his negative experience of a previous firm (one described in similar terms by several of our informants):

> Basically I think it was a very hard crack of the whip type of management there, you couldn't really do a lot, they were always there spying on you. It was pretty bad in that respect, no leeway, they are very racist, a lot of bad things. I don't think there was anything good I can say.... After being there, this was like, I don't know really, luxury.

Another man drew a contrast with his experience of humiliation on YTS training by highlighting an emphasis on problem solving rather than blame allocation at Copy-Co:

> Here they're very easy going... I know YTS, you're at the bottom of the pile but here, you know, you don't have people having a go at you so much as you do there. If you make a problem here they'll always say 'Oh what have you done wrong', but being a YTS kid it was slap you round the head and say 'don't do it again' like. They wouldn't know what you'd done, just make sure you didn't do it again.... [Here] it's very laid back, too nice to people at times. I mean some of the lads will say it's like being treated like a kid, they won't give you a going over if you've done something wrong, they always try and find out what's going wrong like.

At Copy-Co, then, work discipline and the overall work regime were often experienced as more constructive and congenial than at other workplaces.

Often employees were also quite positive about the ways in which managers tried to help those who experienced ill health or other personal problems. For example, one man reported that, after an industrial accident, he was paid through the nine months he was off work and then found a lighter job when he returned, so 'that is one of the areas where the company was very good to me to be quite honest'. Sometimes the company policy of grouping workers with 'problems' on one line did come in for criticism:

> There was a man with a broken ankle, somebody with a broken arm..., and there was a lady that was a total misfit... and there was a man that was waiting for a hernia operation. They used to call it the donkey line. There was myself, I'd had five weeks off with stress, and there was another girl there who had arthritis, and it was like all donkeys, just donkeys, it was totally demoralizing.

However, the dominant interpretation of such arrangements was quite positive and seemed to reinforce the appreciation of management's stance on job security.

Nevertheless, the theme of favouritism, noted earlier, also had significant currency in interpreting relations among operators themselves, expressed in animosities about perceived favours or unequal treatment in the ways in which supervisors, team leaders or even senior operators allocated tasks, exercised discipline or balanced the line. In these contexts friendship patterns but also gender and ethnic distinctions were invoked as bases of unfair treatment, suggesting a pattern of social relations in which mistrust played a significant role. In this atmosphere one man claimed that:

> You do find women tend to get away with more than men, you know what I mean. Women will moan and groan more and they get away with it, and the manager will ease off. Men or anybody else, no chance. 'Just do it'. It's as simple as that, whether you like it or not. That's how it works. They're not fair to everybody here. I think sometimes they have their favourites . . . I know a lot of people know the manager really well . . . and they've all got cushy numbers.

Meanwhile, a woman argued that:

> This is what I think is the most common problem, I've experienced this myself, where it's all boys, all men, and the senior op does the capacity changes. So his mates will say to him 'Oh I don't like doing that, give that to her', and that's quite common. And it's quite common for senior ops to give the best and the least jobs to their friends, but there isn't a balance, it isn't fair.

Finally one white woman claimed that:

> If a line stops for some reason you can get a coloured worker walking around doing nothing, and as long as they're keeping out of sight and not getting found out they're not doing it. But if you get two or three of us stood talking, 'Can't you find these people something to do!' This is the way it goes on, you see. They [minority ethnic workers] like to say what they want to do, 'I'll do this [operation], and I'll do that and I'll do something else'. They like to think that there's not being any more put on them, nothing more than what they're exactly supposed to do, whereas to be honest that's not the point. If you can accept a little bit more work and somebody else is struggling then you should be able to take it.

There are suggestions here of the advantages that might accrue to mates or girlfriends and of the defensive responses of disadvantaged women or ethnic minority workers. There are also hints of patterns of inclusion or exclusion from informal patterns of mutual co-worker support, though our material does not allow us to explore these themes in greater depth. However, the salience of the language of favouritism in discussions of day-to-day work obligations and effort norms suggests that at Copy-Co worker grievances were often articulated in terms of mutual suspicions and antagonisms among shop-floor employees, as well as criticisms of management.

An important illustration of the interplay between these features was provided by widespread criticisms of the ways in which managers awarded merit bonuses, and especially the prominence they gave to records of attendance. A quite typical comment was that it was:

> Completely stupid the way they do it. They come to you and they say they are going to assess you, your job, what grade you are going to be. They show you the list, how you do your job, your attendance and all this is down there, and then they say 'well the assessment is good, you have passed everything, except your attendance'. You say 'well, what's wrong with my attendance?'

> 'You've had eight days off.' So you don't get the assessment, then you find out they've given it to somebody else who they know, and you are wondering why. So half the time you think this assessment is just an attendance assessment. It's not really about your job, because you could have ticks for everything on your job. The assessment always lets you down, which has happened to me.

One aspect of such criticism concerned the way management discretion was exercised: 'I think in a lot of people's cases it all depends on how they get on with the manager, at the end of the day it's at his discretion . . . so I think it's pretty unfair'. Another aspect was the one-sided preoccupation with attendance, a point formulated particularly strongly by a woman who also characterized Copy-Co as 'a very good company', when she claimed that:

> They tend to term loyalty here as good attendance. There's people here who come in and sit on their backside day after day after day. To me this is disloyal.

This captures the preoccupation with fairness and favouritism. Managers were clearly seen as imposing an inflexible policy on attendance, which unreasonably penalized workers, but sometimes they were also seen as tolerating limited efforts in the job itself. To address the ways in which production rates and effort norms were actually negotiated and experienced on the shop-floor, however, it is necessary to distinguish different areas of the factory with distinctive production arrangements and recent histories of restructuring.

Process production

In process production, the area most crucial to the profitability of the whole enterprise, small teams, predominately male, worked rotating twelve-hour 'continental' shifts (three on, three off) to manage a continuous process in relatively hot and dirty conditions. In this context long-standing workers gained considerable expertise in managing the production process, a theme emphasized in the comments of one of the most experienced process workers:

> There is a set procedure in writing, but at the moment it's been altered and changed so much now I don't think it's up-to-date. But I think it all comes down to experience because if a plant is running and you are experienced you can actually tell by sound, from the other end of the department, you can hear something going wrong on one of the machines if you know what you are doing, and you can actually go over and stop it before it starts, if you know what I mean.

Their task was to combine and balance consistent quality standards with high volumes of production, through a combination of effective start-ups, careful monitoring and also problem-solving and repairing when there was a breakdown.

However, there was a feeling that both the work pressures and levels of expertise in this area had increased without commensurate rewards:

> over the years I've noticed the workload had got more, if you know what I mean. Every year there is something added on, like the maintenance, it's getting bigger. We are having to do courses... which makes you better, but there is more work involved at the end of the day with it.

Furthermore, this assessment was explicitly linked to dissatisfactions about pay:

> People don't mind doing it as long as the money was there with it, because when we are actually doing maintenance engineering courses we are on the operators' [rate] now, and we feel the job is quite big for the wage.

In this setting, then, workers were sharply critical of the skill and effort bargain. There was considerable pressure to keep the production rate up: 'if we can't get the production out it's an ear-bashing sort of thing, that's what we get'. At the same time the use of temporary agency workers had placed more pressure and responsibility on the permanent workers, because the temporary workers were neither sufficiently experienced nor motivated to undertake much of the work, 'so that puts more stress on us, we are running around to try to cover the plant'. Furthermore, people in this area also felt that production pressures sometimes compromised regular maintenance:

> We have set schedules for maintenance every month, and there has been times when it's been three months before we've been able to do any maintenance. We haven't been able to shut the plants down, so of course the wear and tear of the stuff has got worse and worse. In turn this made problems and crises more likely.

In this area management had taken the opportunity of the restructuring of supervision to tighten discipline and displace an 'indulgency pattern' (Gouldner 1954), characterized by both camaraderie and horseplay, that had flourished especially during the night shifts. The shift workers themselves emphasized the rigours of the twelve-hour night-shift. One remarked:

> I can't stand working nights. You don't sleep in the day because you are coming on nights. You come here walking about like a zombie all night and the work has still got to get done. You go home the next day, it just takes you for ever to recover.

They also highlighted the alternation of boredom and crisis in dealing with process production, which was the context in which games and pranks were an aspect of nightshift life, especially in quiet periods. However, management felt they had lost control, and used the substitution of team leaders for the leading hands, who had been the senior people on the plant at night, to tighten supervision and discipline. Asked about this one operator commented:

> It's just tightened down really. Before they introduced these team leaders we had what was called leading hands, they were just as bad as everybody else. They would get the cricket out and have a game of cricket. The football would come out. They would even throw buckets of water down off the top of the plants.... They were just as bad as each other so they couldn't say anything. It's calmed down a bit.... The canteen used to be open. We used to go in there, the three of us, cook sausage, bacon, eggs, and wash and wipe up and they wondered where all the stuff had gone next morning! Used to be all right. Those days have gone, they've just gone.

From British management's perspective the implementation of the new structure in such areas inserted 'people management' where a technical focus, combined with reliance on leading hands, had previously left something of a vacuum. In turn workers experienced these developments as a definite tightening up, though the exigencies of process production and night work still encouraged the new team leader, an experienced shift worker, to adopt a relatively relaxed approach, so that 'so long as the work gets done and the stuff's tidy they leave you alone'.

Complex assembly

Here, too, there was some feeling that *British* management initiatives, in particular, had tightened discipline in ways that were regarded as petty, as the example of the enforcement of rigid break times mentioned in Chapter 7 illustrated. Some saw this as part of a wider attempt to tighten work discipline, and again to undermine aspects of an 'indulgency pattern' on the shop-floor. One worker explained that on their existing line the senior operators were 'sort of relaxed older people'. As a result the work got done, but there was also scope to 'sit down and chatter'. On the new line, however, management's intention was to 'cut out all the bad habits' of established workers:

> So you've finished your job, you can go to this canteen early [but] they penalize you for it, get on your back and say you've got to wait until the buzzer goes... so they've got petty things like that going on they want to stop so that [the new line], they'll go when the buzzer goes, so [new employees] won't know what we're like.

Thus the existing repertoire of workers' survival strategies, such as talking on the line or trying to get an early place in the canteen queue, was under threat.

However, the effort bargain itself was seen less negatively than in the process area. Certainly workers commented on the stresses and pressures of the work process, especially for those directly on the line rather than in off-line locations. For example, one woman who had worked at both highlighted the stress of the line compared with sub-assembly, though she also noted the positive aspect of what Baldamus (1961) called 'traction':

> The biggest difference is pressure and stress. For instance I'm still geared to the line, I supply the line and I'm supposed to go in time with the line... I can do two [assemblies] quickly or one slowly and one quickly and still produce the same result. Whereas there [on the line] it's more spontaneous if you like, which I much prefer, I like the continuation, I much prefer that.... But I actually like the atmosphere where I am now because it's far less stressful because the line is very very stressful. It's the pressure that's put upon you to, if you've got a problem you've still only got the same time to do that [task], that is the problem.

However, as we saw in Chapter 7, an emphasis on quality levels, combined with tacit bargaining over job times and informal understandings over work procedures, limited management efforts to push work rates upwards in this area.

The senior operators, experienced workers with some responsibility for sustaining production, provided rich vignettes of the resulting dynamics of surveillance, pressure, survival tactics, and informal bargaining involved in managing the effort bargain on and around these lines. One senior operator recounted a characteristic process of monitoring and implicit bargaining over job timing and manning levels:

> We were supposed to have had seven minutes [cycle time] but we were on fifteen minutes to start off with, but our jobs were taking us like twenty-one minutes and there was no way you could keep up. They worked it out on paper... but it doesn't work. They don't ask the operators how the job is going to go, because they will be standing with the stopwatch and they will say 'we'll time you'. And it's like if we get a part outside our time to put on a machine [they] stop the stopwatch, they don't start the stopwatch, it's just when you put the part on the machine, so you were losing time anyway. Production control... stand around timing, or they would be hiding away behind the glass, because they reckon that the operators will slow down as soon as they see a stopwatch just to gain more time. When he found out we were doing the job at twenty-one minutes he said we were walking it. [We replied] 'You try doing the job yourself'. So we got a relief on the job and he was taking longer than all of us put together, so they had to do something about it.

Another senior operator emphasized the limited acceptability of any close monitoring of experienced workers who knew their jobs well and also suggested that there was some scope to bend job specifications to use modified work routines without clearing this with supervisors or managers. In turn he commented that

> You've got to be careful that you don't get too friendly with the ones at the top because then the lads on the line ain't going to like it, but you can't always side with the lads on the bottom because then you're going to get your own neck chopped. So it's a funny line to walk at times... I'd sooner fall out with the

> managers than I would with the people at the bottom, because half the time the lads know their job anyway so you're on good ground if you're with them. Whereas I mean all managers, they probably know in theory a lot better than I do, but in practice we're the ones that do it.

Thus these accounts suggest that, in the complex assembly area, a broadly accepted effort bargain grew out of a rather uneasy and unsettled relationship between management initiatives directed at controlling production and the practical arrangements through which production was accomplished.

Simple assembly

In the simple assembly area the job cycles were much shorter and the work was very repetitive. Workers noted that 'the pace was quite quick', so 'none of the jobs are difficult, the difficulty is the speed', especially on 'a very very hectic, busy line'. Indeed one of the senior operators believed that 'if they decided to turn the line [speed] up there would be uproar, because really it's doing some now'. She also mentioned that there had been at least one occasion in the past when some people had walked off the line in protest, but had then been coaxed back to work. This suggests that work pressures were quite intense, but awareness of the potential for informal sanctions did set upper bounds to the work rate that could be expected.

However, work pressures also fluctuated according to demand, and there was usually some scope for sociability. Some groups were not so strongly paced:

> Really the line I work on is probably the slowest line up there, and the sort of work, we haven't really got a line as such, we like work on a table, so you can have a natter now and again, so it's very nice and the people are very nice.

Others were more directly paced by a belt but even so:

> People get used to the lines. It's a bit like a home. I know it sounds silly but we do actually live here for a lot of hours a day, and people do tend to get used to who they're working with, the job they're doing, line speed and everything.

Furthermore, it had become increasingly common to rotate people between a range of different tasks, often switching between a couple of jobs each day and around the team through the week. This introduced a degree of flexibility so that absences could be covered, but also made things fairer by sharing better and worse jobs around the group: 'because of the speed of the line some of the jobs are quite tiring, and quite tough on your wrists and shoulders, so we swap them around four times a day'. In turn this mitigated conflicts and accusations of favouritism between workers.

Camaraderie among workers also carried over into helping each other out: 'if you knew somebody was having a bad day then "Oh she's having a bad day, we'll give her a bit of a hand" like', while 'if somebody gets slightly behind then somebody will help them out'. Indeed, a common feature of work in this department was a reliance on informal mutual aid to facilitate the work process. In particular senior operators played a central role in covering for tasks left uncompleted by inexperienced workers ('we can make them look really good when they're not so good'), rectifying faulty assemblies ('if we get an operator that's really turning out a lot of errors then [senior operators] will go to the end of the line and help put it all right, it's all put right') or helping the maintenance engineer during a tool change ('he is supposed to do the changeover but there's quite a lot involved . . . so we get in there and help them out').

Finally this pattern of working, and perhaps also a concentration of women workers in this area, provided the basis for a particularly strong pattern of sociability in this part of the factory, with cakes, flowers or gifts to mark particularly significant events like important birthdays or people leaving. The employment of temporary agency workers potentially cut across these features, but to some extent they were also assimilated into the existing networks of sociability.

Criticisms of management and the absence of a trade union

As we have seen, many workers saw Copy-Co as a relatively good employer, offering job security and a less pressured working environment than some of the comparable firms, but there were grievances about tightening discipline and especially about the scope and bases for progression in the internal labour market. In this context managers at Copy-Co relied entirely on existing management structures to receive and respond to workers' concerns, either through the grievance procedure or through direct approaches to supervisors, personnel or senior management. Many workers were critical of these arrangements, but few felt that there was an obvious alternative other than to quit.

Not everyone felt that it was difficult to address management. Several of our employee interviewees suggested that it was easy to approach management, including the senior British manager. One commented that: 'accessibility is the word, I think, because you can pick up the phone anywhere in the factory and [this manager] is there'. However such positive views tended to be expressed by a minority of employees who had themselves been helped with personal problems, while scepticism about the procedures was much more common when working arrangements or terms and conditions were disputed. Thus another worker, discussing a grievance over overtime premia, argued that the procedure was too formal and legalistic and his section manager tended to ignore complaints, displaying 'a very lackadaisical, don't rock the boat attitude'. Thus on such matters 'there's no neat way where you can ask a reasonable question'.

Indeed quite positive and committed workers could be critical of management in this regard. One such employee argued that:

> There's no support. You know if you've got a problem it won't be resolved. You either let it fester or you leave, and simple problems get out of hand and it's no good.

In particular it was often felt that the internal hierarchy did not provide a satisfactory route for resolving grievances:

> You go through the grievance procedure and you go through your supervisor, your assistant manager.... It never used to get past assistant manager and you know it won't get past [the section manager].... There should be an external outlet, and I think the problem is, personnel is there to promote the company image. My idea of personnel is for the people, that's how I interpret it, to help with people.

Thus there was little confidence that complaints from below would be heard and acted upon through these mechanisms.

As we saw in Chapter 7, there was also considerable scepticism at Copy-Co about management's commitment to QCC activities and in this context, too, workers felt they were not taken seriously. Even when employees became quite engaged in the process they felt that management did not engage with their ideas:

> We were going for it, really going for it, but management didn't, you know, so they let us down badly on that, I think management did, and then you get well 'why should we bother again, what's the point, stuff it'.... And now they've got this suggestion scheme and there's very very few people from [this area] that'll be interested.

Such experiences led one of the skilled maintenance workers, who was very appreciative of the tacit skills of the operators, to turn the argument about QCCs back on management:

> So I ask myself, where's the management quality circle? Are they saying 'Oh, there's absolutely nothing wrong with management'? I mean, the best way to look at things is to look at yourself first, but this has never, ever, come about... they are almost saying that all the problems lie with production, with the shop-floor.

Such comments emphasize that many workers viewed managers as unresponsiveness to shop-floor concerns, whether in relation to suggestions, problems, or grievances.

These findings raised questions about a more formal process of worker representation at Copy-Co, either through a consultative structure or through trade union representation, and such possibilities were raised without prompting by a significant minority of interviewees. However, the dominant response among Copy-Co workers was that summed up in an earlier quote: 'you either let it fester or you leave'. First, there was a certain cynicism about the idea of a company council. Thus the same informant welcomed the idea of such consultation in principle only to dismiss it as unlikely to be effective in practice:

> Well I think something like that would be very good, but the company would then select the people so then it wouldn't be effective.

Second, however, those who considered a potential role for unions were often also sceptical about that option, and rarely saw trade unions as a way of moving beyond the choice of putting up or leaving.

Sometimes this was based on an explicit critique of unions. Thus the person who dismissed a management-dominated consultative process also dismissed the idea of union influence because:

> I don't agree with unions. I'm anti-union because I think in the days of the Tolpuddle Martyrs . . . there was [a need for] a union then, but I think that need has gone. I think unions have destroyed the coal industry. . . . Because it means greed at the end of the day and I don't think that you should have these union dictators that are political. I think if you've got a problem with your workplace you should deal with it in the workplace . . . you can have the best union in the world, if you haven't got a good management relationship you might as well forget it . . . because how could somebody in an office in London or Birmingham thirty or forty miles away know any of your problems? . . . If you can't talk to your manager I think it's time to get out.

This suggests that many standard suspicions of trade unions had some currency among workers at Copy-Co. More often, however, people remained indifferent or simply believed that the firm would not recognize a union: 'I was just always led to believe that they just did not believe in trade unions and that was it'. Moreover, this view had been reinforced when an initial effort to recruit union members prompted the senior British manager to suggest that unionization would undermine existing good relations and jeopardize job security. Indeed some workers held the view that 'I don't think you would ever get a union in this company, they [management] would just shut everything down, just leave, go somewhere else'.

Nevertheless, some workers still regretted the absence of a union. The man just quoted also said 'if we had a union here a lot more would get done, I think you would see changes then, [we could] just stick together more'. Another man, who had been treated unfairly when he applied for promotion and had gained an apology from the personnel department, still felt that if the plant had been unionized 'I could have gone to a union', and on that basis he felt he might have been able to gain more effective redress. Another informant, a woman who 'just loved' working at Copy-Co and felt it was 'difficult to find a problem with it', nevertheless believed that on balance a union might be useful:

> I wouldn't mind seeing a union in here. . . . I think that the workers would have more rights. I mean for instance if somebody didn't get a wage deal then they could approach the union. But in here you don't get it in that sense, there's no argument, no messing, you don't get it. They do say that you can appeal and this, that, and the other, but it's pointless, it's a waste of time. So for things like that I think that perhaps a union might [help]. I mean I've worked with a union before, but then on the other hand unions aren't all good, are they? Sometimes they can stir the muck up when it's unnecessary, so there's good and bad things about unions.

Thus there was a significant reservoir of support for a union presence, but such support was qualified and uneven.

Indeed, some workers in one section of the factory had felt strongly enough about the help a union might provide to make contact with some union officers and activists and encourage them to try to recruit members there. However, the resultant effort to recruit and organize the factory also underlined some of the real difficulties that unions faced in achieving such objectives. First, even some of those workers who were broadly sympathetic to trade unions, such as the person quoted in the previous paragraph, felt that organizing from outside was difficult because the activists involved failed to appreciate conditions within the factory:

> That was quite funny really because we had been given leaflets, we came in through the gate and leaflets were issued, and then they said they'd have a meeting outside the gates at four o'clock. Well, you can't get off your job and just go out to a meeting at four o'clock. They completely messed that one up. But nobody bothered anyhow, because I think that on the whole Copy-Co is not bad. I mean I've never seen them sack anybody unless it's been for a damn good reason. If anybody has a written warning or anything, it's usually for a damn good reason. They don't pick up silly stupid little things and make an example of people.

Not only had the activists failed to appreciate the problems of calling a meeting during factory hours but they had also misjudged the character of workers' grievances, since Copy-Co management had not been draconian in its approach to discipline even though it made threats about the negative consequences of unionization.

In part these difficulties reflected a failure to think through the implications of seeking to organize a quite diverse and fragmented workforce. The activists who talked to workers from the plant met people who were relatively similar to themselves, male workers with some earlier manufacturing and trade union experience, but as such they were quite untypical of the range of employees who worked at Copy-Co. This was underlined when the activists began leafleting the buses bringing workers to the factory and they were surprised at the gender, age, and ethnic composition of these commuters. Beyond this, however, it reflected the lack of experience and resources that were available to such local union enthusiasts, whose unionism had been formed mainly in well-organized factories and during a period of relative union strength. Finally, it also reflected a continuing failure of trade union officials to address the issue of organizing such factories, as they struggled to sustain and service their existing memberships in conditions of state and employer hostility and diminishing resources. In these conditions the small local union offices in such towns as Telford were being closed, and the best that trade union officials could think of was the top-down approach of writing to employers inviting them to consider union recognition.

Finally, however, we should note that in the absence of formal collective representation, the alternatives of 'letting it fester or leaving' did not quite exhaust the possibilities. It will have been evident in our discussion of the effort bargain that shop-floor views did impinge informally on decisions about work pace and manning levels. Furthermore, there had occasionally been more overt protests by workers. One example occurred when a leading hand lost his position and returned to being a plant operator, and management treated this as an opportunity to tighten up discipline:

> I was quite pleased with my shift because they actually went in and had a meeting and they actually backed me up. Couldn't believe it, don't think the management could actually understand it because I mean I was fair, I was always taught to be assertive and also help people, which I did. I didn't just shout at them, if they made a mistake, discuss it and come to some sort of amicable agreement. OK, perhaps things which may be should have gone to the management I didn't actually tell them, but we tried to do it between the team which I think is the best method. Obviously, if they make the same mistake time and again, then obviously you have to go above. But we try to keep it as a team and it worked. I used to get the targets out.... Their view was that I was too soft with them, but anyway I was quite pleased the way the shift reacted when they found I'd lost my position. They actually backed me up, which was good.

This protest actually remained largely ineffective in its immediate objective, as management got their way in appointing a different person as team leader. However, the new appointee was another experienced plant operator who remained aware of the exigencies of process work and quite responsive to the concerns of his team of workers.

CONCLUSIONS

Our assessment of the scope and limits of management hegemony at Part-Co and Copy-Co can usefully begin with our documentation of the absence of any organized 'voice' for employees in these firms. The effective exclusion of trade unions and the superficiality or absence of any organized process of employee consultation meant that there was no scope for the formal and collective articulation of grievances. This meant that employees lacked any independent forum in which they might address differences in their own agendas and priorities, so that rivalries and mutual suspicions remained unchallenged. The absence of a collective agenda also precluded formal negotiations about problems between managers and workers' representatives. As a result managers monopolized authority and power within the workplace, reinforcing the dominance they had gained from their role as inward investors bringing jobs to the locality.

Of course, against the background of wider labour market opportunities for semi-skilled, routine factory work, these companies offered real attractions to shop-floor workers. In particular they provided relatively secure jobs with wages at roughly the going rate for the district. Copy-Co could also claim a relatively relaxed work regime, despite intermittent management efforts to increase work rates, while Part-Co offered opportunities for shop-floor advancement, though at the cost of a more intensive work regime. However, we have also seen that employees at both Part-Co and Copy-Co nurtured significant grievances about management policies and practices, and evinced a predominantly instrumental involvement in work. In both cases there was a sense that managers did not appreciate the realities of shop-floor work, and there was a widespread reluctance to become involved in additional quality and improvement activities on top of being an assembler or machine operator. Furthermore, in both cases worker scepticism was reinforced by the view that such activities were not a real priority for management.

However, there were also important differences between the responses of employees in our two firms. At Part-Co the dominant motif in responses to QCC activities was that workers were not paid sufficient to justify such involvement, while at Copy-Co the emphasis was more on the superficial character of such exercises. As we saw in Chapter 7, further differences arose from the distinctive evolution of internal job ladders in the two firms. At Part-Co opportunities for progression reinforced the commitment of a core of employees, though team leaders remained critical of the pressures they faced. However, the restructuring of supervision at Copy-Co provoked particular shop-floor criticism and fuelled accusations of favouritism, underlining the limits of promotion as an integrative mechanism. Thus differences in the patterns of workplace experience in the two factories gave employee grievances their distinctive character in each case, but workers nevertheless faced similar options and dilemmas in shaping their responses.

In the absence of an effective voice one persistent option for workers in both factories was to quit, and this possibility was discussed quite frequently in our interviews. Periods of high labour turnover underlined the availability of this option, and moments of acute dissatisfaction, arising from such features as an unfair pay grading or being blocked for promotion, appeared likely to precipitate action by hitherto-settled workers. At the same time employees were usually well aware of the constraints within which such moves could be made. For many, even when they negotiated their way past the barriers to transfer, the options were quite limited. Similar wages were on offer for similar routine assembly or process work across the locality, while service sector employment was often more poorly remunerated. Furthermore, older male workers, in particular, were often acutely aware of the risks associated with the external labour market, having had to accept lower wages than they had earned earlier in their working lives.

Nevertheless, the option of quitting remained important and became more salient as the local labour market tightened again in the late 1990s. For some, especially the more skilled and experienced, the alternatives appeared increasingly attractive, especially for those working at Part-Co. For others the risks were greater, but for those without major commitments it could be worth trying elsewhere, especially if continuing recruitment made it possible to return if disappointed. As we have seen, it was also possible in such circumstances for a hint about leaving to be used deliberately as a bargaining chip to gain minor improvements. Beyond this, team leaders were often keen to retain and motivate their most experienced workers, and there was some scope for them to mitigate work pressures through the informal circumvention of stipulated production routines and QC procedures. At the same time relations among co-workers were characterized by patterns of rivalry and accusations of favouritism as well as patterns of mutual support.

Again, however, there were significant differences between Copy-Co and Part-Co in these respects. At Copy-Co it appeared that well-established effort norms were protected through informal understandings between operators and senior operators or team leaders, and this set real limits on efforts to tighten management control of the production process or intensify production. At the same time there was considerable mutual suspicion between employees themselves about the ways in which different people were accommodated within this relatively settled framework, both in terms of task allocation and appraisal. This meant that the linkages between management control systems and informal effort norms were experienced as ambiguous and even contested, features that had been reinforced rather than rectified by the process of reorganization of supervision itself. Nevertheless, quality and productivity levels were sustained relatively effectively on the basis of a fairly settled and tacitly negotiated effort bargain, albeit that 'responsible' workers sometimes felt that they sustained quality and output despite the failings of management. While this might be seen as yet another variant of the 'manufacture of consent' this would, however, fail to capture the tensions and even brittleness of these processes, which involved conflicting concepts of fairness and mutuality.

The pattern at Part-Co was much closer to that at Delbridge's (1998) Nippon CTV. Quite stringent production and QC processes were only modified at the margins, and by informal understandings that often facilitated the overall priorities of quality and output even as they sometimes subverted the precise details of management control systems. Furthermore, prevailing effort norms were sometimes translated into criticisms of the efforts of slower workers, while also encouraging more experienced assemblers to do more when targets were not met. Nevertheless, management hegemony still appeared less secure at Part-Co than at Nippon CTV, not least because of the common view that the wage-effort bargain in the factory was unsatisfactory, combined with an awareness that problems of recruitment and retention provided some leverage in asking for transfers or refusing to participate in additional activities.

In these respects, then, the detailed day-to-day implementation of the effort bargain in these two factories was rather different. However, in the light of our discussion in Chapter 7 it is difficult to interpret this in terms of the age of the respective factories linked to a process of dilution or hybridization of an initially more stringent production regime at Copy-Co. Instead we would suggest that, despite the broad similarities of the establishment of routine assembly work on a greenfield site, managers at the two factories operated with rather different constraints and priorities. At Copy-Co they faced the task of implementing a quite varied range of manufacturing processes which were substantially different in scale from those at the parent plants, but were somewhat sheltered by the investment and marketing structures of the parent firm. Meanwhile, managers at Part-Co were pursuing more ambitious targets for expansion in a market composed of a small number of major final assemblers, using production arrangements which diverged less sharply from those already implemented elsewhere. By comparison the effective installation of a 'high surveillance/low trust' work regime at Nippon CTV appears to have been facilitated by the deployment of a stable, tried-and-tested production technology to produce a mature product to standards and targets set in Japan, and by the relative insulation of the factory from product market fluctuations (especially seasonal ones) through the stocking policy of the wholesale arm of the company.

Once again we do not suggest that the specific patterns of management policies, shop-floor experiences and worker responses at each workplace can be mechanically read off from the wider framework of constraints, priorities and competencies with which management operated. However, we should recognize that in responding to labour market conditions and developing their policies these managers were not operating on the same terrain. Both their different circumstances *and* the cumulative character of the interplay between specific management policies and employee responses must be addressed to understand the distinctive features of life on the line in each of these workplaces.

CHAPTER

12

Theorizing Subsidiary Operations: System, Society, and Dominance Effects Revisited

INTRODUCTION

The purpose of this concluding chapter is to draw out the analytical implications of our research for understanding the organization and activities of the foreign subsidiaries of international manufacturing firms. We start by summarizing the main empirical themes of our research on Japanese subsidiaries in Britain, on which our theoretical arguments are based. We then discuss the implications of our analysis for three dominant images of subsidiary operations, as transplants, hybrids, or branch plants. As we saw in Chapter 4, these images offer contrasting accounts of the linkages and power relations between home and host societies, and give differing emphases to systemic, societal, and dominance effects in understanding the operations of foreign plants. Thus our discussion of these three accounts draws upon the system, society, and dominance framework and also provides a basis for revisiting and refining that framework.

A RÉSUMÉ OF RESEARCH FINDINGS

Our research has provided a detailed analysis of the experience, orientations and actions of managers, supervisors and employees in five varied Japanese manufacturing subsidiaries operating in the United Kingdom. Concentrating on the quartet of greenfield inward investors that operated in the same locality, we have documented important differences in their operations but we have also shown that in some key respects they were quite similar. They were all predominantly involved in routine assembly and materials processing operations, using a comparatively low-paid, semi-skilled workforce. Second, all of these firms were able to avoid union recognition, but alternative mechanisms of worker consultation and involvement were absent or rudimentary. Thus management–worker relations were primarily mediated through informal bargaining within firms and by workers' moves between firms. Third, despite management efforts to coordinate their regulation of employment relations, all these firms found that the recruitment and retention of workers were more problematical than they had expected. Meanwhile, workers remained critical of key features of management policies. Finally, while the rhetoric of management sometimes emphasized the active involvement of workers in problem-solving and continuous improvement, management's own commitment to such policies appeared patchy and inconsistent, and employees were usually sceptical about participation in such 'discretionary' activities.

In these terms, then, our Telford case-studies challenge accounts of the innovativeness of Japanese inward investors in terms of production regimes. They also question the extent to which managers have secured hegemony through distinctive employment practices. Managers in these firms have certainly gained more control over the organization of the production process and the flexible deployment of labour than in British manufacturers of an earlier period, but this control should not be overstated. Furthermore, it has been used in quite mundane and uneven ways to maintain quality and output levels, rather than to deliver anything like innovation-mediated production or high commitment, high performance workplaces. In the terms used by Kenney et al. (1998) in their discussion of Japanese factories in Mexico, our greenfield subsidiaries look like 'reproduction' rather than 'learning' factories. We would also characterize the production operations and employment relations at the manufacturing facility of Computer-Co in similar terms, though this was located in a different new town and was not a greenfield site.

At the same time we have registered important differences between our case-study firms, in the evolution of management micropolitics and management–worker relations and in the particular policy mixes and dilemmas that came to characterize each workplace. In summary, we have compared them in terms of (1) their relationships to their parent firms and their wider commercial environment; (2) the relationships between Japanese and British managers; (3) their efforts to transfer Japanese production recipes; (4) the stringency of the production regime; (5) the precise contours of worker compliance, consent, and dissent; and (6) the relative precariousness or viability of the enterprise (see Table 12.1). While our main fieldwork at each factory was concentrated in a period of three to six weeks, we also sought to develop an analysis of the evolution of management strategies and workplace relations over a longer period. Thus we have been able to

Table 12.1. ***Summary of case-study findings***

Pseudonym	Part-Co	Copy-Co	PCB-Co	Assembly-Co	Computer-Co
Ownership	Japanese (marginal involvement of European company in initial joint venture)	Japanese	Japanese (but parent specialist in higher value production)	Japanese/US joint venture (trading company and sleeping partner respectively)	Failing UK specialist firm bought by major Japanese firm
Establishment and current status	1990 and continuing to expand through period	1983 with model changes but stable production	Opened 1987 and closed 1999	1989, fluctuating and shifting demand	Bought 1990 and closed 1999
Number of employees	1996: 720 employees 2003: 1,400	1996: 550 employees 2003: 650	1996: 92 employees	1996: 180 employees 2003: 370	1996: 475 employees on two main sites
Products	Complex sub-assemblies for car industry	Office equipment and consumables	Printed circuit boards	Plastic parts/ assemblies	Design, development and manufacture of computers and servers
Role of site in commodity chains	Major and powerful first tier supplier to range of car assembly plants across Europe, operating in increasingly competitive sector	Specialist producer that supplies products to marketing division for sale	Supplier to several final assemblers in competition with sister plants in East Asia, pushed towards smaller batch runs	Supplier of parts to shifting range of final assemblers, with initial advantage of patented mechanism	World product division for PCs and servers, to provide capability where parent company had earlier failed
Major areas of task activity	Moulding and machining of components, flow line assembly of complex components on lines dedicated to specific customers	Plastic moulding shop, process production and packaging of consumable product, bench assembly of simple components, flow line assembly of complex machinery, manufacture of complex component, minor design & development role	Automated insertion, manual flow line insertion and rectification	Plastic moulding and routine assembly, with a little 'amateur' development effort	(i) hardware and software design and development of range of computers, servers and IT services; (ii) automated and manual manufacture of PCBs, assembly bay and flow line manufacture of computers and servers

(*Continued*)

Table 12.1. *(Cont.)*

Pseudonym	Part-Co	Copy-Co	PCB-Co	Assembly-Co	Computer-Co
Relations between Japanese and local management	Japanese management cadre substantial and dominant, drawing lessons from US subsidiary; personnel management local responsibility but with limited room for manoeuvre; debate about breaking away from local pay norms	Largely collaborative relationship between Japanese and local management with tensions about quality regime cross-cutting groups, main Japanese role in liaison with HQ and production management, local management responsibility for personnel	Suspicion and conflict between small Japanese management cadre and local managers; failure to become profitable in context of intra-management conflict and squeeze from competing Asian factories prompted closure	Japanese top manager liaises with parents and customers but management of site delegated to local management	UK management dominant in R&D with supportive Japanese cadre, Japanese managers active role in process innovation (but draw on sector recipes), plant & personnel management local; strategy of long-term investment undermined by financial problems of parent company prompting closure.
Dominant features of work organization	Stringent implementation of productivity and quality controls, highly routinized assembly work, training and job rotation limited by pressures for production and worker turnover, process engineers prime movers in work reorganization with worker scepticism about spasmodic and ritualistic QCC activities	Team organization in assembly means rotation between short cycles on bench assembly; line assembly with longer cycles involves fool-proofed task routines but little rotation; active quality control regime but spasmodic and superficial involvement in QCC activities	Routine, line-paced assembly, personalized supervision, idiosyncratic selection from Japanese production repertoire, no time for QCC activity, quality targets varied by customer, ageing equipment, crisis management	Extensive and intensive routine assembly operations on benches and lines, some sub-assemblies at small branch factory, little evidence of Japanese production techniques of any sort, NVQ accreditation of basic skills	(i) matrix organization of project teams with limited resources, juggling quick delivery and robust design; (ii) extensive routine low paid assembly work, with no QCC activities, but some shift to timed off-line 'build through' process; extensive post-production quality checks and rectification

Personnel policies and strategies	Union avoidance, tightly regulated worker consultation process excluding most issues of concern to employees, payment of going rate for the locality but more stringent demands in terms of work pace and compulsory overtime, cursory selection process and use of agency labour influenced by recruitment and retention problems	Active union avoidance, no formal consultation arrangements, pays modest going rate, move from youth recruitment to older workers, cultivation of loyalty through internal promotion (but compromised by external recruitment of new team leaders) and 'caring' attitude, commitment to employment security coupled with use of temporary agency workers	Non-union, low wages, personalized relations, dramatization of competitive pressures originating from Chinese factories, use of agency temps to cover fluctuations and facilitate recruitment	Non-union, modest wages involving 'Payment by Results' system and attendance bonus, face-to-face efforts to cool out problems, use of NVQs to document training, branch factory as escape from constraints of local labour market	Non-union, limited consultation through heavily managed 'one goal committee'; (i) semblance of strong culture, significant training opportunities, but terms and conditions below average for sector; (ii) minimization of personnel function through agency recruitment and training, use of current panaceas from agency temps to zero hours contracts
Dominant features of employment relations and foci of tension	Widespread shopfloor criticism of unfavourable effort bargain, sceptical instrumentalism, informal operator efforts to manage and moderate the impact of management control systems, team leaders under pressure, substantial turnover	Management saw labour turnover as problem, process workers often critical of management's erosion of their relative indulgency pattern, elsewhere tensions around quality and productivity and criticisms of restructuring of supervision and favouritism	Tensions over work pressure, informal resistances, significant turnover of established as well as new workers	Informal fiddles around 'Payment by Results' significant labour turnover	(i) young 'techies' join to gain experience, but tendency to lose experienced staff; (ii) critical view of management fuelled by increased work pressure and treatment of temps

draw on comparisons of developments between firms and over time. On this basis we have sought to understand not only the pattern of current policies but also the social processes and social contexts informing their development, together with any continuing tensions and debates that have surrounded their implementation. In line with a critical realist approach (Pratten 1993; Ackroyd and Fleetwood 2000) it is our analysis of these features of social process and social context, rather than the summary empirical generalizations made earlier, that provides a basis for developing a more adequate theoretical understanding of the operations of Japanese, and indeed other, international manufacturing subsidiaries.

ORGANIZATIONAL STRUCTURES AND MANAGEMENT PROCESSES

Our research has emphasized the ways in which existing templates and repertoires of work organization and employment relations, from whatever source, have been actively modified and reworked in efforts to bring them to bear upon the organization of work and management–worker relations within the subsidiaries we studied. On this basis we have developed an account of the varied social processes of interpretation, negotiation, and often contestation through which both production arrangements and employment relations have been constructed and reconstructed within these workplaces. Such an emphasis arises readily out of detailed empirical research but some may be tempted to treat these processes as incidental to the overall patterns of relationships and activities that are sustained within these factories. Our argument, however, is that they are intrinsic to the operation of such subsidiaries as they underline the problematical character of management, not only in regard to workers and the labour process but also in terms of relations between subsidiaries and their parent firms and wider commercial pressures and exigencies.

All of the factories that we studied were established in localities that appeared to give managers considerable leverage in developing work and employment relations as they saw fit. Telford, in particular, was characterized by supportive local state policies and high levels of unemployment at the time when most of these firms arrived, while all of the companies have pursued successful policies of union avoidance. In this sense our research sites were biased in the direction of conditions that could facilitate the exercise of management prerogatives and the transfer of parent company practices to subsidiaries. Nevertheless, our analysis has drawn attention to a range of problems and uncertainties that beset management policy formation and implementation in each of the factories. In turn, as Chapter 10 shows, responses to these dilemmas and challenges grew out of varied patterns of debate, alliance and conflict among managers in these subsidiaries and in their parent firms, the outcomes of which were influenced by the different priorities, resources, and powers of the protagonists.

The recruitment, retention, control, and motivation of shop-floor workers represented a major focus of management concern across our case-studies, and in this sense labour was an active influence on the making and remaking of work and employment relations within these subsidiaries despite the absence of any collective voice. However, the intractability of labour was not the only source of uncertainties for the managers of these subsidiaries. Others included the problematical relevance of aspects of the established production or design repertoires of parent companies, which arose as much from the commercial role and environment of specific subsidiaries as from the distinctive localities and labour markets in which they operated.

Of course, attention to the micropolitics of management and the tacit negotiation of relations between management and employees has to be placed in the wider context of corporate and competitive relations on the one hand and the social organization of local and national labour markets on the other. Corporate policies beyond the subsidiary, at regional or corporate HQ, clearly had a major impact upon the micropolitics of the workplace. Thus our research has documented the ways in which wider corporate decisions on such matters as the terms of new investments, the allocation of new product lines or wider corporate rationalization influenced the fate of local operations. At this point we have to recognize an important limitation that accompanies the strengths of detailed case-study research at workplace level, namely that we have not explored such wider social processes and power relations in the same way as those within the case-study plants. As Burawoy (1998) emphasizes in his discussion of the extended case-study method, such research focuses upon the social dynamics within the case, and can only treat the wider social context in more summary structural terms, though other studies would reveal the active processes through which such structures are themselves constituted.

In constructing our understanding of these wider relations, however, we have drawn particularly on the accounts and understandings of our subsidiary managers. We recognize that such managers have a partial and selective view of policies and politics in the higher reaches of their parent firms, just as top managers have an incomplete understanding of developments within their subsidiaries (Rubery and Grimshaw 2003: 218–19). Nevertheless, they can be expected to have a well-developed, though partisan, understanding of the pressures that impinge on them. With these qualifications in mind, our case-studies document four important features of the relationship between HQ and overseas operations, which we will return to later in this chapter. First, the subsidiaries we studied were located within rather different corporate structures and their roles were defined in terms of distinctive corporate strategies, and these features made a significant difference to their operations. Second, these different roles not only involved different relations with HQ and 'parent plants' in Japan but also distinctive relationships with overseas 'sister plants', suppliers, customers, and competitors. Third, there were critical junctures when top corporate policies overrode the concerns of subsidiary managers, most obviously when decisions were made to close plants but to some extent also when key investment decisions were made or particular performance targets were defined. Finally, however, within these parameters, subsidiary managers nevertheless had a significant degree of autonomy, as they actively engaged with, interpreted, and negotiated the implications of top corporate policies, including those that substantially constrained their room for manoeuvre.

TRANSPLANTS, HYBRIDS, BRANCH-PLANTS

What, then, are the implications of our analysis for such standard models of the international subsidiary as the transplant, the hybrid, and the branch plant? We will consider each of these models in terms of the claims they make about both the character of workplace social processes and the wider structures of social relations that impinge on these processes.

Transplants

The first image, that of the transplant, was widely used in the 1980s and 1990s, especially to characterize Japanese inward investors. This imagery implied that such enterprises would seek to transfer an unproblematically superior portfolio of Japanese management and production techniques quite directly from home factories to overseas subsidiaries, while any failure of such transfer was to be explained in terms of the obstacles that arose in alien social environments.

In some of our case-studies, certainly, established repertoires of production organization, often drawn from influential home country models, represented central resources and reference points for key actors. In conditions where leading enterprises in the home economy were regarded as successful exponents of contemporary 'best practice', while host country practices were viewed as backward and unsuccessful, such dominant models influenced not only corporate HQ and expatriate managers but also locally recruited managers and possibly shop-floor workers.

Our findings, however, underline the contingent and contested, rather than general and accepted, relevance and impact of such established corporate repertoires. First, our case-study enterprises differed markedly in the degree to which, and the ways in which, existing Japanese production or design operations were seen as models for the subsidiary. In this regard they could be ordered on a spectrum, from Part-Co, where parent plant practices were most closely emulated, through PCB-Co and Copy-Co, to Assembly-Co and finally Computer-Co, where an Anglo-American design and development paradigm was a more dominant reference point. Our research suggests that these differences in the salience of parent company recipes can be explained partly in terms of the role of the subsidiary in wider corporate strategies. For example, among the larger parent firms Electrical-Co clearly sought to acquire key design and development competencies from Computer-Co, its British subsidiary, and this reduced the salience of its existing expertise for the British operation. Meanwhile, Part-Co sought to provide Europe-based motor manufacturers with an equivalent service to that provided to major customers in Japan, making its home model directly relevant. Again, amongst the smaller companies the relevance of Japanese models of best practice was seen differently at PCB-Co and at Assembly-Co. At the latter the limited production experience of the parent company combined with the priority of servicing major customers to provide considerable latitude for British production managers to go their own way. At the former the established production expertise of the parent company was drawn upon in increasingly contentious circumstances.

Second, in each case the salience of parent company practices (and indeed those drawn from sister subsidiaries or domestic companies) had to be worked out in detail among expatriate and local managers within the subsidiary, albeit influenced by varied levels of guidance and pressure emanating from above. The imputation of 'dominance' to leading sectors or whole national economies may be seductive, not only for commentators but also for some of the participants in transnational operations. But such a rhetoric of dominance still had to be translated into concrete forms of work organization and employment relations, and it was at this point that the ramifications of specific product and labour market conditions became pertinent. As Chapter 10 demonstrated, the terms of debate about these matters varied across our case-study factories, as did the related evolution of work and employment policies. At Copy-Co, for example, the mix and scale of production, the existing skills, experience, and orientations of the workforce, and related calculations regarding the balance of capital investment and labour deployment were all implicated in the tailoring of production arrangements in terms of such features as fool-proofing and job rotation. The implications of these circumstances were explored in arguments and discussions among management specialisms and factions with variable leverage at different levels in the firm, while the initiatives and responses of employees also had an indirect influence on the outcomes. In these respects 'transplantation' was inevitably a dynamic and contested process.

At the same time there were important differences between the case-studies in the patterns of management micropolitics through which these matters were addressed, and in the weight given to these different 'contingencies' in the resulting management policies. To understand these differences we need to attend not only to the dynamics of social organization within the plant but to the wider field of forces within which each plant operated. Thus our engagement with the model of the transplant highlights two key arguments that must be carried forward to develop a more adequate theory of the operations of international subsidiaries. The first is that subsidiaries vary in the roles they play within broader corporate structures and this makes a difference to the presumed pertinence of purportedly dominant home country production repertoires. The second is that efforts to draw upon such home country and parent company repertoires inevitably involve debate and tailoring to address the specific commercial and labour market circumstances surrounding the operation of the subsidiary factory. Thus the positioning of the factory within wider corporate structures and strategies, the micropolitical negotiation of the implications of existing management repertoires within the enterprise, and specific product and labour market exigencies are all implicated in the active making of production and employment relations within these overseas subsidiaries, in ways that are neglected by the image of the transplant.

Hybrids

The second image, developed from the late 1990s onwards, is that of the hybrid factory. This metaphor has emphasized the mixing of home and host influences to produce a distinctive set of organizational and production relations, not only in specific subsidiaries and settings but also in the operations of indigenous competitors. Our analysis has important affinities with the image of hybridization, because it problematizes transplantation and does not treat host country conditions merely as an obstacle to the adoption of home country practices. As we saw in Chapter 4, however, the notion of hybridization is not only popular but also rather ambiguous. At one extreme it has simply been used to label the incomplete and diluted character of transplantation, but at the other extreme it has been used to focus on the emergence of new configurations of work and employment relations that may represent viable competitors to existing dominant models. At their best, then, analyses of hybridization have moved beyond the juxtaposition of home and host country effects, to emphasize the evolution of subsidiary operations over time and the emergence of distinctive configurations that may depart from both home-based templates and local practices (Boyer 1998; Liker et al. 1999).

In general, however, analyses of hybridization operate at a fairly high level of abstraction, some distance from the struggles and uncertainties of management policymaking and management–worker relations. One way in which the process of hybridization has been conceptualized in more detail has been in terms of the dynamics of 'organizational learning' involved in the evolution of subsidiary practices. However, much of the literature on organizational learning mixes analytical arguments and prescriptive recommendations in an uneasy fashion. For example, the work of Beechler et al. (1998) maps a range of trajectories of organizational learning within the overseas affiliates of Japanese firms, and usefully identifies some of the influences on the evolution of these patterns. However, they ultimately celebrate one such trajectory, characterized by an 'open hybrid' form that facilitates the explication of tacit knowledge and the reflexive reassessment of the principles of corporate operations. This form, they argue, 'identifies problems more quickly, while problems are still in gestation... is highly proactive, characterized by constant fine tuning... exhibits a willingness to learn from local sources... and [is] often enthusiastic about sharing what they have learned with others' (Beechler et al. 1998: 353).

However, it is unclear how this idealized form relates to their documentation of the much more problematical and contested character of much organizational learning in their own research. For example, they recognized that 'cycles of learning' were often interrupted, so that mistakes were repeated or innovations aborted prematurely. Further, changing circumstances easily rendered earlier solutions problematical, so that 'usually such shifts caught the affiliate off guard, making the subsequent adjustment traumatic' (Beechler et al. 1998: 357). Another limitation is that such analyses often work with a *unitarist* conception of the enterprise, in which effective forms of organizational learning are assumed to offer appropriate joint benefits to all participants. This glosses over enduring conflicts of class interest between management and workers as well as divergences in the status concerns and priorities of different segments and levels of management. As Chapter 10 shows, our case-studies offer a very different perspective on 'organizational learning' because they highlight the uncertainties, contradictions, conflicts, and limitations that characterize management policy formation and enactment, within the constraints surrounding such international subsidiaries. In this sense, our analyses seek to provide a more critical account of the micropolitics of management policymaking and the problematical character of organizational learning in such settings.

From this vantage point the modification and melding of policy repertoires indicated by the concept of hybridization is inevitably characterized by competing claims to expertise and by dilemmas and difficulties in deploying these forms of expertise. In this context British and Japanese managers typically claimed different sources of expertise: Japanese managers in most of the firms could draw upon strong claims to technical expertise grounded in existing corporate activities, while British managers invariably claimed particular expertise in managing a British labour force. However, in neither case could the effectiveness of such claims be taken for granted and their leverage varied between firms and over time. Japanese claims to technical expertise varied in their potency depending upon the specific role of the subsidiary and the related implications of British product and labour markets. Meanwhile, the persistence of problems of labour recruitment and retention weakened the efficacy of British management claims. Thus an adequate theory of subsidiary operations cannot be based on an idealized account of the emergence of new hybrid production and employment regimes (or indeed a simply negative account of dilution) but must address the conflicts and uncertainties that commonly characterize evolving subsidiary operations.

As this discussion implies, such analyses of the micropolitics of hybridization must also address the varied structures, resources and power relations within which such fraught forms of organizational learning have developed. Our research has documented a range of organizational networks and exchanges that may influence policy debates. These include circulating expatriate managers, local management visits to Japanese parent factories, problem-solving teams called in from Japan, exchanges of information and experience with sister subsidiaries in other countries, discussions with other local Japanese firms, and finally comparisons with the practices of other firms operating in the United Kingdom. Among other examples, these various contacts have mediated the transfer of fool-proofing ideas from Japan by Copy-Co; the deployment of quality procedures at PCB-Co; the borrowing of consultative arrangements from the US sister plant by Part-Co; and the influence of practices elsewhere in the United Kingdom on the development of teamworking at Copy-Co. Indeed, in our two major assembly plants the dominance of the Japanese parent firm and the presumed superiority of their production practices did not preclude lateral borrowing or even, in the case of Copy-Co, some modest reverse transfer (Edwards 1998, 2004). Meanwhile, at Computer-Co a central rationale of the takeover was reverse learning, if not transfer.

However, different subsidiaries were differently located in relation to both the extent of such networks and the power relations that characterized them. Thus the larger subsidiaries could draw upon a more developed international management cadre, a wider range of sister plants and more sustained contacts with cluster firms. By comparison the major influences on the smaller subsidiaries tended to be a limited number of parent or sister plants and pressures emanating from customer firms. Even in the larger firms, though, such networks also involved hierarchies of power, with HQ as the dominant partner, sister subsidiaries as more equal partners and other firms having potential influence rather than direct leverage. Thus at Part-Co, and to a lesser extent at Copy-Co, the parent company could call upon a cadre of committed expatriate managers who had experience of managing international operations. At both they could encourage expatriate and local managers to draw upon recipes and comparisons across parent and sister plants in developing initiatives within specific workplaces, and they could both use funding decisions and performance criteria to guide management priorities. Both borrowing from sister plants and instances of reverse transfer took place within these parameters, though subsidiary managers also had scope to make a case for the value of their own policy preferences within this framework.

As we will see in the next section, patterns and processes of hybridization were not simply guided by top management imperatives, not least because they were also influenced by relatively intractable features of existing work and employment relations in the workplace and the local labour market. Nevertheless, our case-studies emphasize that the evolution of 'hybrid' policy repertoires within these subsidiaries was strongly influenced by distinctive organizational networks and power relations, especially within the management structures of the parent firms. In this sense they give support to the argument that corporate organization is often a strong mediator of both home and host country effects (Ferner and Quintanilla 1998; Rubery and Grimshaw 2003), undermining any analysis of hybridization as the direct product of the interaction between such effects. Thus the notion of hybridization may represent a valuable starting point for developing a theoretical understanding of the operations of international subsidiaries, but key features of the dynamics of subsidiary operations risk being obscured by this metaphor. In particular we need to recognize the contested and problematical character of emergent policy repertoires and to locate the micropolitical processes of management policy formation within varied and unequal networks of influence and corporate power relations.

Branch plants

The third image of the subsidiary, that of the branch plant, returns to debates of the 1970s and 1980s about the overseas operations of international firms. This metaphor was developed to emphasize the subordinate role of subsidiary operations within wider corporate structures and strategies orchestrated from the centre. It was also intended to highlight the dependency of regions and localities upon precarious sources of employment because of the capacity of inward investors to shift their operations and investments from place to place. Our research has drawn upon this imagery to underline the importance of top corporate decision-making at critical junctures in both the expansion and closure of such plants. In line with the literature on branch plants, we have also argued that the efforts of national and local states to capture such inward manufacturing investment have often created clusters of routine assembly operations. These have been characterized by the preponderance of low-skilled and low-paid jobs, with the implication that such operations are relatively easily closed and relocated.

However, our analyses have also shown that the specific roles of the different subsidiaries have differed significantly in ways that are not readily accommodated within the branch-plant imagery, as different mandates imply rather different relationships with corporate HQ (Birkinshaw and Hood 1998). One way in which to move away from an undifferentiated branch-plant model is to draw on the various typologies which have been developed of the different types of enterprise structures and strategies associated with international investment. In recent years distinctions have often been made between multidomestic, multinational, international, transnational, and global companies, and such typologies alert us to a spectrum of different relations between HQs and subsidiaries (Dicken 1998; Rubery and Grimshaw 2003: 198–220). However, the immediate utility of these typologies is weakened by inconsistencies in the characterization of these different sorts of enterprise and also by the conflation of analytical and prescriptive categories (especially in discussions of the global networked firm). Furthermore, different subsidiaries of a parent company may actually occupy rather different positions in relation to that parent. This was particularly evident in our research in the cases of PCB-Co (which was quite untypical as a subcontractor subsidiary of the parent company) and Computer-Co (which was untypical in being designated as a product champion in an area of parent company weakness).

Thus, rather than map our cases in terms of such standard typologies, it is more useful to locate them at a lower level of abstraction, in terms of the specific rationales informing their formation as subsidiaries and the distinctive relationships that have developed between them and their HQ, sister companies and the like. For all of our firms the establishment of their operations was primarily an exercise in building market access, rather than delivering immediate profits to the parent company, and this appears to have framed initial relationships with corporate HQ. However, the implications of this priority were interpreted differently in different firms and over time, in ways which were related to the distinctive product markets and relationships with customers and competitors that each company and subsidiary faced. In this regard the concept of the production chain (Gereffi 1996; Gereffi and Korzeniewicz 1994) offers some illumination, as it highlights the salience of distinctions between final assemblers and various tiers of component suppliers, though it does not provide a full characterization of the relationships involved.

The three larger companies each performed distinctive roles within their parent firms. As Chapter 9 demonstrated, Computer-Co was distinctive as a subsidiary in that it was intended to provide the parent company with a capability in the design and production of a specific product range, where that company's domestic efforts had earlier been unsuccessful. Copy-Co was the final assembler of major lines for the European region in a relatively managed market where leasing of complex equipment enhanced scope for profitable sales of consumables, so that local content to underpin market access continued to be an important imperative. We can characterize the position of Part-Co as the key European regional supplier of a dominant Japanese first-tier components firm, supplying powerful and often demanding customers in the highly competitive motor sector. The remaining two factories were both smaller subcontractors, more vulnerable to pressures from both their customer firms and competitor suppliers. However, Assembly-Co gained a degree of protection from its possession of an unexpired patent and its close relationship with one major customer, while PCB-Co occupied the most precarious position as an outrider operation facing direct competition from East Asian factories. Though these varied features are not readily reduced to a simple continuum, our argument is that an understanding of the different ways in which inward-investing subsidiaries are located in these terms is essential to any broader theoretical understanding of the operations and employment relations within such workplaces.

In particular, it is important to locate any discussion of the performance criteria that regulate the relationships between parents and subsidiaries in these terms. In two of our cases, those of Computer-Co and PCB-Co, the parent company eventually closed the subsidiary, after each had operated for about ten years. In each of these cases the closure decision reflected wider pressures that encouraged corporate rationalization and changed the calculus that was applied to the performance of the subsidiary, rather than a distinct change in that performance itself. In other respects, however, the cases differed. At Computer-Co there had been a long-term commitment to investment in a loss-making but innovative enterprise in the hope of developing a viable competitive presence in the PC market, albeit from a marginal and relatively vulnerable position. However, this commitment was curtailed by a wider crisis of corporate profitability arising from changes in other segments of the parent firm's operations and it was this that precipitated closure. By contrast, at PCB-Co an initial tolerance of poor financial performance was underpinned by the prospect of developing business with customers of the parent company, because of the requirements for local content in their overseas operations. However, the relaxation of such regulatory requirements and changes in the sourcing policies of these customers undercut these prospects and exposed the factory more directly to competition from China. As a result the parent company imposed increasingly stringent performance targets and these led to closure.

By comparison the three remaining companies sustained 'good enough' production in the circumstances of their different corporate and commercial settings, though none did this on the basis of a high commitment, high performance workplace. In this context subsidiary managers often sought to consolidate the position of 'their' factories within wider corporate strategies by seeking to extend the capabilities of the enterprise and by bidding for new investment. While their room for doing this was limited by the evolving character of wider corporate strategies, in each case they gained scope for further investments or new product lines, sufficient to sustain production at Copy-Co and Assembly-Co and to continue expansion at Part-Co. As such the sunk costs invested in these firms, and particularly in the larger assemblers, became substantial, and a basis on which subsidiary management could develop a case for further support, though this did not fully guarantee their longer-term performance and viability.

A further implication of the imagery of the branch plant concerns the leverage that location and relocation can provide for management over the workforce. Here, however, our research findings drawn from the Telford cluster are somewhat paradoxical, because they bring out some of the problems as well as the advantages of greenfield locations and deregulated labour markets from the point of view of management. As we showed in Chapter 6 (also Elger and Smith 1998*b*, 1999), conditions in the new town amplified wider features of the 'deregulation' of the labour market and the fragmentation of industrial relations regimes in Britain during the late twentieth century. This provided an attractive site for the location of international inward investors such as our Japanese firms. In turn this created a distinctive set of relations among such firms, based primarily on consultation and concertation in managing the local labour market, rather than the dense linkages between inward investing assemblers and lower tier suppliers that would be characteristic of an integrated production complex. It was in this sense, of mutual learning and active but negotiated employment policy concertation, that these firms constituted a distinctive cluster of Japanese firms. However, our research also underlines some of the contradictory features of the construction of such a new 'production space', and the limits of managerial hegemony in such circumstances.

THE CONSTRUCTION OF NEW PRODUCTION SPACES

Of course, our four case-studies in Telford provide only a partial vantage point for any overall characterization of the operations of Japanese firms in this setting or any general analysis of the structure and dynamics of the local labour market. We have not conducted an ecological study of the growth (or decline) of a full range of subsidiaries in the area, or a sample survey of employees' experiences in major segments of the local labour market. Nevertheless, we have been able to provide a systematic account of how managers and employees in four rather different Japanese subsidiaries perceived and experienced options, dilemmas, and constraints in this locality. In particular, we were able to analyse their perceptions of other Japanese employers, as many of our informants had worked in different

Japanese firms, as well as their views of other employment within the wider labour market. Through these mental maps and experiential rankings, we gained an understanding of the local labour market beyond our immediate case-studies. Overwhelmingly, these accounts (together with those of other key informants) converged on a shared understanding of key features of the labour market, relations between firms and the policy options of Japanese subsidiaries in this locality. In this sense our four case-studies provide the basis for an analysis of the social dynamics of a significant segment of the Telford labour market and an important cluster of Japanese inward investors, as well as broader insights into the town's wider labour market.

There were a variety of incentives for Japanese companies to locate in Telford, including new factory sites, good communications links and the presence of existing Japanese companies. However, the most obvious attraction, emphasized by the local state, was a plentiful supply of relatively cheap labour for routine manufacturing work, while trade unions were relatively quiescent and themselves eager to encourage inward investment. These features promised to facilitate the construction of management's preferred production and employment regimes, and throughout the period of our research the firms were able to retain favourable wage rates and avoid unionization. However, as we saw in each case in Chapters 7 and 8 and again in Chapter 11, managers discovered that the regulation of labour remained more challenging than they had expected. Labour turnover was often substantial, workers were often sceptical about management strategies for employee involvement, and recruitment became difficult as the pace of inward investment and expansion led to a tighter labour market. In some respects these subsidiaries became locked into this pattern. The larger firms sought to sustain their position by collaborating in efforts to manage the local labour market, both by discouraging the movement of labour between their firms and setting guidelines for wage and non-wage costs, while the smaller firms were vicarious participants in the resultant policies. However, this had the consequence of limiting the options of individual subsidiaries in terms of pay rates and to some extent personnel policies. It also encouraged such policies as the reliance upon the 'fool-proofing' of semi-skilled jobs.

For workers the arrival of Japanese inward investors provided increasing job opportunities in an initially slack labour market. This was a particular attraction to older workers who had experienced redundancy from better paying jobs, or those who had worked in more poorly paid service sector work, especially when accompanied by promises of enhanced job security. At the same time the demands of routine factory work, coupled with modest wages, also fed employee grievances. In the absence of effective voice mechanisms, exit in search of modest improvements became a common response, especially for younger or more skilled workers who could be more confident about gaining another job elsewhere. Indeed quitting remained a persistent option of last resort even when workforces became somewhat more stabilized, and as such the possibility remained an implicit basis for informal bargaining over work rates and working conditions in each of these workplaces. As we have seen, in these circumstances selective management efforts to develop enhanced forms of worker involvement through quality circle initiatives tended to be experienced as superficial and inconsistent. And in the more stringent work regimes they were also seen as a further imposition in the context of an already inequitable effort bargain.

Managers in the larger firms could nevertheless gain greater commitment by offering opportunities to progress up internal job ladders (Rubery 1994). However, the attractions of these aspects of employment were qualified by the work pressures involved (especially at Part-Co) and by the perceived unfairness of management's criteria for progression (especially at Copy-Co). Such moves to manage internal job ladders were accompanied by a variety of personnel initiatives, such as broadening recruitment, bussing in workers and prioritizing attendance in bonus calculations. Each of these gave a distinctive inflection to management–worker relations, but none overcame a primarily instrumental orientation among workers or fully stabilized the workforce. Thus these features highlight some real limits to management hegemony in these workplaces, notwithstanding the leverage afforded by greenfield investment and concertation between enterprises. Workers remained heavily reliant on these firms for relatively secure manufacturing employment, while a combination of management policies, differentiation and divisions among workers, and limited trade union initiatives left them with minimal scope for collective voice. Nevertheless, moves between firms, instrumental responses to management policies and informal bargaining over the pace of work set significant limits to management power, a feature underlined by the pressures and sensitivities involved in the work of team leaders and supervisors.

Clearly, managers in the subsidiaries we studied were in key respects subordinate to the wider policies of senior management, while the factory managers had considerable power resources in managing their workforces. In these respects the branch plant model represents an important corrective to characterizations of processes of transplantation or hybridization that abstract from such power relations. However, our case-studies also suggest that the leverage of subsidiary management vis-à-vis HQ varies significantly according to the specific location and role of the subsidiary within wider corporate strategies, features which also evolve over time. Furthermore, even in favourable circumstances the regulation of labour and especially the mobilization of worker cooperation may remain in important respects problematical. Thus a full theory of subsidiary operations must address these features and overcome these limitations of the branch plant model, as well as developing the features we have highlighted in our critical engagement with the transplant and hybrid models.

SYSTEM, SOCIETY AND DOMINANCE REVISITED

The analytical framework of system, societal, and dominance effects grew out of an engagement with recent institutionalist analyses of national production regimes or business systems, rather than a specific discussion of the operations of international firms. However, placing such operations in their wider contexts provides a valuable vantage point from which to review our overall argument about the operations of Japanese manufacturing subsidiaries in the United Kingdom and underline the broader implications of our analysis for theorizing the operations of overseas manufacturing subsidiaries more generally.

Of course, international firms are not the only agencies of the transfer and innovation of management policies and practices, as they operate alongside such other agencies as professional associations, state-sponsored commissions and individual mobility. Nevertheless, such firms represent the dominant means of technology transfer, and offer particular scope for both explicit and tacit knowledge management, learning and the institutional benchmarking of ideas and best practices. These firms, as capitalist enterprises, must accumulate capital, are engaged in competitive rivalry and share definite social relations between labour and capital. However, capitalist firms are necessarily institutionalized within particular societies, so that their strategies and structures remain shaped by their home countries. To some degree international firms transcend their national origins, but for most their operations in other territories and their global competitive strategies are also coloured by the continuing importance of their home base. At the same time firms from the same national territory, while having a common heritage, are nevertheless differentiated through capitalist competitive relations, as well as such features as their sector, size, and position in supply chains, and these features cross-cut national borders. Furthermore, the host societies in which they operate are also heterogeneous in important ways, especially in the receptivity of specific regions towards FDI, and the patterning of FDI clustering (such as the 'locality effect' of new towns in our research).

Against this background we wish to emphasize three key themes that emerge from our research. Our first argument is that any discussion of the transmission of dominant home country recipes from parent to foreign subsidiaries, or of the development of hybrid policies which meld together home and host country influences, must give particular attention to the ways in which specific subsidiaries are positioned within the wider corporate strategies of their parent firms. Corporate 'effects' are important because ostensibly 'national' models and related claims to dominance are developed within specific sectors and firms, and are accorded more or less relevance for specific subsidiaries according to the particular roles that they expected to play within their parent companies. Corporate effects are also important because they involve rather different networks of resources and power relations within and across firms. In turn these condition the activities of subsidiary managers and mediate the implications of a variety of home and host management repertoires (and here the role of sister plants underlines the potential salience of other influences beyond specific home and host countries). Finally, insofar as the emergent corporate strategies and policy repertoires developed by competitor firms, or in rival sectors or national economies, undermine the existing strategies of parent firms, this is indirectly likely to increase the vulnerability of its subsidiary operations. This may be construed as a systemic tendency of corporate rivalry to problematize existing national business systems, even those with current claims to dominance. But it is important to recognize that such tendencies (exemplified in our research by the increasing location of competitor and sister subsidiaries in China) ramify through the global capitalist system in heavily mediated and uneven ways.

Our second argument is that, wherever inward investors are located, the management of the labour process and the regulation of labour are likely to pose significant problems for management. Neither HQ nor subsidiary managers are likely to discover the perfect location or the perfect supports for management hegemony. However, the specific tensions and challenges that managers will confront will be strongly influenced by the specific institutional arrangements and class and gender compromises that characterize particular districts, regions, or countries, that is by differentiated host country effects. Again, as labour process theorists have persistently argued, the underlying intractability of labour may be regarded as a systemic feature of capitalist employment relations. However, our research also helps to document the particular forms and limits of such intractability within a relatively open and supportive locality for capital, within a contradictory and evolving British production regime (Almond and Rubery 2000; Rubery and Grimshaw 2003).

It is plausible to argue that such localities are becoming more common, as national states pursue policies of liberalization and flexibilization and international companies gain more options for relocation of their production operations (Traxler et al. 2001). In this sense system dynamics driven by both states and corporations are recasting and also weakening country effects, making it more likely that the challenges facing management will take the form of an increased volatility of labour and disorganized discontent, rather than organized challenges and compromises (Smith 2001). At the same time, however, it should also be recognized that the specific forms taken by greenfield sites and flexibilized local labour markets continue to vary substantially. Those in the interstices of leading capitalist economies (parts of the United Kingdom), those on the less developed periphery of core capitalist regions (say in Mexico or eastern Europe) and those in the export processing zones of developing countries (say in Indonesia or South China) each have distinctive characteristics. These arise both from different positions in the development hierarchy and specific national features (such as the hybrid capitalist/state socialist form in China). In this sense country effects continue to play a significant role in constituting the terrain on which even the more mobile international subsidiaries may operate.

Finally, our third argument is that, in consequence of the above, the policy repertoires and management practices in specific subsidiaries necessarily develop through micropolitical processes of management debate, alliance and conflict and inevitably involve tacit but somewhat contested bargains with employees. Structures and contexts do not automatically determine outcomes in the enterprise or workplace. Social relations *between* managers and workers and *among* groups of workers and managers animate, articulate and interpret structural pressures and contextual conditions in novel and unanticipated ways. Such processes are clearly framed within the wider parameters of distinctive corporate structures, strategies and power relations on the one hand, and the local and national institutional structuring of labour markets on the other. However, our empirical research suggests that these active processes absorb much of the energy and constitute much of the immediate experience of the managers and workers who work at these subsidiaries. We would also argue that these processes are often more complex than is recognized. They rarely involve a simple clash between, say, Japanese and British managers, and they often sustain patterns of conflict and cooperation between managers and workers that cannot simply be read off from broader relations of power and dependency. Throughout our empirical analysis we have sought to capture these complexities of lived experience whilst locating them within an understanding of the wider structures and power relations discussed in this concluding chapter.

REFERENCES

Abe, E. and Fitzgerald, R. (1995). 'Japanese Economic Success: Timing, Culture and Organisational Capability', *Business History*, special issue [The Origins of Japanese Industrial Power], 37(2): 1–31.

Abegglen, J. (1958). *The Japanese Factory: Aspects of its Social Organisation*. Glencoe, IL.: Free Press.

Abo, T. (ed.) (1990). *Local Production of Japanese Automobile and Electronics Firms in the United States: The 'Application' and 'Adaptation' of Japanese-Style Management*. Tokyo: Institute of Social Science, University of Tokyo.

—— (ed.) (1994*a*). *Hybrid Factory: The Japanese Production System in the United States*. Oxford: Oxford University Press.

—— (1994*b*). 'Sanyo's Overseas Production Activities: Seven Large Plants in the US, Mexico, the UK, Germany, Spain and China', in H. Schutte (ed.), *The Global Competitiveness of the Asian Firm*. London: Macmillan.

—— (1996). 'The Japanese Production System: The Process of Adaptation to National Settings', in R. Boyer and D. Drache (eds.), *States Against Markets: The Limits of Globalisation*. London: Routledge.

—— (1998*a*). 'Hybridization of the Japanese Production System in North America, Newly Industrializing Economies, South-east Asia and Europe: Contrasting Configurations', in R. Boyer et al. (eds.), *Between Imitation and Innovation: The Transfer and Hybridization of Production Models in the International Automobile Industry*. Oxford: Oxford University Press.

—— (1998*b*). 'Changes in Japanese Automobile and Electronic Transplants in the USA: Evaluating Japanese-style Management and Production Systems', in H. Hasagawa and G. D. Hook (eds.), *Japanese Business Management: Restructuring for Low Growth and Globalization*. London: Routledge.

Ackroyd, S. and Fleetwood, S. (eds.) (2000). *Realist Perspectives in Management and Organisation*. London: Routledge.

—— and Procter, S. (1998). 'British Manufacturing Organisation and Workplace Industrial Relations: Some Attributes of the New Flexible Firm', *British Journal of Industrial Relations*, 36(2): 163–84.

—— and Thompson, P. (1999). *Organisational Misbehaviour*. London: Sage.

Adler, P. S. (1993). 'The "Learning Bureaucracy": New United Motor Manufacturing, Inc.', in L. L. Cummings and B. M. Staw (eds.), *Research in Organizational Behaviour*, Vol. 15. Greenwich, CT: JAI Press.

—— (1999*a*). 'Teams at NUMMI', in J. -P. Durand, J. J. Castillo, and P. Stewart (eds.), *Teamwork in the Automobile Industry: Radical Change or Passing Fashion?* London: Macmillan.

—— (1999*b*). 'Hybridization: Human Resource Management at Two Toyota Transplants', in J. K. Liker, W. M. Fruin, and P. S. Adler (eds.), *Remade in America: Transplanting and Transforming Japanese Management Systems*. Oxford: Oxford University Press.

Adler, P. S. and Cole, R. E. (1995). 'Designed for Learning: A Tale of Two Plants', in A. Sandberg (ed.), *Enriching Production: Perspectives on Volvo's Uddevalla Plant as an Alternative to Lean Production*. Aldershot: Avebury.

—— Goldoftas, B., and Levine, D. I. (1995). 'Voice in Union and Non-Union High Performance Workplaces: Two Toyota Transplants Compared', *Industrial Relations Research Association*. Washington, January.

—————— (1998). 'Stability and Change at NUMMI' in R. Boyer et al. (eds.), *Between Imitation and Innovation: The Transfer and Hybridization of Production Models in the International Automobile Industry*. Oxford: Oxford University Press.

Albert, M. (1993). *Capitalism Against Capitalism*. London: Whurr.

Aldridge, M. (1979). *The British New Towns*. London: Routledge & Kegan Paul.

Allen, M. (1994). *Undermining the Japanese Miracle: Work and Conflict in a Coalmining Community*. Cambridge: Cambridge University Press.

Almond, P., Edwards, T., and Clark, I. (2003). 'Multinationals and Changing National Business Systems in Europe: Towards the "Shareholder Value" Model?' *Industrial Relations Journal*, 32(5): 430–45.

—— and Rubery, J. (2000). 'Deregulation and Societal Systems', in M. Maurice and A. Sorge (eds.), *Embedding Organizations: Societal Analysis of Actors, Organizations and Socio-Economic Context*. Amsterdam: John Benjamins.

Amoore, L. (2002). 'Work, Production and Social Relations: Repositioning the Firm in the International Political Economy', in J. Harrod and R. O'Brien (eds.), *Global Unions? Theory and Strategies of Organised Labour in the Global Political Economy*. London: Routledge.

Aoki, M. (1994). 'The Japanese Firm as a System of Attributes: A Survey and Research Agenda', in M. Aoki and R. Dore (eds.), *The Japanese Firm: Sources of Competitive Strength*. Oxford: Clarendon Press.

Armstrong, P. (1984). 'Competition between Organisation Professions and the Evolution of Management Control Strategies', in K. Thompson (ed.), *Work, Employment and Unemployment*. Milton Keynes: Open University.

Babson, S. (1995). *Lean Work: Empowerment and Exploitation in the Global Auto Industry*. Detroit: Wayne State University Press.

—— (1998). 'Mazda and Ford at Flat Rock: Transfer and Hybridisation of the Japanese model', in R. Boyer et al. (eds.), *Between Imitation and Innovation: The Transfer and Hybridization of Production Models in the International Automobile Industry*. Oxford: Oxford University Press.

Bacon, N. (2003). 'Human Resource Management and Industrial Relations', in P. Ackers and A. Wilkinson (eds.), *Understanding Work and Employment: Industrial Relations in Transition*. Oxford: Oxford University Press.

Baldamus, W. (1961). *Efficiency and Effort*. London: Tavistock.

Barrett, R. and Rainnie, A. (2002). 'What's so Special about Small Firms? Developing an Integrated Approach to Analysing Small Firm Industrial Relations', *Work, Employment and Society*, 16(3): 311–23.

Beechler, S. and Bird, A. (eds.) (1999). *Japanese Multinationals Abroad: Individual and Organizational Learning*. New York: Oxford University Press.

———— and Taylor, S. (1998). 'Organisational Learning in Japanese MNCs: Four Affiliate Archetypes', in J. Birkinshaw and N. Hood (eds.), *Multinational Corporate Evolution and Subsidiary Development*. London: Macmillan.

Bélanger, J. and Edwards, P. (2004). 'The Transnational Firm: Systems of Governance and Adjustment to the Institutional Environment', *International Conference on Multinationals and the International Diffusion of Organizational Forms and Practices: Convergence and Diversity within the Global Economy*, IESE Business School, Barcelona.

Benson, J. (1998). 'Labour Management during Recessions: Japanese Manufacturing Enterprises in the 1990s', *Industrial Relations Journal*, 29(3): 207–21.

Berggren, C. (1995). 'Japan as Number Two: Competitive Problems and the Future of Alliance Capitalism after the Burst of the Bubble Boom', *Work, Employment and Society*, 9(1): 53–95.

—— and Nomura, M. (1997). *The Resilience of Corporate Japan*. London: PCP.

Bird, A., Taylor, S., and Beechler, S. (1999). 'Organizational Learning in Japanese Overseas Affiliates', in S. Beechler and A. Bird (eds.), *Japanese Multinationals Abroad: Individual and Organizational Learning*. New York: Oxford University Press.

Birkinshaw, J. and Hood, N. (1998). 'Multinational Subsidiary Evolution: Capabilities and Charter Change in Foreign-Owned Companies', *Academy of Management Review*, 23(4): 773–95.

Blyton, P. and Turnball, P. (2004). *Dynamics of Employee Relations*, 3rd edn. Houndmills: Palgrave.

Boyer, R. (1998). 'Hybridization and Models of Production: Geography, History and Theory', in R. Boyer et al. (eds.), *Between Imitation and Innovation: The Transfer and Hybridization of Productive Models in the International Automobile Industry*. Oxford: Oxford University Press.

—— Charron, E., Jurgens, U., and Tolliday, S. (eds.) (1998*a*). *Between Imitation and Innovation: The Transfer and Hybridization of Productive Models in the International Automobile Industry*. Oxford: Oxford University Press.

—— —— —— —— (1998*b*). 'Conclusion: Transplants, Hybridization and Globalization: What Lessons for the Future?' in R. Boyer et al. (eds.), *Between Imitation and Innovation: The Transfer and Hybridization of Productive Models in the International Automobile Industry*. Oxford: Oxford University Press.

Brinton, M. C. (1993). *Women and the Economic Miracle: Gender and Work in Post War Japan*. California: University of California Press.

Broad, G. (1994). 'The Managerial Limits to Japanisation', *Human Resource Management Journal*, 4(3): 41–61.

Burawoy, M. (1979). *Manufacturing Consent: Changes in the Labor Process under Monopoly Capitalism*. Chicago: The University of Chicago Press.

—— (1985). *The Politics of Production*. London: Verso.

—— (1991). 'The Extended Case Method', in M. Burawoy et al. (eds), *Ethnography Unbound: Power and Resistance in the Modern Metropolis*. Berkeley: California University Press.

—— (1998). 'The Extended Case Method', *Sociological Theory*, 16(1): 4–33.

Burkitt, P. and Hart-Landsberg, M. (1996). 'The Use and Abuse of Japan as a Progressive Model', in L. Panitch (ed.) *Socialist Register 1996*. London: Merlin Press.

Burns, T. (1961). 'Micropolitics: Mechanisms of Institutional Change', *Administrative Science Quarterly*, 6: 257–81.

—— and Stalker, G. M. (1961). *The Management of Innovation*. London: Tavistock.

Campbell, D. (1994). 'Foreign Investment, Labour Immobility and the Quality of Empowerment', *International Labour Review*, 133(2): 185–204.
Carney, L. S. and O'Kelly, C. G. (1990). 'Women's Work and Women's Place in the Japanese Economic Miracle', in K. Ward (ed.), *Women Workers and Global Restructuring*. Ithaca, NY: ILR Press, Cornell University.
Castells, M. (2000). *The Rise of the Network Society*. Oxford: Blackwell.
Castles, S. (2000). *Citizenship and Migration: Globalization and the Politics of Belonging*. London: Macmillan.
Cerny, P. G. (1990). *The Changing Architecture of Politics: Structure, Agency and the Future of the State*. London: Sage.
Chalmers, N. J. (1989). *Industrial Relations in Japan: The Peripheral Workforce*. London: Routledge.
Child, J. (1972). 'Organisation Structure, Environment and Performance: The Role of Strategic Choice', *Sociology*, 6(1): 1–22.
—— (1981). 'Culture, Contingency and Capitalism in the Cross-National Study of Organisations', in B. Staw and L. L. Cummings (eds.), *Research in Organizational Behaviour*, Vol. 3. Greenwich, CT: JAI Press, 303–56.
Clark, P. and Mueller, F. (1996). 'Organisations and Nations: From Universalism to Institutionalism', *British Journal of Management*, 7: 125–40.
Clark, S. (1996). 'A Profile of the Usage of Temporary Labour in Manufacturing Companies in Telford'. MSc dissertation. Personnel Management and Business Administration, Aston University.
Coates, D. (2000). *Models of Capitalism: Growth and Stagnation in the Modern Era*. Cambridge: Polity Press.
Cohen, R. (1997). *Global Diasporas: An Introduction*. London: UCL Press.
Cole, R. (1971). *Japanese Blue Collar: The Changing Tradition*. Berkeley: University of California Press.
—— (1989). *Strategies for Learning: Small-Group Activities in American, Japanese and Swedish Industry*. Berkeley: University of California Press.
Collis, C. and Roberts, P. (1992). 'Foreign Direct Investment in the West Midlands: An Analysis and Evaluation', *Local Economy*, 7(2): 114–29.
Crouch, C. (1993). *Industrial Relations and European State Traditions*. Oxford: Clarendon.
—— (2001). 'Heterogeneities of Practice and Interest', *New Political Economy*, 6: 131–5.
—— and Streeck, W. (eds.) (1997). *Political Economy of Modern Capitalism: Mapping Convergence and Diversity*. London: Sage.
Cusumano, M. A. (1985). *The Japanese Automobile Industry: Technology and Management at Nissan and Toyota*. Cambridge, Mass.: Harvard University Press.
Danford, A. (1999). *Japanese Management Techniques and British Workers*. London: Mansell.
Daskalaki, M. (2001). 'Deconstructing Induction Programmes: Discourses of Organisational Acculturation and Resistance'. Unpublished Ph.D. thesis. Royal Holloway, University of London.
Dedoussis, V. (1994). 'The Core Workforce—Peripheral Workforce Dichotomy and the Transfer of Japanese Management Practices', in N. Campbell and F. Burton (eds.), *Japanese Multinationals: Strategies and Management in the Global Kaisha*. London: Routledge.

—— (1995). 'Simply a Question of Cultural Barriers? The Search for New Perspectives in the Transfer of Japanese Management Practices', *Journal of Management Studies*, 32(6): 731–46.

—— and Littler, C. (1994). 'Understanding the Transfer of Japanese Management Practices: The Australian Case', in T. Elger and C. Smith (eds.), *Global Japanization?* London: Routledge.

Delbridge, R. (1998). *Life on the Line in Contemporary Manufacturing: the Workplace Experience of Lean Production and the 'Japanese' Model.* Oxford: Oxford University Press.

—— Turnbull, P., and Wilkinson, B. (1992). ' Pushing back the Frontiers: Management Control and Work Intensification under JIT/TQC Production Regimes', *New Technology, Work and Employment*, 7(2): 97–106.

De Soissons, M. (1991). *Telford: The Making of Shropshire's New Town.* Shrewsbury: Swan Press.

Dicken, P. (1991). 'The Changing Geography of Japanese Foreign Direct Investment in Manufacturing Industry: A Global Perspective', in J. Morris (ed.), *Japan and the Global Economy: Issues and Trends in the 1990s.* London: Routledge.

—— (1998), *Global Shift: Transforming the World Economy*, 3rd edn. London: Paul Chapman.

DiMaggio, P. and Powell, W. (1983). 'The Iron Cage Revisited: Institutional Isomorphism and Collective Rationality in Organizational Fields', *American Sociological Review*, 48: 147–60.

Dohse, K., Jurgens, U., and Malsch, T. (1985). 'From "Fordism" to "Toyotaism"? The Social Organisation of the Labour Process in the Japanese Automobile Industry', *Politics and Society*, 14(2): 115–46.

Dore, R. (1973/1990). *British Factory, Japanese Factory.* London: Allen and Unwin.

Dunning, J. H. (1986). *Japanese Participation in British Industry.* London: Croom Helm.

—— (1993). *The Globalisation of Business: The Challenges of the 1990s.* London: Routledge.

—— (1997). *Alliance Capitalism and Global Business.* London: Routledge.

Durand, J.-P. and Durand-Sebag, J. (1996). *The Hidden Face of the Japanese Model*, Monash Asia Institute, Japanese Studies Centre, Occassional Paper 27, Monash University.

—— Castillo, J. J. and Stewart, P. (eds.) (1999). *Teamwork in the Automobile Industry: Radical Change or Passing Fashion?* London: Macmillan.

Edwards, P., Armstrong, P., Marginson, P. and Purcell, J. (1996). 'Towards the Transnational Company? The Global Structure and Organisation of Multinational Firms', in R. Crompton, D. Gallie, and K. Purcell (eds.), *Changing Forms of Employment: Organisations, Skills and Gender.* London: Routledge.

—— Hall, M., Hyman, R., Marginson, P., Sisson, K., Waddington, J. and Winchester, D. (1992). 'Great Britain: Still Muddling Through', in A. Ferner and R. Hyman (eds.), *Industrial Relations in the New Europe.* Oxford: Blackwell.

Edwards, P. K. (1986). *Conflict at Work: A Materialist Analysis of Workplace Relations.* Oxford: Blackwell.

—— and Scullion, H. (1982). *The Social Organisation of Industrial Conflict.* Oxford: Blackwell.

Edwards, T. (1998). 'Multinationals, Labour Management and the Process of Reverse Diffusion: A Case Study', *International Journal of Human Resource Management*, 9(4): 696–709.

—— (2004). 'The Transfer of Employment Practices Across Borders in Multinational Companies', in A.-W. Harzing and J. V. Ruysseveldt (eds.), *International Human Resource Management*, 2nd edn. London: Sage.

—— and Ferner, A. (2004). 'Multinationals, Reverse Diffusion and National Business Systems', *Management International Review*, 24(1): 51–81.

—— Almond, P., Clark, I., Colling, T. and Ferner, A. (2003). 'Reverse Diffusion in US Multinationals: Barriers from the American Business System'. International HRM Conference, Limerick.

—— Colling, T. and Ferner, A. (2004). 'Comparative Institutional Analysis and the Diffusion of Employment Practices in Multinational Companies', *International Conference on Multinationals and the International Diffusion of Organizational Forms and Practices: Convergence and Diversity within the Global Economy*, IESE Business School, Barcelona.

Elger, T. (1999). 'Manufacturing Myths and Miracles: Work Reorganisation in British Manufacturing Since 1979', in H. Beynon and P. Glavanis (ed.), *Patterns of Social Inequality: Essays for Richard Brown*. London: Pearson.

—— (2002). 'Analisi critica materialistica del lavoro e dell'occipazione in Gran Bretagna: la terza via tra marxismo ortodosso e postmodernismo', *Sociologia del Lavoro*, 86–87: 61–81.

—— and Burnham, P. (2001). 'Labour, Globalization and the "Competition State"', *Competition and Change*, 5: 245–68.

—— and Edwards, P. (1999). 'An Introduction', in P. Edwards and T. Elger (eds.), *National States and the Regulation of Labour in the Global Economy*. London: Mansell.

—— and Smith, C. (1994). 'Introduction' and 'Global Japanization? Convergence and Competition in the Organization of the Labour Process', in T. Elger and C. Smith (eds.), *Global Japanization? The Transnational Transformation of the Labour Process*. London: Routledge.

—— —— (1998*a*). 'Exit, Voice and "Mandate": Management Strategies and Labour Practices of Japanese Firms in Britain', *British Journal of Industrial Relations*, 36(2): 185–207.

—— —— (1998*b*). 'New Town, New Capital, New Workplace? The Employment Relations of Japanese Inward Investors in a West Midlands New Town', *Economy and Society*, 27: 578–60.

—— —— (1999). 'Japanese Inward Investors and the Remaking of Employment and Production Regimes', in A. Eckardt, H.-D. Kohler, and L. Pries (eds.), *Global Players in Lokalen Bindungen*. Berlin: Edition Sigma.

—— —— (2001). 'The Global Dissemination of Production Models and the Recasting of Work and Employment Relations in Developing Societies: The Case of Japanese TNCs', in J. G. Coetzee and F. Hendricks (eds.), *Development: Theory, Policy and Practice*. Oxford/Cape Town: Oxford University Press.

Endo, K. (1994). 'Satei (personal assessment) and Inter-worker Competition in Japanese Firms', *Industrial Relations*, 33(1): 70–82.

—— (1997). 'Sex and Union Discrimination Under the Satei System in Japanese Firms', *Review of Radical Political Economics*, 29(2) (Spring): 26–44.

Ferner, A. (2003). 'Foreign Multinationals and Industrial Relations Innovation in Britain', in P. Edwards (ed.), *Industrial Relations: Theory and Practice*, 2nd edn. Oxford: Blackwell.

—— and Hyman, R. (eds.) (1992). *Industrial Relations in the New Europe*. Oxford: Blackwell.

—— and Quintanilla, J. (1998). 'Multinationals, National Business Systems and HRM: The Enduring Influence of National Identity or the Process of "Anglo-Saxonisation" ', *International Journal of Human Resource Management*, 9(4): 710–31.

Findlay, P. (1993). 'Union Recognition and Non-unionism: Shifting Fortunes in the Electronics Industry in Scotland', *Industrial Relations Journal*, 24(1): 28–43.

Florida, R., and Kenney, M. (1991*a*). 'Organisation Versus Culture: Japanese Automotive Transplants in the United States', *Industrial Relations Journal*, 22: 181–96.

—— —— (1991*b*). 'Transplanted Organizations: The Transfer of Japanese Industrial Organisation to the United States', *American Sociological Review*, 56(3): 381–98.

Forde, C. (1997). 'Temporary Employment Agency Working: Issues and Evidence', *15th International Labour Process Conference*. Edinburgh, March.

—— (2001). 'Temporary Arrangements: the Activities of Employment Agencies in the UK', *Work, Employment and Society*, 15(3): 63–44.

Foster, J. and Wolfson, C. (1989). 'Corporate Reconstruction and Business Unionism: The Lessons of Caterpillar and Ford', *New Left Review*, 174: 51–66.

Fransman, M. (1990). *The Market and Beyond: Information Technology in Japan*, Cambridge: Cambridge University Press.

—— (1995). *Japan's Computer and Communications Industry: The Evolution of Industrial Giants and Global Competitiveness*. Oxford: Oxford University Press.

—— (1999). 'Where Are the Japanese? Japanese Information and Communications Firms in an Internetworked World', *Telecommunications Policy*, 23: 317–33.

Freyssenet, M. (1998). 'Intersecting Trajectories and Model Changes', in M. Freyssenet et al. (eds.), *One Best Way? Trajectories and Industrial Models of the World's Automobile Producers*. Oxford: Oxford University Press.

—— Mair, A., Shimizu, K., and Volpata, G. (1998). 'Conclusion: The Choices to be Made in the Coming Decade', in M. Freyssenet et al. (eds.), *One Best Way? Trajectories and Industrial Models of the World's Automobile Producers*. Oxford: Oxford University Press.

Frobel, F., Heinrichs, J., and Kreye, O. (1980). *The New International Division of Labour: Structural Unemployment in Industrialized Countries and Industrialization in Developing Countries*. Cambridge: Cambridge University Press.

Fruin, M. (1992). *The Japanese Enterprise System: Competitive Strategies and Cooperative Structures*. Oxford: Oxford University Press.

—— (1997). *Knowledge Works: Managing Intellectual Capital at Toshiba*. Oxford: Oxford University Press.

—— (1999). 'Site-specific Organization Learning in International Technology Transfer', in J. K. Liker, W. M. Fruin, and P. S. Adler (eds.), *Remade in America: Transplanting and Transforming Japanese Management Systems*. Oxford: Oxford University Press.

Fucini, J. L. and Fucini, S. (1990). *Working for the Japanese: Inside Mazda's American Auto Plant*. New York: Free Press.

Fujimoto, T., Nishiguchi, T., and Sei, S. (1994). 'The Strategy and Structure of Japanese Automobile Manufacturers in Europe', in M. Mason and D. Encarnation

(eds.), *Does Ownership Matter? Japanese Multinationals in Europe*. Oxford: Oxford University Press.
Fujimura, H. (1997). 'New Unionism: Beyond Enterprise Unionism?' in M. Sako and H. Sato (eds.), *Japanese Labour and Management in Transition*. London: Routledge.
Gallie, D. (1978). *In Search of the New Working Class*. Cambridge: Cambridge University Press.
Gamble, J. (2003). 'Working for *Laowai*: Chinese Shopfloor Worker's Perceptions of Employment in a Western Multinational', mimeo, *Centre for Workplace Research in Asia Pacific Societies*. School of Management, Royal Holloway, University of London.
Garrahan, P. and Stewart, P. (1992). *The Nissan Enigma: Flexibility at Work in a Local Economy*. London: Cassell.
Gereffi, G. (1996). 'Commodity Chains and Regional Divisions of Labor in East Asia', *Journal of Asian Business*, 12(1): 75–112.
—— and Korzeniewicz, M. (eds.) (1994). *Commodity Chains and Global Capitalism*. Westport, CT: Praeger.
Glaser, B. G. and Strauss, A. L. (1967). *The Discovery of Grounded Theory*. London: Weidenfeld and Nicolson.
Goldthorpe, J. (2000). *On Sociology: Numbers, Narratives and the Integration of Research and Theory*. Oxford: Oxford University Press.
Gordon, A. (1985). *The Evolution of Labor Relations in Japan: Heavy Industry 1853–1945*. Boston: Harvard University Press.
—— (1993). 'Contests for the Workplace', in A. Gordon (ed.), *Post-war Japan as History*. Berkeley: University of California Press.
—— (1996). 'The Emergence of a Labour-Management Settlement in Japan 1945–60', *International Labor and Working Class History*, 50: 133–9.
Gottfried, H. and Graham, L. (1993). 'Constructing Difference: The Making of Gendered Subcultures in a Japanese Automobile Transplant', *Sociology*, 27: 611–28.
—— and Hayashi-Kato, N. (1998). 'Gendering Work: Deconstructing the Narrative of the Japanese Economic Miracle', *Work, Employment and Society*, 12(1): 25–46.
Gouldner, A. W. (1954). *Patterns of Industrial Bureaucracy*. New York: Free Press.
Graham, L. (1995). *On the Line at Subaru-Isuzu: The Japanese Model and the American Worker*. New York: ILR/Cornell University Press.
Grant, D. (1994). 'New Style Agreements at Japanese Transplants in the UK', *Employee Relations*, 16(2): 65–83.
—— (1996). 'Japanization and New Industrial Relations', in I. Beardwell (ed.), *Contemporary Industrial Relations: A Critical Analysis*. Oxford: Oxford University Press.
Gronning, T. (1995). 'Recent Developments at Toyota Motor Co', in A. Sandberg (ed.), *Enriching Production: Perspectives on Volvo's Uddevalla plant as an Alternative to Lean Production*. Aldershot: Avebury.
—— (1997). 'The Emergence and Institutionalization of Toyotism: Subdivision and Integration of the Labour Force at the Toyota Motor Corporation from the 1950s to the 1970s', *Economic and Industrial Democracy*, 18(3): 423–56.
—— (1998). 'Whither the Japanese Employment System? The Position of the Japan Employers' Federation', Industrial Relations Journal, 29(4): 295–303..
Gunnigle, P., Collins, D. G., and Morley, M. J. (2004). 'Innovators or Disrupters? An Exploration of the Polemic on American MNCs and their HRM and Industrial

Relations Practices in Ireland'. *Multinationals and the International Diffusion of Organizational Forms and Practices: Convergence and Diversity within the Global Economy,* IESA Business School Barcelona, Spain.

Haitani, K. (1976). *The Japanese Employment System.* Lexington, MS: D.C. Heath & Co.

Halford, S., Savage, M., and Witz. A. (1997). *Gender, Careers and Organizations.* Basingstoke: Macmillan.

Hall, P. A. and Soskice, D. (2001). 'An Introduction to Varieties of Capitalism', in P. A. Hall and D. Soskice (eds.), *Varieties of Capitalism: The Institutional Foundations of Comparative Advantage.* Oxford: Oxford University Press.

Halliday, J. and McCormack, G. (1973). *Japanese Imperialism Today: Co-prosperity in Greater East Asia.* Harmondsworth: Penguin.

Hallier, J. and Leopold, J. (2000). 'Managing Employment on Greenfield Sites: Attempts to Replicate High Commitment Practices in the UK and New Zealand', *Industrial Relations Journal,* 31(3): 177–91.

Hanada, M. (1998). 'Nissan: Restructuring to Regain Competitiveness', in M. Freyssenet et al. (eds.), *One Best Way? Trajectories and Industrial Models of the World's Automobile Producers.* Oxford: Oxford University Press.

Hanami, T. (2000). 'Equal Employment Revisited', *Japan Labour Bulletin,* 39(1): 1–5.

Hantrais, L. and Walters, P. (1994). 'Making It in and Making Out: Women in Professional Occupations in Britain and France', *Gender, Work and Organisations,* 1(1): 23–32.

Harrison, B. (1994). *Lean and Mean.* New York: Basic Books.

Harvey, D. (1982). *The Limits to Capital.* Oxford: Blackwell.

Harvey-Jones, J. (with Masey, A.) (1990). *Trouble Shooter.* London: BBC Books.

Hazama, H. (1987). *The History of Labour Management in Japan.* London: Macmillan Press.

Henderson, J. (1989). *The Globalisation of High Technology Production.* London: Routledge.

—— (1994). 'Electronics Industries and the Developing World: Uneven Contributions and Uncertain Prospects', in L. Sklair (ed.), *Capitalism and Development.* London: Routledge.

—— (1999). 'Uneven Crisis: Institutional Foundations of East Asian Economic Turmoil', *Economy and Society,* 28(3): 327–68.

Hill, S. and Munday, M. (1994). *The Distribution of Foreign Manufacturing Investment in the UK.* London: Macmillan.

Hollingsworth, J. R., Schmitter, P. C., and Streeck, W. (eds.) (1994). *Governing Capitalist Economies: Performance and Control of Economic Sectors.* Oxford: Oxford University Press.

Hudson, R. (1989). 'Labour-Market Changes and New Forms of Work in Old Industrial Regions', *Environment and Planning D: Society and Space,* 7: 5–30.

Hyman, R. (2004). 'Varieties of Capitalism, National Industrial Relations Systems and Transnational Challenges', in Anne-Wil Harzing and Joris Van Ruysseveldt (eds.), *International Human Resource Management.* London: Sage.

Igarashi, M. (2000). 'The Management of Japanese Firms in Telford'. MBA dissertation. School of Management, Royal Holloway, University of London.

Inagami, T. and Whittaker, D. H. (2005,). *The New Community Firm: Employment, Governance and Management Reform in Japan.* Cambridge: Cambridge University Press.

Industrial Bank of Japan (1994). 'Copy Machine Market: Present Condition and Future Outlook', *Quarterly Survey: Japanese Finance and Industry*, 100: iv.

Ishida, H. (1989). 'Transferability of Japanese Human Resource Management Abroad', *Human Resource Management*, 25(1): 103–20.

Itagaki, H. (ed.) (1997). *The Japanese Production System: Hybrid Factories in East Asia*. London: Macmillan.

JETRO (Japan External Trade Organisation) (2003). *Japanese Affiliated Manufacturers in Europe/Turkey—Survey 2002*. London: JETRO.

Jones, C. S. (1996). 'The Growth and Development of Employment Agencies in Telford since 1980'. M.Sc. dissertation. Personnel Management and Business Administration, Aston University.

Katz, H. C. and Darbishire, O. (2000). *Converging Divergences: Worldwide Changes in Employment Systems*. Ithaca, New York: ILR Press.

Kelly, J. (1985). 'Management's Redesign of Work', in D. Knights, H. Willmott and D. Collinson (eds), *Job Redesign: Critical Perspectives on the Labour Process*. Aldershot: Gower.

Kenney, M. and Florida, R. (1988). 'Beyond Mass Production: Production and the Labor Process in Japan', *Politics and Society*, 16(1): 121–58.

—— —— (1993). *Beyond Mass Production: the Japanese System and its Transfer to the US*. Oxford: Oxford University Press.

—— —— (1995). 'The Transfer of Japanese Management Styles in Two US Transplant Industries: Autos and Electronics', *Journal of Management Studies*, 32(6): 789–802.

—— Goe, W. R., Contreras, O., Romero, J. , and Bustos, M. (1998). 'Learning Factories or Reproduction Factories? Labor–Management Relations in the Japanese Consumer Electronics Maquiladoras in Mexico', *Work and Occupations*, 25(3): 269–304.

—— —— —— —— —— ——(1999). 'Labor–Management Relations in the Japanese Consumer Electronics Maquiladoras', in S. Beechler and A. Bird (eds.), *Japanese Multinationals Abroad: Individual and Organizational Learning*. New York: Oxford University Press.

Kim, Young-Chan (1999). 'Japanese Inward Investment in UK Car Manufacturing: A Case Study of International Business–National Government Relations within the Context of the European Union'. Ph.D. thesis. Royal Holloway, University of London.

Kinzley, W. D. (1991). *Industrial Harmony in Modern Japan: The Invention of a Tradition*. London: Routledge.

Kogut, B. and Parkinson, D. (1993). 'The Diffusion of American Organising Principles to Europe', in B. Kogut (ed.), *Country Competitiveness: Technology and the Organizing of Work*. Oxford: Oxford University Press.

Koike, K. (1988). *Understanding Industrial Relations in Modern Japan*. Basingstoke: Macmillan.

Kondo, D. K. (1990). *Crafting Selves: Power, Gender and Discourses of Identity in a Japanese Workplace*. London: The University of Chicago Press.

Krugman, P. (1994). 'Competitiveness: A Dangerous Obsession', *Foreign Affairs* (March/April): 28–44.

Kumazawa, M. (1996). *Portraits of the Japanese Workplace: Labor Movements, Workers and Managers*. Boulder: Westview Press.

Kusumoto, M. (2003). 'Japanese Multinationals and the European Market: Changes in Investment Motivations, Progress of Localization, Suitability of Management Style and the Restructuring of Networks'. MBA dissertation. Royal Holloway, University of London

Kyotani, E. (1999). 'New Managerial Strategies of Japanese Corporations', in A. Felstead and N. Jewson (eds.), *Global Trends in Flexible Labour*. London: Macmillan.

Lam, A. (1992). *Women and Japanese Management*. London: Routledge.

—— (1995). 'Building Integrated Workforces across National Borders: The Case of British and Japanese Engineers', *International Journal of Human Resource Management*, 6(3): 508–26.

—— (1996*a*). 'Work Organisation, Skills Development and Utilisation of Engineers: A British–Japanese Comparison', in R. Crompton et al. (eds.), *Changing Forms of Employment: Organisations, Skills and Gender*. London: Routledge.

—— (1996*b*). 'Engineers, Management and Work Organization: A Comparative Analysis of Engineers' Work Roles in British and Japanese Electronics Firms', *Journal of Management Studies*, 33(2): 183–212.

—— (2003). 'Organizational Learning in Multinational Companies: R&D Networks of Japanese and US MNEs in the UK', *Journal of Management Studies*, 40(3): 673–703.

Lane, C. (1989). *Management and Labour in Europe*. Aldershot: Edward Elgar.

—— (1995). *Industry and Society in Europe: Stability and Change in Britain, Germany and France*. Aldershot: Edward Elgar.

Lapavitsas, C. (1997). 'Transition and Crisis in the Japanese Financial System: An Analytical Overview', *Capital and Class*, No. 62: 21–47.

Lauchlan, J. (1993). 'How to Attract Japanese R&D to Europe: A Study of the Determinants and Effects of Japanese R&D Activities in Europe', *Institute for Japanese–European Technology Studies*, University of Edinburgh.

Legge, K. (1995). 'HRM: Rhetoric, Reality and Hidden Agendas', in J. Storey (ed.), *Human Resource Management: A Critical Text*. London: Routledge.

Leopold, J. W. and Hallier, J. (1997). 'Start-up and Ageing in Greenfield Sites', *Human Resource Management Journal*, 7(2): 72–88.

Leyshon, A. (1994). 'Under Pressure: Finance, Geo-economic Competition and the Rise and Fall of Japan's Postwar Growth Economy', in S. Corbridge and N. J. Thrift (eds.), *Money, Power and Space*. Oxford: Blackwell.

Liddle, J. and Nakajima, S. (2000). *Rising Suns, Rising Daughters: Gender, Class and Power in Japan*. London: Zed Books.

Liker, J. K., Ettlie, J. E., and Campbell, J. C. (1995). *Engineered in Japan: Japanese Technology Management Practices*. New York: Oxford University Press.

—— Fruin, W. M., and Adler, P. S. (1999). 'Bringing Japanese Management to the United States: Transplantation or Transformation? in J. K. Liker, W. M. Fruin, and P. S. Adler (eds.), *Remade in America: Transplanting and Transforming Japanese Management Systems*. Oxford: Oxford University Press.

Lincoln, J. R. and Nakata, Y. (1997). 'The Transformation of the Japanese Employment System: Nature, Depth and Origins', *Work and Occupations*, 24(1): 33–55.

Littler, C. R. (1982). *The Development of the Labour Process in Capitalist Societies*. London: Heinemann.

Machin, S. (2000). 'Union Decline in Britain', *British Journal of Industrial Relations*, 38(4): 631–45.

Mair, A. (1994). *Honda's Global Local Corporation*. London: Macmillan.

Mair, A. (1998). 'The Globalization of Honda's Product-Led Flexible Mass Production System', in M. Freyssenet et al. (eds.), *One Best Way? Trajectories and Industrial Models of the World's Automobile Producers*. Oxford: Oxford University Press.
Mann, S. (1991). 'The Significance of Japanese Manufacturing Investment in the UK: An Overview and Case-study of Telford New Town'. MA dissertation. Labour Studies, Department of Sociology, University of Warwick.
Marginson, P. (1994). 'Multinational Britain: Employment and Work in an Internationalised Economy', *Human Resource Management Journal*, 4(4): 63–80.
Marsh, D. (1992). *The New Politics of British Trade Unionism: Union Power and the Thatcher Legacy*. London: Macmillan.
Massey, D. (1984). *Spatial Divisions of Labour*. London: Macmillan.
Maurice, M., Sellier, F., and Silvestre, J. J. (1986). *The Social Foundations of Industrial Power: A Comparison of France and Germany*. Cambridge, MA: The MIT Press.
—— and Sorge, A. (eds.) (2000*a*). *Embedding Organizations: Societal Analysis of Actors, Organisations and Socio-Economic Context*. Amsterdam: John Benjamin.
—— —— (2000*b*). 'Conclusions', in M. Maurice and A. Sorge (eds.), *Embedding Organizations: Societal Analysis of Actors, Organisations and Socio-Economic Context*. Amsterdam: John Benjamin.
Mayer, M. C. J. and Whittington, R. (1999). 'Strategy, Structure and "Systemness": National Institutions and Corporate Change in France, Germany and the UK, 1950–1993', *Organization Studies*, 20: 933–59.
McCormick, B. and McCormick, K. (1996). *Japanese Companies, British Factories*. Aldershot: Avebury.
McCormick, K. (1996). 'Japanese Engineers as Corporate Salarymen', in P. Meiksins and C. Smith (eds.), *Engineering Labour: Technical Workers in Comparative Perspective*. London: Verso.
Meiksins, P. and Smith, C. (1996). *Engineering Labour: Technical Workers in Comparative Perspective*. London: Verso.
Milkman, R. (1991). *Japan's California Factories: Labor Relations and Economic Globalisation*. Los Angeles: Institute of Industrial Relations, University of California.
—— (1992). 'The Impact of Foreign Investment on US Industrial Relations: The Case of California's Japanese-Owned Plants', *Economic and Industrial Democracy*, 13: 151–82.
—— (1997). *Farewell to the Factory: Auto Workers in the Late Twentieth Century*, California: University of California Press.
Morgan, G., Sharpe, D. R., Kelly, W., and Whitley, R. (2002). 'The Future of Japanese Manufacturing in the UK', *Journal of Management Studies*, 39(8): 1023–45.
Morris, J. (1988). 'The Who, Why and Where of Japanese Manufacturing Investment in the UK', *Industrial Relations Journal*, 19(1): 31–40.
—— (1991*a*). 'Globalisation and Global Localisation: Explaining Trends in Japanese Foreign Manufacturing Investment', in J. Morris (ed.), *Japan and the Global Economy: Issues and Trends in the 1990s*. London: Routledge.
—— (1991*b*). 'Japanese Foreign Manufacturing Investment in the EC: An Overview', in J. Morris (ed.), *Japan and the Global Economy: Issues and Trends in the 1990s*. London: Routledge.
—— Munday, M. and Wilkinson, B. (1993). *Working for the Japanese: The Economic and Social Consequences of Japanese Investment in Wales*. London: Athlone.

—— and Wilkinson, B. (1995). 'The Transfer of Japanese Management Techniques to Alien Institutional Environments', *Journal of Management Studies*, 32(6): 719–30.

Morris-Suzuki, T. (1992). 'Japanese Technology and the New International Division of Knowledge in Asia', in S. Tokunaga (ed.), *Japan's Foreign Investment and Asian Economic Interdependence: Production, Trade and Financial Systems.* Tokyo: Tokyo University Press.

Mueller, F. (1996). 'National Stakeholders in the Global Contest for Corporate Investment', *European Journal of Industrial Relations*, 2(3): 345–68.

Munday, M. (1995). 'The Regional Consequences of the Japanese Second Wave: A Case Study', *Local Economy*, 10(1): 4–20.

—— Morris, J., and Wilkinson, B. (1995). 'Factories or Warehouses? A Welsh Perspective on Japanese Transplant Manufacturing', *Regional Studies*, 29: 11–17.

Murphy, R. T. (2000). 'Japan's Economic Crisis', *New Left Review*, 1 (2nd series): 25–52.

Nagai, A. (1985). 'Establishment of Telford Factory of Maxell (UK) Ltd', in *An Autobiography: Life of Thomas Telford* (Japanese text). Tokyo.

Naruse, T. (1991). 'Taylorism and Fordism in Japan', *International Journal of Political Economy*, 21(2): 31–48.

Nohara, H. (1999). 'The Historic Reversal of the Division of Labour? The Second Stage of the Toyota Production System', in J.-P. Durand, J. J. Castillo, and P. Stewart (eds.), *Teamwork in the Automobile Industry: Radical Change or Passing Fashion?* London: Macmillan.

Nonaka, I. (1995). 'The Development of Company-Wide Quality Control and Quality Circles at Toyota Motor Corporation and Nissan Motor Co. Ltd.', in H. Shiomi and K. Wada (eds.), *Fordism Transformed: The Development of Production Methods in the Automobile Industry.* Oxford: Oxford University Press.

Odagiri, H. and Yusada, H. (1996). 'The Determinants of Overseas R&D by Japanese Firms: An Empirical Study at the Industry and Firm Levels', *Research Policy*, 25: 1059–79.

—— —— (1999). 'Overseas R&D Activities of Japanese Firms', in A. Goto and H. Odagiri (eds.), *Innovation in Japan*. Oxford: Oxford University Press.

Okayama, R. (1986). 'Industrial Relations in the Japanese Automobile Industry 1945–70: The Case of Toyota', in S. Tolliday and J. Zeitlin (eds.), *The Automobile Industry and its Workers: Between Fordism and Flexibility.* Cambridge: Polity.

Okimoto, D. and Nishi, Y. (1994). 'R&D Organization in Japanese and American Semiconductor Firms', in M. Aoki and R. Dore (eds.), *The Japanese Firm*. New York: Oxford University Press.

Oliver, N. and Wilkinson, B. (1988). *The Japanisation of British Industry.* Oxford: Blackwell.

—— —— (1992). *The Japanisation of British Industry: New Developments in the 1990s*, 2nd edn. Oxford: Blackwell.

Ouchi, W. G. (1981). *Theory Z.* Reading, MA: Addison-Wesley.

Palmer, G. (1996). 'Reviving Resistance: The Japanese Factory Floor in Britain', *Industrial Relations Journal*, 27: 129–43.

—— (2000). Embeddedness and Workplace Relations: A Case-Study of a British-based Japanese Manufacturing Company. Ph.D. thesis. University of Warwick.

Papanastassiou, M. and Pearce, R. (1995). 'The Research and Development of Japanese Multinational Enterprises in Europe', in F. Sachwald (ed.), *Japanese Firms in Europe*. Luxemburg: Harwood.

Parker, M. and Slaughter, J. (1988). 'Management-by-Stress: The Team Concept in the US Automobile Industry', *Technology Review*, October: 37–44.

Pascale, R. T. and Athos, A. G. (1982). *The Art of Japanese Management*. Harmondsworth: Penguin.

Peck, J. (1996). *Work-Place: The Social Regulation of Labor Markets*. New York: Guilford.

—— and Miyamachi, Y. (1995). 'Regulating Japan? Regulation Theory versus the Japanese Experience', *Environment and Planning D: Society and Space*, 12: 639–74.

Pratten, S. (1993). 'Structure, Agency and Marx's Analysis of the Labour Process', *Review of Political Economy*, 5(4): 403–26.

Price, J. (1997). *Japan Works: Power and Paradox in Postwar Industrial Relations*. Ithaca, NY: ILR Press, Cornell University.

Ram, M. and Edwards, P. (2003). 'Praising Caesar not Burying Him: What We Know about Employment Relations in Small Firms', *Work, Employment and Society*, 17(4): 719–30.

Reinhart, J., Robertson, D., Huxley, C., and Wareham, J. (1994). 'Reunifying Conception and Execution of Work under Japanese Production Management? A Canadian Case Study', in T. Elger and C. Smith (eds.), *Global Japanization?* London: Routledge.

—— Huxley, C., and Robertson, D. (1997). *Just Another Car Factory? Lean Production and its Discontents*. New York: Cornell University Press.

Roy, D. (1955). 'Efficiency and "the Fix": Informal Intergroup Relations in a Piecework Machine Shop', *American Journal of Sociology*, 60: 255–66.

Rubery, J. (1994). 'Internal and External Labour Markets: Towards an Integrated Analysis', in J. Rubery and F. Wilkinson (eds.), *Employer Strategies and the Labour Market*. Oxford: Oxford University Press.

Ruigrok, W. and van Tulder, R. (1995). *The Logic of International Restructuring*. London: Routledge.

Sako, M. (1992). *Prices, Quality and Trust: Inter-firm Relations in Britain and Japan*. Cambridge: Cambridge University Press.

Sayer, A. (1986). 'New Developments in Manufacturing: The Just-in-Time System', *Capital and Class*, 30: 43–72.

Scott, A. (1994). *Willing Slaves? British Workers Under Human Resource Management*. Cambridge: Cambridge University Press.

Seton, C. (1994). 'Targeting the Favourite Asian Tiger', *Daily Telegraph*, 27 April.

Sewell, G. and Wilkinson, B. (1992). ' "Someone to Watch Over Me": Surveillance, Discipline and the JIT Labour Process', *Sociology*, 26(2): 271–89.

Sharpe, D. (1997). 'Managerial Control Strategies and Sub-cultural Processes: On the Shop-floor in a Japanese Manufacturing Organisation in the UK', in A. Sackmann (ed.), *Cultural Complexity in Organisations: Inherent Contrasts and Contradictions*. London: Sage.

—— (1998). 'Shop Floor Practices Under Changing Forms of Management Control: A Comparative Ethnographic Study'. Ph.D. thesis. University of Manchester.

—— (2001). 'Globalization and Change: Organizational Continuity and Change within a Japanese Multinational in the UK', in G. Morgan, P. H. Kristensen, and R. Whitley (eds.), *The Multinational Firm: Organizing Across Institutional and National Divides*. Oxford: Oxford University Press.

Shimizu, K. (1995). 'Humanization of the Production System and Work at Toyota Motor Co', in A. Sandberg (ed.), *Enriching Production*. Aldershot: Avebury.

—— (1998). 'A New Toyotaism?', in M. Freyssenet et al. (eds.), *One Best Way? Trajectories and Industrial Models of the World's Automobile Producers*. Oxford: Oxford University Press.

Shirai, T. (ed.) (1983). *Contemporary Industrial Relations in Japan*. Wisconsin: University of Wisconsin Press.

Sklair, L. (2001). *The Transnational Capitalist Class*. Oxford: Blackwell.

—— (2002). *Globalization: Capitalism and its Alternatives*. Oxford: Oxford University Press.

Smith, C. (1987). *Technical Workers*. London: Macmillan.

—— (1990). 'How are Engineers Formed? Professionals, Nation and Class Politics', *Work, Employment and Society*, 3(4): 451–67.

—— (1996). 'Japan, the Hybrid Factory and Cross-National Organisational Theory', *Osterreichische Zeitschrift fur Soziologie*, 3: 105–30.

—— (2001). Should I Go or Should I Stay? The Double Indeterminacy of Labour Power: Labour Process and Labour Mobility, Towards a Theoretical Integration. A paper presented to the *19th International Labour Process Conference*. Royal Holloway, University of London, 26–28 March.

—— (2003). 'Living at Work: Management Control and the Chinese Dormitory Labour System', *Asia Pacific Journal of Management*, 20(3): 333–58.

Smith, C., Child, J., and Rowlinson, M. (1990). *Reshaping Work: The Cadbury Experience*. Cambridge: Cambridge University Press.

—— Daskalaki, M., Elger, T., and Brown, D. (2004). 'Labour Turnover and Management Retention Strategies in New Manufacturing Plants', *International Journal of Human Resource Management*, 15(2): 371–96.

—— and Elger, T, (1997). 'International Competition, Inward Investment and the Restructuring of European Work and Industrial Relations', *European Journal of Industrial Relations*, 3: 279–304.

—— —— (2000). 'The Societal Effects School and Transnational Transfer: The Case of Japanese Investment in Britain', in M. Maurice and A. Sorge (eds.), *Embedding Organizations: Societal Analysis of Actors, Organizations and Socio-Economic Context*. Amsterdam: John Benjamins.

—— and Meiksins, P. (1995). 'System, Society and Dominance Effects in Cross-National Organisational Analysis', *Work, Employment and Society*, 9: 241–68.

—— and Thompson, P. (1998). 'Re-evaluating the Labour Process', *Economic and Industrial Democracy*, 19(4): 551–78.

Smith, P. and Morton, G. (1993). 'Union Exclusion and the Decollectivisation of Industrial Relations in Contemporary Britain', *British Journal of Industrial Relations*, 31(1): 97–114.

Sorge, A. (1991). 'Strategic Fit and the Societal Effect: Interpreting Cross-National Comparisons of Technology, Organisation and Human Resources', *Organisation Studies*, 12: 161–90.

Spender, J. C. (1989). *Industrial Recipes*. Oxford: Blackwell.

Stephenson, C. (1996). 'The Different Experience of Trade Unionism in Two Japanese Plants', in P. Ackers et al. (eds.), *The New Workplace and Trade Unionism*. London: Routledge.

Steven, R. (1991). 'Structural Origins of Japan's Direct Foreign Investment', in J. Morris, (ed.), *Japan and the Global Economy.* London: Routledge.

—— (1996). *Japan and the New World Order: Global Investments, Trade and Finance.* London: Macmillan.

Storey, J., Edwards, P. and Sisson, K. (1997). *Managers in the Making: Careers, Development and Control in Corporate Britain and Japan.* London: Sage.

Stubbs, R. and Underhill, G. R. D. (eds.) (2000). *Political Economy and the Changing Global Order,* Oxford: Oxford University Press.

Sugayama, S. (1995). 'Work Rules, Wages and Single Status: the Shaping of the Japanese Employment System', *Business History,* 37(2): 120–39.

Suzuki, A. (1998). 'Union Politics in Hard Times: The Restructuring of Japanese Style Employment Relations and the Internal Politics of the Japanese Labour Movement in the 1990s', International Sociological Association Conference, Montreal.

Sey, A. (2000). 'Team Work in Japan: Revolution, Evolution or No Change at All?' *Economic and Industrial Democracy,* 21: 475–503.

Taylor, B. (2001). 'Labour Management in Japanese Manufacturing Plants in China', *International Journal of Human Resource Management,* 12(4): 600–20.

Teague, P. (1997). 'Review Essay: New Institutionalism and the Japanese Employment System', *Review of International Political Economy,* 4(3): 587–607.

TDA (Telford Development Agency) (1997). *Telford Workforce: Key Facts and Figures 1997–98.* TDA.

TDA (Telford Development Agency)/Wrekin Council (1996). '1995/96 Telford and Wrekin Employment Survey'. Unpublished.

Tejima, S. (1998). 'Japanese International Investment in the Regions of East Asia and the Pacific: A Horizontal Division of Labour', in H. Mirza (ed.), *Global Competitive Strategies in the New World Economy: Multilateralism, Regionalisation and the Transnational Firm.* Cheltenham: Edward Elgar.

Telford and Wrekin EDU (2004). *Telford Workforce 2003–2004.* Telford and Wrekin Economic Development Unit, www.cometotelford.co.uk/business/population and workforce.html (accessed 10–12–04).

Thompson, P. (2002). 'Per una critica del quadro di riferimento: lavora, occupazione e politica economica nella ed oltre la Labour Process Theory', *Sociologia del Lavoro,* 86–87: 40–60.

—— and Ackroyd, S. (1995). 'All Quiet on the Workplace Front: A Critique of Recent Trends in British Industrial Sociology', *Sociology,* 29(4): 615–33.

Tickell, A. and Peck, J. A. (1995). 'Social Regulation after Fordism: Regulation Theory, Neo-liberalism and the Global-local Nexus', *Economy and Society* 24(3): 357–86.

Tolliday, S. (1998). 'The Diffusion and Transformation of Fordism: Britain and Japan Compared', in R. Boyer et al. (eds.), *Between Imitation and Innovation: The Transfer and Hybridization of Production Models in the International Automobile Industry.* Oxford: Oxford University Press.

—— and Zeitlin, J. (1986). 'Introduction: Between Fordism and Flexibility', in S. Tolliday and J. Zeitlin (eds.), *The Automobile Industry and its Workers:Between Fordism and Flexibility.* Cambridge: Polity.

Too Keizai (1992). *Japanese Overseas Investment, A Complete Listing of Firms and Countries, 1992–1993* [*sic*]. Tokyo: Too Keizai Inc.

Traxler, F., Blaschke, S., and Kittel, B. (2001). *National Labour Relations in Internationalized Markets.* Oxford: Oxford University Press.

Trevor, M. (1983). *Japan's Reluctant Multinationals: Japanese Management at Home and Abroad.* London: Francis Pinter.

—— (1988). *Toshiba's New British Company. Competitiveness through Innovation.* London: Policy Studies Institute.

Trinder, B. (1973). *The Industrial Revolution in Shropshire.* London: Phillimore.

Tsurumi, P. (1990). *Women in the Thread Mills of Meiji Japan.* Princeton, NJ: Princeton University Press.

Tsutsui, W. M. (1998). *Manufacturing Ideology: Scientific Management in Twentieth-Century Japan.* Princeton, NJ: Princeton University Press.

Turner, C. L. (1995). *Japanese Workers in Protest: an Ethnography of Consciousness and Experience.* Berkeley, CA: University of California Press.

Udagawa, M. (1995). 'The Development of Production Management at the Toyota Motor Corporation', *Business History,* 37(2): 105–19.

Vaughan, D. (1992). 'Theory Elaboration: The Heuristics of Case Analysis', in C. C. Ragin and H. S. Becker (eds.), *What is a Case? Exploring the Foundations of Social Inquiry.* Cambridge: Cambridge University Press.

Visser, J. and Ruysseveldt, J. V. (1996). 'From Pluralism to Where? Industrial Relations in Great Britain', in J. V. Ruysseveldt and J. Visser (eds.), *Industrial Relations in Europe.* London: Sage.

Waye, J. (1983). 'Workplace Industrial Relations in Telford New Town'. MA dissertation. Industrial Relations, University of Warwick.

Webb, M. and Palmer, G. (1998). 'Evading Surveillance and Making Time: An Ethnographic View of the Japanese Factory Floor in Britain', *British Journal of Industrial Relations,* 36(4): 611–27.

Weiss, L. (1993). 'War, State and the Origins of the Japanese Employment System', *Politics and Society,* 21(3): 325–54.

Westney, D.E. (1987). *Imitation and Innovation.* Cambridge, MA.: Harvard University Press.

—— (1999). 'Organization Theory Perspectives on the Cross-Border Transfer of Organizational Patterns', in J. K. Liker, W. M. Fruin, and P. S. Adler (eds.), *Remade in America: Transplanting and Transforming Japanese Management Systems.* Oxford: Oxford University Press.

White, M. and Trevor, M. (1983). *Under Japanese Management: The Experience of British Workers.* London: Heinemann.

Whitley, R. (1992*a*). *Business Systems in East Asia.* London: Sage.

—— (ed.) (1992*b*). *European Business Systems: Firms and Markets in Their National Contexts.* London: Sage.

Whittaker, D. H. (1997). *Small Firms in the Japanese Economy.* Cambridge: Cambridge University Press.

Wilkinson, B., Morris, J., and Munday, M. (1993). 'Japan in Wales: A New Industrial Relations', *Industrial Relations Journal,* 24(4): 273–83.

—— Gamble, J., Humphrey, J., Morris, J., and Anthony, D. (2001). 'The New International Division of Labour in Asian Electronics: Work Organization and Human Resource Management in Japan and Malaysia', *Journal of Management Studies,* 38: 675–95.

Williams, K., Haslam, C., Johal, S., and Williams, J. (1994*b*). *Cars: Analysis, History, Cases.* Providence, RI: Berghahn.

—— —— Williams, J., Adcroft, A., and Johal, S. (1991). 'Factories versus Warehouses: Japanese Manufacturing Foreign Direct Investment in Britain and the US',

Occasional Papers on Business, Economy and Society 6, London: Polytechnic of East London.

——Mitsui, I. and Haslam, C. (1994*a*). 'How Far From Japan? A Case study of Japanese Press Shop Practice and Management', in T. Elger and C. Smith (eds.), *Global Japanization?* London: Routledge.

Williamson, H. (1994). *Coping with the Miracle: Japan's Unions Explore New International Relations.* London: Pluto Press.

Womack, J. D., Jones, P. T., and Roos D. (1990). *The Machine that Changed the World: The Triumph of Lean Production.* New York: Rawson Associates.

Wood, S. (1992). 'Japanization and/or Toyotaism?', *Work, Employment and Society,* 5(4): 567–600.

——(1993). 'The Japanization of Fordism', *Economic and Industrial Democracy,* 14: 535–55.

Wrekin Council (1996). '1995/96 Telford and Wrekin Employment Survey'. Unpublished.

INDEX

N.B. Tables and figures are indicated by bold type.